Administration

A Bibliography on
Historical Organization Practices

Administration

Edited by

Frederick L. Rath, Jr.
and
Merrilyn Rogers O'Connell

American Association for State and Local History
Nashville, Tennessee

We are grateful for the generous support of the American Conservation Association, Inc., and the Surdna Foundation for their assistance in the preparation of this volume.

Publication of this book was made possible in part by funds from the sale of the Bicentennial State Histories, which were supported by the National Endowment for the Humanities.

Library of Congress Cataloguing-in-Publication Data (Revised)

Rath, Frederick L
  A bibliography on historical organization practices.
  Vols. 2– compiled by R. S. Reese.
  Includes index.
  Contents: v.1. Historic preservation.—v.2. Care and conservation of collections. [etc.]
—v.5. Administration.
  1. Historic buildings—United States—Conservation and restoration—Bibliography. 2. Historic sites—United States—Conservation and restoration—Bibliography. 3. Historic buildings—Conservation and restoration—Bibliography. 4. Historical museums—Bibliography. 5. Museum techniques—Bibliography.
I. O'Connell, Merrilyn Rogers, joint author.
II. Title.
Z1251.A2R35 [E159] 016.973   75–26770
ISBN 0–910050–17–1 (v. 1)
ISBN 0–910050–44–9 (v. 5)

Printed in the United States of America

Contents

Preface

It was relatively easy once. A group of gentlemen (never gentlewomen, who were not expected to take part in reflective discussions) met and decided to form a society, an association to deal with the history of their community, their region, or their state. They elected officers, including a secretary whose lot usually was to serve as chief executive officer. From his study in his home, he assumed the mantle and played the role. It was, by the way, an invaluable service, for it assured the saving of a part of the American heritage of incalculable value.

It is not so easy today. The administration of a historical organization, even though it begins frequently with the determined effort of a few enthusiastic volunteers, eventually demands the services of a staff of men and women who have been trained to blaze the paths that lead to carefully conceived goals.

This volume, the fifth in a series of separate but related volumes that amass selected references applying to the full scope of historical organization practices, deals with administration. It ranges from a discursive chapter on the national and international organizations serving the field through the effect of contemporary issues on those who seek to preserve the cultural and historical heritage to every aspect of administration: governing boards, management, ethics, personnel, fund raising, tax and legal issues, insurance problems, buildings, printing and publishing, public relations, collections management, and the administration of libraries and archives. It is comprehensive because nothing less will do in a field that has become increasingly complex.

What has happened in the last fifty years is an acceleration of interest not only in the heritage of nations but also their culture. In Europe and Canada as well as in the United States we have witnessed official attention to a broad field that hitherto had been largely the concern of individuals. The voices of a minority have been heard and even heeded in governmental chambers, and the legislation that has proliferated has brought not only largesse but also problems. A need has been created for administrative managers: men and women with more skills; administrators able to deal with public funds; and staff and volunteers with an awareness of the "plurality of professions," as Albert Eide Parr phrased it, intertwined in the management of both large and small nonprofit educational institutions. No one expects the administrator to know all the answers, but he or she had better know where to look to find the answers—whether from the printed page, an individual expert, or a clearinghouse of information.

Many of the answers, most of the answers are in the citations given here. This volume, like its predecessors, seeks to offer the better reference, whether that is a book, an article, a leaflet, an agency, or a service organization. Also like its predecessors it is selective rather than definitive. It seeks to include all the most significant references but some older materials have been omitted in order to accommodate a growing amount of new literature. The compilers, aided by their expert advisors, have also exercised an arbitrary discretion in not listing monographs or articles in obscure or unattainable editions or periodicals. Although some early definitive references are still included, the concentration is on materials published between 1945 and mid-1979. Researchers should be reminded to refer frequently to *Books in Print: An Author-Title-Series Index to the Publishers' Trade List Annual* . . . (New York: R. R. Bowker, annual) and *Ulrich's International Periodicals Directory* (New York: R. R. Bowker, biennial and quarterly supplements) to keep abreast of the growing number of revised editions, reprints of important works, and current periodicals.

As before, all entries for books and pamphlets follow the Library of Congress catalog card information. Thus, all include the following: number of pages or number of volumes; illustrations (if any), including drawings, plans, photographs, or other graphic materials; bibliography or bibliographical footnotes (if any).

The primary purpose of the bibliography is to be a working tool, providing the first steps on research trails. To add to its practicality, this volume includes more annotations with the entries. At the end of many sections, the notes and periodicals descriptions have been expanded to include more information sources and services that cannot be listed as standard bibliographic references. Listed in the appendix are all the periodicals cited throughout the volume, with addresses and subscription information, and notations where necessary if a journal has ceased, been superseded, or renamed. The index, derived from a punch card retrieval system, is deliberately comprehensive so that the most obscure references, coauthors, editors, notes or even allusions can be tracked down easily.

There are two other departures from what may be considered standard bibliographic practice which have become integral parts of the entire *Bibliography* . . . series. An annotated Basic Reference Shelf is provided in order to give an immediate listing of the most useful guides and handbooks that cover all aspects of administration. There is also a discursive section on the purposes and programs of national, foreign, and international organizations serving the profession.

To produce a bibliography of this kind, the advice and assistance of many individuals and organizations is necessary. Rosemary S. Reese, Associate Editor of the Bibliographic Project, was instrumental in compiling and verifying references for numerous sections. The Smithsonian Institution, as administrator of National Museum Act funds, initially made the expanded Bibliographic Project possible. We are especially grateful to the Advisory Council and to Paul N. Perrot. The New York State Historical Association provided the first office for the Project, and continues to offer the full services of its fine library.

We are deeply indebted to Dr. William T. Alderson, Director of Museum Studies at the University of Delaware, and Holman J. Swinney, Director of the Margaret Woodbury Strong Museum, for their special assistance in determining the scope and content of the entire volume. Invaluable guidance and advice on specialized areas were generously given by Larry L. Belles, Sandra R. Stone, and Roger W. Zaenglein of the Margaret Woodbury Strong Museum; Dr. Robert G. Chenhall, Buffalo Museum of Science; Susan Filupeit, New York State Historical Association; Gary G. Gore and Martha I. Strayhorn, American Association for State and Local History; Daniel R. Porter, Director of the Cooperstown Graduate Programs; and B. W. Thibault, Alexander & Alexander, Inc., Utica, New York. Since the references for such a complex subject have been drawn from many related sources and organizations as well as other professions, we extend our thanks to all the individuals who responded promptly to our inquiries about publications, programs, and services. And we wish to take this opportunity to acknowledge and express our gratitude to the staffs of the American Association of Museums, the National Trust for Historic Preservation, and the Museum Reference Center of the Smithsonian Institution for their continuing cooperation in making the *Bibliography* . . . series a more complete and useful handbook for the entire profession.

As we noted in the earlier four volumes, the American Association for State and Local History undertook the support of the Bibliographic Project in recognition that this growing profession must have a reference guide to the myriad of books and articles that are defining and refining the field. We are grateful to Association Director Gerald W. George for continuing to oversee the total Project; and to the Association's publications department, under the direction of Gary G. Gore, without which there would be no finished product.

Finally, we are grateful to the American Conservation Association, Inc., and the Surdna Foundation for partial support of the publication of this and other volumes in this series. Additional publication support came from the sale of the Bicentennial State Histories series.

To all those who have assumed the mantle of administration for a historical organization we offer our good wishes. We know there are burdens as well as joys. It simply is not possible to satisfy all of the people all of the time when there are so many areas to cover, to protect, to enhance. But even in the smallest operations there is rich reward—in personal satisfaction at least—when basic goals are established, are worked on, sometimes for many years, and are attained. It is our hope, of course, that this volume, like its predecessors, will make your jobs a little easier.

Frederick L. Rath, Jr.
Executive Secretary
Eastern National Park
and Monument Association

Merrilyn Rogers O'Connell
Director, Bibliographic Project

A Bibliography on Historical
Organization Practices

Administration

Basic Reference Shelf

The Basic Reference Shelf includes handbooks, guidelines, and technical leaflets that should be part of the working library of every historical organization administrator. Most of the references cover a range of administrative considerations; books and articles on narrower or technical aspects are included in their respective chapters and subchapters. Each entry includes extensive annotation, with special note of glossaries, sample forms, and additional bibliography. For several areas, such as security, codes of ethics, and collections management, basic manuals by more than one professional organization have been cited.

Also recommended is institutional and/or individual membership in one or more professional organizations in order to keep up with current trends and special developments, and to receive their important publications. Professional journals have been listed separately in Chapter 4.

Alderson, William T., Jr. "Securing Grant Support: Effective Planning and Preparation," *History News*, 27:12 (December 1972), Technical Leaflet no. 62. ◆ General guidelines which have been found successful by agencies that have received grants and notes on pitfalls. Emphasis on elements of a project proposal: planning the program, choosing the right foundation or agency, preparing the budget and steps in submitting the request. Includes sample budget and checklist of considerations.

Alexander, Edward P. *Museums in Motion: An Introduction to the History and Functions of Museums*. Nashville, Tenn.: American Association for State and Local History, 1979. 308 pp., illus. ◆ Comprehensive history of the various kinds of museums and offers sound practices for administering the museum of today. Includes collections, conservation, research, exhibition, interpretation, cultural center, and the museum profession.

American Association of Museums. *Professional Standards for Museum Accreditation*. Rev. ed. Edited by H. J. Swinney. Washington, D.C.: 1978. 80 pp. ◆ Subtitled: The Handbook of the Accreditation Program of the American Association of Museums. Includes modified and expanded accreditation procedures; discussion of re-accreditation, refinements and clarification of standards; revisions in the requirements governing the confidentiality of the accreditation process.

American Association of Museums. Committee on Ethics. *Museum Ethics*. Washington, D.C.: 1978. 31 pp. ◆ Guidelines for ethical conduct concerning the collection, the staff, museum management policy, and museum governance. See also: *Museum News*, 56:4 (March/April 1978), pp. 21-30. Refer also to the codes of ethics formulated by the Canadian Museums Association and The Museums Association of Great Britain.

Canadian Museums Association. Training Committee. *Basic Museum Management*. Edited by George MacBeath and S. James Gooding. Ottawa: Canadian Museums Association, 1969. 80 pp., illus., bibliog. ◆ Clear and practical advice; includes museum world; museum's purposes; legal status; governing body and staff; planning; fundraising; budgets; collections; research and record keeping; conservation; exhibition; the museum and its community.

1

Chambers, J. Henry. *Cyclical Maintenance for Historic Buildings.* Washington, D.C.: Interagency Historic Architectural Services Program, Office of Archeology and Historic Preservation, National Park Service, 1976. 125 pp., illus., appendices, notes, bibliog. ◆ Technical advice on starting a maintenance program, professional services, employee training, and maintenance techniques for specific materials.

Creigh, Dorothy Weyer. *A Primer for Local Historical Societies.* Nashville, Tenn.: American Association for State and Local History, 1976. 153 pp., illus., bibliog., appendices, index. ◆ Basic handbook on all aspects of organization including publicity, beginning projects, tours, establishing a library, restorations, museums, and financing.

Cunha, George D.M., and Dorothy Grant Cunha. *Conservation of Library Materials: A Manual and Bibliography on the Care, Repair and Restoration of Library Materials.* 2nd ed. Metuchen, N.J.: Scarecrow Press, 1971 -. Vols. 1 and 2, 406 and 414 pp., illus., diagrams, graphs, appendices, glossary, index. ◆ Contents: History of Bookbinding; Materials; Enemies of Books; Conservation (environmental); Conservation (of materials); Conservation in the Tropics; Repair and Restoration; Book Repair; Map Repair; Restoration of Manuscripts, Prints, Drawings, Seals, Films, Tapes and Discs.

Duckett, Kenneth W. *Modern Manuscripts: A Practical Manual for Their Management, Care and Use.* Nashville, Tenn.: American Association for State and Local History, 1975. 375 pp., illus., notes, glossary, bibliog., appendices, index. ◆ Focuses on practical and technical aspects of the management of manuscript collections; role of the curator from fundraiser to microfilmer and conservator; mechanics and ethics of acquisitions; physical care and conservation; bibliographic control; information retrieval; non-manuscript material; use of collections; and public service.

Dudley, Dorothy; Irma B. Wilkinson; et al. *Museum Registration Methods.* 3rd ed. rev. Washington, D.C.: American Association of Museums, 1979. 346 pp. ◆ Updated, expanded and redesigned, and includes computerizing collections and a glossary of terms. Added appendix on "Shipping, Packing and Insurance."

Evans, Frank B. *Modern Archives and Manuscripts: A Select Bibliography.* Washington, D.C.: Society of American Archivists, 1975. 209 pp., indexes. ◆ Guide to writings in archival administration with new chapters on machine-readable records and archives; three chapters on international aspects of archives. Additional subheadings and a system of decimal numbering has been adopted for the subheadings to facilitate revisions and indexing.

Felt, Thomas E. *Researching, Writing, and Publishing Local History.* Nashville, Tenn.: American Association for State and Local History, 1976. 165 pp., bibliog., index. ◆ Contents are presented in three major chapters: researching, including note taking and organization, use of libraries, oral history, other research sources; writing, including the writing process, footnotes and quotes, editing; publishing, including design and type styles, production processes, promotion and marketing. Annotated bibliography.

Ferguson, Rowena. *Editing the Small Magazine.* 2nd ed., rev. New York: Columbia University Press, 1976. 221 pp., bibliog., index. ◆ Covers the editorial process from planning and editorial policy, procuring and processing manuscripts to pictures, layout and design, and printing. Also includes "The Editor's Bookshelf."

Gross, Malvern J., Jr., and William H. Daughtrey. *Museum Accounting Handbook.* Washington, D.C.: American Association of Museums, 1978. 158 pp., illus., glossary, bibliog., index. ◆ How-to manual to span the gap between minimal or nonexistent accounting background of most museum administrators; problems created by increased government support and tightened tax requirements to which private foundations and donors must now adhere. Includes introduction to the use of the handbook and a glossary; basic concepts of financial reporting and accounting; bookkeeping systems; aspects of fund accounting; budgeting; contributed services and materials; optional procedures; and includes the entire ASTC *Museum Accounting Guidelines* (1976).

Harrison, Raymond O. *The Technical Requirements of Small Museums.* Rev. ed. Technical Papers no. 1. Ottawa: Canadian Museums Association, 1969. 27 pp., illus., bibliog. ✦ Includes building materials and equipment, principles of building and interior space planning, site selection, building costs and capital budgets. Illustrated with basic floor plans. Appendix on small art gallery requirements by Archie F. Key.

International Paper Company. *Pocket Pal: A Graphic Arts Production Handbook.* 11th ed. New York: International Paper Company, c1974. 191 pp., illus. ✦ A basic handbook on printing and publishing; includes history, printing processes, composition, photoengraving, printing inks, binding, graphic arts terms, printing papers. Revised periodically to include recent innovations in printing; sections of earlier editions still helpful. .

Keck, Caroline K.; Huntington T. Block; Joseph Chapman; John B. Lawton; and Nathan Stolow. *A Primer on Museum Security.* Cooperstown, N.Y.: New York State Historical Association, 1966. 85 pp., illus., graphs, forms, bibliog. ✦ An essential handbook on methods of building security. Includes chapters on insurance and environmental security.

Lee, Marshall. *Bookmaking: The Illustrated Guide to Design and Production.* 1965. Reprint. New York: R. R. Bowker Co., 1972. 399 pp., bibliog., index. ✦ Covers every step in the process of designing and producing a book, including creative and practical details on designing, layout, costs, and paper. Definition of terms; illustrated with examples and diagrams.

Lewis, Ralph H. *Manual for Museums.* Washington, D.C.: National Park Service, U.S. Department of the Interior; for sale by the Superintendent of Documents, U.S. Government Printing Office, 1976. 412 pp., illus., bibliog., index. ✦ An outgrowth of the 1941 volume, *Field Manual for Museums* by Ned J. Burns. Contents in four parts: Museum Collections; Museum Records; Furnished Historic Structure Museums; Exhibit Maintenance and Replacement, and also eight specialized appendices.

Menzeńska, Mary Jane. *Archives and Other Special Collections: A Library Staff Handbook.* New York: School of Library Service, Columbia University, 1973. 87 pp., forms, glossary, bibliog., appendices. ✦ Includes introduction to rare books, manuscripts and archives; handling and care, general policies; acquisitions and disposal; arrangement; control, access and publicity; sample copies of finding aids; sample of a record groups classification for archives.

Miller, Ronald L. *Personnel Policies for Museums: A Handbook for Management.* Rev. ed. Washington, D.C.: American Association of Museums, 1980. 200 pp., reading list. ✦ Manual, based on a survey of museum personnel policies, intended as a source of information and alternative approaches in writing, revising, evaluating policies and procedures. Includes staffing, affirmative action, termination of employment, leaves of absence, due process, benefits, work assignments, compensation administration, pay practices, education and training, supplemental employment, personnel files, performance appraisal, use of museum property and facilities. First edition published by Smithsonian Institution, 1977; revised and updated for publication by the American Association of Museums.

National Fire Protection Association. Committee on Libraries, Museums and Historic Buildings. *Protecting Our Heritage: A Discourse on Fire Prevention in Historic Buildings and Landmarks.* 2nd ed. Edited by Joseph F. Jenkins. Boston: National Fire Protection Association with the assistance of the American Association for State and Local History, 1970. 39 pp., illus., glossary of fire protection equipment, appendices. ✦ Prepared by NFPA Committee to assist persons who are in any way responsible for or interested in protecting historic properties from fire. Includes ideas and directions regarding losses, evaluation of risk and protection measures, good housekeeping, emergency planning and cost consideration. Appendices include list of NFPA publications, and glossary of fire protection equipment.

National Trust for Historic Preservation. *Do-It-Yourself Press Kit.* Washington, D.C.: The Trust, 1977. folder, six insertions. ✦ Guide to types of news; assistance in obtaining media coverage of group activities; sample press releases for radio, television and publications.

National Trust for Historic Preservation. *Legal Considerations in Establishing a Historic Preservation Organization.* Washington, D.C.: Preservation Press, 1977. 24 pp. ✦ Information sheet on planning and objectives, impact of federal tax laws on nonprofit organizations; descriptions of organizations structures (corporate, unincorporated association, "sister organization", charitable trust). Outlines steps in forming an organization, sample articles of incorporation, qualifying for federal income tax exemption, sample bylaws.

Nauert, Patricia, and Caroline M. Black. *Fine Arts Insurance: A Handbook for Art Museums.* Washington, D.C.: Association of Art Museum Directors, distr. by American Association of Museums, 1979. 100 pp., appendices, glossary, bibliog. ◆ Contents include risk management, insurance management, responsibility of the museum, policy design, insurance documents, rates and premiums, evaluating policies, procedures for handling loss. Separate chapter on special areas of fragile items, contemporary art, indemnity, U.S. Federal Indemnity Program, and loans. A project of the Fine Arts Insurance Committee of the Association of Art Museum Directors.

Pizer, Laurence R. "Financing Your History Organization: Setting Goals," *History News,* 33:7 (July 1978), Technical Leaflet no. 106. ◆ Discusses need to outline goals, suggests sources for permanent funding, and financing short-term projects.

Reibel, Daniel B. *Registration Methods for the Small Museum: A Guide for Historical Collections.* Nashville, Tenn.: American Association for State and Local History, 1978. 160 pp., illus., bibliog., appendices. ◆ How-to manual covering entire registration process; examines role of registrar or curator, collections committee, and board of directors; acquisition, numbering, cataloging, documentation and loans; and includes sample forms.

Schellenberg, Theodore. R. *Modern Archives: Principles and Techniques.* 1956. Reprint. Chicago: University of Chicago Press, 1975. 247 pp. ◆ Examines the management of governmental records at all levels; offers valuable background material for archivists.

Suhler, Sam A. *Local History Collection and Services in a Small Public Library.* Chicago: American Library Association, 1970. 11 pp.,

bibliog. ◆ Small Libraries Project Pamphlet no. 19. Useful suggestions for small local libraries, including local historical society libraries, and deals with newspapers, magazines, books, manuscripts, maps, vertical file materials, tape recordings, and pictorial materials.

Thompson, Enid T. *Local History Collections: A Manual for Librarians.* Nashville, Tenn.: American Association for State and Local History, 1978. 100 pp., illus., bibliog., appendix, index. ◆ Contents: collecting local history; materials of local history; legal aspects; conservation, cleaning, mending and other chores; processing local history; services; training volunteers; special projects. Appendix includes organizations, sources of supplies, and publication addresses.

Tillotson, Robert G. *Museum Security.* Edited by Diana D. Menkes. Washington, D.C.: American Association of Museums and International Council of Museums, 1977. 256 pp., illus., bibliog., appendices, index. ◆ Includes architectural planning; psychological aspects of guarding; anti-intrusion devices and detectors; protection against fire, vandalism and environmental damage; internal security; and inventory control.

United Nations Educational, Scientific and Cultural Organization. *The Organization of Museums: Practical Advice.* Museums and Monuments, IX. Paris: UNESCO, 1960. 188 pp., illus., bibliog. ◆ Chapters by museum experts on museum and its functions, administration, staff, research, visitors, education, museum laboratory, collections, exhibitions, and museum architecture.

Wilson, Marlene. *The Effective Management of Volunteer Programs.* Boulder, Colo.: Volunteer Management Associates, c1976. 197 pp., diagrams, bibliog. references. ◆ Includes: Look at Volunteerism; Role of a Manager; Motivation; Organizational Climate; Planning and Evaluation; Designing Jobs and Recruiting to Fill Them; Interviewing and Placing Volunteers; Training; Communications; Putting It All Together—Client/Staff/Volunteer/Board.

1

Historical Organizations

The wise administrator of an historical organization belongs to most of the major associations serving the profession and pays careful heed to what is developing in the principal agencies and international bodies representing the profession. It is only in this manner that one is able to keep up with trends, innovations and progress in an increasingly complex field. Periodicals, seminars and workshops, technical bulletins, legal reports, consultant services, all provide administrators, trustees, and staff with information necessary to run an efficient educational and cultural institution.

The major associations and agencies serving the profession in the United States, Canada, and Great Britain, as well as two international organizations, are described below in terms of their purposes, services, publications, meetings, and training programs. This section is followed by a selection of publications giving an overview of regional, state, and local historical organizations. Further information about individual history museums, historical societies, historic sites and buildings, or outdoor museums—large and small, public and private—may be found in the major directories listed in Chapter 3 and by writing directly for their descriptive brochures and publications.

Finally, acknowledging the increasing importance of their role in the last two decades, the arts councils and community centers are treated by references in the last section.

National Organizations

American Association for State and Local History (AASLH), 1400 Eighth Avenue South, Nashville, Tennessee 37203.

The American Association for State and Local History, founded in 1940, is a nonprofit educational organization dedicated to advancing knowledge, understanding, and appreciation of localized history in the United States and Canada. It serves amateur and professional historians, individuals and organizations, and includes in its broad spectrum such groups as historical museums and libraries, junior history clubs, historic sites, manuscript collections, and large as well as small historical societies.

To encourage the development of popular knowledge about American history, the Association launched the magazine *American Heritage* in 1949. Within five years it became a bimonthly, hardcover magazine published professionally by American Heritage Publishing Company and cosponsored by the Association. Royalties help provide some of the financial resources needed to carry out the Association's broad educational and professional programs. In recent years, the National Endowment for

5

the Humanities, the National Endowment for the Arts, the Council on Library Resources, the National Museum Act and private grants have provided funds to the Association to support special training programs, seminars for historical agency personnel, consultant services, and publications.

Membership in the Association is open to professionals, institutions, libraries, and individuals.

PROFESSIONAL SERVICES: Clearinghouse for inquiries from individuals and organizations; research surveys about the profession; job placement service; consultant service to historical societies and museums; annual awards of merit and commendation for outstanding contributions to the field by individuals and organizations; cooperative programs with state and regional conferences of historical organizations; annual meeting; joint meetings with related historical organizations.

PUBLICATIONS: *History News,* monthly magazine of up-to-date news of members, events, new ideas, reviews of books, and a Technical Leaflet series of how-to articles (with three-ring binder available); *Directory of Historical Societies and Agencies in the United States and Canada,* biennial; Bicentennial State Histories series; books and booklets; careers brochure; catalog of Association publications and Technical Leaflets. *History News* and out-of-print volumes of Association *Bulletins,* a series of booklets published between 1941 and 1973 which preceeded the Technical Leaflet series, are available in microfilm from Xerox University Microfilms, 300 N. Zeeb Road, Ann Arbor, Michigan 48106.

TRAINING PROGRAMS: Cosponsor of annual Williamsburg Seminar for Historical Administrators; Independent Study Program (brochure available); seminars on publications, administration of historical agencies and museums, historical museum techniques, management and interpretation of history museums and historic sites; training seminars and regional workshops for beginning professionals and small agency directors; cassette lectures and slide/tape training kits (catalog available).

American Association of Museums (AAM), 1055 Thomas Jefferson Street, N.W., Washington, D.C. 20007.

Organized in 1906, the American Association of Museums is a nonprofit service organization that promotes museums as major cultural resources and represents the interests of the museum profession on a national level. The Association is supported primarily by dues and contributions from its membership, which includes museums of every size and discipline, museum employees and others concerned with the future of museums. Membership benefits include subscriptions to publications, services of the Professional Relations Committee, and use of the placement service.

The Association functions with Administrative committees and special committees, including AAM/ICOM Committee, and Accreditation Commission; Advisors to the AAM Council; and Standing Professional Committees for Curators, Educators, Trustees, and Security.

REGIONAL GROUPS: A network of six regional affiliate groups helps to disperse information about museums and encourages cooperation among institutions, museum professionals, and the general public. Yearly meetings for members are sponsored in each of the regional conferences, and all publish a newsletter. The regions and their newsletters are: New England Museums Association (*NEMA News*); Northeast Museums Conference (*The Museologist*); Midwest Museums Conference (*The Quarterly*); Mountain-Plains Museums Conference (*MPMC Newsletter*); Western Regional Conference (*WRC Newsletter*); Southeastern Museums Conference (*SEMC Notes; Inside SEMC*).

PROGRAMS: Professional Relations Service provides formal, objective third-party inquiry and reporting in employment disputes. Service is available only to voting members who file a formal request. Placement Service provides timely information on employment opportunities within the museum profession. The service is available to members and consists of advertisements of institutional positions open and individuals seeking employment in *AVISO*, the monthly newsletter. Accreditation sets prescribed professional criteria by which a museum's quality and performance may be judged. Accreditation certifies that a museum currently meets accepted standards established by the profession, but does not grade achievement or excellence beyond established minimum requirements. The program is administered by a seven-member commission that is representative of a range of geographic areas and professional disciplines. Travel Programs are arranged for groups of Association members. Special charter flights are planned for attendance at international events of special importance to the museum profession. Tours are also arranged in conjunction with AAM annual meetings. The Association sponsors special seminars in conjunction with regional conferences; and holds an annual meeting.

TRUSTEES COMMITTEE: The Museum Trustees Committee helps trustees fulfill their vital responsibilities to museums. It provides a forum for communication about federal and state programs, legislation and tax concerns, museum accreditation, sources of funding, and the preservation of our cultural and educational heritage. AAM trustee members receive all the benefits of individual membership, as well as a special quarterly newsletter directed to trustee interests. They may attend seminars for trustees on taxes, trustee responsibilities, finances, legislation and other topics pertaining to the trustee's role. Trustees are encouraged to attend AAM annual meetings and regional conferences. The Association offers special liability insurance for trustees and officers.

PUBLICATIONS: *Museum News*, bimonthly journal on a range of subjects, special features and theme sections; *AVISO*, monthly newsletter, including current issues, "Washington Report," Placement Service, classified listings, and news of regional conferences and AAM professional committees (succeeds *AAM Bulletin*); *Official Museum Directory*, biennial; books, major reports, reprints of Technical Supplements and special articles (brochure available).

AAM/ICOM: In June 1973, with the merger of the U.S. National Committee of the International Council of Museums (ICOM) and the AAM, the U.S. Committee became an integral part of the Association as the AAM/ICOM Committee. Through this committee, the Association participates in international museum activities. AAM members may join AAM/ICOM and receive such benefits as the *AAM/ICOM Newsletter;* the Paris-published quarterly magazine *ICOM News;* a membership card honored for free or reduced admission at many museums in Europe and the U.S.; use of the ICOM Documentation Centre in Paris; help in planning museum trips abroad; invitations to attend ICOM international meetings and the Triennial World Conference; and a discount on subscriptions to *Museum,* UNESCO's quarterly magazine. The AAM/ICOM office also sponsors, with the cooperation of the U.S. Department of State, annual visits to the United States by museum professionals from other countries.

National Trust for Historic Preservation (NTHP), 1785 Massachusetts Avenue, N.W., Washington, D.C. 20036.

The National Trust for Historic Preservation was chartered by Congress in 1949 "to further the national policy of preserving for public use America's heritage of historic districts, sites, buildings, structures and objects; to facilitate public participation in the historic preservation movement and to serve that movement through educational and advisory programs; and to accept and administer for public benefit and use significant historic properties."

Membership in the National Trust is open to individuals, organizations, and businesses interested in historic preservation. Programs are supported by membership dues, endowment funds, contributions, and matching grants from the U.S. Department of the Interior, Heritage Conservation and Recreation Service, under provisions of the National Historic Preservation Act of 1966.

Programs are carried out under seven departments: Office of the President, Finance, Preservation Services, Historic Properties, Real Estate and Legal Services, Public Affairs, The Preservation Press. Advisory services are provided to preservation groups, community leaders, and city planning officials, and special liaison is maintained with federal programs. The National Trust is also in contact with numerous related groups, both national and international, concerned with architecture, urban history, landscape architecture, and other special interests. Information on preservation legislation, architectural surveys, and preservation projects is distributed throughout the country.

Field services are provided through six regional offices: Midwest Regional Office, 407 South Dearborn Street, Suite 710, Chicago, Illinois 60605; Western Regional Office, 681 Market Street, Suite 859, San Francisco, California 94105; Northeast Regional Office, 100 Franklin Street, Boston, Massachusetts 02110 (sponsored jointly with the Society for the Preservation of New England Antiquities); Southwest/Plains Regional Office, 903 Colcord Building, Oklahoma City, Oklahoma 73102; Mid-Atlantic Regional Office, 1600 H Street, N.W., Washington, D.C. 20006; and, Southern Regional Office, Aiken House, 456 King Street, Charleston, South Carolina 20403.

PROFESSIONAL SERVICES: Clearinghouse of current information on preservation theories, techniques, standards, legislation; advisory services and visits by professional staff and consultants; lectures and visual aid materials; preservation library services (brochure available); employment opportunities clearinghouse and "WORK" column published in *Preservation News;* consultant service grants and National Historic Preservation Fund (brochure available); annual meeting and preservation conference; tours in the U.S. and abroad, annual awards.

PUBLICATIONS (THE PRESERVATION PRESS): *Preservation News,* monthly newspaper of preservation activities, also available in xerographic print and microfilm from Xerox

University Microfilms, 300 N. Zeeb Road, Ann Arbor, Michigan 48106; *Historic Preservation,* illustrated bimonthly journal; *Member Organizations and Their Properties,* annual directory; *Annual Report;* Consultant Service Grant reports; conference proceedings; information leaflet series; Trust property brochures. The Preservation Bookstore is located at 1600 H Street, N.W., Washington, D.C. 20006; and a catalog is available. Landmarks and Historic District Commission *Newsletter* (begun in 1975, bimonthly, subscription), is available from Landmarks and Preservation Law Division, Office of Preservation Services, National Trust headquarters.

EDUCATION PROGRAMS: Cosponsor of annual Williamsburg Seminar for Historical Administrators; annual Woodlawn Conference for Historical Museum Associates; technical conferences and seminars; youth work-study programs.

NATIONAL TRUST MUSEUMS: Andalusia (Pa.); Chesterwood (Mass.); Cliveden (Pa.); Decatur House (D.C.); Drayton Hall (S.C.); Lyndhurst (N.Y.); Oatlands (Va.); Pope-Leighey House (Va.); Shadows-on-the-Teche (La.); Woodlawn Plantation (Va.); Woodrow Wilson House (D.C.); descriptive brochures available. Five historic properties: Belle Grove (Va.); Casa Amesti (Calif.); Filoli (Calif.); Frank Lloyd Wright Home and Studio (Ill.); Mount Harmon Plantation (Md.).

U.S. National Park Service (NPS), Department of the Interior, Washington, D.C. 20240.

The National Park Service was created as a bureau of the Department of the Interior by Congress in 1916 and was charged with the administration of the small number of existing national parks and monuments, including some archeological and historical areas. The Historic Sites Act of 1935 established "a national policy to preserve for public use, historic sites, buildings and objects of national significance for the inspiration and benefit of the people of the United States." With new powers and responsibilities, the National Park Service embarked on a national preservation program.

Added to this legislative lineage is the National Historic Preservation Act of 1966 which significantly broadened the scope of national preservation policy. Under this new authority, the National Register of Historic Places was greatly expanded, a national Advisory Council on Historic Preservation was appointed, and a system of matching grants-in-aid to the states and the National Trust for Historic Preservation was established. An Office of Archeology and Historic Preservation (OAHP) was organized in 1967 to manage the increased responsibilities.

NATIONAL PARK SYSTEM: The Park System is composed of natural, historical, and cultural areas, totaling 298 as of January 1, 1979. Field direction is provided through eight regional offices: New England Region, Boston; Northeast Region, Philadelphia; Southeast Region, Atlanta; Midwest Region, Omaha; Southwest Region, Santa Fe; Western Region, San Francisco; Pacific Northwest Region, Seattle; parks and memorials in Washington, D.C., are administered by the Office of National Capital Parks. Functions of planning, design and construction of physical facilities in the parks are carried out by the Denver Service Center. Production of publications, museum exhibits, and audiovisual programs is carried out by the Harpers Ferry Center. Cooperative research programs are conducted in conjunction with several universities throughout the country.

PUBLICATIONS: The National Park Service publication program is as varied as the parks it serves, from archeological studies and architectural records to maps and posters. There is an informational folder published for most of the parks. Over one hundred of the parks have interpretive handbooks and folders, all reasonably priced and sold in the visitor centers. The program further serves the public with fishing, boating, and camping information booklets; and, with the Administrative Policy series, it opens to the public rules, regulations and standards by which the parks are managed and maintained.

TRAINING CENTERS: The Albright Training Center, Grand Canyon National Park, Arizona, is maintained for orientation and skills training for all new employees; the Mather Training Center, Harpers Ferry, West Virginia, is maintained for teaching interpretive methods. There are also a number of short courses at both centers for new and experienced rangers and interpreters. The Park Service maintains career and seasonal employment services for the Park System.

ADMINISTRATION: Because of the expansion of nonpark programs such as the National Register, grants, surveys, and interagency services, the National Park Service reorganized its divisions in the historic preservation field into two major offices in 1973. The Cultural Resources Management Division was, and remains, responsible for historic preservation programs within the park system; the Office of Archeology and Historic Preservation managed all nonpark preservation programs. The Advisory Council on Historic Preservation was established as an independent federal agency in 1976 (P.L. 94-422).

In 1978 a new agency, the Heritage Conservation and Recreation Service (HCRS), was created within the Department of the Interior and combined the natural and historic preservation activities of the NPS Natural Landmarks Program and Office of Archeology and Historic Preservation, and the recreation responsibilities of the Bureau of Outdoor Recreation.

The *Cultural Resources Management Division* of the National Park Service comprises branches of history, historical architecture, and archeology. It sets the overall policies and standards for NPS research in these fields and for the preservation of cultural resources (historic and prehistoric sites, structures, and objects) in all areas of the National Park System. It maintains Servicewide listings of historic structures and research reports. It publishes the results of selected research for public distribution. It participates in training programs for cultural resource management and preservation maintenance. The research and preservation projects themselves are for the most part executed by National Park Service archeological centers, planning centers, and regional offices throughout the country.

The *Office of Archeology and Historic Preservation,* now part of the Heritage Conservation and Recreation Service, was first organized in 1967 from existing professional staffs within the National Park Service. Its purpose was to carry out more fully the preservation policies of the federal acts of 1906, 1935, and 1966. In 1973 all nonpark programs in historic preservation were reorganized under the Office and included four main divisions: National Register, Grants, Historic and Architectural Surveys, Interagency Services. The organization of the Office as of 1978 consists of seven divisions whose programs remain the same under the HCRS: National Register of Historic Places, Grants Administration, National Historic Sites Survey, Historic American Buildings Survey, Historic American Engineering Record, Interagency Archeological Services, and Technical Preservation Services. Located within the Chief's office is the Automatic Data Processing Section.

The *National Register of Historic Places* is divided into three branches: Registration, Planning, and Publications and Archives. The Registration Branch is responsible for establishing criteria and professional standards for nominations and assessing the significance of properties nominated by the states and federal agencies, determining the eligibility of properties for inclusion in the National Register at the request of federal agencies and individuals, assisting federal agencies in the development of internal procedures for the implementation of laws pertaining to historic preservation, and administering certain provisions of the Tax Reform Act of 1976. The Planning Branch is responsible for reviewing the State Historic Preservation Plan of each state, the District of Columbia, and the territories, providing standards and guidelines for the development of comprehensive plans, and giving guidance to communities acting as federal agencies under the Block Grant Program of the Housing and Community Development Act of 1974. The Publications and Archives Branch is responsible for maintaining the National Register of Historic Places, and making the contents available to other federal agencies, the states, the territories, and the general public through announcements in the "Federal Register," and publication of hardcover editions of the National Register.

The *Grants Administration Division* develops criteria and guidelines for fiscal management and administers the matching grants-in-aid program accordingly. Working in close cooperation with the State Historic Preservation Officers appointed by the governors, it recommends apportionments of funds to the states for plans and surveys and to the states and National Trust for Historic Preservation for project grants. It monitors the expenditure of grant funds, reviews and processes fiscal aspects of project initiation letters, and conducts audits.

The *Historic Sites Survey Division* is responsible for identifying and preparing factual studies of historical properties of potential national significance under themes ranging from prehistoric man to the 20th century, presenting these studies for evaluation by two boards of experts that make a recommendation to the Secretary of the Interior, who designates those possessing national significance as National Historic Landmarks. Properties so designated are automatically listed in the National Register of Historic Places. This division is also responsible for encouraging the preservation of landmarks by inviting owners to accept a bronze plaque and certificate at appropriate ceremonies, giving advisory assistance through biennial visits, and increasing public awareness of the importance of preserving their historic heritage through the publication of a Landmark Series. In the evaluation process, an additional recommendation identifies National Historic Landmarks that merit further study for possible future addition to the National Park System.

The *Historic American Buildings Survey* is responsible for identifying and documenting the design and construction of architecturally or historically important structures; encouraging public interest and action in the preservation of the historic environment through publications, exhibits, and other projects carried out in cooperation with state and local governments, preservation groups, educational institutions, historical societies, and private individuals; and providing information and assistance to federal agencies concerning HABS standards and procedures of recording and documenting historic structures.

The *Historic American Engineering Record* is responsible for identifying and documenting the engineering and industrial heritage of the United States; advising and assisting state and local organizations on matters concerning engineering history and industrial archeology; advising federal agencies on the documentation of federally owned engineering and industrial sites; and increasing public awareness of industrial, engineering, and technological history through publications, exhibits, and programs carried out in cooperation with preservation groups, educational institutions, professional organizations, and private individuals.

The *Automatic Data Processing* project is automating Office survey files (National Register, Historic American Buildings Survey, Historic American Engineering Record, National Historic Landmarks) in order to coordinate them and to facilitate the use of their information. It is also automating the fiscal and management records of the Grant-in-Aid Program and will establish a case-tracking system to assist in the Office work under the Tax Reform Act of 1976. It will assist states in planning for automation of survey records, and will answer technical questions on the UTM grid reference system.

Interagency Archeological Services is responsible for conducting a nationwide program for salvage of archeological remains (outside National Park Service areas). It develops policies, standards, and procedures for the professional conduct of this archeological program. The division also develops and disseminates information on archeological research methods, including archeological salvage techniques; advises as requested on legislative proposals, proposed area studies, and Congressional and Presidential requests; and participates in programs of historical and archeological societies and commissions. The Chief is designated as the Departmental Consulting Archeologist; in support thereof, the division issues permits for archeological exploration on federally owned or controlled lands, except lands under the jurisdiction of the Department of Agriculture. It also coordinates the program to meet the requirements of Executive Order 11593. Field offices are located in Atlanta, Georgia; Denver, Colorado; and San Francisco, California.

Technical Preservation Services is responsible for developing and disseminating technical information on the preservation and restoration of cultural properties; advising federal agencies in the preservation, improvement, restoration, and maintenance of cultural properties; reviewing and evaluating the plans of transferees of surplus federal property for historic monument purposes; and evaluating and advising preservation grantees on preservation methods, monitoring grant-assisted projects to foster professional standards and techniques, and ensuring compliance with federal regulations and accountability for appropriated funds. The Division Chief is designated as the Departmental Consultant for Historic Architecture.

PARK PRACTICE PROGRAM: Begun in 1957, the Park Practice Program is a mutual program of service to park and recreation people, cosponsored by the National Conference on State Parks, National Recreation and Park Association, and the National Park Service. The Program is a series of publications for individuals and organizations concerned with parks, recreation, and conservation. It seeks to communicate interesting and high quality practical information on planning, designing, operating, and administering recreation facilities. The Park Practice Program is located at the National Recreation and Park Association, 1601 North Kent Street, Arlington, Virginia 22209.

The publications, available through full membership or individual subscriptions, include: *Grist*—bimonthly, tested time-, effort-, and money-saving technical ideas and devices for more effective park operation; *Guideline*—bimonthly, members exchange methods of management, administration, and interpretation of park and recreation facilities; *Trends*—quarterly, features new and important issues relating to parks, recreation, and conservation; *Design*—semiannual, innovative structural designs and layout plans for park and recreation sites to better serve visitor needs.

EASTERN NATIONAL PARK AND MONUMENT ASSOCIATION: The Association is a private, nonprofit cooperating association formed in 1947 to promote the historical, scientific, educational, and interpretive activities of the National Park Service, principally in the eastern half of the United States, through grants-in-aid for research, publication of historical literature, development of park libraries, acquisition of lands needed to prevent intrusions on present areas. Its principal office is located at 339 Walnut Street, Philadelphia, Pennsylvania 19106. It is a consortium of agencies with sales counters or small bookstores ranging from Maine to Minnesota and from Louisiana to the Virgin Islands. Its publications include a newsletter; *Annual Report;* books, booklets, pamphlets and leaflets for sale at National Park Service sites.

SOUTHWESTERN MONUMENTS ASSOCIATION: The Association is also a nonprofit cooperating association supporting historical, scientific, and educational activities of the National Park Service. It was formed in 1946 to provide accurate information concerning the Southwest to the traveling public; to stimulate and encourage scientific research in the historical and natural sciences within the National Park System areas in the Southwest; to publish information and technical papers dealing with various historical and natural sciences; to develop and maintain in the National Park Service areas reference libraries available to the public; and to assemble and safeguard in the National Park Service areas of the Southwest study collections and exhibits germane to these areas. The Association publishes a catalog listing items distributed through its sales centers.

Foreign and International Organizations

Canadian Museums Association (CMA), 331 Cooper Street, Suite 400, Ottawa, Ontario K2P 0G5 Canada.

The Canadian Museums Association was incorporated in 1947 to promote, on a national basis, the interests of all Canadian museums and the welfare of their staffs. Its purposes are to advance public museum and art gallery services in Canada by promoting among museums a greater consciousness of their responsibilities as cultural institutions; acting as a clearinghouse for information of special interest and relevance to the Canadian museum scene; promoting and supporting museum training programs; extending assistance to museums in securing competent staff; and cooperating with regional, national and international associations to serve better the museum community in Canada.

The Association is governed by a national council of sixteen members, elected by individual, institution and association members. The Executive Committee is composed of the President, Vice President, and Secretary-Treasurer, and is aided by committees on education, elections, finance, membership, publications, and training.

Membership includes the voting categories of individual, association and institution, and nonvoting categories of student and affiliate. The Association sponsors regional meetings and seminars, and holds an annual conference.

PUBLICATIONS: *CMA gazette/AMC gazette,* quarterly beginning Winter 1975 (succeeds bimonthly magazine published 1966-1974); *museogramme,* monthly, newsletter begun 1973 for members; *Basic Museum Management; The Technical Requirements of Small Museums; Directory of Canadian Museums; CMA Bibliography;* annual report; conference proceedings; *CMA Booklist* (current edition, 5th, 1978).

MUSEUM DOCUMENTATION CENTRE: The Centre was established to provide documentary resources on all aspects of museum operations, to assist wherever possible in museum research requirements, and to provide the necessary resource materials for the training of museum personnel. The Resource Library of the Centre maintains, as a prerequisite, a comprehensive and specialized collection of museological and related documentation in both French and English, as well as various foreign language publications. The Centre continues to seek out materials related to museum operations and activities in order to increase both its scope and efficiency as a clearinghouse for the museum community. The *CMA Bibliography,* begun in 1976 and supplemented with six-month updates, has been entered into the computer network of the National Inventory System. A brochure describing the services of the Centre is available.

TRAINING RESOURCES PROGRAM: The Association has revised its correspondence course to serve as an introduction to basic museum principles and practice with certification being awarded upon successful completion; a resource center with a library and publications order service; and a resource services program to aid those involved in training programs that includes lists of instructors, a seminar procedures manual, and audiovisual training aids. The Program also has a national seminar program including seminars for professionals in addition to a special session at the annual conference; a training publications program including materials published in the quarterly or in separate pamphlets; and limited financial aid for travel, special research projects, and internships.

Heritage Canada, P.O. Box 1358, Station B, Ottawa, Ontario K1P 5R4, Canada.

Heritage Canada is a nonprofit corporation formed in 1973 to promote, preserve and develop articles, buildings and landscapes for the enjoyment of present and future generations. It also holds in trust for the nation buildings and landscapes that are its heritage. It works closely with provincial representatives, other voluntary organizations and individuals concerned with heritage preservation, and enlists the support of individuals and groups in the protection of old buildings and natural areas. Policies are directed by a Board of Governors, and its work complements the National and Historic Parks Branch, Parks Canada, of the Department of Indian and Northern Affairs.

Membership is open to anyone interested in the preservation of individual buildings, groups of buildings, and areas of historical and natural value that are of national significance. Members are entitled to voting privileges, periodicals and reports, and use of research services.

REGIONAL COUNCILS: Comprised of one representative from each participating organization, eight councils were created in 1975 under the guidance of the regional governors of Heritage Canada. The Councils hold regional meetings, publish newsletters, take initiative in local legislation and studying techniques of area conservation, and sponsor workshops. The Regional Councils with numbers of organizations are: Atlantic Provinces—Newfoundland, Nova Scotia, Prince Edward Island, New Brunswick (22); Quebec Region—entire Province (19); Eastern Ontario—Ottawa Valley, National Capital Region, Cornwall area (17); Central Ontario—Kingston, Peterborough areas (8); Western Ontario—Toronto, Niagara Peninsula, North and West Ontario (42); Manitoba—entire Province (7); Alberta-Saskatchewan—entire Provinces (17); British Columbia-Yukon—Province and Territory (25).

PROFESSIONAL SERVICES: Communications center for voluntary associations and individuals; information and program material for local associations; advice and technical assistance to local associations; public education programs; cooperation with the Canada Council, the provinces, universities and technical colleges to provide training courses for restoration specialists; resource and clearinghouse for exchange of technical information at the national and international level; Awards program.

PUBLICATIONS: *Heritage Canada,* bimonthly magazine of activities; *Annual Report;* proceedings of symposia; monographs and studies on conservation areas; posters and brochures; bibliography; do-it-yourself publications. A publications list is available.

PROPERTY: Property may be acquired by donation, bequest, purchase, lease, or exchange and may include real and personal property. Real property of special significance, "Heritage Property," is held in trust and not sold or mortgaged, but may be leased or transferred to federal, provincial, or municipal departments or agencies or private agencies for appropriate use. Worthwhile buildings renovated for adaptive use are placed under restrictive covenants for protection. Acquired property, of commercial value only may be operated for its revenue, sold, leased, or mortgaged. Personal property may be declared "Heritage Property" and retained as an integral part of a building or landscape, or such collections may be turned over to appropriate federal agencies.

National Historic Parks and Sites Branch, Parks Canada, Department of Indian Affairs and Northern Development, Ottawa, Ontario K1A OH4 Canada.

The national park concept, which began in 1872 with Yellowstone National Park in the United States, was applied to Canada in 1885 when the Canadian government reserved from private ownership the mineral hot springs of Sulphur Mountain in what is now Banff National Park. Two years later it was expanded and named Rocky Mountain Park, the first federal park in Canada. By 1907 four other reserves were added; this formed the nucleus of the park system after the Dominion Forest Reserves and Parks Act was passed in 1911. A National Parks Branch was created to protect, administer and develop the parks which include national parks, national historic parks and sites, historic waterways, wild rivers and byways. Headquarters for Parks Canada is in Ottawa; five regional offices are: Atlantic Regional Office, Halifax; Quebec Regional Office, Quebec City; Ontario Regional Office, Cornwall; Prairie Regional Office,

Winnipeg; Western Regional Office, Calgary. A complete listing of parks is included in the 1972 and 1973 editions of *Canada Year Book;* details and maps are available in *Canada's National Parks,* published by the Department of Indian Affairs and Northern Development.

NATIONAL HISTORIC PARKS AND SITES BRANCH: The Dominion Forest Reserves and Parks Act of 1911 created in the Department of the Interior a Dominion Parks Board to administer national and historic parks. In 1917, Fort Anne at Annapolis Royal, Nova Scotia, was declared Canada's first National Park of historic significance. A seven-member Historic Sites and Monuments Board of Canada was formed to advise the minister on sites of national historical interest. The National Parks Act of 1930 provided that the Governor in Council may set apart any land as a National Historic Park to commemorate an historic event, or preserve any historic landmark or any object of historic, prehistoric or scientific interest of national importance. The Historic Sites and Monuments Act of 1953 provided the statutory base for the operation of the Historic Sites and Monuments Board and defined the role of the board as adviser to the minister. Further legislation in 1955 and 1959 amended and broadened the scope of the original act. The Canadian Historic Sites Division was created in the Department in 1955 to develop, interpret, operate and maintain historic parks and sites and to act as secretariat for the board. It was later renamed the National Historic Sites Service; in 1973 it became the National Historic Parks and Sites Branch.

The *National Historic Parks and Sites Program* consists of some 80 national historic parks and major sites, over 53 operational, and in the commemoration with plaques of over 650 persons and events of national (as opposed to local or regional) significance. The department has entered into 40 cost-sharing agreements with provincial and municipal governments and with incorporated nonprofit societies for the acquisition and restoration of architecturally or historically significant buildings and structures on the understanding that the other party will pay the balance of the acquisition and restoration costs and will maintain the buildings in perpetuity. A number of monuments which commemorate people and events significant in the nation's history are maintained by the Branch. Full details on location and characteristics of parks and sites are available from the Department.

The 1953 Act provides for a board of 15 members: two representatives each from Ontario and Quebec and one from each of the eight other provinces appointed by the Governor in Council, the Dominion Archivist, one representative from the National Museums of Canada and one from the Department of Indian Affairs and Northern Development as ex officio members. The board may recommend that sites, buildings and other structures of national importance be developed as National Historic Parks or Historic Sites or that commemoration be carried out by the erection of plaques of the Historic Sites and Monuments Board of Canada, or in exceptional circumstances, of distinctive monuments. Suggestions for the establishment of parks and sites come from many sources including historical societies and other groups, the general public and board members themselves. Before a site is referred to the board for consideration, a background paper is prepared by the Branch research staff. The board then determines the significance of the site, makes its recommendation and, if approved, a development plan is prepared. A policy statement in 1968 specified that for commemoration, a site or structure must be closely associated with a person, place or event of national historical importance, or it must illustrate the cultural, social, political, economic or military patterns of history or of a prehistoric people or archeological discovery, or be valuable as an example of architecture. The statement included guidelines for the provision of visitor services, interpretative programs and information to the public. Standards were established for the preservation, restoration and reconstruction of structures which stressed authenticity in the materials used and in the furnishings and artifacts. The policy recognized the need for a comprehensive program to give full thematic and geographical representation and to establish a long-range planning program.

The *Canadian Inventory of Historic Building,* another Branch undertaking begun in 1970, is a computerized program to survey, analyze and categorize old buildings in Canada. The three-phased project consists of the recording of the exteriors of nearly 100,000 buildings and producing a complete view of the architectural heritage; recording in detail the interiors and analyzing the structures of the best 5,000 buildings selected from the results of the first phase; and selecting from Phase II particularly significant structures for study for eventual consideration by the Historic Sites and Monuments Board for further commemoration.

RESEARCH AND PUBLICATION: The Branch carries out extensive archeological and historical research in support of the identification and development of national historic parks and sites. Unpublished research papers have been grouped together in the *Manuscript Report* series and copies have been deposited with the Public Archives of Canada and the provincial archives for the use of the public. Research results are published in *Canadian Historic Sites,* a series of occasional papers in archeology and history available for sale through Information Canada, Ottawa. Parks folders and information leaflets are available for all operational parks.

National Museums of Canada (NMC), Ottawa, Ontario K1A 0M8 Canada.

Established by Act of Parliament in 1968, the National Museums of Canada is a crown corporation governed by a fourteen-member Board of Trustees composed of Canadians from various backgrounds and all regions of the country. The NMC administers Canada's four National Museums: The National Gallery of Canada, the National Museum of Man (which includes the Canadian War Museum), the National Museum of Natural Sciences, and the National Museum of Science and Technology (which includes the National Aeronautical Collection).

NATIONAL MUSEUM POLICY: In 1972 the corporation was charged with the implementation and administration of the National Museum Policy whose objectives are to give the Canadian public easier access to the objects and collections that form the Canadian cultural heritage, and to preserve them for future generations. The Policy involves large and small museums in all regions of the country. Smaller institutions are encouraged to improve the abilities of their professional staff and improve the museum facilities so they can better preserve and display their artifacts. Larger institutions are encouraged to develop advisory services for smaller institutions, to help them improve the quality of their exhibitions and loans for people in remote areas of the country. The Policy consists of four major programs.

The *National Inventory of Collections* is a computerized inventory of the art and artifacts across Canada that compose the national cultural heritage.

The *Museumobiles Program* provides a number of mobile museum units that can be transported to rural and remote regions of the country not now served by museological institutions.

The *Canadian Conservation Institute* provides laboratories across the country to help museums and art galleries to preserve and conserve their collections.

The *Museum Assistance Program* provides financial and other assistance to museological institutions for projects that train and develop museum staff, improve facilities, support education and extension programs within museums, and other projects such as traveling exhibitions, that increase public viewing of collections.

PUBLICATIONS: Catalog available from Publishing Division, 200 Laurier Avenue West, 21st Floor, Ottawa, Ontario K1A 0M8 Canada.

The Museums Association, 87 Charlotte Street, London W1P 2BX, England.

Founded in 1889, The Museums Association is an organization comprising and representing museums and art galleries and those who work in them both in the British Isles and overseas. The purposes of the Association are to promote the establishment and better administration of museums and art galleries and to improve the qualifications and status of members of museum staffs.

Its activities include the collection and publication of information about museums and the subjects they deal with, and the arrangement of courses of study in these subjects. The Association endeavors to represent the interests of museums and the profession in dealings with governmental and other outside bodies, whether public or private, national or foreign, and also to assist such bodies to establish a closer relationship with museums. It maintains links, in the interests of international cooperation, with related organizations in all parts of the world, including UNESCO and the International Council of Museums.

The Museums Association works in collaboration with the Carnegie United Kingdom Trust, which has made grants for the improvement of the museum service in the British Isles. Assistance from the Trust is available for the provision of expert reports on the development or reorganization of museums and art galleries, towards the provision of new facilities or projects in the museum field, including countryside schemes under the aegis of museums, and collaboration between museums. Grants are also available for training projects for students at the Leicester University Department of Museum Studies and other approved training bodies, and for study tours to enable members of museum staffs to gain experience relevant to their museum duties. In addition, the Trust makes a contribution towards the cost of the educational services provided by the Association.

Membership is open to persons connected with or interested in museums. There are eight classes of members including fellows, students, and institutions. The Association sponsors an annual five-day conference, and other meetings to promote exchange of information between members of museum staffs.

PUBLICATIONS: *Museums Journal,* quarterly, technical index for 1930-55 and 1955-66 available and vols. 1-75 available in microfilm; *Bulletin,* monthly newsletter for members;

Museums Yearbook annual (succeeds *Calendar*), directory of museums and art galleries in the British Isles; Handbook for Museum Curators series, published 1956-1967; Information Sheet series, begun 1967.

TRAINING PROGRAMS: The Diploma of the Association is the recognized qualification in curatorship within the museum profession, and is awarded on the recommendation of the Association's Education Committee to those members who have had at least three years' fulltime experience in a museum or art gallery (or two years, if university graduates), have completed the required courses of study, and have passed the prescribed examinations. By the institution of the Diploma, which is the essential qualification for Associateship, and by the election of suitably qualified Associates as Fellows, the Association endeavors to set standards of curatorship and professional ability that will be recognized both inside and outside the profession. A Conservation Certificate has been instituted for those museum staff whose work is primarily concerned with the conservation and restoration of museum objects. The Technical Certificate of the Association is the qualification for museum workers whose duties are primarily technical, and is awarded after examination to candidates who have not less than five years' experience in museum work.

SPECIAL GROUPS: Information Retrieval Group of the Museums Association, organized in 1968; Group for Education Services in Museums.

International Council of Museums (ICOM), 1 rue Miollis, 75732 Paris 15, France.

Founded in 1946, the International Council of Museums is the international, non-governmental, and professional organization representing museums and the museum profession. It maintains close consultative and cooperative relations with UNESCO, International Council of Monuments and Sites (ICOMOS), and the International Centre for the Study of the Preservation and the Restoration of Cultural Property (Rome Centre), and other national, regional, or international, intergovernmental or nongovernmental organizations, with the authorities responsible for museums and with specialists of other disciplines. The primary aims are: to define, support and aid museums and the museum institution; to establish, support, and reinforce the museum profession; to organize cooperation and mutual assistance between museums and between the members of the museum profession in the different countries; to emphasize the importance of the role played by museums and the museum profession within each community and in the promotion of a greater knowledge and understanding among peoples.

The General Assembly is the governing body of ICOM. Activities are carried out through the Paris-based Secretariat, National Committees, and International Committees. The Secretariat conducts the day-to-day operation of the organization and world-wide coordination of its activities and programs. Through its National Committees, ICOM coordinates a vast international effort between all countries aimed at a thorough and progressive transformation of the concept of a museum; toward an increase of its scientific role; improvements in display and exhibition; the modernization and expansion of its educational and cultural activities, and the preservation of the cultural heritage through conservation.

The International Committees are composed of the leading authorities in a given type of museum discipline, or in an activity common to all museums. These groups of professionals come together regularly to discuss latest developments, familiarize themselves with new techniques, and make recommendations which serve the interest of ICOM members throughout the world. The Committees are: Archaeology and History; Architecture and Museum Techniques; Applied Art; Modern Art; Conservation; Costume; Documentation; Education; Ethnography; International Art Exhibitions; Training of Personnel; Musical Instruments (CIMCIM); Regional Museums; Public Relations; Natural History; Science and Technology (CIMUSET); Museum Security (ICMS); Glass. Affiliated International Associations include: Agricultural Museums (IAMA); Arms and Military History; Association of European Open-Air Museums; Performing Arts (SIBMAS); Transport Museums (IATM).

Membership is open to individuals and institutions. The support and services of ICOM are most required by museums in countries least able to afford them, and for this an independent tax-exempt foundation has been established to obtain and make available funds in support of ICOM, its members and their associations, as well as other organizations with similar aims. ICOM holds a Triennial World Conference; meetings of National and International Committees; and special conferences and seminars.

REGIONAL AGENCIES: ICOM maintains the ICOM Regional Agency in Asia, in New Delhi, India; and encourages regional programs in cooperation with other related organizations in Africa, Latin America, and Arab countries.

PUBLICATIONS: *ICOM News,* quarterly; *International Museological Bibliography,* annual; Reports and Papers on Museums series; papers from symposiums and general conferences; *ICOM Education,* annual, information on current events in museum education published by the ICOM International Committee for Education and Cultural Action (formerly *Museums' Annual: Education-Cultural Action,* 1968-1975); results of surveys, technical research, and committee recommendations; contributions to and cooperation in planning, distribution and sale of the UNESCO magazine, *Museum.*

UNESCO/ICOM DOCUMENTATION CENTRE: The Centre is an outgrowth of a library established in 1947 by the Museums and Monuments Division of UNESCO for its own research and documentation. The following year it was turned over to the International Council of Museums. It is administered by a small staff and maintains the largest library of its kind in existence. The responsibilities of the Centre are for: acquiring and conserving all documentation of any nature concerning subjects of interest to ICOM; making use of such information for purposes of diffusion and communicating the same to the personnel of UNESCO and to the members of ICOM, as well as, where possible, to all experts, students or qualified researchers; studying and using all means of improving and increasing the diffusion of information; encouraging the creation of regional documentation centers and coordinating their activities; assisting the National Committees and professional associations in the fields of documentation and information, more particularly by the instruction of trainees; assisting the International Committees in their documentary tasks (directories, questionnaires, cataloging), etc.; assisting the ICOM Secretariat in its tasks of a documentary, informative or bibliographical nature.

Documentation is received from all over the world and includes directories, manuals, treatises, monographs, guidebooks, exhibition catalogues, photographs, architectural plans, bulletins and brochures. The material is analyzed, cross-referenced and classified in an extensive scheme based on the Library of Congress method. A card index system (Synoptic) permits the entire literature of a given museum subject to be consulted at the flip of a finger. The system can be readily adapted to a mechanical, microfilm or electronic system of documentation. Documents are then placed at the disposal of visitors at the Centre and correspondents. The Centre is able to furnish photocopies on request at cost price.

The Centre has established an international directory of museums, and index of suppliers; and is developing technical bibliographies. It publishes annually an international bibliography of basic museum writing covering publications appearing two years before. It also maintains an Archive of National Legislations for the Protection of Cultural Property on microfiche to keep up to date material compiled for the handbook by Bonnie Burnham (cited under Management of Collections chapter).

AAM/ICOM: The United States National Committee merged with the American Association of Museums in 1973 to become AAM/ICOM. It is headquartered at the Association, 1055 Thomas Jefferson Street, N.W., Washington, D.C. 20007. For details, see AAM description.

United Nations Educational, Scientific and Cultural Organization (UNESCO), Place de Fontenoy, 75700 Paris, France.

The development of UNESCO programs began in 1924 when the League of Nations established the International Institute for Intellectual Cooperation, with a section designated the International Office of Museums. IOM published the bulletin *Mouseion;* a two-volume work, "Museographie"; and a number of technical manuals. Many of its projects were subsequently carried on by its successor, UNESCO.

UNESCO is an independent agency of the United Nations and has over 140 member states which contribute to its program. Its member states meet biennially and review and vote upon its program and budget. The program concerned with the preservation and presentation of cultural property is administered by the Cultural Heritage Division which in turn is divided into three sections: studies and exchange of information; international norms and standards; and operations and training.

The *Section for Studies* carries out a series of projects in this field, frequently in cooperation with The International Centre for the Study of the Preservation and Restoration of Cultural Property, Rome, Italy (Rome Centre); the International Council of Museums (ICOM); the International Council of Monuments and Sites (ICOMOS); and the International Federation of Landscape Architects (IFLA). It is responsible for the publication of the quarterly, *Museum;* manuals in the Museums and Monuments series; *The Cultural Heritage Bulletin;* and brochures and books. Seminars and symposia are also worked out in cooperation with international and regional organizations.

The *Section on Norms and Standards* is responsible for the preparation and application of international instruments (recommendations and conventions) for the protection and conservation of the cultural and natural heritage. To date, they include conventions: for the protection of cultural property in the event of armed conflict (The Hague, 1954); on the means of prohibiting and preventing the illicit import, export and transfer of ownership of cultural property (1970); on the international principles applicable to archaeological excavations (1956); concerning the most effective means of rendering museums accessible to everyone (1960); concerning the safeguarding of the beauty and character of landscapes and sites (1962); on the means of prohibiting and preventing the illicit export, import and transfer of ownership of cultural property (1964); concerning the protection, at national level, of the cultural and natural heritage (1972); concerning the safeguarding and contemporary role of historic areas (1976); on the international exchange of cultural property (1976); on the protection of movable cultural property (1978). In addition the Section supplies secretarial services for the World Heritage Committee (1972 Convention) and prepares specialized studies and publications in this field.

The *Section for Operations and Training* carries out the following types of projects at the request of the governments concerned: (1) International Campaigns for the Preservation and Presentation of some of the world's outstanding monuments and sites. As of 1980 the General Conference of UNESCO has carried out twenty-eight campaigns including the Nubian monuments (Arab Republic of Egypt); City of Venice (Italy); Borobudur (Indonesia); Moenjodaro (Pakistan); Kathmandu Valley (Nepal); Citadel of la Ferrìre (Haiti); Neolithic monuments (Malta); (2) Projects financed under the United Nations Development Programme (UNDP) for which UNESCO is the executing agency such as the preservation and development of sites and monuments in Peru and Mongolia; (3) Projects financed by the World Bank for which UNESCO provides advisory services such as for the preservation and presentation of the Island of Gorée, off Dakar, Senegal; the modernization of the National Museum in Cairo (Arab Republic of Egypt); the preservation of Petra (Jordan). Many other projects are financed under UNESCO's Programme of Participation through which consultants, fellowships and equipment are furnished. It also has a small budget for emergency rescue for property damaged by natural or other causes. Projects approved under the World Heritage Fund are also carried out by this Section.

TRAINING PROGRAMS: Courses are given in national training programs and regional centers such as in Jos, Nigeria; The International Louis Leakey Memorial Institute for African Prehistory (TILLMIAP); and Churubusco, Mexico. Centers also exist which receive part of their support from Regional UNDP budgets such as the one for the Andean countries in South America; and for South Asia in Lucknow, India. International courses include those given for the training of architect/restorers at the Rome Centre; courses financed by UNESCO in the preservation of stone in Venice, Italy (with the cooperation of the Rome Centre and the Italian National Services); the exchange of specialists in the conservation of historic quarters of cities between Eastern and Western Europe and North America (in collaboration with ICOMOS).

INTERNATIONAL COOPERATION: UNESCO works closely with national, regional and international bodies in these fields. It provides contracts to the Rome Centre, and subventions and contracts to ICOM, ICOMOS, and IFLA. It provides subventions to the UNESCO/ICOM and the UNESCO/ICOMOS Documentation Centers and contributes towards the development of a computer lined service between these units and the library of the Rome Centre. It also carries out projects in cooperation with U.S. institutions and organizations such as the Advisory Council for Historic Preservation; the Smithsonian Institution and national ICOM, ICOMOS and IFLA Committees as well as private committees and foundations contributing to UNESCO's program. UNESCO/

ICOMOS Documentation Centre is headquartered at 75 rue du Temple, 75003 Paris, France. The UNESCO/ICOM Documentation Centre is located at 1 rue Miollis, 75732 Paris 15, France; for details, see ICOM description.

Regional, State and Local

Adamson, Anthony. "New Solutions to Old Problems, Upper Canada Village," *The Museologist,* 82 (March 1962), pp. 8-15. ♦ Describes how buildings and history were preserved as a folk museum.

Allen, Jon L. *Aviation and Space Museums of America.* New York: Arco Publishing Co., 1975. 287 pp., illus. ♦ Pictorial survey of 57 collections from vintage and World War II planes to Apollo mooncraft. Arranged by region; includes Canada.

American Heritage. *The American Heritage Book of Great Historic Places.* Narrative by Richard M. Ketchum, introduction by Bruce Catton. New York: American Heritage Publishing Co., 1957. 376 pp., illus., maps.

Angle, Paul M. *The Chicago Historical Society, 1856-1956: An Unconventional Chronicle.* New York: Rand McNally & Co., 1956. 256 pp., illus., index.

Arizona Historical Society. *The Arizona Historical Society Today.* By Sybil Ellinwood. Tucson, Ariz.: The Society, 1973. 56 pp., illus. ♦ Describes history of the society and its programs (museum, library, archives, publications, historic sites, educational programs, affiliates).

Atkinson, Frank, and Michael Holton. "Open Air and Folk Museums," *Museums Journal,* 72:4 (March 1973), pp. 140-142. ♦ Paper based on interim report of the Working Party on Open Air Museums set up in 1972. Includes definition, scope and role, potential.

Aymar, Brandt. *A Pictorial Treasury of the Marine Museums of the World.* A Guide to the Maritime Collections, Restorations, Replicas, and Marine Museums in Twenty-three Countries. New York: Crown Publishers, 1967. 244 pp., illus.

Ball, Laurel. "Swedish Folk Museums," *Museums Journal,* 70:1 (June 1970), pp. 19-23. ♦ Report given in a course in folk life studies for British Museum curators.

Black, Mary. "Museum of American Folk Art: A Quinquennial Report," *Curator,* XII:2 (1969), pp. 96-109.

Boatner, Mark M., III. *Landmarks of the American Revolution: A Guide to Locating and Knowing What Happened at the Sites of Independence.* Harrisburg, Pa.: Stackpole Books, 1973. 608 pp., illus. ♦ Directory arranged by state; includes houses, cemeteries, geographical sites.

Boesen, Gudmund. *Danish Museums.* Edited by Kristjan Bure. English text by Reginald Spink. Copenhagen: Committee for Danish Cultural Activities Abroad, 1966. 247 pp., illus.

Cardiff, Wales. National Museum of Wales. Welsh Folk Museum. *Handbook.* St. Fagans: The Museum, 1970. 54 pp., illus., plans.

Carmichael, Leonard, and J. C. Long. *James Smithson and the Smithsonian Story.* New York: G. P. Putnam's Sons, 1965. 316 pp., illus., bibliog.

Carson, Hampton Lawrence. *A History of the Historical Society of Pennsylvania.* Philadelphia: Published by the Society under the special centennial publication fund, 1940. 2 vols., illus., bibliog. footnotes, index.

Chamberlain, Samuel, and Henry N. Flynt. *Historic Deerfield: Houses and Interiors.* Rev. ed. New York: Hastings House, 1965. 182 pp., illus., map, index. ♦ Revised and enlarged edition of the authors' "Frontier of Freedom."

Coleman, Laurence Vail. *College and University Museums; A Message for College and University Presidents.* Washington, D.C.: American Association of Museums, 1942. 73 pp., plates, plans.

Coleman, Laurence Vail. *Company Museums.* Washington, D.C.: American Association of Museums, 1943. 173 pp., photos, directory, index. ♦ Includes chapters on management, collecting, exhibition, and interpretation. Appendices: Parent Companies; Company Museums in U.S.; Company Museums in Canada.

Collins, James L., Jr. "The U.S. Army Museum System," *Curator*, XVII:4 (December 1974), pp. 264-279.

Colonial Williamsburg Foundation. *Official Guidebook and Map.* 7th ed. Williamsburg, Va.: The Foundation, c1972, 1975. 108 pp., illus.

"Conference on Countryside Centres, Leiscester, 1968," *Museums Journal*, 69:2 (September 1969), pp. 63-73.

Cummings, Abbott Lowell, ed. "Restoration Villages," *Art in America*, 43:2 (May 1955), entire issue.

Davidson, Marshall B. *The American Heritage History of Notable American Houses.* New York: American Heritage Publishing Co., 1971. 383 pp., illus. ◆ See also: *Historic Houses of America Open to the Public* (An American Heritage Guide).

Edison Institute (Henry Ford Museum and Greenfield Village), Dearborn, Mich. *Folk Art and the Street of Shops, Henry Ford Museum.* Dearborn: Edison Institute, c1971. 47 pp.

Edison Institute (Henry Ford Museum and Greenfield Village), Dearborn, Mich. *Greenfield Village and the Henry Ford Museum.* New York: Crown Publishers, 1972. 247 pp., illus., index. ◆ Photographic essay on the collections and events of the museum village. A combined edition of two separately published works: *Greenfield Village*, and *The Henry Ford Museum.*

Eleutherian Mills-Hagley Foundation, Greenville, Del. *The Hagley Museum: A Chronicle of America's Industrial Heritage.* Greenville, Del.: The Foundation, 1963. 48 pp., illus., maps.

Engelstad, Eivind S. *Norwegian Museums: Museums of Art and Social History.* Oslo: Royal Norwegian Ministry of Foreign Affairs, Office of Cultural Relations, 1959. 53 pp., illus.

Greene, Richard Lawrence, and Kenneth Edward Wheeling. *A Pictorial History of the Shelburne Museum.* Shelburne, Vt.: Shelburne Museum, 1972. 127 pp., illus.

Groff, Sibyl McC. *New Jersey's Historic Houses: A Guide to Homes Open to the Public.* South Brunswick, N.J.: A. S. Barnes, 1971. 247 pp., illus., index. ◆ Descriptions of towns and houses with times of admission.

Haas, Irvin. *America's Historic Houses and Restorations.* New York: Hawthorn Books, 1967. 271 pp., illus. ◆ Arranged by geographic region.

Haas, Irvin. *America's Historic Inns and Taverns.* New York: Arco Publishing Co., c1972. 182 pp., illus., bibliog.

Haas, Irvin. *America's Historic Villages and Restorations.* New York: Arco Publishing Company, 1974. 149 pp., illus.

Hamarneh, Saml Khalaf. *Pharmacy Museums and Historical Collections on Public View, U.S.A.* Madison, Wisc.: American Institute of the History of Pharmacy, 1972. 49 pp., illus., bibliog. ◆ Its Publication no. 1.

Hice, Charles A. "History and Hospitality, Canadian Style," *Western Museums Quarterly*, 4:4 (December 1967), pp. 17-20. ◆ Report of the American Association of Museums meeting in Toronto.

Hinshaw, Merton E. "The Museum in a Small City," *Western Museums Quarterly*, 4:2 (June 1967), pp. 1-6. ◆ Description of role and activities.

Historic Houses of America Open to the Public. By the editors of American Heritage; editor in charge, Beverley DaCosta. New York: American Heritage Publishing Co., 1971. 320 pp., illus. ◆ An American Heritage Guide.

Illustrated Guide to the Treasures of America. Pleasantville, N.Y.: Reader's Digest Association, 1974. 624 pp., illus. ◆ Regional Guide to architecture, sites and objects.

Karp, Walter. *The Smithsonian Institution; An Establishment for the Increase and Diffusion of Knowledge Among Men.* Washington, D.C.: Smithsonian Institution, 1965. 125 pp., illus.

Katz, Herbert, and Marjorie Katz. *Museum Adventures: An Introduction to Discovery.* New York: Coward-McCann, 1969. 253 pp., illus. ◆ Descriptions of visits to museums of art, science, nature, history and special places.

Kocher, Alfred Lawrence, and Howard Dearstyne. *Colonial Williamsburg, Its Buildings and Gardens: A Descriptive Tour of the Restored Capital of the British Colony of Virginia.* Rev. ed. Williamsburg, Va.: Colonial Williamsburg; distributed by Holt, Rinehart & Winston, New York, 1961. 104 pp., illus., bibliog.

Lathrop, Elise L. *Historic Houses of Early America.* New York: Tudor Publishing Co., c1927, 1941. 464 pp., illus., bibliog. ♦ Photographs and architectural history. "A Record of Historic Houses by Towns and States," pp. 453-464.

Lea, John S., comp. *Brief Guide to the Smithsonian Institution.* Washington, D.C.: Smithsonian Institution Press, 1972. 96 pp., maps, floor plans, index. ♦ Illustrated guide to the museums and galleries that comprise the Institution; brief history and information on each building.

Lerman, Leo. *The Museum, One Hundred Years and the Metropolitan Museum of Art.* New York: Viking Press, 1969. 400 pp., illus., map, index. ♦ Brief text accompanied by plans and diagrams of the buildings, photographs of the interiors and personalities of each era, and selected reproductions of its collections.

Lindsley, James Elliott. *A Certain Splendid House: The Centennial History of the Washington Association of New Jersey.* Morristown, N.J.: Washington Association of New Jersey, 1974. 136 pp., illus., map, bibliog. ♦ History of an historical society.

Lord, Clifford L. *Reuben Gold Thwaites and the Progressive Historical Society.* Madison, Wisc.: State Historical Society of Wisconsin, 1963. 15 pp. ♦ The Burton Lecture.

Lord, Clifford L., and Carl Ubbelohde. *Clio's Servant: The State Historical Society of Wisconsin, 1846-1954.* Madison, Wisc.: State Historical Society of Wisconsin, 1967. 598 pp., illus., bibliog. references.

Lyngby, Denmark. Frilandmuseet. *Frilandmuseet/The Open Air Museum.* 7th Department of the National Museum. English Guide by Kai Uldall. Kobenhaven, Denmark: Nordlunde, 1966. 87 pp., illus., map.

Marine Historical Association, Inc. *Mystic Seaport Guide.* Mystic, Conn.: The Association, 1974. 64 pp., illus.

Mariners' Museum, Newport News, Va. *The Mariners' Museum, 1930-1950: A History and Guide.* Compiled by Alexander C. Brown. Newport News, Va.: The Museum, 1953. 264 pp., illus., map. ♦ Its Publication no. 20.

Matthews, William H., III. *A Guide to the National Parks; Their Landscape and Geol-* ogy. Garden City, N.Y.: Doubleday, 1973. 259 pp., illus., bibliog.

Merrimack Valley Textile Museum, North Andover, Mass. *The Housing of a Textile Collection.* Occasional Reports, no. 1. North Andover, Mass.: The Museum, 1969. 32 pp., illus., bibliog.

Murfin, James V. *National Park Service Guide to the Historic Places of the American Revolution.* Washington, D.C.: Office of Publications, National Park Service, for sale by U.S. Government Printing Office, 1974. 135 pp., illus., maps, reading list. ♦ Guide to existing sites and structures relating to the Revolutionary War, grouped by states and areas, and including associated history.

New York State Historical Association. *The New York State Historical Association and Its Museums: An Informal Guide.* Edited by Frederick L. Rath, Jr. Cooperstown, N.Y.: The Association, 1968. 96 pp., illus., map.

Newark Museum Association, Newark, N.J. *A Survey: 50 Years of the Newark Museum: History, Paintings, Sculpture, Decorative Arts, Oriental, Ancient, Coins, Ethnological, Science, Trustees.* Newark: The Association, 1959. 136 pp., illus. ♦ Brief history and catalog; includes the record of the country's first museum training program initiated in 1925 under John Cotton Dana.

Old Sturbridge Village, Sturbridge, Mass. *Old Sturbridge Village: A Guidebook.* By Catherine Fennelly. 5th ed. Sturbridge, Mass.: The Village, 1966. 77 pp., illus., map. ♦ Old Sturbridge Village Booklet series no. 6. Out of print.

Perrin, Richard W. E. *Outdoor Museums.* Milwaukee, Wisc.: Milwaukee Public Museum, c1975. 83 pp., illus. ♦ Overview of American and European museums and recommendations for an outdoor museum in Wisconsin. A series of articles originally published in *Lore.* Milwaukee Public Museum Publications in Museology no. 4.

Petersen, Eugene T. *The Preservation of History at Mackinac.* Lansing, Mich.: Mackinac Island State Park Commission, 1972. 224 pp., illus.

Quimby, Maureen O'Brien. *Eleutherian Mills.* Greenville, Del.: Hagley Museum, 1973. 87 pp., illus. ♦ History of the house, guide to its contents and story of restoration of the Mills.

Reibel, Daniel B. *A Guide to Old Economy: Third and Final Home of the Harmony Society.* Harrisburg: Pennsylvania Historical and Museum Commission, 1972. 43 pp., illus., bibliog. ◆ Written in response to requests for a more comprehensive guide and history of the Harmony Society and Old Economy.

Reid, William; John Tanner; and Margaret Weston. "The Financing and Administration of New National Museums," *Museums Journal,* 73:3 (December 1973), pp. 114-119. ◆ Three reports given at the Annual Conference of The Museums Association, England, 1973. National Army Museum: development and fund raising, stabilization and consolidation, staff and budget analysis, works services. Royal Air Force Museum: building, finance, collections. The new National Railway Museum: progress report.

Richards, William N. "The William Penn Memorial Museum and Archives Building," *The Museologist,* 124 (September 1972), pp. 8-17.

Schlebecker, John T. *Living Historical Farms: A Walk into the Past.* Washington, D.C.: Smithsonian Institution, 1969. 31 pp., illus.

Schwartz, Alvin. *Museum; The Story of America's Treasure Houses.* 1st ed. New York: E. P. Dutton and Co., 1967. 256 pp., illus., bibliog. ◆ General overview of museums and their function and organization. Includes art museums, history museums, natural history museums, and museums of science and industry.

Shoemaker, Floyd C. *The State Historical Society of Missouri: A Semicentennial History.* Columbia: The State Historical Society of Missouri, 1948. 193 pp., illus., appendices, bibliog., index.

Stewart, John J. "Historic Gardens in Canada and the United States," *Newsletter of APT,* 2:3 (June 1973), entire issue. ◆ Initial study includes location and description of gardens, historic garden experts, sources of plant materials and seeds.

Stockholm. Nordiska Museet. *The Nordiska Museet and Skansen: An Introduction to the History and Activities of a Famous Swedish Museum.* By Mats Rehnberg. Stockholm: The Museum, 1957. 194 pp., illus., bibliog.

Strawbery Banke, Inc. *Strawbery Banke in Portsmouth, New Hampshire: Official Guidebook.* Edited by Nancy R. Beck. 3rd rev. ed. Portsmouth, N.H.: Strawbery Banke, Inc., c1971. 83 pp., illus., map.

Tishler, William H. "Saving Ourselves: Our Rural Heritage," *Museum News,* 55:4 (March/April 1977), pp. 21-25 ◆ Description of Old World Wisconsin.

Tomkins, Calvin. *Merchants and Masterpieces: The Story of the Metropolitan Museum of Art.* 1st ed. New York: E. P. Dutton, 1970. 383 pp., illus., appendices, index. ◆ History of the museum given by introducing the personalities of its directors, curators, and trustees. Also provides an understanding of the development of other museums and their interrelationships.

Uldall, Kai. "Open Air Museums," *Museum,* X:1 (1957), pp. 68-96. ◆ Variety of national types.

Vail, Robert W. G. *Knickerbocker Birthday, A Sesqui-Centennial History of the New-York Historical Society, 1804-1954.* New York: New-York Historical Society, 1954. 547 pp., illus., maps, bibliog., index.

Wall, Alexander J. "The Case for Popular Scholarship at Old Sturbridge Village," *Museum News,* 47:5 (January 1969), pp. 14-19.

Westrate, J. Lee. *European Military Museums: A Survey of Their Philosophy, Facilities, Programs, and Management.* Washington, D.C.: Smithsonian Institution, 1961. 206 pp., illus. ◆ A model study of the problems of organizing and maintaining specialized museums, with implications for museums in general.

Whitehill, Walter M. *Museum of Fine Arts, Boston; A Centennial History.* Cambridge, Mass.: Belknap Press, 1970. 2 vols. (888 pp.), illus., bibliog. references. ◆ A continuous narrative rather than an historical survey, coupled with works of art from the museum's collection and a personal acquaintance with the museum and the city.

Williams, Henry Lionel, and Ottalie K. Williams. *A Treasury of Great American Houses.* 1st ed. New York: G. P. Putnam's Sons, 1970. 295 pp., illus., plans.

Williams, Patricia M. *Museums of Natural History and the People Who Work in Them.* New York: St. Martin's Press, c1973. 120 pp., illus. ◆ Describes the purposes, contents, functions and personnel of a natural history museum. Includes a list of natural history museums in the U.S.

Winterthur Portfolio. One. Winterhur, Del.: Henry Francis du Pont Winterthur Museum, 1964. 255 pp., illus. ◆ First volume in the series is a description of Winterthur. See also: *The Winterthur Story*, reprinted from *Winterthur Portfolio One* (1965), 165 pp., illus.

Zook, Nicholas. *A Guide to Gardens of New England Open to the Public.* Barre, Mass.: Barre Publishers, 1973. 96 pp., illus.

Zook, Nicholas. *Houses of New England Open to the Public.* Barre, Mass.: Barre Publishers, 1968. 126 pp., illus. ◆ Brief introduction and section on architecture; includes Fruitlands, Old Sturbridge Village, and Strawbery Banke.

Zook, Nicholas. *Houses of New York Open to the Public.* Barre, Mass.: Barre Publishers, 1969. 143 pp., illus., index. ◆ Discusses New York houses in general, and the Dutch influence on New York architecture, then goes on to list houses around the state and their backgrounds.

Zook, Nicholas. *Museum Villages U.S.A.* Barre, Mass.: Barre Publishing Co., c1970, 1971. 136 pp., illus., dictionary of museum villages. ◆ Descriptive guide to museum complexes arranged to illustrate growth and expansion of this country.

Arts Councils and Community Centers

Adams, William Howard. *The Politics of Art– Forming a State Arts Council.* New York: Arts Councils of America, 1966. 49 pp. ◆ Covers organization, programming, and financing of state arts councils. Appendices include definitions of terms, art survey forms, cultural facility surveys and program procedures.

American Council for the Arts. *Community Arts Agencies: A Handbook and Guide.* Ellen S. Daniels and Robert Porter, eds. New York: The Council, 1978. 408 pp.

Arey, June B. *State Arts Agencies in Transition: Purpose, Program, and Personnel.* Wayzata, Minn.: Spring Hill Conference Center, 1975. 267 pp., illus. ◆ Derived from

eight meetings held at the Center between December 1972 and December 1973.

Arts Council of Great Britain. *The Arts Council of Great Britain: What It Is and What It Does.' Twenty-five Questions and Answers about the Structure and Work of the Council.* 11th ed. London: Arts Council of Great Britain, 1975. 23 pp.

Arts Councils of America. *The Arts: A Central Element of a Good Society; Eleventh National Conference.* New York: 1966. 145 pp. ◆ Joint Conference of the Arts Councils of America and the American Symphony Orchestra League, held in Washington, D.C., June 16-19, 1965.

Associated Councils of the Arts. *The Arts: Planning for Change; Proceedings of the Twelfth National Conference, Associated Councils of the Arts, formerly Arts Councils of America, May 19-21, 1966, New York.* New York: 1966. 131 pp. ◆ A collection of articles on education and the arts, industry and the arts, arts centers, and leadership in the arts.

Biddle, Ludy. "Keeping Tradition Alive," *Museum News,* 55:5 (May/June 1977), pp. 35-42. ◆ Report on growth of Native American cultural centers.

Bird, Peter. "The Role of the Arts Council," *Museums Journal,* 68:2 (September 1968), pp. 84-86.

Burgard, Ralph. *Arts in the City: Organizing and Programming Community Arts Councils.* New York: Associated Councils of the Arts, 1968. 150 pp., bibliog., appendices. ◆ Appendices include community arts surveys, incorporation and by-laws, bibliography, arts agencies and ACA publications.

Burgard, Ralph. *The Creative Community: Arts and Science Programs for New and Renewing Communities.* New York: Associated Councils of the Arts, 1973? 70 pp. ◆ Report of a creative plan that outlines the potential role of future community arts councils or their alternatives.

Garton, Anthony V. "Community Arts Centers are Alive and Well," *Museum News,* 53:1 (September 1974), pp. 20-23. ◆ Argues that community arts centers serve a vast and varied audience and are able to relate to their communities in a way that large metropolitan museums often cannot.

27

Kimche, Lee. "Federal-State Conference on the Arts," *Museum News,* 48:3 (November 1969), pp. 26-28. ◆ Report on a three day conference on governmental action at federal and state levels, attended by executive directors of artistic and academic communities, Arts Endowment and congressional leaders. The purpose of the meeting was to exchange information on programs of the state arts councils and to provide information on programs currently receiving federal support.

McLanathan, Richard. "A Venturesome Idea,"*Museum News,* 41:1 (September 1962), pp. 29-34. ◆ Details of the formation of the New York State Council on the Arts that served as a model for other states.

Martin, Keith. "A New Museum Concept," *Museum News,* 45:4 (January 1967), pp. 23-28. ◆ Description of the Roberson Center for the Arts and Sciences, Binghamton, New York, a cooperative cultural center.

National Endowment for the Arts. *The State Arts Agencies in 1974: All Present and Accounted For.* Research Division Report no. 8. New York: distr. by Publishing Center for Cultural Resources, 1978. 160 pp. ◆ Information and data on 55 official arts agencies covering their basic organization and structure; relationships with other government agencies; staffing patterns; their functions, practices and programs; and sources of funds and expenditures for program projects.

National Research Center of the Arts. *State Arts Councils.* Special editors: Janet English Gracey and Sally Gardner. New York: Associated Councils of the Arts, 1972. 80 pp., illus.

Newton, Michael, and Scott Hatley. *Persuade and Provide: The Story of the Arts and Education Council in St. Louis.* New York: Associated Councils of the Arts, 1970. 249 pp. ◆ Story of fundraising in St. Louis through the Arts and Education Fund.

Sennema, David C.; Nancy B. Call; and, Richard D. Collins. "State Arts Councils and Museums," *Museum News,* 49:10 (June 1971), pp. 24-28. ◆ Three reports of state arts commission support for museums, including program summaries and recommendations, in South Carolina, California and Maine.

NOTES

Advocates for the Arts, c/o Jack Duncan, 2210 Massachusetts Avenue, N.W., Washington, D.C. 20008. Originally a program of the American Council for the Arts in 1974, Advocates for the Arts has become a separate organization and continues its role of handling legal and legislative issues related to the arts. Its purpose is to assemble a national constituency of citizens to support economic, public and legal action for the arts, and to increase financial support of the arts by federal, state and local legislative bodies, and to improve the general artistic climate, e.g. financing through bond issues, promoting better architecture through zoning incentives, and finding funding for experimental work. Memberships are available. Published *The Arts Advocate,* a quarterly newsletter, from 1974-1976, and a Resource Kit.

American Council for the Arts, 570 Seventh Avenue, New York, New York 10018. Organized in 1960, the ACA is a nonprofit organization formed to provide professional guidance for state and community agencies and to act as a national advocate for the arts. It provides a central source of information and education and special assistance. Its work is supported by membership dues from individuals, state and community councils, municipal arts commissions, and by contributions from individuals, foundations and corporations. It does not make grants to individuals or organizations. It conducts research and surveys, and holds an annual assembly and seminars and conferences. Publications include: *Cultural Affairs,* quarterly (1967-1971); *ACA Report,* monthly, resource kit; *Arts in Common,* monthly, newsletter; *Word from Washington,* monthly; *Advocates for the Arts Resource Kit; Resource Kit for Community Arts Agencies.* Formerly: Community Arts Councils, 1960-1964; Arts Councils of America, 1965; Associated Councils of the Arts, 1966-1977.

Community Arts Management Program, Sangamon State University, Springfield, Illinois 62708. The Community Arts Management Program offers "Conversations on Arts Management," a project of videotaping leading arts administrators in informal conversations concerning their various areas of expertise. The video cassettes are available to arts organizations and interested individuals. The tapes are on three-quarter inch video cassettes and on audio cassettes for a modest charge; a brochure of the tapes and ordering instructions are available from the Program. Topics include issues in the arts; National Endowment for the Arts; Regional Arts Agencies/Regionalism, State Arts Agencies; Local Arts Agencies; Arts in General; Money for the Arts; Public Relations and Promotion; Arts Festivals; Arts and Recreation; Art and the Artist; Law and the Arts.

2
History and Contemporary Issues

Mankind's inclination to look back for answers is not new, nor is his inclination to lay to one side, for a future look as it were, those objects, materials and even structures that have special meaning or special value.

This chapter deals with perspectives and some of the more significant issues that confront those who are the principal conservators of the art, architecture, history, and culture of localities, nations, and the world. It deals first with a history of the development of historical organizations but moves quickly to the present, giving an overview of the growing body of literature about the relationships between the structures of today's society and the historical organizations. The range is wide, touching on most social and educational issues besetting our society today. The effective administrator today must be alert to "the passions of his times," to use Justice Oliver Wendell Holmes' apt phrase. The environment, aging, urban blight, technological change, obligations to the disadvantaged are only a few of the interest areas being explored today.

What such concern leads to is a re-examination of what is happening as more and more government agencies crowd the stage to lend their support to the often-beleaguered historical organization. The result frequently is a sense of obligation, not to mention a sense of panic, as one views the competition for public support. And that in turn leads to a need to examine the current economic issues that are affecting all historical and cultural organizations. There are discussions ranging from taxes to tourism in the final section of this chapter.

History and Definition

Adam, Thomas R. *The Civic Value of Museums.* 1937. Reprint. Ann Arbor, Mich.: University Microfilm, 1974. 114 pp. ◆ Studies in the Social Significance of Adult Education in the U.S., no. 4. Contents include: The Purpose of Museums; The Independent Visitor; Art and the Public; Art and Technology; American Art; Science in Cases; Technology and Education; History on Parade; Instruments of Adult Education; Reflections.

Adam, Thomas R. *The Museum and Popular Culture.* 1939. Reprint. Ann Arbor, Mich.: University Microfilm, 1974. 177 pp. ◆ Contents include: Perspective; Vested with a Public Interest; The Education Function; Art and Culture; Art and Society; The Revival of Nature

Study; Science, Industry and Commerce; History as a Hobby; Beyond Museum Walls; For Greater Public Support.

Alexander, Edward Porter. *The Museum: A Living Book of History.* Detroit: Published for Detroit Historical Society by Wayne State University Press, 1959. 22 pp., bibliog.

Alexander, Edward P. *Museums in Motion: An Introduction to the History and Functions of Museums.* Nashville, Tenn.: American Association for State and Local History, 1979. 308 pp., illus. ◆ Comprehensive history of the various kinds of museums and offers sound practices for administering the museum of today. Includes collections, conservation, research, exhibition, interpretation, cultural center, and the museum profession.

Alexander, Edward P. *What Should Our Historical Society Do?* Bulletins of the American Association for State and Local History, vol. 1, no. 1. Washington, D.C.: American Association for State and Local History, 1941. 22 pp. ◆ Out of print. Available from Xerox University Microfilms. Discusses the historical development of historical societies and four main ways of achieving purposes: meeting activities, publications, library, and museum.

American Association for State and Local History. *Ideas in Conflict: A Colloquium on Certain Problems in Historical Society Work in the United States and Canada.* Edited by Clifford L. Lord. Harrisburg, Pa.: The Association, 1958. 181 pp. ◆ Appraisal of certain aspects of the historical society movement, including merit of local history, effectiveness of historical societies, competition between state and local societies, new techniques in preserving and recording historical evidence.

American Association for State and Local History. *The Present World of History: A Conference on Certain Problems in Historical Agency Work in the United States.* Edited by James H. Rodabaugh. Madison, Wisc.: The Association, 1959. 129 pp. ◆ Includes sessions on educational function of historical societies, role of archivists, competition between agencies, the artifact as an historical source, developments in local history, and status of the history profession in general.

American Association of Museums. *Museum Accreditation: Professional Standards.* By Marilyn Hicks Fitzgerald. Washington, D.C.: The Association, 1973. 116 pp., illus. ◆ Contains the details of the development of the museum accreditation program since its implementation in June 1970. The history of the program, principles of accreditation, the procedures for achieving accreditation, evaluation instructions, and checklists for the visiting committees, case studies, statistics and testimonials are all included. First published in 1970: American Association of Museums, *Museum Accreditation: A Report to the Profession.* 39 pp.

Bazin, Germain. *The Museum Age.* Translated by Jane van Nuis Cahill. 1st American edition. New York: Universe Books, Inc., 1967. 302 pp., illus., facsims, plans. ◆ General listing of the development of the museum from ancient times to the present.

Bourne, Henry E. "Development and Work of American Historical Societies." In *American Historical Association, Annual Report for the Year 1904* (Washington, D.C.: U.S. Government Printing Office, 1905), pp. 117-127. ◆ Reviews types of historical societies and their activities as of 1904, and notes the diversity and inquires about the increase in cooperation between them.

Brown, Henry D. "Heritage—An Open Door," *History News,* 22:3 (March 1967), pp. 55-66. ◆ Traces development of historical societies and their purposes. Concludes that local history is an open door for scholarship, learning, enjoyment and identification with reality.

Burns, William A. "What's Right with Museums?" *Western Museums Quarterly,* 8:1 (December 1971), pp. 4-9. ◆ Museum functions.

A Cabinet of Curiosities: *Five Episodes in the Evolution of American Museums.* Described by Whitfield J. Bell, Jr., and others. With an introduction by Walter Muir Whitehill. Charlottesville, Va.: University Press of Virginia, 1967. 166 pp., illus., bibliog. footnotes. ◆ Five studies on: American Antiquarian Society, American Philosophical Society, Clark's Indian Museum (St. Louis), Western Museum of Cincinnati, Smithsonian Institution. See also: Whitehill, Walter Muir, et al., "History of the Museums in the United States . . . ," cited below.

Colbert, Edwin H. "What Is a Museum?" *Curator,* IV:2 (1961), pp. 138-146.

Coleman, Laurence Vail. *The Museum in America: A Critical Study.* 1939. Reprint. Washington, D.C.: American Association of Museums, 1970. 480 pp., appendices, index. ◆ Somewhat out of date, but still the most comprehensive study of museums in the United States, providing an historical perspective through the 1930's. Original three volumes published in one volume with volume 3 abridged and tables omitted.

Dunlap, Leslie W. *American Historical Societies, 1790-1860.* 1944. Reprint. Philadelphia, Pa.: Porcupine Press, 1974. 238 pp., bibliog. references, index. ◆ Perspectives in American History, no. 7. Reprint of the edition privately printed, without thesis note, in Madison, Wisconsin.

Ellis, Richard P. "The Founding, History, and

Significance of Peale's Museum in Philadelphia, 1785-1841," *Curator,* IX:3 (September 1966), pp. 235-258.

Ellsworth, Lucius F., and Maureen O'Brien, eds. *Material Culture: Historical Agencies and the Historian.* Philadelphia: Book Reprint Service, 1969. 336 pp. ♦ Consists of photoreproduced articles and parts of books previously published elsewhere. One section on material culture (theory, method, and application), one on historical agencies (definition and history). Discusses the value of studying artifacts to construct past cultures.

Foundoukidis, Euripede. *The Work of the International Museums Office and Associated Organizations During the Period June 1940-January 1945.* Paris: International Museums Office, 1946. 32 pp.

Gilman, Benjamin I. *Museum Ideals of Purpose and Method.* 1923. Reprint. Ann Arbor, Mich.: Finch Press, 1973. 462 pp., illus., plans, index. ♦ Useful as a period piece which explores the broad scope of the philosophical aspects of the arts and its functional uses in the museum situation. Written for the Trustees of the Museum of Fine Arts, Boston.

Guthe, Carl E., and Grace M. Guthe. *The Canadian Museum Movement.* Ottawa: Published by the Canadian Museums Association, 1958. 48 pp. ♦ Permanently out-of-print, 1974.

Hesseltine, William B. *Pioneer's Mission: The Story of Lyman Copeland Draper.* 1954. Reprint. Westport, Conn.: Greenwood Press, 1970. 384 pp., illus., bibliog. references.

Hudson, Kenneth. *A Social History of Museums: What the Visitors Thought.* Atlantic Highlands, N.J.: Humanities Press, 1975. 210 pp., illus., bibliog., index. ♦ Surveys history of establishment and growth of museums in Europe; museums' search for a purpose and a function; and discerns current trends.

Katz, Herbert, and Marjorie Katz. *Museums, U.S.A.: A History and Guide.* Garden City, N.Y.: Doubleday, 1965. 395 pp., illus., bibliog. notes. ♦ History of the museum in America: Art, Science, History, Children, Variety. Includes bibliographic notes and an appendix which is a directory of museums.

Key, Archibald F. *Beyond Four Walls: The Origins and Development of Canadian Museums.* Toronto: McClelland and Stewart,

1973. 384 pp., bibliog., appendix, index. ♦ Source book on Canadian museums, includes a listing of museums and related institutions. Four sections: foreign developments, American developments, Canadian beginnings, and World War II to the present. Examines way in which Canadian museums have been influenced by social, religious and political events from early colonial times to the present, and predicts their future role.

Lewis, Ralph H. "Museum." Reprinted from *Encyclopedia Britannica,* 1971. 22 pp., illus., bibliog. ♦ In alphabetical volume, pages 1033-1054. Article is divided into five sections: Purposes and Activities, History of Museums, Functions of Modern Museums, Organization of Modern Museums, Types of Museums.

Low, Theodore. *The Museum as a Social Instrument.* New York: Metropolitan Museum of Art for the American Association of Museums, 1942. 70 pp., bibliog. ♦ Out of print. A study undertaken for the Committee on Education of the American Association of Museums. Review of social and educational problems which museums are facing in a rapidly changing world.

Low, Theodore. "The Museum as a Social Instrument: Twenty Years After," *Museum News,* 40:5 (January 1962), pp. 28-30.

Montgomery, Charles F. "The Historic House—A Definition," *Museum News,* 38:1 (September 1959), pp. 12-16.

O'Connor, Francis V. *Federal Support for the Visual Arts: The New Deal and Now.* Greenwich, Conn.: New York Graphic Society, 1969. 226 pp., charts, graphs, tables, bibliog. ♦ A report on the New Deal Art Projects in New York City and New York State with recommendations for present-day federal support for the visual arts to the National Endowment for the Arts, Washington, D.C., October 1968.

Schneider, Evžen. "The Way of Museums: An Exhibition at the Moravian Museum, Brno," *Museum,* XXXIX:4 (1977), pp. 183-191. ♦ Exhibit on the history of and future for museums.

Sukel, William M. "Museums as Organizations," *Curator,* XVII:4 (December 1974), pp. 299-301. ♦ Discusses similarities of museums to business organizations: goals, organizational structure, functional specialists; also, striking differences.

Swinney, Holman J. *Historical Museums.* AASLH Cassette Tape no. 11. Nashville, Tenn.: American Association for State and Local History, 1971. 56 minutes. ◆ Discusses the historical museum and its unique function in society, the division of history museums into four types, consideration of the uniqueness of the objects and their use in interpretive exhibits, and the history of the museum's place in the education system.

Swinney, Holman J. "Introductory Essay." In Arminta Neal, *Exhibits for the Small Museum: A Handbook* (Nashville, Tenn.: American Association for State and Local History, 1976), pp. 1-8. ◆ Statement on understanding what a museum is in order to go on to a sound analysis of capabilities, and then to sound planning.

Taylor, Francis H. *Babel's Tower: The Dilemma of the Modern Museum.* New York: Columbia University Press, 1945. 53 pp., illus. ◆ Six essays on the choice of becoming temples of learning and understanding, or perpetuating the pleasures of aestheticism with the conclusion that overhauling museums must be intellectual as well as physical.

Washburn, Wilcomb E. *Defining the Museum's Purpose.* New York State Historical Association's Monographic Studies no. 1. Cooperstown, N.Y.: New York State Historical Association, 1975. 20 pp., illus. ◆ Urgent need for museums to define their purpose in order that they may better organize their resources to accomplish that purpose and to evaluate the extent to which they have achieved it.

"What Are Museums For?" *Museums Journal,* 69:3 (December 1969), pp. 102-105. ◆ Session at Annual Conference of the Museums Association, Leicester, 1969. Articles by John V. H. Eames and W. W. Taylor.

Whitehill, Walter Muir. "Cerebration Versus Celebration," *The Virginia Magazine of History and Biography,* 68:3 (July 1960), pp. 259-270.

Whitehill, Walter Muir. *Independent Historical Societies: An Enquiry Into Their Research and Publication Functions and Their Financial Future.* Boston: The Boston Athenaeum, distributed by Harvard University Press, 1962. 593 pp., bibliog., footnotes, index. ◆ First ten chapters describe the principal independent historical societies with historical background designed to suggest the manner in which they became what they are. Other organizations,

save the State Historical Society of Wisconsin which is treated in some detail as the prototype of the publicly supported society, are described more briefly with greater emphasis on their present activities. Final chapters consist of general observations and conclusions derived from the facts set forth earlier in the book.

Whitehill, Walter Muir. "The Scholarly Responsibility of an Independent Historical Society," *Maryland Historical Magazine,* 56:4 (December 1961), pp. 321-334.

Whitehill, Walter Muir; Clifford K. Shipton; Louis L. Tucker; and Wilcomb E. Washburn. "History of Museums in the United States: Report of a Session of the American Historical Association, December 28, 1964," *Curator,* 8:1 (1965), pp. 5-54. ◆ See also: *A Cabinet of Curiosities: Five Episodes in the Evolution of American Museums* (cited above).

Wittlin, Alma S. *Museums: In Search of a Usable Future.* Cambridge, Mass.: MIT Press, 1970. 299 pp., illus., bibliog. references, index. ◆ Historical survey on museums, with special attention to their current problems.

Wrenn, George L., III. "What Is a Historic House Museum?" *Historic Preservation,* 23:1 (January-March 1971), pp. 55-58.

NOTES

Elementary and Secondary Education Act of 1965, as amended, 1974 (P.L. 93-380), explicitly mentions museums as educational institutions, since museums serve as resources for schools.

Role in Society

Alderson, William T. "Answering the Challenge," *Museum News,* 53:3 (November 1974), pp. 9, 63. ◆ The challenge to history museums is helping American people understand themselves and their shared experience.

American Association for State and Local History. *Life is a Local Story: A Collection of Talks Concerning Local History, Historic Sites, and History Museums.* Edited by Clement M. Silvestro. Nashville, Tenn.: The Association, 1964. 85 pp. ◆ Topics: "Importance of Local History . . ."; "What's New and Effective in Museum Interpretation?"; "Museum Interpretation of Western History"; "Dollars and Cents and the Historic Site"; "Preservation of Historic Sites: Whose Responsibility?"

American Council for Arts in Education. Arts, Education and Americans Panel. *Coming to Our Senses: The Significance of the Arts for American Education, A Panel Report.* New York: McGraw-Hill, c1977. 334 pp., illus., bibliog., index. ◆ Two-year study on the arts in education in America.

Arts and the Aging: An Agenda for Action. A National Conference convened by the National Council on the Aging, Inc., and its National Center on the Arts and the Aging in cooperation with the Minnesota Arts Board and the Minnesota Governor's Citizens Council on Aging, October 17-19, 1976, Minneapolis, Minnesota. Washington, D.C.: National Council on the Aging, 1977. 90 pp., appendix. ◆ Edited transcripts of sessions on workshops on building the arts/aging alliance, expanding cultural services, theater arts, music, visual arts, museums—opening the doors, intergenerational programming, the vulnerable and institutionalized aged.

Baghli, Ahmed. "Museums and Development," *ICOM News,* 22:2 (June 1969), pp. 42-44. ◆ Subject of the Year; discusses difficult stage through which museums are passing and seeking new concepts which will enable them to adapt to the requirements of modern times.

Bodine, John W.; Kyran M. McGrath; Julia Hare; and Samuel C. Miller. "New Urban Opportunities for the Museum." In *Papers, 64th Annual Meeting, American Association of Museums* (San Francisco, Calif.: 1969), pp. 175-189. ◆ Discussion of museum response to inner city needs.

Boulding, Kenneth E. "The Future of Museums," *Museum News,* 52:2 (October 1973), pp. 51-52. ◆ Questions whether museums should expand their clientele, cooperate with other institutions, take adequate opportunity of new technologies.

Burns, William A. "Mostly About Museums," *The Museologist,* 120 (September 1971), pp. 12-19. ◆ Reviews some philosophy about museums with particular emphasis on the middle sized and smaller institution.

Burns, William A. "Museums and the Social Crisis," *Western Museums Quarterly,* 7:2 (March 1971), pp. 1-4.

Cameron, Duncan F. "The Creative Audience," *The Museologist,* 114 (March 1970), pp. 12-19. ◆ Museum is a product of social evolution; its social function is constant.

Cameron, Duncan F. "The Museum, a Temple or the Forum," *Curator,* XIV:1 (March 1971), pp. 11-24. ◆ The museum as a temple is valid but there is also argument for museum reform to make them better and more effective. Also in *Journal of World History,* XIV:1 (1972), pp. 189-202.

Cameron, Duncan F. "Museums and the World of Today," *ICOM News,* 23:2 (June 1970), pp. 41-45 ◆ Subject of the Year; includes museum reform in the 1950's and 1960's, the creative museum, the role of the museum in contemporary society.

Canadian Museums Association. *Conference Proceedings for '2001: The Museum and the Canadian Public'.* Edited by Ted Poulos. Ottawa: The Association, 1977. 100 pp., illus., appendices. ◆ Report on a major conference held at Lake Couchiching, Ontario, September 1976. Complete set of conference working papers, a number of presentations given at the conference, and a list of over 35 recommendations for action.

Coffey, Katherine. "Operation of the Individual Museum," *Museum News,* 40:2 (October 1961), pp. 26-29. ◆ Discusses educational role of museum in relation to its scholarly role and function of a dual role. One of three points of view; see also articles by Wilcomb E. Washburn and Clark C. Evernham.

Cox, Merridy. "Nationalism and Museums," *gazette,* 11:3 (Summer 1978), pp. 7-10.

Dennis, Emily. "Seminar on Neighborhood Museums," *Museum News,* 48:5 (January 1970), pp. 13-19. ◆ Prospects for direct museum-community involvement, including planning and operation, and broadening the museum's social function.

Dixon, Brian; Alice E. Courtney; and Robert H. Bailey. *The Museum and the Canadian Public.* Edited by John Kettle. Toronto: Published for the Arts and Culture Branch, Department of Secretary of State, Government of Canada, by Culturcan Publications, 1974. 381 pp. ◆ Discusses public ignorance concerning the role and nature of museums at all socio-economic levels, the result of a statistical report.

Duhamel, Jacques. "Museums and Government," *ICOM News,* 25:2 (June 1972), pp. 92-95. ◆ The Year's Topic; is culture to be a consumer commodity or a product of participation, with choice independent of political government to which everything tends to be reduced.

Edwards, R. Yorke. "Tomorrow's Museum," *gazette,* 10:1 (Winter 1977), pp. 6-11. ◆ Overview of all aspects of museums—audience, collections, building, staff, exhibits, security, publishing, conservation, research, extension.

Engstrom, Kjell. "Museums and Development," *ICOM News,* 22:3 (September 1969), pp. 33-35. ◆ Subject of the Year; task of every museum, no matter what subject it deals with, to document and illustrate a process of development, be it cultural, industrial, economic, or biological.

ERIC Clearinghouse on Media and Technology. *Museums and Media: A Status Report,* prepared by Richard Grove; and *Museums and Media: A Basic Reference Shelf,* by Philip C. Ritterbush. Stanford, Calif.: ERIC Clearinghouse on Educational Media and Technology at the Institute for Communication Research, Stanford University, 1970. 15 pp. ◆ Based on a paper prepared for the President's Commission on Instructional Technology in 1968. Bibliography lists books, papers, periodicals, and reports to help show the important role museums play in elementary and secondary education.

Evernham, Clark C. "Science Education: A Museum Responsibility," *Museum News,* 40:2 (October 1961), pp. 20-22. ◆ One of three points of view on the role of museums: ever-changing technology must always be clearly and simply presented to the people and the museum is a popular force with a liberal education program for the community it serves. See also articles by Wilcomb E. Washburn and Katherine Coffey.

Finlay, Ian. *Priceless Heritage: The Future of Museums.* London: Faber and Faber, 1977. 183 pp., bibliog., index. ◆ Includes ideas, problem of presentation, museums as a profession, who should run museums, and planning buildings.

Fishel, Leslie H., Jr. "The Role of the Historical Society in Contemporary America," *History News,* 30:12 (December 1975), pp. 283-290.

Frantz, Joe B. "The Relationship of the Historical Society to the Community," *Texas Libraries,* 29:3 (Fall 1967), pp. 181-186. ◆ A clearinghouse for the preservation and use of materials.

Galicia, Yolanda Ramos. "Creating a Museum—A Community Venture," *ICOM News,* 29:4 (1977), pp. 38-42. ◆ Description of a local museum program based on the social needs of the community and the kinds of solutions they themselves advocated.

Gaudibert, Pierre, et al. "Exchange of Views of a Group of Experts," *Museum,* XXIV:1 (1972), pp. 5-32. ◆ Other authors: Pontus Hulton, Michael Keeston, Jean Leymarie, Francois Mathey, Georges Henri Rivière, Harald Szeemann, Eduard de Wilde. Contents include: "Introduction"; "The Principle and Function of the Museum"; "New Art Forms and the 'Museum' Explosion"; "Information Centre"; "The Museum and the Artist"; "Museums and the Public"; "Museums and Art Dealers"; "Museums and Authorities"; "The Director and His Team"; "The Collection"; "The Building."

Gauthier, Georges-E. "Museum Development in Canada's Centennial Year," *Museum News,* 45:7 (March 1967), pp. 11-16.

Guthe, Alfred K. "The Role of a University Museum," *Curator,* IX:2 (June 1966), pp. 103-105. ◆ The distinctive role of a university museum lies in the nature of the community it serves; fulfills a role as a public museum as well.

Heckscher, August. "Museums in a New Age," *Museum News,* 41:1 (September 1962), pp. 22-28. ◆ Discusses the new demands being made upon museums and the realization of how great the enterprise is.

Hindle, Brooke. "Museum Treatment of Industrialization: History, Problems, Opportunities," *Curator,* XV:3 (September 1972), pp. 206-219.

Howland, Richard H. "What Is Past, Is Prologue," *Museum News,* 43:3 (November 1964), pp. 34-39. ◆ Discusses what the preservation movement means to museums—a whole population becoming more conscious of its heritage.

Hudson, Kenneth. *Museums for the 1980's: A Survey of World Trends.* London: Macmillan for UNESCO, 1977. 198 pp., illus., bibliog.

references, index. ◆ Describes and evaluates the major changes in theory and practice which characterize the museum world today. Available from Unipub, New York.

Hughes, Robert. "The Museum on Trial," *New York Times Magazine* (September 9, 1973), pp. 34ff. ◆ Suggests that museums are trying to be too "relevant", competing with television and movies for a share of public attention.

Hyatt, Jim. "Troubled Museums: Many U.S. Exhibitors Reel Under Burden of Own Popularity," *The Museologist,* 121 (December 1971), pp. 10-13. ◆ Reprinted from *The Wall Street Journal,* November 1, 1971. Discusses problems of museum popularity: security, financial crisis, staff dissatisfaction with salaries.

International Council of Museums. *The Museum and the Modern World.* Papers from the Tenth General Conference of ICOM. Paris: ICOM, 1975. 119 pp. ◆ Text in English and French. Contents: addresses; Introducing ICOM '74, Progrès or on Croissance?; The Environment; Society; Le Musée et L'Avenir; Conclusions.

International Council of Museums. *The Museum in the Service of Man, Today and Tomorrow: The Museum's Educational and Cultural Role.* The Papers from the Ninth General Conference of ICOM. Paris: ICOM, c1972. 195 pp., illus. ◆ English or French. Includes: museums in contemporary educational and cultural systems; the third dimension in education; chance and task of the museum; the museum and society; intermediaries between the museum and the community; conclusions.

International Council of Museums. *Museums and Research.* Papers from the Eighth General Conference of ICOM, Cologne-Munich, 1968. Reports and Papers on Museums, 8. Munich: Deutsches Museum for ICOM, 1970. 126 pp. ◆ Contents include: museums and research, university museums, collections and research, utilization of collections, scientific documentation, training, the curator-university professor.

Jelinek, Jan. "Museums and the World of Today," *ICOM News,* 23:1 (March 1970), pp. 38-40. ◆ Subject of the Year; science and technology play a major role in the tasks and responsibilities of museums; museums cannot stand aloof from developmental changes, in structure of the organization or in methods and activities.

Johnston, Donald. " 'The Old Gray Museum, She Ain't What She Used to Be,' " *The Museologist,* 128 (September 1973), pp. 5-12. ◆ Reprinted from *The New York Times,* The Week in Review Section, Sunday, June 17, 1973. Discusses current influences on museums and changes in appearance, action and participation, education, relevance, permanent collections.

Jones, Louis C. "The Trapper's Cabin and the Ivory Tower," *Museum News,* 40:7 (March 1962), pp. 11-16. ◆ In outdoor museums there is a need for research and cooperation with the research activities of universities.

Jordan, Joye E. "The History Museum: Poor Relation?" *Museum News,* 43:3 (November 1964), pp. 17-19. ◆ Why the history museum has long been considered the poor relation in the museum family, and what it is doing to change this public image.

Larrabee, Eric. "Education and the Arts," *The Museologist,* 119 (June 1971), pp. 5-11. ◆ Emphasizes the common features between education and the arts, and between them both and museums.

Larrabee, Eric. "A 'Silent Spring' for the Arts?" *Curator,* XVI:2 (June 1973), pp. 89-98. ◆ Discusses status of the arts in the U.S.; must forestall destruction with an active campaign that is non-apologetic, exemplify bent toward excellence, be self-critical and self-renewing.

Lemieux, Louis. "Canadian Museums and Their Role in Social Issues," *Curator,* XIV:1 (March 1971), pp. 50-55.

McGrath, Kyran M. "Environmental Education Act," *Museum News,* 49:4 (December 1970), pp. 22-25. ◆ Discusses provisions of the act to establish educational programs to encourage understanding of policies and support of activities designed to preserve and enhance environmental quality and maintain ecological balance. Museums included within the definition of educational institutions on a federal level.

Molloy, Lawrence. "The City History Museum: Challenges and Opportunities." In *Papers, 64th Annual Meeting, American Association of Museums* (San Francisco, Calif.: 1969), pp. 83-86. ◆ City museum must have more vital concern in human affairs if it is to fulfill a useful purpose.

Mostny, Grete. "Museums and the Problems of Everyday Life," *Museum,* XXV:1/2 (1973), pp. 108-111. ◆ Museums can play essential part in community, arousing legitimate concerns through interpretation of natural and cultural environment.

Murphy, Judith. *The Place of the Arts in New Towns: A Report.* New York: Educational Facilities Laboratories, 1973. 72 pp., illus., bibliog. references. ◆ Reviews approaches and experiences for developing arts programs and facilities in new towns and established communities. Gives insights and models for the support of the arts, including the role of the arts advocate, the use of existing space, and financing. Available from the American Council for the Arts, New York.

A Museum for the People. A Report of Proceedings at the Seminar on Neighborhood Museums, held November 20, 21 and 22, 1969, at MUSE, the Bedford Lincoln Neighborhood Museum in Brooklyn, New York. Edited by Emily Dennis Harvey and Bernard Friedberg. New York: Arno Press, 1971. 86 pp., illus. ◆ Demonstrates the re-evaluation American museums are undertaking in establishing inner-city programs. Paperback available from Acanthus Press, Cambridge, Massachusetts.

"The Museum in 1980: Questions, Problems, Signs," *Museum News,* 45:9 (May 1967), pp. 28-31. ◆ A report on the 1966 Aspen Conference.

"Museums in Contemporary Society," *Journal of World History,* XIV:1 (1972), entire issue. ◆ Articles on the role of museums; museums, science and technology; museums of the world; the museum crisis. Designed to highlight the relationship between museums and the structures of society and knowledge in the contemporary world.

Museums in Crisis. Edited with an introduction by Brian O'Doherty. New York: G. Braziller, 1972. 178 pp., illus., bibliog. references. ◆ A dialogue on problems facing museums in the 1970's including staffing, financing, scholarship, goals, popularity, and ethics. Articles first appeared in a special museum issue of *Art in America,* 59:4 (July-August 1971).

Nason, James D. "Museums and American Indians: An Inquiry into Relationships," *Western Museums Quarterly,* 8:1 (December, 1971), pp. 13-17.

National Endowment for the Arts. *Creative America: Arts and the Pursuit of Happiness.* Washington, D.C.: The Endowment, for sale by the Superintendent of Documents, U.S. Government Printing Office, 1976. 32 pp., illus. ◆ Discusses growing interest in the arts, the historical background of the American artistic impulse, and the relationship of the NEA to the arts today.

"New York Annual Meeting: Going to Meet the Issues," *Museum News,* 49:1 (September 1970), pp. 18-22. ◆ Excerpts from speeches made at American Association of Museums annual meeting, June 1-3, New York City, relating to awareness of issues outside the "internal" business of museums.

Newton, Earle W. "Cultural Institutions as Learning Resources," *Curator,* XVII:3 (September 1974), pp. 225-230. ◆ Discusses American Studies curricula developed in coordination with museum and historical agencies.

Nicholson, Thomas D. "A Question of Function," *Curator,* XIV:1 (March 1971), pp. 7-10. ◆ Questions whether society's demands are just cause for forcing museums to become something they are not, for expecting them to take on responsibilities for which they are poorly equipped.

"1984 Minus 10," *Museum News,* 52:9 (June 1974), pp. 49-51. ◆ Interviews with several prominent people whose careers and interests touch on museum work, on what the museum world is heading for.

Noble, Joseph V. "More Than a Mirror to the Past," *Curator,* XVI:3 (September 1973), pp. 271-275. ◆ Must explain the past as if it were a prologue.

Noble, Joseph V. "Museum Manifesto," *Museum News,* 48:8 (April 1970), pp. 16-20. ◆ Discusses five areas of basic museum responsibility—acquisition, conservation, study, interpretation, and exhibition—to be carried out so that institutions are complete and balanced.

Noble, Joseph V. "Museum Prophecy: The Role of Museums in the 1970's," *Curator,* XIV:1 (March 1971), pp. 69-74. ◆ Deals with problems of the world and the methods of museums in facing them.

Older Americans: *The Unrealized Audience for the Arts.* By Alton C. Johnson, et al. Madison, Wisc.: Center for Arts Administration, Graduate School of Business, University of Wisconsin—Madison, 1976. 51 pp., tables, bibliog. references. ◆ Includes a national survey of arts administrators, an audience development and model, and illustrative senior citizen programs.

Olson, James C. "Viewpoint–The Historical Agency: Relevance and Responsibility," *History News*, 25:1 (January 1970), pp. 9-12.

Outhwaite, Leonard. *Museums and the Future: An Inquiry Into the Life and Welfare of American Museums and Other Cultural Institutions.* New York: Institute of Public Administration, 1967. 144 pp.

Parr, Albert Eide. "The Functions of Museums: Research Centers or Show Places," *Curator*, VI:1 (1963), pp. 20-31.

Parr, Albert Eide. "History and the Historical Museum," *Curator*, XV:1 (March 1972), pp. 53-61. ◆ Argues that museums should take responsibility for completing our image of former days.

Parr, Albert Eide. "The Importance of Being Public," *Curator*, IV:3 (1961), pp. 252-256. ◆ Contends that museums suffer and decline from lack of response to changing trends of public interest and genuine educational needs.

Parr, Albert Eide. *Mostly About Museums.* New York: American Museum of Natural History, 1959. 112 pp. ◆ Writings covering the period 1939-1959 on such subjects as natural history museums, trends and conflicts in museum development, museum and the people, thoughts on design for museums and cities.

Parr, Albert Eide. "Museums: Enriching the Urban Milieu," *Museum News*, 56:4 (March/April 1978), pp. 46-51. ◆ Discusses museums shifting aim from authoritative evaluations of truths toward selecting messages for popular appeal which may result in loss of public esteem and support; cultural functions become secondary to business management.

Parr, Albert Eide. "Museums in Megalopolis," *History News*, 27:6 (June 1972), pp. 129-132. ◆ Discusses the future of museums in megalopolis. See also: *gazette*, 4:4/5 (August-November 1970), pp. 19-25.

Pisney, Raymond, ed. *Historical Resources: Finding, Preserving and Using.* Verona, Va.: McClure Press, 1976. 116 pp. ◆ Techniques for discovering and preserving local historic resources; includes a chapter on youth and museums and one on historical agencies and communities.

Potamkin, Meyer P. "Is Outreach a Cop-out?" *Museum News*, 51:4 (December 1972), p. 25. ◆ Argues that the museum's most important program must be "inreach" to help train the disadvantaged within the museum.

Pott, Peter H. "The Role of Museums of History and Folklife in a Changing World," *Curator*, VI:2 (1963), pp. 157-170.

Pratt, George, Jr. "The Consequences of Activism," *Museum News*, 49:1 (September 1970), pp. 26-29. ◆ Discusses small museums and involvement in present problems, e.g. environmental education.

Rao, V.K.R.V. "Museums and the World of Today," *ICOM News*, 23:4 (December 1970), pp. 41-44. ◆ Subject of the Year; illustrates how a politician tries to promote in his country present day ideas in museology.

Richardson, Edgar P. "The Museum in America 1963," *Museum News*, 42:1 (September 1963), pp. 20-28.

Ripley, S. Dillon. "Museums: Evolution or Revolution," *The Museologist*, 122 (March 1972), pp. 4-12. ◆ Museums are at a stage of either a great leap forward or a state of quiescence.

Ripley, S. Dillon. *The Sacred Grove: Essays on Museums.* New York: Simon and Schuster, 1969. 159 pp., bibliog. references. ◆ Nine essays on the evolution of museums, and a close look at today's museums. Topics include new ideas and concepts placed in perspective; application of communications theory; evaluation of museum functions; relationship between research and exhibition; and the place of the museum in the community.

Rivard, Paul. "Done by the Old Mill Scheme," *Museum News*, 49:10 (December 1970), pp. 18-21. ◆ A history museum and environmental action in Pawtucket, Rhode Island represent a major shift in traditional priorities and goals.

Rivière, Georges-Henri. "Museums and the World of Today," *ICOM News*, 23:3 (September 1970), pp. 33-35. ◆ Subject of the Year; an examination of the anticipated dangers of a changing world and of the way in which museums could answer their challenge.

Rivière, Georges-Henri, ed. "New Aspects of the History Museum," *Museum,* XXIX:2/3 (1977), entire issue. ◆ Articles by various authors on problems of general history; descriptive surveys of three museums devoted to the history of nations; three museums devoted to the history of towns; seven museum variations on historical themes; and an album of eleven shorter essays. Includes a selective bibliography.

Robbins, Michael W. "The Neighborhood and the Museum," *Curator,* XIV:1 (March 1971), pp. 63-68. ◆ Comments on Seminar on Neighborhood Museums, November 1969, New York City, held at MUSE. Asks basic questions about culture and the quality of life and what kinds of cultural institutions can work.

Sabloff, Jeremy A. "The Buck Stops Here," *Museum News,* 51:9 (May 1973), pp. 46-48. ◆ Suggests that museum personnel and archeologists should develop a program of public education to end pillaging of archeological sites throughout the world.

Selig, J. Daniel. "A Voice for Small Museums," *The Museologist,* 138 (September 1976), pp. 16-19. ◆ Discusses purposes and areas of activity of the Small Museums Committee of the Northeast Museums Conference.

Sheon, Aaron. "Museums and Development," *ICOM News,* 22:2 (March 1969), pp. 34-37. ◆ Subject of the Year; how roles of museums will change in developing countries where cultural, economic and social frameworks are transformed.

Sunderland, Jacqueline T. "Museums and Older Americans," *Museum News,* 55:3 (January/February 1977), pp. 21-23.

Sunderland, Jacqueline T. *Older Americans and the Arts: A Human Equation.* Rev. ed. Washington, D.C.: National Council on the Aging, Inc., c1976. 64 pp. ◆ Updated and reprinted edition, published in 1973 by the National Center for Older Americans and the Arts, National Council on the Aging, and the John F. Kennedy Center for the Performing Arts.

Thomas, W. Stephen. "Today's Museums are Arenas for Action," *The Museologist,* 120 (September 1971), pp. 19-22.

Thompson, G. B. "A Museum's Role in a Changing Society," *Museums Journal,* 78:1 (June 1978), pp. 2-4.

Turner, Evan. *Ideals and Realities: The Museum's Looming Conflict.* Ottawa: Canadian Museums Association, 1977. 60 pp. ◆ Fellows Lecture 1976; discusses the looming administrative, financial, and curatorial problems of museums.

Tyler, Barbara Ann. "Art in the American History Museum." In *Papers, 64th Annual Meeting, American Association of Museums* (San Francisco, Calif.: 1969), pp. 75-80. ◆ Discusses lack of appreciation of art in history museums, and recommends joining forces with art museums to present history as a whole.

United Nations Educational, Scientific and Cultural Organization. *International Symposium on Museums in the Contemporary World.* Unesco House, Paris, 24-28 November 1969. Final Report. Paris: 1970. 41 pp. ◆ Translated from French.

Varine-Bohan, Hughes de. "The Modern Museum: Requirements and Problems of a New Approach," *Museum,* XXVIII:1 (1976), pp. 131-143.

Varine-Bohan, Hughes de. "Museums and Development," *ICOM News,* 22:4 (December 1969), pp. 35-38. ◆ Subject of the Year: museums must aid scientific and technological development (science museums); balance technical development (art museums); and integrate the sciences and the arts in the service of man's development (history museums).

Veillard, Jean-Yves. "The Problem of the History Museum, from an Experiment in the Musée de Bretagne, Rennes," *Museum,* XXIV:4 (1972), pp. 193-203. ◆ Maintains that the object of a history museum is not merely to add to the store of knowledge, but to foster the dynamic assimilation of knowledge in order to better challenge the values of the contemporary world.

Washburn, Wilcomb E. "Grandmotherology and Museology," *Curator,* X:1 (March 1967), pp. 43-48. ◆ Contends that the emergence of a powerful new administrative element has led to confusion of aim and purpose.

Washburn, Wilcomb E. "The Museum Responsibility in Adult Education," *Curator,* VII:1 (1964), pp. 33-38.

Washburn, Wilcomb E. "Scholarship and the Museum," *Museum News,* 40:2 (October 1961), pp. 16-19. ♦ One of three points of view on role of the museum: museums are losing their best scholars to universities because of preoccupation with the public. See also articles by Clark C. Evernham and Katherine Coffey.

Wertheimer, Barbara M. *Exploring the Arts: A Handbook for Trade Union Program Planners.* New York: New York State School of Industrial and Labor Relations, Cornell University, Division of Extension and Public Service, c1968. 61 pp., illus., bibliog. ♦ A handbook to assist unions and community organizations in planning arts programs, courses and field trips. Includes discussion of leadership role, evaluation of programs, specific resources in New York City.

Whitehill, Walter Muir. " 'The Bed of Procrustes'," *The Museologist,* 129 (December 1973), pp. 6-16. ♦ The new museum cannot be an all-inclusive organization that would provide possibility of self-instruction in science and technology through exhibits and lectures; so diverse in aims and resources that few principles are of universal application.

Williams, Richmond D. "Challenges to State and Local History Administrators," *History News,* 32:1 (January 1977), supplement. ♦ Emphasizes challenges of the Bicentennial, of history, of administration, and of professionalism.

Wittlin, Alma S. *Museums: In Search of a Usable Future.* Cambridge, Mass.: MIT Press, 1970. 299 pp., illus., bibliog. references, index.

NOTES

National Center on the Arts and Aging, National Council on the Aging, 1828 L Street, N.W., Washington, D.C. 20036. The National Center is a program of the National Council on the Aging to enrich the lives of older persons through their increased participation in and broader access to cultural programs and services. The Center seeks to make cultural administrators more aware of how their organizations, public and private, can serve and be served by older people. It believes that older people can be participants, supporters, volunteers, paid professionals, molders of public opinion, and an important part of a new, expanded audience for the arts. The Center is a clearinghouse for program ideas and information. It sponsors workshops, seminars and conferences, and offers technical assistance and consultation to individuals and organizations interested in developing a closer relationship between older persons and the arts.

Public Policy

American Association of Museums. *America's Museums: The Belmont Report.* A Report to the Federal Council on the Arts and Humanities by a Special Committee of the American Association of Museums. Washington, D.C.: American Association of Museums, 1969. 81 pp. ♦ Study of the financial needs and educational role of museums in the 1960's; includes demands on museums, present condition of museums, case for federal support, mechanism for federal support, and appendices.

American Council for the Arts. *The Arts and Public Policy: A Summary of Hearings on a White House Conference on the Arts.* New York: The Council, 1978. 96 pp. ♦ Nine sections; listing of major recommendations presented by witnesses for consideration by planners of state and national conferences on arts issues.

American Council for the Arts. *Local Government and the Arts.* By Luisa Kreisberg. New York: The Council, 1979. 296 pp. ♦ Strategies for mayors, city managers, council members, and other locally elected officials wishing to incorporate arts in municipal planning programs. Relates arts to such municipal priorities as economic development, environmental quality, public safety, transportation, education, recreation, and human resources. Includes extensive listing of resources for city officials.

Associated Councils of the Arts. *Carter on the Arts.* Introduction by Joan Mondale. New York: ACA Publications, 1977. 48 pp. ♦ Views on federal support for the arts; importance of the arts in the economy; and the arts and foreign policy.

Atkinson, Richard, et al. "Federal Points of View," *Museum News,* 57:1 (September/October 1978), pp. 16-27. ◆ Interviews with directors of federal agencies about future museum funding, the notion of cultural policy, and legislative concern over funding overlap.

Balter, Lori A. "Six Years and Four Hearings Later," *The Museologist,* 142 (September 1977), pp. 17-28. ◆ Reviews the process and hearings involved in passage of the Arts, Humanities and Cultural Affairs Act of 1976: Title II-Museum Services. Article is concluded in *The Museologist,* 143 (December 1977), pp. 3-20.

Brademas, John. "The American Museum of the Future: The Federal Role," *Museum News,* 48:1 (September 1969), pp. 14-17. ◆ Reviews museums and their needs, museums as educational institutions, financial pressures, the federal role, guns and welfare priorities, specific proposals on the federal level for immediate action.

Broadland, Bob. "National Museum Policy," *gazette,* 6:4 (October 1972), pp. 12-15. ◆ Committee report on the progress of the new National Museum Program.

"Canada and the Arts," *Cultural Affairs,* 6 (1969), special issue. ◆ Contents: "An Essential Grace"; "Federal Support"; "Canada's Public Media"; "Reportwrighting."

Cheetham, Francis W. "A National Museum Service for Britain," *Museums Journal,* 68:2 (September 1968), pp. 70-73.

"Congressional Hearings on the Arts and Humanities," *Cultural Affairs,* 10 (Spring 1970), entire issue. ◆ Edited statements of individual witnesses as well as responses to questions given at Congressional hearings on National Foundation on the Arts and Humanities.

Earl of Rosse. "Museums and Local Government," *Museums Journal,* 68:2 (September 1968), pp. 67-69. ◆ Partnership with government to help realize museum potential.

Eccles, The Rt. Hon. Viscount. "The Report of the Committee on Provincial Museums and Galleries," *Museums Journal,* 73:3 (December 1973), pp. 120-124. ◆ The Wright Report regarding support of museums in Great Britain and services provided through Area Museum Councils.

Educational Facilities Laboratories. *Arts and the Handicapped: An Issue of Access.* A Report from the Educational Facilities Laboratories and the National Endowment for the Arts. New York: Educational Facilities Laboratories, 1975. 79 pp., illus. ◆ Techniques for eliminating physical and social barriers to the handicapped in various arts facilities.

Gilborn, Craig. "What a Friend We Have in (A) John Brademas (B) Nancy Hanks (C) Douglas Dillon (D) Jo Stewart Randel, Part I," *The Museologist,* 137 (June 1976), pp. 3-9. ◆ Calls attention to lack of comparative data and the absence of open discussion about aid programs to museums, and continues with examination of testimony concerning proposed legislation to provide operating funds for museums (Museum Services Act) from September 1972-November 1975. See also: "Part II," *The Museologist,* 138 (September 1976), pp. 3-9; "Part III," *The Museologist,* 139 (December 1976), pp. 12-18.

"Government and the Arts: How Much to Whom?" *Newsweek,* 68 (July 18, 1966), pp. 56-58. ◆ Special report on the beginnings of federal aid to the arts provided by the Arts and Humanities Bill (P.L. 89-209), passed on September 29, 1965.

Greyser, Stephen A., comp. *Cultural Policy and Arts Administration.* Cambridge, Mass.: Harvard Summer School Institute in Arts Administration, distr. by Harvard University Press c1973. 173 pp., bibliog. references. ◆ International colloquium focusing on a variety of viewpoints on cultural and public policy issues germane to arts administrators.

Hanks, Nancy. "The Arts in America: A Single Fabric," *Museum News,* 52:3 (November 1973), pp. 42-47. ◆ Report on history and funding of National Endowment for the Arts.

Hightower, John. "Museums and Government," *Museum News,* 46:1 (September 1967), pp. 22-23. ◆ As more government support becomes available for museums, their role as public institutions will become increasingly emphatic.

Keeney, Barnaby C. "Viewpoint," *History News,* 25:4 (April 1970), pp. 81-82 ◆ An account of the efforts and philosophy of the National Endowment for the Humanities.

Kenney, Alice P. "Museums from a Wheelchair," *Museum News,* 53:4 (December 1974), pp. 14-17. ◆ Through government action and funding pressure, museums are made increasingly aware of responsibilities in making resources available to the handicapped; a personal view of the problem and specific recommendations.

Kenney, Alice P. "Open Door for the Handicapped," *Historic Preservation,* 30:3 (July/September 1978), pp. 12-17. ◆ Examples of meeting specific problems of handicapped visitors; reference to Section 504 of the Rehabilitation Act of 1973 and the May 1977 guidelines.

Malone, Alice R. "Establishing Museum Guidelines for Educational Programs for Handicapped Students," *The Museologist,* 140 (March 1977), pp. 12-14. ◆ Report of survey to be done on programs and services for the handicapped student visitor.

Mark, Charles C. *A Study of Cultural Policy in the United States.* Paris: UNESCO, 1969. 43 pp. ◆ Evaluation of cultural needs, administrative structures and management, planning and financing, budgeting, the training of personnel, international cultural cooperation and other related topics. Studies and Documents on Cultural Policy, 2.

Molloy, Larry. "504 Regs: Learning to Live by the Rules," *Museum News,* 57:1 (September/October 1978), pp. 28-33 ◆ Discusses implementation of Section 504 of the Rehabilitation Act of 1973; for museums that receive federal money, full accessibility will require long-term planning and ingenuity.

"Museums and Government: ICOM Secretariat," *ICOM News,* 25:1 (March 1972), pp. 34-36. ◆ The Year's Topic; from ICOM experience, enumerates points for discussion on political meaning of the museum, responsibilities of government, relationship between politicians and museum professionals.

"Museums and the Handicapped," *gazette,* 11:3 (Summer 1978), pp. 2-6. ◆ Identifies four levels of educational needs in the world of the handicapped; action by museum educators applies at all levels.

Museums Association. *A Museum Service for the Nation.* London: The Association, 1971. 6 pp. ◆ Proposals to make new non-metropolitan counties the statutory authorities for the provision of museum services; a system for improving inter-relationships between national institutions and principal local museums and galleries.

Owens, Gwendolyn J., comp. "A Guide to Information on Accessibility," *Museum News,* 55:3 (January/February 1977), pp. 38-39. ◆ Sources and addresses for information and/or publications about accessibility for children, elderly, and handicapped.

Pelletier, Gerard. "Museums and Government: Democratization and Decentralization, A New Policy for Museums," *ICOM News,* 25:4 (December 1972), pp. 219-222. ◆ The Year's Topic; notes from a speech on cultural policy of the Canadian government.

Pelletier, Gerard. "A New Policy for Museums," *gazette,* 6:2 (April 1972), pp. 3-13. ◆ Increasing access to the products of cultural activity for all taxpayers and making cultural activities available to all Canadians through such programs as National Museums Corporation, National Loan Collection, National Exhibition Centers, National Inventory, Canadian Conservation Institute.

Purcell, Ralph. *Government and Art, A Study of American Experience.* Washington, D.C.: Public Affairs Press, 1956. 129 pp. ◆ History of the efforts of the federal government to support the arts in America.

Regents of the University of the State of New York. "Culture and Education: A Statement of Policy and Proposed Action," *Curator,* XV:3 (September 1972), pp. 173-188. ◆ Identifies the nature of museums as essential agencies of society, in what they are and in their potential.

"Setting Priorities," *Museum News,* 55:3 (January/February 1977), pp. 30-31, 45. ◆ Experiences of museum administrators in developing programs for the handicapped including priorities, limits to accessibility, working with limited staff and resources.

Snider, Harold. "The Inviting Air of An Accessible Space," *Museum News,* 55:3 (January/February 1977), pp. 18-20. ◆ Consultation with handicapped in planning accessible programs at National Air and Space Museum.

Stevens, S. K. "Museum Building as a Responsibility of State Governments," *Museum News,* 45:1 (September 1966), pp. 31-32.

U.S. Congress. House. Committee on Education and Labor. Select Subcommittee on Education. *Arts, Humanities and Cultural Affairs*

Act of 1975. Joint Hearings before the Subcommittee on Select Education of the Committee on Education and Labor, House of Representatives, and the Special Subcommittee on Arts and Humanities of the Committee on Labor and Public Welfare, United States Senate, Ninety-fourth Congress, first session, on H. R. 7216 and S.1800 . . . November 12, 13, 14, 1975. Washington, D.C.: U.S. Government Printing Office, 1976. 489 pp., bibliog. ♦ "National Report on the Arts, by the National Committee for Cultural Resources," pp. 249-283.

U.S. Congress. House. Committee on Education and Labor. Select Subcommittee on Education. *Museum Services Act.* Ninety-second Congress, Second Session, on H.R. 8677 . . . Hearings held in Washington, D.C., September 19, 1972, and Chicago, Ill., September 23, 1972. Washington, D.C.: U.S. Government Printing Office, 1972. 205 pp., tables.

U.S. Library of Congress. Education and Public Welfare Division. *Survey of United States and Foreign Government Support for Cultural Activities.* By Lilla M. Pearce. Washington, D.C.: U.S. Government Printing Office, 1971. 245 pp. ♦ Prepared for Special Subcommittee on Arts and Humanities of the Committee on Labor and Public Welfare, U.S. Senate, 92nd Congress, first session. Attempts to consolidate a universal catalog of federal and state cultural programs.

Van Meter, Elena C. "The Developing Federal Government-Museum Relationship," *Museum News*, 45:9 (May 1967), pp. 20-22.

"The Washington Connection," *Museum News*, 54:5 (May/June 1976), entire issue. ♦ Focuses on some congressional and federal agency activities which directly influence museum interests. Museums and other nonprofit arts organizations are beneficiaries or victims of decisions made in Washington regarding tax reforms, occupational health and safety standards, employee pension benefits, postal regulations, etc.

NOTES

Architectural Barriers Act, 1968 (P.L. 90-480), provides that new or renovated buildings financed in whole or in part with federal funds must be designed and constructed to be accessible to the handicapped. Since passage of federal regulations, all states have passed similar legislation.

The National Arts and the Handicapped Information Service, Box 2040, Grand Central Station, New York, New York 10017. The Service provides information that can be used to make arts programs and facilities more accessible to handicapped persons. The material covers a variety of topics such as funding sources, conferences, architectural barriers, and technical assistance. Enrollment in the Service is open to everyone interested in arts and the handicapped; there is no fee. The Service is a joint project of the National Endowment for the Arts, and Educational Facilities Laboratories, a nonprofit organization that disseminates information on facilities for educational, social, and cultural services. Information packets are made available to enrollees.

Rehabilitation Act, 1973 (P.L. 93-112), passed September 26, 1973, includes among services to be developed and implemented, new approaches and requirements regarding barrier-fee construction of public facilities, and study and development of solutions to existing architectural and transportation barriers impeding handicapped individuals. Title 5 provides for an Architectural and Transportation Barriers Compliance Board to insure compliance with standards prescribed in the Architectural Barriers Act of 1968, as amended by the Act of March 5, 1970 (P.L. 91-205).

UNESCO Recommendations. Recommendation Concerning the Most Effective Means of Rendering Museums Accessible to Everyone, Adopted by the General Conference at Its Eleventh Session, Paris, 14 December 1960.

Economic Issues

American Association of Museums. *America's Museums: The Belmont Report.* A Report to the Federal Council on the Arts and Humanities by a Special Committee of the American Association of Museums. Washington, D.C.: American Association of Museums, 1969. 81 pp. ♦ Study of the financial needs and educational role of museums in the 1960's.

Boorstin, David. "Art Book Publishing in the 70s," *Museum News*, 54:5 (January/February 1975), pp. 36-37ff. ♦ Discusses effects of recessionary economy on art book publishing.

"The Business of Culture," *Saturday Review*, 53:9 (February 28, 1970), pp. 17-34. ◆ Special issue on the economic crisis in the arts.

Cirre, Richard J. *Estimating User Benefits from Historic Sites and Museums.* Ithaca, N.Y.: Cornell University, Program in Urban and Regional Studies, 1977. 119 pp., illus. ◆ Study undertaken to develop a method for predicting future visitation at historic properties and the economic benefits. Model related visitation from various origin zones to the population, mean annual income, education level, and cost of travel from the zones.

Davis, Gordon. "Financial Problems Facing College and University Museums," *Curator*, XIX:2 (June 1976), pp. 116-122. ◆ Results of a study of 49 campus museums.

Elder, Betty Doak. "Proposition 13 Clouds Local History Future: A Special Report," *History News*, 33:9 (September 1978), pp. 197-200. ◆ Reviews effects of property tax cuts on publicly-financed historical organizations.

Gasser, James. "Why Cities Need Museums," *Museum News*, 57:5 (May/June 1979), pp. 26-28. ◆ As sources of ancillary spending and as businesses that employ professional and service based staffs, museums offer substantial economic benefits to the nation's cities.

Gold, Seymour M. *The Impact of Fees and Charges on the Use of Urban Parks, Recreation and Cultural Facilities.* Monticello, Ill.: Council of Planning Librarians, 1978. 17 pp. ◆ Exchange Bibliography no. 1496.

Howard, Robert. "Museums in a Period of Inflation," *Museums Journal*, 54:3 (December 1975), pp. 118-120.

Martin, J. Lynton. "Doing More With Less," *gazette*, 11:4 (Fall 1978), pp. 33-36. ◆ Discusses economic status of museums—competition for limited funding available means improved performance, and a level of professionalism for all museums must be achieved by cooperative action.

Matthai, Robert A. "The Real Crunch: Energy or Inflation?" *Museum News*, 53:1 (September 1974), pp. 24-27. ◆ Discusses two long-term problems facing museums.

Moskow, Michael, and Karl F. Price. "On Walls, With Figures," *Cultural Affairs*, 7 (1969), pp. 14-17. ◆ Summary of a survey of economic data on the visual arts done by the Associated Councils of the Arts with the Brookings Institution, assisted by the American Association of Museums.

"Museums' Earning Gap Widens," *AVISO*, 9 (September 1976), pp. 1, 6-7. ◆ Brief review of survey conducted by the Council on Foundations focusing on the issue: as costs continue to rise, will funds coupled with increased earnings as attendance goes up, compensate for reported loss of municipal and state monies. Survey covered organizations in performing arts, folk arts, public media, summer festivals, and museums, science and technology centers and historical restorations.

National Committee for Cultural Resources. *National Report on the Arts: A Research Report on the Economic and Social Importance of Arts Organizations and Their Activities in the United States, with Recommendations for a National Policy of Public and Private Support.* New York: The Committee, 1975. 36 pp., graphs, bibliog.

National Endowment for the Arts. *Economic Impact of Arts and Cultural Institutions: A Model for Assessment and a Case Study in Baltimore.* Research Division Report no. 6. New York: distr. by Publishing Center for Cultural Resources, 1977. 96 pp.

National Endowment for the Arts. *Museums, U.S.A.* Washington, D.C.: for sale by the U.S. Government Printing Office, 1974. 203 pp., tables, appendix, index. ◆ Survey of approximately 700 art, history, science museums in the U.S. with emphasis on comprehensive picture of museum operations. Parent study done by National Research Center of the Arts, cited below.

National Research Center of the Arts. *Museums U.S.A.: A Survey Report.* Research conducted by National Research Center of the Arts. Washington, D.C.: National Endowment for the Arts, for sale by Superintendent of Documents, U.S. Government Printing Office, 1975. 592, 87, 7 pp.

Nicholas, D.A. "Recession Money-Managing Pointers," *Museum News*, 54:1 (September/October 1975), pp. 50-51.

Parkhurst, Charles. "America's Museums: Prices and Priorities," *Cultural Affairs*, 7

(1969), pp. 9-12. ◆ Discusses the Belmont Report.

Sansweet, Stephen J. "Proposition 13's Impact on the Arts," *Wall Street Journal,* CXCII:9 (July 14, 1978), p. 11.

Steere, William C. "One More Problem for Municipally Supported Museums." In *Papers, 64th Annual Meeting, American Association of Museums* (San Francisco, Calif.: 1969), pp. 158-160. ◆ Discusses attempts of cities to curtail cultural activities.

U.S. Conference of Mayors. Standing Committee on the Arts. *The Taxpayers Revolt and the Arts.* Maynard Jackson, Chairman. Washington, D.C.: The Conference, 1978. 12 pp. ◆ Position paper developed by the Urban Arts Project of the Conference's Standing Committee on the Arts; promotes cultural institutions as economically vital to the future of urban centers and the necessity of keeping the arts and museums as a high priority for funding by municipalities faced with budget cutbacks or standstills.

Waters, Somerset R. "Museums and Tourism," *Museum News,* 44:5 (January 1966), pp. 32-37. ◆ Includes relationship between museums and tourism; services and dollars spent in a community; steps taken by travel industry to support museums and vice versa; ways to improve on travel/museum relationship.

Weiner, Louise W. "Economic Perspective— Impact of Museums to Community," Midwest Museums Conference *Quarterly,* 37:5 (1977), pp. 7-8. ◆ Brief outline of some concerns of the Office of Cultural Resources, U.S. Department of Commerce.

Wescott, Richard. "Who Speaks for the Little Guy?" *The Museologist,* 131 (July/September 1974), pp. 4-6. ◆ Discusses problems of small but effective community facilities facing great demands for additional services and being called upon to support legislative measures where there is no significant government relief for them under present or future funding structures.

Wheeler, Robert C. "Museums or Tourist Traps?" *Museum News,* 40:8 (April 1962), pp. 11-16.

"Will Small Museums Survive the Recession?" *Museum News,* 53:6 (March 1975), pp. 28, 46. ◆ Discusses effects of inflation-recession which have forced modifications in programs or cutbacks.

3

Governing Boards

It may well be that there never was and never will be an absolutely perfect relationship between a Board of Trustees and all members of a staff. Perhaps there shouldn't be, for their roles are to interact, to stimulate, to provoke thought, and to carve out their respective turfs and to ward off trespass. The basic premise of their relationship is simplistic: the Board, under the direction of its chairman, makes policy; the staff, under the direction of its chief administrative officer, carries out policy. The permutations and combinations, however, are well-nigh infinite and, therefore, frequently troublesome. There cannot be, however, a well-administered historical or cultural organization that does not at least try to understand and come to grips with this relationship.

The references cited here deal with the qualifications of trustees, with their roles and responsibilities individually and collectively, with the liabilities they are likely to incur and with their immunities, and with the difficult problems raised by potential conflicts of interest. The bibliography is scant and here reaches over into allied fields for further assistance. But it is vital, for too many historical organizations have foundered on the shoals of misunderstanding of the nature and role of the trustee.

Ahmanson, Caroline. "Trustees and Directors," *Museum News*, 50:1 (September 1971), pp. 35-36. ♦ Excerpt from session at 66th Annual Meeting, American Association of Museums, Denver, Colorado, June 1-5, 1971.

ALI-ABA Course of Study, Winston-Salem, N.C., 1975. *Officers' Powers and Duties in Nonprofit Organizations.* No. V377. Philadelphia: American Law Institute-American Bar Association, 1975. 5 cassettes, study materials. ♦ The program, designed for the general practitioner, provides about 7½ hours of instruction. It examines the selection or election of officers, statutory powers and duties of officers, liabilities and immunities of officers, the effect of officers serving concurrently as directors and trustees, and the problem of conflicts of interest of officers and employees serving in nonprofit organizations. The faculty also discusses the liability of officers and directors of condominiums and other forms of residence associations, and officers' problems in charitable, cultural, and membership organizations. Included with the series are a 284-page Course Study Book and several outlines.

Anderson, Elmer L. *Trustees and Responsibilities.* AASLH Cassette Tape no. 1. Nashville, Tenn.: American Association for State and Local History, 1971. 1 cassette tape, 50 minutes. ♦ Covers qualifications in a trustee that will most benefit the historical society, and includes the roles and responsibilities of the individual trustee and what he or she is expected to do as a member of the Board.

Budd, Edward G., Jr. "Museum Organization and Personnel Policies," *Museum News*, 44:1 (September 1965), pp. 22-24. ♦ Role of museum trustee with respect to organization and personnel.

Burns, Gerald. *Trustees in Higher Education, Their Function and Coordination.* New York: Independent College Funds of America, 1966. 194 pp., illus., bibliog. ♦ A general guide to trustee organization and operation with emphasis on the smaller college. Contains useful bibliography.

46

Burns, William A. "Trustees: Duties and Responsibilities," *Museum News*, 41:4 (December 1962), pp. 22-23.

Chudleigh, Ann, ed. *The Role of the Trustee in the 70's.* A Report of the Proceedings of a Seminar Organized by The Ontario Association of Art Galleries. Ottawa: Ontario Association of Art Galleries, 1971. 86 pp. ♦ Addresses by participants on: "Role of the Trustee as Seen by a Trustee," "Role of the Trustee as Seen by a Director," and "Who Runs the Museum—Director or Trustee?"

Conrad, William R., Jr., and William E. Glenn. *The Effective Voluntary Board of Directors: What It Is and How It Works.* Chicago: Swallow Press, c1976. 184 pp., illus., bibliog. ♦ Describes function and roles of a volunteer board in terms of the overall management and planning process of volunteer organizations. Covers specifics of board agendas, committee structures, guidelines and proceedings.

Copeland, Mrs. Lammot DuPont. "The Role of Trustees: Selection and Responsibilities," *History News*, 29:3 (March 1974), Technical Leaflet no. 72.

"Duties of Charitable Trust Trustees and Charitable Corporation Directors," *Real Property, Probate and Trust Journal*, 2:4 (Winter 1967), pp. 545-564.

Erpf, Armand. "AAM Trustee Advisory Committee," *Museum News*, 48:9 (May 1970), p. 21. ♦ Chairman of Committee comments on rationale and goals of the committee.

Fenn, Dan H., Jr. "Executives as Community Volunteers," *Harvard Business Review*, 49:2 (March-April 1971), pp. 4-16. ♦ Also available in Reprint Series, no. 21123, Management of Nonprofit Organizations Series. Address: Reprint Service, *Harvard Business Review*, Boston, Massachusetts 02163.

"Foundations, Charities and the Law: The Interaction of External Controls and Internal Policies," *UCLA Law Review*, 13:4 (May 1966), entire issue. ♦ Issue devoted to foundations and the law. Nine papers on such subjects as Treasury Department Report on Private Foundations, law of trusts, use for perpetuity, duties and responsibilities of trustees.

Getlein, Frank. "Points of View: Trustees," *Museum News*, 42:7 (March 1964), p. 9. ♦ Discusses tendency of trustees to get out of fiscal grind and dabble with operating policy.

Guthe, Carl E. "Governing Board." In *So You Want a Good Museum?* (Washington, D.C.: American Association of Museums, 1967), pp. 11-13.

Hassard, Howard. "Legal Responsibilities of Historical Society Trustees," *History News*, 17:4 (February 1962), pp. 57-59.

Hawkins, Ashton. "Improving Governance at the Metropolitan Museum," *Museum News*, 50:10 (June 1972), p. 35. ♦ Metropolitan Museum of Art point of view regarding allegations of discrimination against women staff members. Written by the Secretary and Counsel of the museum.

Heneman, Harlow J., et al. "Responsibilities of an Arts Trustee." In *The Arts: Planning for Change* (New York: Associated Councils of the Arts, May 1966), pp. 73-85. ♦ Contents include: basic obligations of the governing body; characteristics, selection and orientation of board members; composition of governing boards; composition of a community council; qualifications of a museum trustee; raising funds; vitality of the board.

Hess, John L. *The Grand Acquisitors.* Boston: Houghton Mifflin Company, 1974. 178 pp., illus. ♦ An inquiry into the acquisition/disposal policy of the Metropolitan Museum of Art.

Horowitz, Harvey. *Responsibilities and Liabilities of Directors and Officers of Non-Profit Corporations.* New York: Associated Councils of the Arts, 1976. 5 pp., mimeo.

Kimche, Lee. "The AAM Trustee Committee," *Museum News*, 49:6 (February 1971), pp. 26-30.

Knoll, Alfred P. "Museums—A Gunslinger's Dream," *The Museologist*, 136 (March 1976), pp. 3-8, 17-25. ♦ Explores legal responsibilities and public accountability of museums today. Points out areas of concern to museum administrators and trustees that have historically been relatively immune from public scrutiny but are now prime targets for outside attack. Reviews recent court actions relating to acquisition and deaccessioning cases. Reprinted, c1975, Bay Area Lawyers for the Arts, Inc., 2446 Durant Avenue, Berkeley, California 94704.

McGrath, Kyran M. "A Landmark Court Decision," *Museum News*, 53:4 (December 1974), pp. 40-41. ◆ A recent District Court decision delineates the responsibilities of trustees of nonprofit institutions.

McGreevy, Milton. "The Trustee–Professional Staff Relationship," *Museum News*, 44:1 (September 1965), pp. 27-29.

Meneely, Clinton. "Try It! You'll Like It!" *Museum News*, 53:6 (March 1975), pp. 34-35, 45. ◆ Points out opportunities in serving as volunteer treasurer of a small nonprofit arts organization.

Museums Association. *Code of Practice for Museum Authorities.* London: The Association, 1977. 6 pp., appendix, bibliog. ◆ Adopted at the Association's Annual General Meeting in July 1977 and recommended to Boards of Trustees, local authorities, museum committees, senior staff and others involved in management of museums and art galleries. Includes statement of purpose; definition of a museum; minimum requirements of museums and art galleries; acquisitions to museum and art gallery collections; disposal of collections; museum organization. Appendix lists relevant policy statements of the Association adopted between 1968 and 1975, some of which are reprinted in *Museums Yearbook 1977.*

Naumer, Helmuth J. *Of Mutual Respect and Other Things.* Washington, D.C.: American Association of Museums, 1977. 31 pp., bibliog., appendix. ◆ An essay on trusteeship. Includes definition; constitution and bylaws; board responsibilities, conflicts, composition; Trustee–Director responsibilities; Board and officer selection; board orientation; committees; museum director; trustee–staff relations. Appendix is a suggested Board of Trustees–Director Employment Agreement.

Nelson, Charles A. "Trusteeship Today," *Curator,* XIX:1 (March 1976), pp. 5-16.

Noble, Joseph Veach. "Open Letter to the Members of Arts Councils," *Museum News*, 54:2 (November/December 1975), pp. 46-47. ◆ Ten new commandments essential for successful fulfillment of an arts council's mission.

On Understanding Art Museums. Edited by Sherman Lee. Englewood Cliffs, N.J.: Prentice-Hall, 1975. 212 pp., bibliog., index. ◆ Background papers prepared for the

46th American Assembly, Arden House, November 1974.

Peat, Wilbur D. "Trustees and Museum Staff," Midwest Museums Conference *Quarterly,* 24:3 (Summer 1964), pp. 6-8.

Prentice, Ann E. *The Public Library Trustee: Image and Performance on Funding.* Metuchen, N.J.: Scarecrow Press, 1973. 176 pp., bibliog.

Ripley, S. Dillon. "The Governance of Museums," *Museum News*, 48:4 (December 1969), pp. 9-10.

Rose, Mrs. Reginald P. "The Trustee and Museum Collections and Exhibition Policy," *Museum News*, 44:1 (September 1965), pp. 31-33.

Smieton, Dame Mary, and Sir Denis Hamilton. "The Trustee and the National Museums," *Museums Journal,* 77:3 (December 1977), pp. 117-120.

Smith, William H. "The Care and Feeding of Trustees," *Western Museums Quarterly,* 5:2 (June 1968), pp. 10-14.

Spaeth, Eloise. "The Fine Art of Being a Trustee," *Museum News*, 44:2 (October 1965), pp. 39-40.

Swann, Peter C. "The Director Preserved?" *The Museologist,* 117 (December 1970), pp. 4-11. ◆ Criticisms discussed are: museum response to demands of modern society, directors and public issues, trustees out of touch with needs of democratic society. Each demand puts professional director in different position.

Thomas, M. W., Jr. "The Historic House and Education–Need and Opportunities." In *Section Papers, 63rd Annual Meeting, American Association of Museums* (New Orleans, La.: May 1968), pp. 80-84. ◆ Discusses "inward education" of trustees, founders and staff; and the outward educational function.

Thomas, Robert E. "The Trustee and the Institution," *The Museologist,* 123 (June 1972), pp. 5-9. ◆ Text of a talk given at Museums' Trustees Workshop, September 25, 1971. Includes what makes an effective trustee; duties and responsibilities of trustees.

Trenbeth, Richard P. "Ideas in the Market Place," *Museum News*, 45:1 (September 1966), pp. 29-31.

"Trustee–Employee Relations: Report of Committee, Louis C. Jones and Richard E. Fuller, Co-Chairmen," *Museum News*, 33:5 (September 1955), pp. 5-6.

Welles, Chris. *Conflicts of Interest: Nonprofit Institutions.* Report to The Twentieth Century Fund Steering Committee on Conflicts of Interest in the Securities Market. New York: The Twentieth Century Fund, 1977. 93 pp., bibliog. notes. ◆ Contents include educational endowments, the trustees, the portfolio, investments managers, brokers and bankers, foundations, the donors.

Wicke, Myron F. *Handbook for Trustees.* Rev. ed. Nashville, Tenn.: Division of Higher Education, Board of Education, Methodist Church, 1962. 101 pp. ◆ Church and college trustees.

Woods, Lawrence C., Jr. "The Trustee's Role in Community–Museum Relations," *Museum News*, 44:1 (September 1965), pp. 29-31.

Young, Virginia G., ed. *The Library Trustee, A Practical Guidebook.* 3rd ed. New York: R. R. Bowker, 1978. 256 pp., bibliog., appendix, index. ◆ Covers latest problems facing libraries and their supporters—paid library, user services, changes in technology, space planning, new copyright law and the photocopying of materials; censorship; finances; staffing; public relations.

NOTE

American Association of Museums, Trustees Committee. The Museum Trustees Committee helps trustees fulfill their vital responsibilities to museums. It provides a forum for communication about federal and state programs, legislation and tax concerns, museum accreditation, sources of funding, and the preservation of our cultural and educational heritage. AAM trustee members receive all the benefits of individual membership, as well as a special quarterly newsletter directed to trustee interests. They may attend seminars for trustees on taxes, trustee responsibilities, finances, legislation and other topics pertaining to the trustee's role. Trustees are encouraged to attend AAM annual meetings and regional conferences. The Association offers special liability insurance for trustees and officers.

4

Resources for Administration

There are still far too many historical organizations that do not have a management plan or indeed a knowledgeable and effective administrator. The spate of references in the first two sections of this chapter are proof not only of that fact but also of the fact that help is near at hand—if only one knows where to look. The first section lists the best of the directories and guides, bibliographies, professional periodicals, and even the organizations that serve as clearinghouses of information on administration. The next section deals with the art of effective management in general, although it should be remembered that what follows in the remainder of the volume constitutes the whole of the primer on administration.

Then there are sections on three specialized topics. The first concerns itself with standards and ethics, always a problem for a developing profession. It deals with criteria for professionalism, with accreditation programs in the United States and Canada, with the ethical codes that have been devised by the professional national organizations.

The second explores the surveys that are being made of museums and their audiences. No administrator can succeed until he or she comes to understand the explosion of interest that brings millions more each year into the cultural centers of the country.

And finally there is a section that deals with the growing movement to bring cultural institutions out of their singular stance into cooperative effort: locally, regionally, nationally, and internationally.

Directories, Bibliographies, Periodicals

Directories

Alegre, Mitchell R. *A Guide to Museum Villages: The American Heritage Brought to Life.* New York: Drake Publishers, 1978. 160 pp., illus. ◆ Details on more than 100 museum villages; what to see and do, directions, hours, prices, restaurants and lodging.

American Association of Museums. "Guide to Museum-Related Resource Organizations," *Museum News,* 57:2 (November/December 1978), Supplement. ◆ Revised edition of March 1975 "Handbook. . . ." Reprints available.

American Council for the Arts. *Community Arts Agencies: A Handbook and Guide.* Ellen S. Daniels and Robert Porter, eds. New York: The Council, 1978. 408 pp.

Associated Councils of the Arts. *ACA Arts Yellow Pages.* Prepared by Margot Honig and Raymond Baron. New York: Associated Councils of the Arts, 1977. 128 pp. ◆ Directory of national, regional and state arts centers and agencies; arts advocacy groups; national and regional arts service organizations; fundraising organizations; national arts publications; volunteer legal aid for the arts.

Canadian Museums Association. *Directory of Canadian Museums/Repertoire des Musées Canadiens,* 1978. Ottawa: The Association, 1978. 270 pp. ◆ Includes museums and related institutions, nonprofit museums and art galleries, government departments and agencies, and associations.

Center for Arts Information. *Directory for the Arts.* New York: Center for Arts Information, 1978. 83 pp., index. ◆ Guide to 145 organizations offering free or low-cost services, programs and funds for nonprofit arts organizations, artists and local sponsors in New York State and the nation.

Christensen, Erwin O. *A Guide to Art Museums in the United States.* New York: Dodd, Mead & Co., 1968. 303 pp., illus.

Directory of Historical Societies in the United States and Canada. Nashville, Tenn.: American Association for State and Local History, 1956 -. 1 vol., biennial. ◆ Current edition, 11th, 1978.

Fedden, Henry Romilly, and Rosemary Joekes, eds. *The National Trust Guide.* 2nd ed. London: Jonathan Cape, 1977. 608 pp., illus., maps, glossary, index. ◆ Official guide to the properties of the English National Trust, arranged by type of property.

Gale Research Company. *Encyclopedia of Associations.* Detroit: 1967 -. 3 vols. ◆ Vol. 1—National Associations of the U.S.; Vol. 2—Geographic and Executive Index; Vol. 3—New Associations and Projects (periodical supplements). Current edition, 13th, 1979.

Hudson, Kenneth, and Ann Nicholls, eds. *The Directory of Museums.* New York: Columbia University Press, 1975. 864 pp., illus., bibliog., glossary, index. ◆ Includes introductory essay for each country; planning, finance and administration; description of museum contents; location, hours, admission.

International Directory of Arts. Edited by Helmut Rauschenbusch. Berlin: Deutsche Zentraldruckerei, 1952/53 -. 1 vol., annual. ◆ Current Edition, 13th, 1977-78, now 2 vols., biennial. Available from Marquis Who's Who, Chicago.

Katz, Herbert, and Marjorie Katz. *Museums, U.S.A.: A History and Guide.* Garden City, N.Y.: Doubleday, 1965. 395 pp., illus., bibliog. notes. ◆ History of the museum in America: Art, Science, History, Children, Variety. Includes bibliographic notes and an appendix which is a directory of museums.

The Libraries, Museums and Art Galleries Year Book. London: J. Clarke & Co., Ltd., distr. in U.S. by R. R. Bowker, New York, 1897 -. 1 vol., annual. ◆ Includes libraries and branches in the United Kingdom and Eire, plus special and industrial libraries and museums. Entries give name, address, chief librarian or curator, special collections, expenditures. Current edition, 1978.

McDarrah, Fred W. *Museums in New York: A Descriptive Reference Guide to Ninety Fine Arts Museums, Local History Museums, Specialized Museums, Natural History and Science Museums, Libraries, Botanical and Zoological Parks, Commercial Collections, and Historic Houses and Mansions Open to the Public Within the Five Boroughs of New York City.* Special landmarks checklist edited by Gloria S. McDarrah. New York: Quick Fox, 1978. 349 pp., illus., index.

Museums and Galleries in Great Britain and Ireland. London: Index Publishers, 1955 -. 1 vol., annual. ◆ Title varies; British Historic Guides series. Current edition, 1978.

Museums Association. *Museums Yearbook, 1978.* London: 1976 -. 1 vol., annual. ◆ Annual reports and program; directory of museums and galleries in the British Isles. Supersedes *Museums Calendar.*

Museums of the World: A Directory of 17,500 Museums in 150 Countries, Including a Subject Index. 2nd ed., enl. Pullach (Isartal): Verland Documentation, 1975. 808 pp., indexes. ◆ English text; lists and describes art museums and galleries, natural science museums, technical and archeological museums, historic buildings, specialized collections, and exhibits. Available from R. R. Bowker, New York.

National Trust for Historic Preservation. *Library Resources in Washington, D.C. Relating to Historic Preservation.* Compiled by Lelahvon Lugo. Washington, D.C.: The Preservation Press, 1977. 55 pp., index. ◆ Guide to libraries and resources; entries include general information, materials, accessibility, subjects, and comment.

National Trust for Historic Preservation. *Member Organizations and Their Historic*

Properties. Washington, D.C.: The Trust, 1966 -. 1 vol., annual. ◆ Includes description of Trust programs and properties; directory of U.S. member organizations and foreign preservation organizations; State Historic Preservation Officers; American Institute of Architects State Preservation Coordinators; NTHP Board of Advisors; NTHP Board of Trustees; NTHP staff; sponsoring organizations.

The Official Museum Directory 1978/79. Skokie, Ill.: National Register Publishing Co., 1978. 942 pp. ◆ Biennial; begun 1971, imprint varies.

Restored Village Directory: *An Illustrated Directory Listing Restored, Recreated and Replica Villages of Historic Interest in the United States and Canada.* 3rd ed. New York: Quadrant Press, Inc., 1973. 80 pp., illus.

Selected Living Historical Farms, Villages and Agricultural Museums in the United States and Canada. Washington, D.C.: Association for Living Historical Farms and Agricultural Museums, 1976. 62 pp., illus., map.

U.S. Department of the Army. Center of Military History. *Guide to U.S. Army Museums and Historic Sites.* Compiled by Norman M. Cary, Jr. Rev. ed. Washington, D.C.: U.S. Government Printing Office, 1975. 116 pp., illus., maps. ◆ Supersedes 1968 *Official Directory of U.S. Army Museums.*

Wynar, Lubomyr, and Lois Buttlar. *Guide to Ethnic Museums, Libraries and Archives in the United States.* Kent, Ohio: Kent State University Press, 1978. 378 pp.

Bibliographies

Art Index; *An Author and Subject Index to Domestic and Foreign Art Periodicals and Museum Bulletins Covering Archaeology, Architecture, Art History, Arts and Crafts, City Planning, Fine Arts, Graphic Arts, Industrial Design, etc.* Bronx, New York: H. W. Wilson Co., 1929 -. 1 vol. ◆ Quarterly, service basis from H. W. Wilson Co., 950 University Avenue, Bronx, New York 10452.

Bibliographie Muséologique Internationale/International Museum Bibliography. Prague: Museological Cabinet of the National Museum in Prague for International Council of Museums, 1969 -. 1 vol., annual. ◆ Each number covers publications which appeared two years beforehand. Entries arranged according to the Unesco/ICOM Museum Documentation Centre's classification scheme and each issue includes a geographical index and index of museum material referring to articles about the nature of the object or the substance of which it is made. For the years 1967-1970 (1969-1972), published as a supplement to *ICOM News;* beginning *For the Year 1972-1973* (1975), published by the Centre.

Canadian Museums Association. *CMA Bibliography.* Ottawa: The Association, 1976. 233 pp. ◆ An extensive listing of published material on the subjects of museology, museography, and museum and art gallery administration. Available as a complete work or in sets. Supplements published twice a year, beginning 1977, include all changes and additions with no alteration to complete bibliography. Fourth Supplement, September 1978, 84 pp.

Clapp, Jane. *Museum Publications.* New York Scarecrow Press, 1962. 2 vols. ◆ Part I—Anthropology, Archeology and Art, includes museums and museum work, museum directories, museum catalogs, guides and history, anthropology and archeology, and art; Part II—Biology and Earth Sciences.

De Borhegyi, Stephan F., and Elba A. Dodson. *A Bibliography of Museums and Museum Work, 1900-1960.* Publications in Museology no. 1. Milwaukee, Wisc.: Milwaukee Public Museum, 1960. 72 pp.

De Borhegyi, Stephan F.; Elba A. Dodson; and Irene A. Hanson. *Bibliography of Museums and Museum Work, 1900-61, Supplementary Volume.* Publications in Museology no. 2. Milwaukee, Wisc.: Milwaukee Public Museum, 1961. 102 pp.

Georgi, Charlotte. *The Arts and the World of Business.* Rev. 2nd ed. Metuchen, N.J.: Scarecrow Press, 1979. 175 pp., index. ◆ Revised and updated bibliography which supersedes all previous publications. Arranged in sixteen subject areas and five form sections with index by author and a section on publishers' addresses.

Griffin, Appleton P.C. "Bibliography of American Historical Societies." 2nd ed., rev. and enl. In *American Historical Association, Annual Report for the Year 1905* (Washington, D.C.: U.S. Government Printing Office, 1907), Volume II. ◆ Includes publications of historical societies through 1905.

Hawkins, Barbara A. *A Selected Bibliography for Park and Recreation Planners, 1969-1977.* Exchange Bibliography, 1558. Monticello, Ill.: Council of Planning Librarians, 1978. 30 pp.

Michigan. University. Museum of Art. *Selective Bibliography on Museums and Museum Practice; Museums of Art and History in the United States.* Ann Arbor, Mich.: The University, 1974. 34 pp.

National Endowment for the Arts. *Arts Management: An Annotated Bibliography.* Compiled by Linda Coe and Stephen Benedict. New York: distr. by Publishing Center for Cultural Resources, 1978, 76 pp., indexes. ◆ Includes references on management. planning and program development, fund raising and technical assistance, marketing and public relations, governing boards, research and public policy.

New York City. Metropolitan Museum of Art. Library. *Bibliography of Museums and Museology.* Compiled by William Clifford, librarian. New York: The Museum, 1923. 98 pp.

Paris. International Museum Documentation Centre. *Bibliographie Muséographique pour les Années 1951 et 1952/Museographical Bibliography for the Years 1951 and 1952.* Paris, 1956. 82 pp.

Prieve, E. Arthur, and Daniel J. Schmidt. *Administration in the Arts: An Annotated Bibliography of Selected References.* Rev. ed. Madison, Wisc.: Center for Arts Administration, Graduate School of Business, University of Wisconsin, 1977. 177 pp. ◆ Includes references to books and articles dealing with arts administration and management arranged in four basic sections: management in the arts, financial management, marketing the arts in society, publications in business and the arts.

Rath, Frederick L., Jr., and Merrilyn Rogers O'Connell. *A Bibliography on Historical Organization Practices.* Nashville, Tenn.: American Association for State and Local History, 1975 -. 6 vols., appendix, index. ◆ Vol. 1—Historic Preservation; Vol. 2—Care and Conservation of Collections, compiled by Rosemary S. Reese; Vol. 3—Interpretation, compiled by Rosemary S. Reese; Vol. 4—Documentation of Collections, compiled by Rosemary S. Reese; Vol. 5—Administration; Vol. 6—Research (in prep.).

Smith, Ralph C. *A Bibliography of Museums and Museum Work.* Washington, D.C.: American Association of Museums, 1928. 310 pp.

U.S. National Park Service. "Bibliography." In *Field Manual for Museums* (Ann Arbor, Mich.: Finch Press, 1974), pp. 318-342.

NOTES

Museum Documentation Centre, Canadian Museums Association, 331 Cooper Street, Suite 400, Ottawa, Ontario K2P 0G5, Canada. The Center was established to provide documentary resources on all aspects of museum operations, to assist wherever possible in museum research requirements, and to provide the necessary resource materials for the training of museum personnel. The Resource Library of the Centre maintains, as a perequisite, a comprehensive and specialized collection of museological and related documentation in both French and English, as well as various foreign language publications. The Centre continues to seek out materials related to museum operations and activities in order to increase both its scope and efficiency as a clearinghouse for the museum community. The *CMA Bibliography,* begun in 1976 and supplemented with six-month updates, has been entered into the computer network of the National Inventory System. A brochure describing the services of the Centre is available.

Museum Reference Center, A & I Building, Room 2235, Office of Museum Programs, Smithsonian Institution, Washington, D.C. 20560. The Center was established in 1974 as a working collection of resources on all aspects of museum operations for museum personnel and researchers. It provides reference assistance from its files on such fields as museum organization, administration and management, legislation, museum programs, activities and exhibitions, support services, museum architecture, exhibit design, history and philosophy of museums, management of museum collections, conservation, museum education, and related areas. The Center offers the following services to museum professionals and qualified researchers: literature searching, bibliographies on selected subjects, information on current museum activities, information on current issues in the profession, selected materials from OMP workshops, files on professional activities and training opportunities, access to the collection for search use.

UNESCO/ICOM Documentation Centre. The Centre is an outgrowth of a library established in 1947 by the Museums and Monuments Division of UNESCO for its own research and documentation; the following year it was turned over to the International Council of Museums. It is administered by a small staff and maintains the largest library of its kind in existence. The responsibilities of the Centre are for acquiring and conserving all documentation of any nature concerning subjects of interest to ICOM; making use of such information for purposes of diffusion and communicating the same to the personnel of UNESCO and to the members of ICOM, as well as, where possible, to all experts, students or qualified researchers; studying and using all means of improving and increasing the diffusion of information; encouraging the creation of regional documentation centers and coordinating their activities; assisting the National Committees and professional associations in the fields of documentation and information, more particularly by the instruction of trainees; assisting the International Committees in their documentary tasks (directories, questionnaires, cataloging); assisting the ICOM Secretariat in its tasks of a documentary, informative or bibliographical nature.

Documentation is received from all over the world and includes directories, manuals, treatises, monographs, guidebooks, exhibition catalogues, photographs, architectural plans, bulletins and brochures. The material is analyzed, cross-referenced and classified in an extensive scheme based on the Library of Congress method. A card index system (Synoptic) permits the entire literature of a given museum subject to be consulted at the flip of a finger. The system can be readily adapted to a mechanical, microfilm or electronic system of documentation. Documents are then placed at the disposal of visitors at the Center and correspondents; photocopies can be furnished at cost price.

The centre has established an international directory of museums and index of suppliers; and is developing technical bibliographies. It publishes annually an international bibliography of basic museum writing covering publications appearing two years before. It also maintains an Archive of National Legislations for the Protection of Cultural Property on microfiche to keep up to date material compiled for the handbook compiled by Bonnie Burnham (cited in Management of Collections chapter).

Periodicals

Association Management. 1949, monthly, subscription. American Society of Association Executives, 1101 16th Street, N.W., Washington, D.C. 20036. Formerly American Society of Association Executives, *Journal.* Absorbed Society's *ASAE News* and *Here's How,* January 1963.

AVISO. September 1975, monthly, membership. American Association of Museums, 1055 Thomas Jefferson Street, N.W., Washington, D.C. 20007. Succeeds *AAM Bulletin.*

Curator. 1958, quarterly, subscription. American Museum of Natural History, 79th Street at Central Park West, New York, New York 10024. Vol. 20, no. 4 (December 1977) contains cumulative index to Vols. 1-20, arranged by author, title, and subject.

gazette. 1975, quarterly, membership. Canadian Museums Association, Box 1328, Station B, Ottawa, Ontario K1P 5R4, Canada. Supersedes *What's New(S);* published bimonthly 1966-1974.

Heritage Canada. 1974, bimonthly, membership. Heritage Canada, P.O. Box 1385, Station B, Ottawa, Ontario K1P 5R4, Canada. Combines *Heritage Canada* (quarterly) and *Heritage Conversation.*

Historic Preservation. 1949, bimonthly, membership. National Trust for Historic Preservation, 1785 Massachusetts Avenue, N.W., Washington, D.C. 20036.

History News. 1941, monthly, membership, includes Technical Leaflet. American Association for State and Local History, 1400 Eighth Avenue South, Nashville, Tennessee 37203.

ICOM News/Nouvelles de L'ICOM. 1948, quarterly, membership. International Council of Museums, 1 rue Moillis, 75732 Paris, France.

Inside SEMC. bimonthly, membership/subscription. Maralynn Troutmann, Editor, Arkansas Arts and Humanities Office, Continental Building, Suite 500, Markham and Main Streets, Little Rock, Arkansas 72201. Newsletter of the Southeast Museums Conference, American Association of Museums.

Living Historical Farms Bulletin. 1970, bimonthly, membership. Association for Living Historical Farms and Agricultural Museums, c/o John T. Schlebecker, Smithsonian Institution, Washington, D.C. 20560.

Midwest Museums Conference. *The Quarterly.* 1941, quarterly, membership/subscription. L. G. Hoffman, Editor, Davenport Municipal Art Gallery, 1737 West 12th Street, Davenport, Iowa 52804: Newsletter of the Midwest Museums Conference, American Association of Museums.

MPMC Newsletter. 1960, quarterly, membership/subscription. David L. Hartman, Editor, Denver Museum of Natural History, City Park, Denver, Colorado 80205. Newsletter of the Mountain-Plains Museums Conference, American Association of Museums.

museogramme. April 1973, monthly, membership. Canadian Museums Association, Box 1328, Station B, Ottawa, Ontario K1P 5R4, Canada.

The Museologist. 1935, quarterly, membership. Robert W. Ott, Editor, Division of Art and Museum Education, 273 Chambers Building, Pennsylvania State University, University Park, Pennsylvania 16802. Quarterly magazine of the Northeast Museums Conference, American Association of Museums.

Museum. 1948, quarterly, subscription. UNESCO, 7 Place de Fontenoy, 75700 Paris, France. Also available from UNIPUB, Box 433, Murray Hill Station, New York, New York 10016.

Museum News. 1924, 6 issues/yr., membership. American Association of Museums, 1055 Thomas Jefferson Street, N.W., Washington, D.C. 20007.

Museum Scope. 1976, bimonthly, subscription. Alden Redfield, Editor, Suite 5, Strollway Centre, 111 South 9th Street, Columbia, Missouri 65201.

Museums Journal. 1901, quarterly, membership. Museums Association, 87 Charlotte Street, London W1P 2BX, England.

NEMA News. 1976, quarterly, membership/subscription. Katherine Smith, Editor, DeCordova Museum, Sandy Pond Road, Lincoln, Massachusetts 01773. Newsletter of the New England Museums Association, American Association of Museums.

Parks and Recreation: Journal of Park and Recreation Management. 1903, monthly, subscription. National Recreation and Park Association, 1601 N. Kent Street, Arlington, Virginia 22209.

Preservation News. 1961, monthly newspaper, membership. National Trust for Historic Preservation, 1785 Massachusetts Avenue, N.W., Washington, D.C. 20036.

WRC Newsletter. 1975, quarterly, membership/subscription. Joan Pursell, Editor, Santa Barbara Museum of Natural History, 2559 Puesta del Sol Road, Santa Barbara, California 93105. Newsletter of the Western Regional Conference, American Association of Museums.

NOTES

American National Standards Institute, 1430 Broadway, New York, New York 10018. Founded in 1918, the Institute serves as a clearinghouse for nationally coordinated, voluntary safety, engineering and industrial standards. It approves and drafts standards in the fields of library work, documentation and related publishing practices, standards adopted under OSHA, information and processing, construction and demolition operations, photography and motion pictures, security equipment, textiles, and many others. A catalog of a complete set of all American National Standards, and special series, is available from the Institute; brochures listing standards in special fields also available. Formerly American Engineering Standards Committee (1928), American Standards Association (1965), United States of America Standards Institute (1969).

American Society of Association Executives, 1101 16th Street, N.W., Washington, D.C. 20036. The Society is the professional organization of executives who manage trade, education, technical, business, civic, fraternal, and professional associations and societies. The society, founded in 1920 as the American Trade Association Executives, adopted its present name in 1956. The basic purpose is to help the association executive improve his management skills and grow in his profession, and to help him develop and strengthen his organization. ASAE membership categories include trade, individual and federation memberships on local, state, regional and national levels. The services of the Society include educational programs and seminars; a government relations program; an international relations program; professional counseling; executive employment services; and special studies and reports. It also offers a certified association executive program, insurance programs, and retirement program. Its publications include *Association Management* (monthly); membership directory (annual); books, manuals, reports, brochures, and audio visual materials relating to association management (catalog available).

Arts Reporting Service, Charles C. Mark, Editor, 9214 Three Oaks Drive, Silver Spring, Maryland 20901. The Service, available through an annual subscription, is a biweekly newsletter begun in 1970 summarizing top stories in the arts, new programs, problems and trends.

Center for Arts Information, 152 West 42nd Street, Room 1239, New York, New York 10036. The Center serves as a clearinghouse of information for and about the arts in New York State. Its services are available to all members of the arts community, as well as the general public. It maintains a library and researches inquiries ranging from addresses and telephone numbers to location of arts services and guidelines for eligibility for government funds. The staff is available by appointment to assist in use of the library resources. The Center publishes specialized directories, news bulletins, and *Directory for the Arts* (1978). Current projects include a study on management assistance programs offered by national service organizations; and other resource guides.

Community Arts Management Program, Sangamon State University, Springfield, Illinois 62708. The Program offers "Conversations on Arts Management," a project of videotaping leading arts administrators in informal conversations concerning their various areas of expertise. The video cassettes are available to arts organizations and interested institutions and individuals. The tapes are available on three-quarter-inch video cassettes and on audio cassettes for a modest charge; a brochure of the tapes and order instructions is available from the Program. Topics include issues in the arts; National Endowment for the Arts; Regional Arts Agencies/Regionalism; State Arts Agencies; Local Arts Agencies; Arts in General; Money for the Arts; Public Relations and Promotion; Arts Festivals; Arts and Recreation; Art and the Artist; Law and the Arts.

Cultural Resources Development Project, National Endowment for the Arts, Washington, D.C. 20506. Begun in 1975, the Project has issued a periodic *Bulletin on Federal Economic Programs and the Arts*. The bulletins are intended to encourage and assist cultural leaders' efforts to obtain local allocations of Comprehensive Employment and Training Act (CETA) funds for arts programs and cultural institutions, and to provide information on federal revenue sharing, antirecession fiscal assistance and emergency jobs programs. Two special bulletins are: "Building a Local Base for Federal Arts Support" (July 5, 1977), a four-page outline on effective use of locally administered federal funds; and, "The Uses of Public Service Employment in the Arts," (October 28, 1977), which describes some of the CETA/Arts projects being undertaken in various regions of the country.

National Recreation and Park Association, 1601 N. Kent Street, Arlington, Virginia 22209. Founded in 1965, the Association is a public interest organization dedicated to improving the human environment through improved park, recreation and leisure opportunities. Activities include programs for the development and upgrading of professional and citizen leadership in the park, recreation and leisure field; dissemination of innovations and research; technical assistance to affiliated organizations, local communities and members; providing information on public policy; public education; and an extensive publications program. Regional service centers are located in Atlanta, Chicago, Denver, White Plains, N.Y., and Fresno, California. It also maintains a library. The Association was formed by a merger of American Association of Zoological Parks and Aquariums (again independent), American Institute of Park Executives, American Recreation Society, National Conference of State Parks, and National Recreation Association.

Effective Management

Alderson, William T. "Using Consultants Effectively," *History News*, 30:3 (March 1975), Technical Leaflet no. 82.

Allan, Douglas A.; D. E. Owen; and F. S. Wallis. *Administration*. Handbook for Museum Curators, A1. London: Museums Association, 1960. 51 pp.

American Association for State and Local History. *101 Ideas from History News.* Nashville, Tenn.: The Association, 1975. 151 pp., illus., diagrams. ◆ A compilation of practical ideas for historical societies including money making, exhibits and displays, collections, publicity, security, special programs, administration, publications, education programs, and maintenance.

Association for Living Historical Farms and Agricultural Museums. *Proceedings of the Annual Meeting, June 16-18, 1974, University of ·California, Davis.* Edited by Virginia W. Briscoe and Jay A. Anderson. Washington, D.C.: The Association, Smithsonian Institution, 1975. 63 pp. ◆ Contents include interpretive themes; establishing basic programs; descriptions of farms and museums; reports and membership list.

Atkinson, Frank. "The Administration of Museums by Librarian-Curators," *Museums Journal,* 63:3 (December 1963), pp. 147-155. ◆ Survey and comparisons with charts.

Baxi, Smita J., and Vinod P. Dwivedi. *Modern Museum: Organization and Practice in India.* New Delhi: Abhinav Publications, 1973. 208 pp., illus., bibliog. ◆ Also available from International Publications Service, New York.

Blundell, John D. "Go Metric Now," *Museums Journal,* 70:2 (September 1970), pp. 61-62.

Canadian Museums Association. Training Committee. *Basic Museum Management.* Edited by George MacBeath and S. James Gooding. Ottawa: Canadian Museums Association, 1969. 80 pp., illus., bibliog. ◆ Clear and practical advice; includes museum world; museum's purposes; legal status; governing body and staff; planning; fundraising; budgets; collections; research and record keeping; conservation; exhibition; the museum and its community.

Cases in Arts Administration. Edited by Thomas C. Raymond, Stephen A. Greyser, and Douglas Schwalbe. Rev. ed. Cambridge, Mass.: Arts Administration Research Institute, 1975. 389 pp., illus., bibliog. references.

Chedister, Ron. "You Have to Shop Around," *Museum News,* 52:5 (January/February 1974), pp. 63-64. ◆ Suggestions for locating outside consultants.

Coleman, Laurence Vail. *Historic House Museums.* 1933. Reprint. Detroit, Mich.: Gale Research Co., 1973. 187 pp., illus., maps, directory, bibliog. ◆ A manual for people concerned with establishing or administering historic house museums which includes origins, methods, and prospects. Originally published by the American Association of Museums.

Coleman, Laurence Vail. *Manual for Small Museums.* New York: G. P. Putnam's Sons, 1927. 395 pp., illus., diagrams, bibliog. ◆ Includes organization, administration, curatorial work, education work, research, building, and appendices.

Conflict in the Arts: The Relocation of Authority: The Museum. Edited by Douglas Schwalbe and Janet Baker-Carr. Cambridge, Mass.: Arts Administration Research Institute, c1976. 81 pp. ◆ Collections of interviews on management and art museums. Also in the series: *The Arts Council* (1977); *The Orchestra* (1977).

Corey, Albert B. "A Decalogue for State and Local Historical Societies," *Nebraska History,* 34:4 (December 1953), pp. 245-255. ◆ Outlines duties of a historical society.

Coy, Roy E. "Developing a Community Museum in America," *Curator,* XI:3 (September 1968), pp. 223-233. ◆ Describes growth and development from a project, to incorporated museum, membership drive, city tax support, and building headquarters.

Creigh, Dorothy Weyer. *A Primer for Local Historical Societies.* Nashville, Tenn.: American Association for State and Local History, 1976. 153 pp., illus., bibliog., appendices, index. ◆ Chapters include organizing, publicity, beginning projects, tours, establishing a library, restorations, museums, and publishing.

"Do or Die: Historical Societies, Problems and Solutions," *History News,* 18:2 (December 1962), pp. 24-25.

Drucker, Peter F. *Management: Tasks, Responsibilities, Practices.* 1st ed. New York: Harper & Row Publishers, 1974. 839 pp., bibliog., index. ◆ Study of management as an organized body of knowledge; deals with techniques of effective management, and looks at management from outside and studies its tasks and requirements.

Educational Facilities Laboratories. *Hands-on Museum: Partners in Learning, A Report from Education Facilities Laboratories.*

New York: EFL, 1975. 44 pp., illus. ✦ Study of museums as experience-oriented centers; includes examples from museums across U.S. and general administrative advice.

Endter, Ellen A. "Technical Assistance: How to Get It When You Need It," *Museum News,* 53:6 (March 1975), pp. 33, 46. ✦ Discusses museums, arts related organizations, local colleges, technical institutes and federal agencies as potential sources.

"Folk Parks: A Report of a Seminar Organized on the 8th and 9th October 1966, by the Institute of Advanced Architectural Studies," *Museums Journal,* 66:3 (December 1966), pp. 220-224. ✦ Meeting focused on establishment and running of folk museums, and discussion of basic problems.

Friedman, Renee. "The Museum-Media Contractor Relationship," *Museum News,* 57:4 (March/April 1979), pp. 17-20.

Greenhill, Basil. "New Patterns in Museum Management," *Museums Journal,* 77:3 (December 1977), pp. 123-125. ✦ Brief summaries of nine general principles of management practices.

Guthe, Carl E. *The Management of Small History Museums.* 2nd ed. Nashville, Tenn.: American Association for State and Local History, 1964. 78 pp., bibliog. ✦ Manual on the fundamentals of good museum operation; discusses procedures and technical advice on physical facilities, the collections, interpretive exhibits, and supplementary services.

Guthe, Carl E. *So You Want a Good Museum: A Guide to the Management of Small Museums.* 1957. Reprint. Washington, D.C.: American Association of Museums, 1967. 37 pp., bibliog. ✦ Short bulletin on the fundamental elements of good museum management especially for those least familiar with museum work. Includes collections records and care; organization pattern; administration of plant and budget; exhibits and other activities.

Hilferty, Gerald, and Elizabeth Hilferty. "Planning a Local Museum: An Approach for Historical Societies," *History News,* 29:9 (September 1974), Technical Leaflet no. 78. ˙

"Historical Administrators Can Tap Variety of Sources for Consultation Services," *History News,* 27:9 (September 1972), pp. 202-203.

Horwitz, Tom. *Arts Administration: How to Set Up and Run a Successful Nonprofit Arts Organization.* Chicago: Chicago Review Press, 1978. 256 pp., appendix. ✦ Brief handbook for novice or volunteer administrator; lists of agencies and organizations; boards of directors; bylaws and incorporation proceedings; fundraising; taxation; financial management; marketing.

Hyslop, Julie. "Planning the Small Museum," *Western Museums Quarterly,* 7:1 (July 1970), pp. 5-7.

International Council of Museums. Rumanian National Committee. *Organization of Open-Air Ethnographic Museums–Principles and Methods, The Symposium, Bucharest, September 7-15, 1966, Papers.* Bucharest: 1966. 116 pp.

Inverarity, Robert Bruce. "Thoughts on the Organization of Museums," *Curator,* II:4 (1959), pp. 293-303. ✦ Factors to be considered in planning and administering museums.

Kittleman, James M. "Museum Mismanagement," *Museum News,* 54:5 (March/April 1976), pp. 44-46. ✦ Suggests that sound business management principles should be applied to museum administration.

Knoll, Alfred P. "Museums—A Gunslinger's Dream," *The Museologist,* 136 (March 1976), pp. 3-8, 17-25. ✦ Reprinted, c1975, Bay Area Lawyers for the Arts, Inc., 2446 Durant Avenue, Berkeley, California 94704. Explores legal responsibilities and public accountability of museums today; points out areas of concern to museum administrators and trustees that have historically been relatively immune from public scrutiny; reviews recent court actions relating to acquisition and deaccessioning cases.

Kotler, Philip. *Marketing for Non-Profit Organizations.* Englewood Cliffs, N.J.: Prentice-Hall, c1975, 1974. 436 pp., illus., bibliog. references. ✦ How museums, universities, symphony orchestras and social agencies can analyze their impact on the community and creatively tailor programs and fundraising activities to meet and fulfill their needs. Assists in defining goals and objectives.

Lemaire, Ingrid. *Resource Directory of the Funding and Managing of Non-Profit Organizations.* New York: Edna McConnell Clark

Foundation, 1977. 127 pp. ◆ Intended for use as a reference tool on where to secure funds, how to secure funds, and where to secure technical assistance for more effective management.

Levitt, I. M. "Inching Toward the Metric System," *Museum News,* 49:4 (December 1970), pp. 30-31.

Lewis, Ralph H. *Manual for Museums.* Washington, D.C.: National Park Service, U.S. Department of the Interior; for sale by the Superintendent of Documents, U.S. Government Printing Office, 1976. 412 pp., illus., bibliog., index. ◆ An outgrowth of the 1941 volume, *Field Manual for Museums* by Ned Burns. Includes museum collections; museum records, furnished historic structure museums, exhibit maintenance and replacement, and eight specialized appendices.

Lewis, Ralph H. "NPS Assistance to Museums," *Museum News,* 49:6 (February 1971), pp. 13-17. ◆ Assistance in the form of specimens, training, technical advice, and in planning and development.

McConkey, Dale D. *MBO for Nonprofit Organizations.* New York: AMACOM, 1975. 223 pp., bibliog., index. ◆ Guide to management by objectives approach; case studies of representative nonprofit organizations which demonstrate how MBO improves organizations and managerial effectiveness.

"Mail Goes Through . . . Slowly," *History News,* 34:2 (February 1979), pp. 41-43. ◆ Reviews problems in mailing periodicals, reasons for post office delays, special services, and mailing tips.

Marshall, William E. *Museum Planning.* AASLH Cassette Tape no. 8. Nashville, Tenn.: American Association for State and Local History, 1971. 59 minutes. ◆ Review of museum planning including philosophical reasons for the museum, functions, programs, and prospective audience of the museum in terms of space needed for these activities.

New York (State). Office of State History. *A Quiz for Local Historians.* Albany: 1967. 21 pp., mimeo. ◆ Outline of duties and responsibilities of officially appointed historians in New York State.

Parker, Arthur C. *A Manual for History Museums.* New York State Historical Associa-

tion Series . . . no. III. New York: American Museum of Science Books, c1935. 204 pp., illus., maps, bibliog.

Parkinson, Cyril Northcote. *Parkinson's Law and Other Studies in Administration.* New York: Ballantine Books, 1969. 112 pp., illus.

Parr, Albert Eide. "Origins, Nature and Purposes of Museum Policy," *Curator,* V:3 (1962), pp. 217-220. ◆ Discusses issues of policy; primary responsibility for initiating development of policies and plans rests with the administration.

Perry, Mary-Ellen Earl. "Problems of Small Museums," *The Museologist,* 122 (March 1972), pp. 15-17. ◆ Discusses lack of funds, public relations, maintenance of collections, and security.

Randel, Jo Stewart. "When Starting a Small Museum," *Museum News,* 49:7 (March 1971), pp. 21-22.

Reiss, Alvin H. *Arts Management Handbook.* 2nd rev. ed. New York: Law-Arts Publishers, 1974. 802 pp., bibliog. ◆ Articles which appeared in *Arts Management,* 1962-1972, on fundraising techniques, analyzing and building audiences, publicity and advertising, corporate support, free community services.

Rigney, Eugene D. "Experiences in Operating a Museum," *History News,* 11:10 (August 1956), pp. 78-80.

Schlebecker, John T., and Gale E. Peterson. *Living Historical Farms Handbook.* Washington, D.C.: Smithsonian Institution Press, 1972. 91 pp., directories, bibliog. references, index. ◆ Includes chronology of the movement; starting a living historical farm; financing; historical research; staff and equipment; visitors and interpretation; capital and overhead; income; state directory.

Selby, Cecily Cannan. "Better Performance from 'non-profits'," *Harvard Business Review,* 56:5 (September-October 1978), pp. 92-98. ◆ Experienced administrator shows how the unique characteristics of rich personal resources and strong motivation can, together with established business practices, convert nonprofit weaknesses into strengths.

"Setting Priorities," *Museum News,* 55:3 (January/February 1977), pp. 30-31, 45. ◆ Review of experiences in developing and administering programs for the handicapped, including priorities, limits to accessibility, becoming accessible with limited staff and resources.

Silvestro, Clement M. *Organizing a Local Historical Society.* Rev. ed. Nashville, Tenn.: American Association for State and Local History, 1968. 40 pp. ◆ Basic outline for planning and organizing a local historical society including guidelines for preliminary meetings, the statement of purpose and scope, the organizational meeting, incorporation and tax exemption, and sample articles of incorporation, constitution and bylaws.

Sinnick, A. [Lucas, Frederic Augustus]. "Modern Principles of Museum Administration," *Curator,* IV:1 (1961), pp. 49-57.

"The Small Museum: Some Reflections," *Museum News,* 49:7 (March 1971), pp. 15-18. ◆ Four administrators reflect on the present and future state of the small museum, its functions and place in its community, and its strengths and weaknesses.

Stone, Ron. "Developing Objectives in Museums," *gazette,* 10:1 (Winter 1977), pp. 20-23. ◆ Discusses goals and planning, and translation into tasks.

Swinney, Holman J. "Common Sense Advice in Planning an Historical Museum," *The Museologist,* 112 (September 1969), pp. 8-16. ◆ Defines concept of what a museum is, responsibilities of museum, practical/technological planning, collections and exhibiting.

Texas Historical Commission. Museum Services Department. *Thoughts on Museum Planning.* Austin, Tex.: The Commission, 1976. 55 pp., mimeo. ◆ Collection of material written for small historical museums: planning for a new museum in an old building; problems to consider when planning a museum; three articles of gallery space; organization structure; function and responsibilities of a trustee; examples of bylaws and selective bibliography.

Texas Historical Commission. Museum Services Department. *Thoughts on the Museum and the Community.* Austin, Tex.: Texas Historical Commission and Texas Historical Foundation, 1976. 19 pp., bibliog. ◆ Includes definitions, elements of a museum, contributions of a museum to a community, and a business bibliography for administration, security, insurance, and financing.

Texas State Historical Survey Committee. *Museum Memorabilia.* Texas Small Museum Institutes, 1966, 1968. Austin, Tex.: The Committee, 1969. 104 pp. ◆ Includes summaries of the Institutes which were established to assist new museums and to disseminate information on museum methods and techniques.

Texas State Historical Survey Committee. *1973 Museum Seminars.* Technical Information Supplement. Austin, Tex.: The Committee, 1973. 59 pp., bibliog. ◆ Recommendations on the founding and financing of a museum, and a series of short articles on storage and handling, conservation and exhibition planning.

United Nations Educational, Scientific and Cultural Organization. *The Organization of Museums: Practical Advice.* Museums and Monuments—IX. Paris: UNESCO, 1960. 188 pp., illus., bibliog. ◆ Chapters by museum experts on museum and its functions, administration, staff, research, visitors, education, museum laboratory, collections, exhibitions, and museum architecture.

U.S. National Park Service. *Administrative Policies for Historical Areas of the National Park System.* Rev. 1973. Washington, D.C.: for sale by the U.S. Government Printing Office, 1973. 170 pp., appendices. ◆ Includes administrative policies of historical areas and the historic resources of other areas, and background and philosophy on which policies are based. Helpful in long-range planning.

U.S. National Park Service. *Field Manual for Museums.* 1941. Reprint. Ann Arbor, Mich.: Finch Press, 1974. 426 pp., illus., plans, bibliog. ◆ Includes role of museums in national parks; planning; exhibit room and equipment; exhibits; study collection room; collections; technical methods; library; historic house museum; museum in use; administrative relationships in the National Park Service; bibliography and appendix.

U.S. Postal Service. *Mailers Guide.* Publication 19. Washington, D.C.: U.S. Government Printing Office, January 1978. 43 pp., appendix. ◆ Includes regulations for all classes of mail, service delivery standards, express mail service, special services, money order, postage applications and payment, delivery and collection, address procedures and ZIP code, metered mail. Postage rates and fees, which are subject to change, are not included but are available in the *Postal Service Manual* and the *Postal Bulletin* at all post offices. Also, monthly publication *Memo to Mailers,* advises business mailers of all rate and classification changes and is available free from P.O. Box 1600, LaPlata, Maryland 20646. Appendix includes letter mail dimensional standards.

Winterthur Seminar on Museum Operation and Connoisseurship: A Resumé of Papers and Discussions. Winterthur, Del.: Henry Francis duPont Winterthur Museum, 1956. 49 pp., bibliog., mimeo. ◆ The first seminar in 1954 was prepared for Fellows of the Winterthur Program in Early American Culture, and later expanded to include other museum professionals. Topics feature problems in administration and research and technical aids for preservation and identification of artifacts; succeeding conferences have focused on specific topics in the fields of decorative and fine arts.

Museum/Audience Surveys

American Association of Museums. *Museums: Their New Audience.* A Report to the Department of Housing and Urban Development by a Special Committee of the American Association of Museums. Washington, D.C.: American Association of Museums, 1972. 108 pp., illus., bibliog. ◆ An investigation of museums and their efforts at reaching their new audience: the inner-city population, the ethnic groups, and the suburban audience. Includes results and recommendations; and 22 case studies of American museums.

American Association of Museums. *A Statistical Survey of Museums in the United States and Canada.* 1965. Reprint. New York: Arno Press, 1976. 52 pp.

Cheney, Terry. "Canadians and Museums: Statistics on Interest and Resources," *gazette,* 10:3 (Summer 1977), pp. 15-29. ◆ Includes tables and graphs by region for adult population, income, characteristics.

Damm, Robert L. "What's Your Status?" *Museum News,* 51:7 (March 1973), pp. 45-49. ◆ Survey of 50 state-supported museums regarding the place of the historical agency in the government structure. Includes purposes, governing board and functions, chief administrative officer, budget, people served, involvement in government reorganization.

De Borhegyi, Stephan F., and Irene A. Hanson. "Chronological Bibliography of Museum Visitor Surveys." In *Museums and Education: Papers* (Washington, D.C.: Smithsonian Institution, 1968), pp. 239-251.

Christensen, Erwin O. "Evening Hours for Museums: A Preliminary Statistical Survey," *Museum News,* 43:3 (November 1964), pp. 40-41.

Christensen, Erwin O. "A Generation of Museum Growth," *Museum News,* 39:10 (June 1961), pp. 31-35. ◆ Report of results of a survey of museum resources and information.

DiMaggio, Paul, and Michael Useem. "Opinion Polls: A Finger on the Public Pulse," *Museum News,* 57:5 (May/June 1979), pp. 29-33. ◆ Discusses research on local public's attitudes toward the arts to enable museum administrators to assess the political climate and identify the needs of the community.

Franceschini, Jane. "Audience Research: Solving the Visitor Identity Crisis," *gazette,* 10:4 (Fall 1977), pp. 35-37. ◆ Discusses the purpose and usefulness of audience research in Canadian museums.

Loomis, Ross J. "Please! Not Another Visitor Survey," *Museum News,* 52:2 (October 1973), pp. 21-26.

"Museums USA," *Museum News,* 53:2 (October 1974), pp. 36-41. ◆ Review of major findings of a survey sponsored by National Endowment for the Arts and scope of information found in the publication.

Nash, George. "Art Museums as Perceived by the Public," *Curator,* XVIII:1 (March 1975), pp. 55-67. ◆ Visitor survey at Whitney Museum of American Art and Memorial Art Gallery at the University of Rochester.

National Endowment for the Arts. *Audience Studies of the Performing Arts and Museums: A Critical Review.* By Paul DiMaggio, Michael Useem, and Paula Brown. Research Division Report no. 9. New York: distr. by Publishing Center for Cultural Resources, 1978. 102 pp., tables.

National Endowment for the Arts. *Museums, U.S.A.* Washington, D.C.: for sale by U.S. Government Printing Office, 1974. 203 pp., tables, appendix, index. ◆ Survey of approximately 700 art, history, science museums in the U.S. covering all areas of museum operation—programs, attendance, collections, personnel, facilities, and finances. Presented and analyzed by museum type, budget size, governing authority, and region with emphasis on comprehensive picture of museum operations. Parent survey conducted by National Research Center of the Arts.

National Endowment for the Arts. *Museums U.S.A.: Highlights–Finance, Programs, Attendance, Trustees, Personnel, Facilities.* Washington, D.C.: 1973. 20 pp., charts, graphs. ◆ Summary of the results of a survey conducted by the National Research Center of the Arts, Inc., in 1972.

National Research Center of the Arts, Inc. *Americans and the Arts: A Survey of Public Opinion.* Tulsa, Okla.: Associated Councils of the Arts, 1974. 36 pp. ◆ Highlights from *A Survey of Public Opinion,* a parent study covering interest in the arts, preferences in the arts, major obstacles to participation and attendance, effects of childhood exposure to the arts and attitudes toward teaching of the arts, and support of the arts.

National Research Center of the Arts, Inc. *Americans and the Arts: Highlights from a Survey of Public Opinion.* New York: Associated Councils of the Arts, 1975. 28 pp. ◆ Summary of survey which updates 1974 survey; includes statistics on national attendance at cultural events and institutions, as well as public attitudes toward the arts.

National Research Center of the Arts, Inc. *Arts and the People: A Survey of Public Attitudes and Participation in the Arts and Culture in New York State.* New York: available from Cranford Wood, Inc., c1973. 124 pp., tables, appendix. ◆ Survey conducted for the American Council for the Arts in Education, Inc., with support from the New York State Council on the Arts, to provide information about the cultural community, its audience and potential audience.

National Research Center of the Arts, Inc. *Museums USA: A Survey Report.* Research conducted by National Research Center of the Arts. Washington, D.C.: National Endowment for the Arts, for sale by Superintendent of Documents, U.S. Government Printing Office, 1975. 592, 87, 7 pp. ◆ Parent study of the National Endowment for the Arts publication, 1974, cited above.

National Research Center of the Arts, Inc. *A Study of the Non-Profit Arts and Cultural Industry of New York State.* New York: 1972. 194 pp., map.◆ A computer survey of 543 organizations in New York State, conducted for the Performing Arts Association of New York State, Inc., in cooperation with the New York State Association of Museums.

New York (State). Commission on Cultural Resources. *Cultural Resource Development: Planning Survey and Analysis.* 2nd ed. New York: Praeger, 1976. 219 pp., bibliog. references.

New York (State) University, State Education Department. Division of Evaluation. *The 1966 Audience of the New York State Museum: An Evaluation of the Museum's Visitors Program.* Albany: The University, 1968. 160 pp. ◆ Conducted jointly by the State Education Department and Janus Museum Consultants, Ltd., Toronto, Canada, to study geographic distribution, characteristics (sex, age, occupation, education, income, etc.), and visitor behavior.

O'Hare, Michael. "The Audience of the Museum of Fine Arts," *Curator,* XVII:2 (June 1974), pp. 126-158. ◆ Report on a series of visitor surveys.

O'Hare, Michael. "Why Do People Go to Museums? The Effect of Prices and Hours on Museum Utilization," *Museum,* XVII:3 (1975), pp. 134-146. ◆ Includes experiments in rationalizing prices and hours policy, statistical survey of historical attendance behavior, experiment with piggy-backed admission price/administration for a special exhibit.

Older Americans: The Unrealized Audience for the Arts. By Alton C. Johnson, et al. Madison, Wisc.: Center for Arts Administration, Graduate School of Business, University of Wisconsin-Madison, 1976. 51 pp., tables, bibliog. references. ◆ Contents include summary of findings, national survey of arts administrators, an audience development and model, illustrative senior citizen programs.

Prague, Rochelle H. "The University Museum Visitor Survey Project," *Curator,* XVII:3 (September 1974), pp. 207-212.

Rogers, Lola Eriksen. *Museums and Related Institutions: A Basic Program Survey.* Washington, D.C.: U.S. Office of Education, for sale by the U.S. Government Printing Office, 1969. 120 pp., illus., forms. ◆ Purpose of the study was to establish a screened universe of museums and related operations; to determine the types of supporting resources of these museums; and to ascertain the nature and extent of museum program activities.

Screven, Chandler. "A Bibliography on Visitor Education Research," *Museum News,* 57:4 (March/April 1979), pp. 56-59, 86-88.♦ Entries categorized: audience survey; behavior studies; experimental research; evaluation studies and methods; theoretical papers, description of methods; and resource materials.

Silvestro, Clement M., and Richmond D. Williams. *A Look at Ourselves: A Report on the Survey of the State and Local Historical Agencies in the United States.* Madison, Wisc.: American Association for State and Local History, 1962. 53 pp.

Wells, Carolyn. *Smithsonian Visitor.* Washington, D.C.: Smithsonian Institution, 1970. 77 pp., bibliog., appendices. ♦ Results of a visitor survey in the National Museum of History and Technology and the National Museum of Natural History, Smithsonian Institution.

NOTE

National Endowment for the Arts, Research Division Reports. Since 1976, the Research Division has been studying matters of interest to the arts community and issuing reports on its surveys. Subjects studied include: "Arts and Cultural Organizations"—economic impact, state arts agencies, condition and needs of American theatre, five planning studies for the establishment of an economic data series; "Artists"—employment, and unemployment, minorities and women, American crafts planning survey, self-employment/migration/household/family; "Audience and Consumers of Arts and Cultural Services"—programs on radio and television, studies of performing arts and museums, theatre and symphony in four southern cities. All three areas have additional survey projects in process or planning stages. Published reports are available from the Publishing Center for Cultural Resources, 625 Broadway, New York, New York 10012.

Standards and Ethics

Alderson, William T. "Accreditation Commission: After One Year," *Museum News,* 49:9 (May 1971), pp. 17-19.

American Association for State and Local

History. "Committee Makes Final Report on Professional Standards," *History News,* 12:3 (January 1957), pp. 19-22. ♦ Included training and experience, compensation, tenure, professional productivity, summary and recommendations.

American Association of Museums. *Code of Ethics for Museum Workers, Being the Report of a Committee of the American Association of Museums Adopted Unanimously at the Twentieth Annual Meeting of the Association.* Washington D.C.: The Association, 1925. 8 pp. ♦ Reprinted in *Museum News,* 52:9 (June 1974), pp. 26-28.

American Association of Museums. *Museum Accreditation: A Report to the Profession.* Washington, D.C.: American Association of Museums, 1970. 39 pp. ♦ Includes history of the accreditation program, procedure, record of meetings held by the accreditation committee, biographies of committee members, visiting committee instructions.

American Association of Museums. *Museum Accreditation: Professional Standards.* By Marilyn Hicks Fitzgerald. Washington, D.C.: The Association, 1973. 116 pp., illus. ♦ A more comprehensive report on the development of the program, principles of accreditation, procedures, case studies and statistics.

American Association of Museums. *Professional Standards for Museum Accreditation.* Rev. ed. Edited by H. J. Swinney. Washington, D.C.: The Association, 1978. 80 pp. ♦ Subtitled: The Handbook of the Accreditation Program of the American Association of Museums. Includes modified and expanded accreditation procedures; discussion of re-accreditation, refinements and clarification of standards; revisions in the requirements governing the confidentiality of the accreditation process.

American Association of Museums. Committee on Ethics. *Museum Ethics.* Washington, D.C.: The Association, 1978. 31 pp. ♦ Guidelines for ethical conduct concerning the collection, the staff, museum management policy, and museum governance. Also in *Museum News,* 56:4 (March/April 1978), pp. 21-30.

Association of Art Museum Directors. "Code of Ethics," *Museum News,* 52:8 (May 1974), p. 22.

Association of Art Museum Directors. Professional Practice Committee. *Professional Practices in Art Museums: Report.* New York: The Association, 1971. 28 pp. ◆ Analysis of the purposes of art museums and the relationships that should obtain between governing boards and directors, and includes acquisition and disposal policies, finances, legal matters, and personnel and labor relations. Reprinted in full in *Museum News,* 51:2 (October 1972), pp. 15-20.

Boylan, Patrick J. "Museum Ethics: Museums Association Policies," *Museums Journal,* 77:3 (December 1977), pp. 106-111. ◆ Includes introduction, code of practice for museum authorities, and guidelines for professional conduct; appendix includes additional sources. See also Museums Association references, cited below.

Buckley, Charles E. "Museum Accreditation, An Interim Report," *Museum News,* 48:3 (November 1969), pp. 16-17.

Calvert, Monte A. *The Mechanical Engineer in America, 1830-1940: Professional Cultures in Conflict.* Baltimore: Johns Hopkins University Press, 1967. 296 pp., illus., selected bibliog. ◆ Important introductory chapter on professionalism and list of six criteria which distinguish the professional in any field.

Canadian Museums Association. *The Ethical Behavior of Museum Professionals.* Ottawa: The Association, 1979. 10 pp. ◆ Policy covers personal relationships with self, fellow workers, superiors, institutions, peers, and associations; and institutional relationships with collections, presentations, the public, specific outsiders, other institutions, and associations. Approved at the Annual Meeting, Calgary, Alberta, 1977. French and English.

Constable, W. G. "Museum Ethics," *Museums Journal,* 41:7 (October 1941), pp. 145-151.

Cubbon, A. Marshall. "Museum Standards: Accreditation," *Museums Journal,* 73:3 (December 1973), pp. 97-98.

Donson, Jerome Allan. "Current Trends in Professional Standards for Museums," *Curator,* II:2 (1959), pp. 157-161.

Douglas, R. Alan. "Museum Ethics: Practice and Policy," *Museum News,* 45:5 (January 1967), pp. 18-21. ◆ Code of Ethics devised by the Museums Section, Ontario Historical Society.

Grove, Richard. "You Don't Need a Weatherman to Tell Which Way the Wind's Blowing," *Museum News,* 52:9 (June 1974), pp. 33-34. ◆ Reviews 1925 Code of Ethics, Association of Art Museum Directors report, and Code of the Museums Section of the Ontario Historical Society; recommends updating 1925 code and providing for an ethical practices committee.

Hess, John L. *The Grand Acquisitors.* Boston: Houghton Mifflin Company, 1974. 178 pp., illus.

Hicks, Marilyn. "Accreditation: Two Years After," *Museum News,* 52:7 (April 1974), p. 14.

Howarth, A. J. "Curators and Politics: A Strand Where Corals Lie?" *Museums Journal,* 77:3 (December 1977), pp. 113-114.

Inglis, Robin. "Editorial [Proposal for Accredited Membership in the C.M.A.]," *gazette,* 12:1 (Winter 1979), pp. 4-6. ◆ See also, "President's Message," by George MacBeath, same issue, pp. 8-9.

Leavitt, Thomas W. "The Need for Critical Standards in History Museum Exhibits: A Case in Point," *Curator,* X:2 (June 1967), pp. 91-94.

McNab, Margaret C. *Ethics for a Town Historian.* Albany, N.Y.: Office of State History, 1972. 4 pp.

Madison, H. L. "Tentative Code of Ethics," *Museums Journal,* 25:1 (July 1925), pp. 19-23.

Miquelon, Patricia A. "The Fiduciary Obligations of Museum Personnel," *gazette,* 10:1 (Winter 1977), pp. 17-19. ◆ Discusses obligations of employees and directors, conflict of interest situations such as collecting.

Museums Association. *Code of Practice for Museum Authorities.* London: The Association, 1977. 6 pp., bibliog., appendix. ◆ Adopted at the Association's Annual General Meeting in July 1977 and recommended to Boards of Trustees, local authorities, museum committees, senior staff and others involved in management of museums and art galleries. Includes statement of purpose, definition of a museum, minimum requirements of museums and art galleries, acquisitions to museum and art gallery collections, disposal of collections, museum organization. Appendix lists relevant policy statements of the Association adopted between 1968 and 1975, some of which are reprinted in *Museums Yearbook 1977*.

Museums Association. *Guidelines for Professional Conduct*. London: The Association, 1977. 3 pp. ◆ Policy adopted at the Association's Annual General Meeting in July 1977, as a suggested code of conduct for members of the museum profession. Includes personal responsibility of the curator to the collections, personal responsibility of the curator to the public, professional confidence, untrue or misleading identification or certification, relationship with colleagues, personal activities, abuse of professional position to further improper associations, sanctions.

Neal, Arminta; Kristine Haglund; and Elizabeth Webb. "Evolving a Policy Manual," *Museum News*, 56:3 (January/February 1978), pp. 26-30.

Rorimer, James J. "Our Motto Should Be: Standards Without Standardization," *Museum News*, 36:3 (June 1, 1958), pp. 3-4.

Rosenbaum, Lee. "The Scramble for Museum Sponsors: Is Curatorial Independence for Sale?" *Art in America*, 65:1 (January-February 1977), pp. 10-14. ◆ Discusses influence of growth of outside support for museums from corporations, foundations and government; interviews museum directors and curators.

Shaffer, Dale E. *The Maturity of Librarianship as a Profession*. Methuchen, N.J.: Scarecrow Press, 1968. 166 pp., bibliog. references. ◆ A study of professionalism.

Swinney, H. J., et al. "Looking at Accreditation" *Museum News*, 55:2 (November/December 1976), pp. 15-41. ◆ Six articles by professionals who have been involved in all stages of the program; review of its growth, development, and importance to the profession. Includes listing of accredited museums as of May 1976. Available as a 24-page reprint from American Association of Museums.

Swinton, William E. "Museum Standards," *Curator*, I:1 (January 1958), pp. 61-65.

Ullberg, Alan D., and Patricia Ullberg. "A Proposed Curatorial Code of Ethics," *Museum News*, 52:8 (May 1974), pp. 18-22.

Vaughan, Thomas. "A Simple Matter of Standards," *Museum News*, 55:3 (January/

February 1977), pp. 32-34, 45. ◆ Commentary on professional ethics.

NOTE

American Association of Museums, Accreditation Program. The program sets prescribed professional criteria by which a museum's quality and performance may be judged. Accreditation certifies that a museum currently meets accepted standards established by the profession, but it does not grade achievement or excellence beyond the established minimum requirements. An applicant for accreditation undergoes a confidential evaluation by experienced professionals, and upon achieving accredited status is eligible to display a special certificate that publicly identifies the institution as meeting professional standards of quality and performance set by the AAM. The accreditation program is administered by a seven-member Accreditation Commission that is representative of a range of geographic areas and professional disciplines.

Cooperative Services

Agrawal, O. P. "Technical Cooperation, Its Philosophy and Practice," *ICOM News*, 24:2 (June 1971), pp. 35-40. ◆ Subject of the Year; reviews kinds of technical cooperation, the need and role of cooperation, tools and structure, experts and training, creating institutions, international/regional meetings, receiving assistance, evaluation.

Atkinson, Frank. "Regional Museums," *Museums Journal*, 68:2 (September 1968), pp. 74-77.

Bell, Wayne. "The American History Museum and Historical Commissions." In *Papers, 64th Annual Meeting, American Association of Museums* (San Francisco, Calif.: 1969), pp. 73-74. ◆ Discusses services and areas of cooperation among state and local agencies.

Booth, Malcolm A. "Museums: The Regional Concept," *The Museologist*, 102 (March 1967), pp. 4-7. ◆ Describes Orange County Community of Museums and Galleries, Goshen, New York, a regional federation formed in 1961.

Burnham, Sophy. "Competition or Cooperation: Six Ideas for Museum Monies," *Curator*,

VII:1 (1964), pp. 51-62. ◆ Discusses cooperation and shared facilities for conservation laboratories, dating laboratories, taxidermy shops, publicity, membership drives, publications, film and television.

Clover, R. A. "Area Councils and Regionalization," *Museums Journal,* 68:2 (September 1968), pp. 78-79. ◆ A system of specialized museum services.

Cohen, M. L. "Cooperation Between Museums of the Rich Countries and Those of the Third World," *ICOM News,* 24:3 (September 1971), pp. 54-55. ◆ Subject of the Year; advantages and disadvantages of direct collaboration and other forms of assistance in training of staff, collection and conservation of exhibits, study and scientific research.

Daifuku, Hiroshi. "Museums and International Cooperation," *Curator,* IV:1 (1961), pp. 15-28. ◆ Describes international cooperative agencies since World War II: International Office of Museums of the International Institute for Intellectual Cooperation, League of Nations, continued as Museums and Historic Monuments Division of UNESCO.

Dunhill, Patricia. "Museums Collaborative," *The Museologist,* 123 (June 1972), pp. 9-11. ◆ Describes purposes of the organization in New York City to decentralize museum resources and use them in new ways and to ease individual burdens through collective services.

Friedberg, Bernard. "Museums Collaborative: A Broker for Cooperation," *Museum News,* 52:7 (April 1974), pp. 20-24.

Gilborn, Craig. "Toward a Balance: University-Museum Cooperation," *Curator,* XIV:1 (March 1971), pp. 36-40. ◆ Describes growing collaboration especially with museum training programs.

Hanks, Nancy. "Co-operation: A Key to Professional Development." In *Papers, 64th Annual Meeting, American Association of Museums* (San Francisco, Calif.: 1969), pp. 47-50. ◆ Discusses professional development of own institution at four levels of cooperation: institutional, community, state, federal.

Harrison, Richard. "Local and Regional Cooperation in Museums," *ICOM News,* 24:4 (December 1971), pp. 43-46. ◆ Subject of the Year; problems and advantages on local and

regional levels regarding personal contact, pooling of resources, influence on public opinion, rationalization, training.

Harrison, Richard. "The First Seven Years 1963-1970: Reflection on the Work of Area Councils," *Museums Journal,* 71:1 (June 1971), pp. 20-24. ◆ Reviews early development, exhibitions, technical services, and other projects and activities.

Kley, Ronald J. "Curatorial Centers: Strength in Numbers," *Museum News,* 53:7 (April 1975), pp. 14, 27.

"RCHA Offers Helping Hands to 23 Counties in New York," *History News,* 33:8 (August 1978), pp. 173-174. ◆ Describes services and programs of the Regional Conference of Historical Agencies in central New York.

Spock, Michael. "Museums in Collaboration," *Museum News,* 48:8 (April 1970), pp. 21-23. ◆ Reviews various forms of regional cooperation: business office, production shop, educational reference center, exhibition and auditorium facility, development and public relations service, manpower service, warehouse structure.

Stott, F. J., and T. A. Walden. "Area Councils and the Future Role," *Museums Journal,* 71:3 (December 1971), pp. 102-104 ◆ Problems and achievements of a regional system of government aid for museums.

Varine-Bohan, Hughes de. "Cooperation," *ICOM News,* 24:1 (March 1970), pp. 32-36. ◆ Subject of the Year; cooperation on the institutional level, intergovernmental, bilateral or multilateral, and non-governmental.

Zimmerman, John D. "Viewpoint–Under One Umbrella," *History News,* 25:5 (May 1970), pp. 105-106 ◆ Example of several cultural organizations pooling resources and problems for common economic advantage in York, Pennsylvania.

NOTE

Museums Collaborative, Inc., 15 Gramercy Park South, New York, New York 10003. Museums Collaborative is a private, not-for-profit organization founded in 1970 to promote broader public understanding and utilization of the resources of cultural institutions, and to sponsor joint activities which strengthen the capacity of the institutions to serve the public more efficiently and economically. Its activities bring perspectives and expertise from beyond the museum profession to bear on museum problems, in addition to fostering greater communication among the staff members of cultural institutions. It offers programs in the areas of public education and continuing professional education. Through voucher systems designed to reach public schools and community organizations which serve adult constituents, the Collaborative brings new audiences into contact with the resources of cultural institutions. The Collaborative sponsors courses, symposia and publications on, topics central to the museum profession including basic management principles, marketing and audience development, and financial management and controls.

5

Personnel Training and Management

Not too many years ago there were few professional positions in historical organizations. And just as well too, for there were few men and women who had been professionally trained. Perhaps after having taken some general courses, an applicant might obtain an apprenticeship. Personnel training and management was haphazard, opportunistic.

Not so today in the majority of cases. This chapter cites the literature that deals first with the new formal training programs at all levels, undergraduate, graduate, and even continuing education, and in all of the associated disciplines that are part of a well-rounded historical and education program.

There follows a section on personnel management that touches the many facets of this increasingly complex aspect of historical organization administration: job descriptions, salaries and benefits, federal and state regulations, tenure, unionization, communications, policies and procedures, new types of manpower programs. The administrator's lot is no longer a simple one.

Finally, there is a section on the unpaid—and priceless—volunteer. In many institutions volunteers are the force that gives character, tone, quality. But when they are very, very good there is always a reason: a well-managed program of recruitment, training, and administration. The references here explain how it is done.

Career Planning and Training Programs

Alexander, Edward P. "Museum Studies at Delaware," *Curator,* XV:1 (March 1972), pp. 34-38.

Alexander, Edward P. "Seminar at Williamsburg," *Museum News,* 47:2 (October 1968), pp. 21-24.

Alexander, Edward P. "The Seminar for Historical Administrators: A Special Report," *History News,* 20:12 (December 1965), pp. 261-264.

Alexander, Edward P. "The Williamsburg Seminar," *Museum News,* 57:2 (November/December 1978), pp. 4ff.♦ Brief review of history and purposes of the Seminar for Historical Administrators.

American Association for State and Local History. *So You've Chosen To Be a History Professional . . . .* Nashville, Tenn.: The Association, 1978. 20 pp., appendix ♦ Careers in the field of history, directed towards undergraduate and graduate students and others interested in pursuing jobs in the profession.

American Association of Museums. *Museum Training Courses in the United States and Canada.* Compiled by G. Ellis Burcaw. Rev. ed. Washington, D.C.: The Association, 1971. 51 pp.♦ Museum training is used to cover all preparation aimed specifically at providing those attitudes and skills which are the mark of the museum professional. Not included are college and university courses which use museums as resources but which have educational aims other than the training of the student for employment by a museum. Also excluded are fields such as architectural preservation, scientific classification, public relations, commercial arts; and training of non-professional staff such as guards, volunteers, office staff. Entries include state and location, name of sponsoring institution, actual name of training program, brief description, prerequisites and credit details, address for correspondence.

American Association of Museums. Museum Studies Committee. "Museum Studies," *Museum News,* 57:2 (November/December 1978), pp. 19-26.♦ In-depth report, based on two-year examination of training for a museum career. Includes "Statement on Preparation for Professional Careers"; "Minimum Standards for Professional Museum Training Programs"; "Museum Positions—Duties and Responsibilities."

American Association of Museums. Museum Studies Curriculum Committee. *Museum Studies: A Curriculum Guide for Universities and Museums: A Report.* By Edward P. Alexander. Washington, D.C.: The Association, 1973. 28 pp., bibliog., appendices. ♦ Evaluates the effectiveness of current museum education programs and presents a comprehensive list of recommended standards and guidelines for museums, colleges, and universities which offer museum studies. Describes the educational potentials available to museums and the need for college-trained museum personnel. Out of print.

Barton, K. J. "Technical Training," *Museums Journal,* 73:3 (December 1973), p. 99.♦ Discusses proposed programs by Museums Association.

Bethel, David. "The Training of Museum Personnel: The Contribution of Colleges of Art," *ICOM News,* 25:2 (June 1972), pp. 103-105. ♦ Suggests number of topics of museum education which could be pursued by art colleges on a short course basis.

Burcaw, G. Ellis. "Films for Teaching Museology, A Guide to Where They Are," *Museum News,* 46:3 (November 1967), pp. 25-26.

Burcaw, G. Ellis. *Introduction to Museum Work.* Nashville, Tenn.: American Association for State and Local History, 1975. 202 pp.♦ Basic manual in the development of professional attitudes and standards for students, beginning professionals, and devoted amateurs. Emphasizes theory, definitions, philosophical issues, and orientation to the entire field of museum work. Each chapter (20) constitutes one lesson with practical exercises.

Burcaw, G. Ellis. "Museum Training: The Responsibility of College and University Museums," *Museum News,* 46:3 (November 1967), pp. 25-26.

Burns, William A. *Your Future in Museums.* 1st ed. New York: Richard Rosen Press, 1967. 154 pp., illus.♦ Somewhat dated but still good general treatment of different jobs found in museums.

Canadian Museums Association. *A Curriculum for Museum Studies Training Programs.* Ottawa: 1979. 16 pp., bibliog.♦ Outline of topics encompassed by the discipline of museology.

Canadian Museums Association. *Guide to Museum Positions.* Ottawa: 1979. 28 pp.♦ Companion to *Curriculum . . . ,* cited above; describes 14 core positions in museum work, along with type of training and skills recommended for each one. Includes C.M.A. Statement on the Ethical Behavior of Museum Professionals.

Canadian Museums Association. Training and Standards Division. *Museum Studies Programmes in Canada.* Ottawa: 1979. 24 pp.♦ Alphabetical listing by province with organizations operating with a regional or national scope; supplementary list of foreign programs; index of training opportunities by type.

Capstick, Brenda. "The Museum Profession in the United Kingdom," *Museum,* XXIII:2 (1970-71), pp. 154-162.♦ Status of the profession and description of the Museums Association training program.

Clarke, David. "Professional Training," *Museums Journal,* 73:3 (December 1973), pp. 98-99.♦ Discusses diploma and training program of the Museums Association.

Cushman, Bigelow. "The Winterthur Program," *Museum News,* 47:8 (April 1969), pp. 11-14.

Dailey, Charles A. "Bringing a Unique Perspective to Museum Work," *Museum News,* 55:5 (May/June 1977), pp. 53-54.♦ Training Native Americans to assume an active role in preservation, documentation and exhibition of their cultural heritage.

Eisler, Colin. "Curatorial Training for Today's Art Museums," *Curator,* IX:1 (March 1966), pp. 51-61.

Fitch, James Marston. "Professional Training for the Preservationist." Reprinted from the *AIA Journal,* 51:4 (April 1969), pp. 57-61.

Fleming, E. McClung. "Accent on Artist and Artisan: The Winterthur Program in Early American Culture," *American Quarterly,* 22:2, part 2 (Summer 1970), pp. 571-596.

International Council of Museums. Committee for the Training of Personnel. "[Report]: Leicester Symposium, 17-19 July 1969, held at Department of Museum Studies, University of Leicester," *ICOM News,* 22:3 (September 1969), pp. 45-46. ◆ Brief review of discussions, conclusions and recommendations relating to training programs.

International Council of Museums, 7th Conference, New York, 1965. *Papers from the Seventh General Conference of ICOM.* Reports and Papers on Museums, no. 3. New York: Metropolitan Museum of Art, 1965. 98 pp.◆ Papers relating to professional training.

International Council of Museums. Training Unit. *Professional Training of Museum Personnel in the World: Actual State of the Problem.* Paris: 1972. 85 pp.◆ Statement on curriculum; also representative examples of professional training centers.

Jobling, Patricia L. "Where to Find— Continuing Education Programs," *Museum News,* 57:2 (November/December 1978), pp. 11-15.◆ Listing of regional and national continuing education opportunities for museum professionals; included on basis of applicability to museum work and regularity with which they are offered; excludes university and college programs.

Jones, H. G.; T. R. Schellenberg; John C. Olson; and W. Kaye Lamb. "Training of Archivists," *The American Archivist,* 31:2 (April 1968), entire issue.

Jones, Louis C. "Twiggery and Tomorrow's Museums." In *Papers, 64th Annual Meeting, American Association of Museums* (San Francisco, Calif.: 1969), pp. 161-173.◆ Discusses training of young people for museum work and effect on quality and character of institutions tomorrow.

Keck, Sheldon. "A Little Training Can Be a Dangerous Thing," *Museum News,* 52:4 (December 1973), pp. 40-42.◆ Advocates extended course in curatorial conservation responsibilities in regular museum training programs.

Lewis, Ralph H. "Museum Training in the National Park Service," *Curator,* VI:1 (1962), pp. 7-13.

Lunn, John. "Training Committee Chairman's Report to the Annual Meeting," *gazette,* 6:3 (July 1972), pp. 4-8.

Marvel, Bill. "How A Love of Art Can Become a Career," *The Museologist,* 115 (June 1970), pp. 12-19.

Mindlin, Freda. "Writing a Résumé that Opens Doors," *Museum News,* 57:6 (July/August 1979), pp. 54-55.◆ Analyzes elements of a good résumé for the job-seeker in an arts related field.

Munroe, John A. "The Museum and the University," *Curator,* II:3 (1959), pp. 252-258.◆ Describes University of Delaware and the Hagley and Winterthur Programs.

Museums Association. *Careers In Museums.* 4th ed. London: The Association, 1975. 4 pp.

National Trust for Historic Preservation. *Conference on Training for the Building Crafts, November 19-20, 1971, Washington, D.C.: A Summary Report.* Washington, D.C.: The Trust, 1972. 68 pp.

Newton, Earle W. "Interdisciplinary Training for Learning Resource Institutions," *Curator,* XVI:4 (December 1973), pp. 342-345.

Nutter, Carolyn F. *The Résumé Workbook: A Personnel Career File for Job Applications.* 5th ed. Cranston, R.I.: The Carroll Press, 1978. 128 pp., forms, bibliog.◆ Advice and worksheets covering self-analysis, career analysis, educational background, work experience, military record, activities and interests, personal background, salary and location requirements, reference, potential audience; sample résumés and letters.◆

Papageorge, Maria. "A World View of Museum Studies," *Museum News,* 57:2 (November/December 1978), pp. 7-9.

Place, Linna Funk; Joanna S. Zangrando; James W. Lea; and John Lovell. "The Object as Subject: The Role of Museums and Material Culture Collections in American Studies,"

American Quarterly, 26:3 (August 1974), pp. 281-294 ♦ Contents include possibilities at university and museum; locating and making contact with museums; making use of the resources of the local museum; community museum program; museum and the university; bibliography.

"Preservation and Higher Education," *Preservation News,* 18:10 (October 1978), Supplement.♦ Includes listing of directories and guides, and chart of programs offering a degree.

Quimby, George I., and James D. Nason. "New Staff for a New Museum," *Museum News,* 55:5 (May/June 1977), pp. 50-52.♦ Discusses training Native Americans.

Rodeck, Hugo G. "The Role of the University in Education Towards Museum Careers," *Curator,* IV:1 (1961), pp. 69-75.

Rowinski, L. J. "Workshops and Seminars for Small Museums," *Western Museums Quarterly,* 5:4 (December 1968), pp. 13-17.

Segger, Martin. "A New Museum Training Programme in British Columbia," *gazette,* 8:2 (Spring 1975), pp. 18-20.

Seggar, Martin. "Standards and Criteria for the Training of Canadian Museum Workers: Toward Some Definition of the Problem," *gazette,* 11:3 (Summer 1978), pp. 20-25.♦ Earlier version of article formed, in part, a study for the National Museums Corporation, Museums Assistance Program. Proposes conceptual framework toward clarifying some of the issues and problems as to what constitutes training, who is being trained, and why.

Seggar, Martin. *Training Opportunities for Museum Workers in Canada.* Ottawa: National Museum of Canada, 1976. 59 pp., bibliog., appendices.♦ Out of print; photocopies available.

Shenker, Mary Claire. "Professional Opportunities in History Museums: A Seminar," *Museum News,* 46:3 (November 1967), pp. 22-24.

Singleton, H. Raymond. "Professional Education and Training," *Museums Journal,* 71:3 (December 1971), pp. 99-101.♦ Brief review of the postgraduate course in Gallery and Museum Studies, Department of Art History, University of Manchester, England.

Slaney, Jill Penelope. "The Leicester Course: A Student's View," *Museums Journal,* 70:2 (September 1970), pp. 75-77.

Smithsonian Institution. Office of Museum Programs. *Museum Studies Programs in the United States and Abroad.* Washington, D.C.: Smithsonian Institution, April 1976. 81 pp., indexes; addendum, 11 pp.♦ A directory of museum training programs including affiliate museum or university (where appropriate), type of program offered, program description, and contact person. Addendum, February 1977, updates the edition and future updates are planned.

A Survey of Arts Administration Training in the United States and Canada. Rev. ed. Edited by Ellen Stofolsky Daniels. Madison, Wisc.: Center for Arts Administration, University of Wisconsin, 1977. 69 pp.♦ Updates and summarizes information about arts administration programs in the U.S. and Canada, initially compiled by William H. Donner Foundation in 1975. Includes graduate arts administration programs, graduate museum studies programs including administration, seminars and workshops in museum administration.

Teather, Lynne. *Professional Directions for Museum Work in Canada: An Analysis of Museum Jobs and Museum Studies Training Curricula.* Ottawa: Canadian Museums Association, 1978. 412 pp., illus., tables, diagrams.♦ Analysis of 19 museum job areas and comprehensive listing of current training programs.

Thompson, Enid. "Commentary on Archival Management and Special Libraries," *Special Libraries,* 69:12 (December 1978), pp. 491-492.♦ Discusses need for dual training, history and library science, for museum librarians.

Training Arts Administrators: Committee of Enquiry Report. London: Arts Council of Great Britain, 1972. 76 pp., tables.

Training of Museum Personnel. Published with the help of the Smithsonian Institution, Washington, D.C. Reports and Papers on Museums no. 5. London: Hugh Evelyn for International Council of Museums, 1970. 242 pp. ♦ Discussions of the philosophy of museum studies programs together with a selective list of programs throughout the world. Text in English and French.

"Training Programs," *Preservation News,* 18:1 (January 1978), Supplement.♦ Articles on tools for students and professionals, National Trust programs, and a listing of programs on the basis of applicability to preservation work under the categories of management, subjects, U.S. and foreign organizations, internships. College and university training programs are not included.

Waller, Bret. "Museum Training: Who Needs It?" *Museum News,* 52:8 (May 1974), pp. 26-28.♦ Review of results of studies on museum training programs in the U.S.

Walsh, John, Jr. "Training Young Curators," *Metropolitan Museum of Art Bulletin,* 27:10 (June 1969), pp. 442-444.

"What Should We Train Our Curators To Do?" *Museums Journal,* 69:3 (December 1969), pp. 133-135. ♦ Session at Annual Conference of the Museums Association, Leicester, 1969; articles by A. J. Duggan and Raymond H. Singleton.

Whitehill, Walter Muir. "Education and Training for Restoration Work." In *Historic Preservation Tomorrow:* ... (Williamsburg, Va.: National Trust for Historic Preservation and Colonial Williamsburg, 1967), pp. 31-36.

NOTES

American Association for State and Local History, Audio-Visual Training Kits. A series of slide-tape cassettes developed with grant funds from the National Museum Act. The Series covers topics ranging from security to museum exhibits. Available for sale or a minimum rental. Includes supplementary materials and instructions. Equipment needed are a Kodak carousel projector and a cassette tape recorder.

American Association for State and Local History, Independent Study Program. The Program offers independent, home study courses in four major areas of interpretation: Research and Collection, Exhibits and Education, Historic Site Interpretation, and Publications. Courses now available are Collection, Research and Interpretation of Historical Photographs; Documents: Interpretation and Exhibition; Interpretation through Effective Labels; Education: School Programs and the Museum; Basic Interpretation of Historic Sites; and Basic Layout and Design of Publications.

Additional courses are planned; write for current list of titles and description of programs.

American Association for State and Local History, Job Placement Service. As part of its general service to the profession, the Association maintains a job placement service for its members. Institutional members notify the Association of vacancies and individual members may register with the placement service without charge. Job openings are printed in *History News.*

American Association of Museums, Placement Service. The Association's placement service includes a placement listing section in *AVISO.* Appearing monthly, the listing offers institutional members the opportunity to list positions they have available and offers individual members the chance to announce their qualifications on a nationwide basis. For those individuals desiring confidential replies, the Association provides a box number, and forwards the replies to the box holder. Charges to place a listing are available on request.

American Studies Programs. An annual listing of current American Studies curricular programs in colleges and universities in the U.S. is published in the bibliography issue of *American Quarterly,* no. 3. The quantitative study includes undergraduate and graduate courses, degrees offered, person in charge and departmental affiliation, and availability of summer work.

Canadian Museums Association, Training Resources Program. The Association has revised its correspondence course to serve as an introduction to basic museum principles and practice with certification being awarded upon successful completion. The program also includes a resource center with a library and publications order service; a resource services program to aid those involved in training programs with lists of instructors, seminar procedures manual, audiovisual training aids; and a national seminar program to include two seminars for professionals in addition to a special session at the annual conference. A training publications program includes materials published in the *gazette* or in separate pamphlets. Limited financial aid is available for special research projects and internships. Descriptive pamphlets about the program are available.

Civil Service Examination Passbooks, National Learning Corporation, 212 Michael

Drive, Syosset, New York 11791. Study guides, in paperback and hard cover for civil service examinations, include an examination section and questions and answers. Series includes museum positions: attendant, instructor, technician, laboratory technician, exhibits technician, intern, and curator.

Institute in Arts Administration, Harvard Summer School, 1350 Massachusetts Avenue, Cambridge, Massachusetts 02138. The Institute's Annual Management Development Program is a four-week intensive program. Its primary mission is to provide individuals with skills in management and problem-solving relevant to administering arts organizations and activities. The goal is an understanding of the fundamentals of managing arts organizations, including community arts centers and councils, orchestras and other musical organizations, theaters, ballet and modern dance companies, museums, university arts programs, and the expansion arts. The curriculum focuses on basic management subjects, administering arts organizations, impact on management of artistic criteria, and public policy and the arts administrator. Eligible are persons with arts administration experience who seek a more thorough grounding in fundamentals, practitioners in the arts interested in being exposed to the administrator's view, and non-professionals (trustees, volunteers) concerned with the administration of organizations in the arts.

Museum Access Planning Seminars. A project developed by Skye Pictures, Inc., 2225 Floyd Avenue, Richmond, Virginia 23220, a nonprofit media organization, to encourage training programs in museums in light of compliance with Section 504 of the Rehabilitation Act of 1973. The project consists of films, training materials and technical information designed to introduce museum staff, volunteers and security personnel to the problems people with disabilities encounter in participating in museum activities.

Museums Association, Diploma and Certificate Program. The Diploma of the Association is awarded on the recommendation of the Association's Education Committee to those members who have had at least three years fulltime experience in a museum or art gallery (or two years, if university graduate), have completed the required courses of study, and have passed the prescribed examinations. A Conservation Certificate is also given to those whose work is primarily concerned with the conservation and restoration of museum objects. The Technical Certificate is awarded to those whose duties are primarily technical, and is given after examination of candidates who have not less than five years experience in museum work.

Opportunity Resources for the Arts, 1501 Broadway, New York, New York 10036. An independent, nonprofit corporation created to provide placement, counseling, and information for organizations seeking administrative, technical, and professional personnel, and for individuals who wish to learn of employment opportunities in the arts. The Performing Arts Placement Program was begun in 1972 and the Visual Arts Placement Program in 1974. The programs are funded with grants from private foundations, the National Endowment for the Arts, the New York State Council on the Arts. The Field Service and Evaluation Program, established in 1974, enables individuals residing outside of New York City to benefit from personal contact with a staff member of the organization. The services are available to theatre, opera and ballet companies, orchestras, museums, science/technology centers, festivals, arts councils, arts centers, and other nonprofit organizations serving the visual and performing arts. Opportunity Resources does not attempt to place performers, stage directors, or other creative personnel, nor does it handle positions normally associated with academic instruction or administration. Organizations and individuals pay an annual registration fee; organizations pay a placement fee when a candidate is hired. A brochure is available on request.

Smithsonian Institution Workshop Series, Office of Museum Programs, Smithsonian Institution, Washington, D.C. 20560. The series of workshops is designed to introduce and improve professional skills for individuals employed in museums and related institutions. All workshops are held at the Smithsonian Institution with its professional staff members serving as faculty for most workshops. In some cases, outside experts are brought in to supplement the program. There are no tuition or registration fees, and the Smithsonian supplies most of the materials used in class. Participants must defray their own travel, lodging and meals. Workshop topics range from all aspects of museum exhibits, fundamentals of museum management, principles of conservation, interpretive and membership programs, museum–school relations to training docents, museum insurance, administering grants, publications and museum library administration.

Personnel and Employment Practices

Alexander, Edward P. "A Handhold on the Curatorial Ladder," *Museum News,* 52:8 (May 1974), pp. 23-25.♦ Discusses need for curators to be familiar with museum management and overall function.

Allan, Douglas A. "The Staff." In *The Organization of Museums: Practical Advice* (Paris: UNESCO, 1960), pp. 52-67.

American Association for State and Local History. "Salaries in Historical Agencies, An Updated Report: 1974-75," *History News,* 30:2 (February 1975), pp. 37-46.♦ Third survey in a series: 1966, 1972-73, 1974-75; see also fourth survey, reported by Patricia Hall, cited below.

Arth, Malcolm. "Two Different Cultures," *Museum News,* 52:9 (June 1974), pp. 39-40.♦ Compares differences between museum and university regarding concept of tenure, audience, and role of the trustee.

Atkinson, Frank. "A Report on Job Creation in Museums 1976 to 1978," *Museums Journal,* 77:4 (March 1978), pp. 158-160.♦ Summarizes the effectiveness and problems of the two-year Job Creation Project developed by Great Britain's Manpower Services Commission, aimed at alleviating the effects of recession and unemployment.

Bingham, Judith. "Giving Your Interns a Piece of the Action," *Museum News,* 52:4 (December 1973), pp. 33-39.♦ Discusses need for federally subsidized internships and giving interns responsibility as well as subsidized wages; gives general information on Urban Corps programs throughout the country.

Burns, William A. "The Curator-as-Canary," *Curator,* XIV:3 (September 1971), pp. 213-220.♦ Discusses need for the curator who will bridge the artificial chasm that has been created between and among museums and will correlate joint offerings of science, art and history museums.

Capstick, Brenda. "The Museum Profession in the United Kingdom," *Museum,* XXIII:2 (1970-71), pp. 154-162. ♦ Reviews problems of the museum profession with galleries and museums of varying character, size and administration, and earlier reports, surveys and training programs.

Colbert, Edwin H. "On Being a Curator," *Curator,* I:1 (1958), pp. 7-12.

"A Conversation with: Peter Swann," *gazette,* 9:1 (Winter 1976), pp. 17-27. ♦ Questions and answers about the structure and membership of an Association of Cultural Executives and comparisons with a union.

Conger, John; Ronald Egherman; and Gail Mallard. "The Museum as Employer," *Museum News,* 57:6 (July/August 1979), pp. 22-28.♦ Three museum managers discuss certain legal and ethical obligations of museums and how museums could better fulfill them.

"The Curator: A Symposium Held at the Annual Meeting of the American Association of Museums, Seattle, Washington, May 26-29, 1963," *Curator,* VI:4 (1963), pp. 280-302.

"A Curator is 'a cross between a magpie and a housewife'," *Museums Journal,* 71:2 (September 1971), pp. 73-75.♦ Two student essays on the definition of a curator.

Dribin, Eileen. "Museums Get a Taste of PASTA," *Museum News,* 50:10 (June 1972), pp. 21-26.♦ Discusses union activity in American museums and the spiritual split between museum professionals and management.

Drucker, Peter F. *The Effective Executive.* 1st ed. New York: Harper & Row, 1967. 178 pp.♦ Discusses two premises: the executive's job must be effective, and effectiveness can be learned.

Endter, Ellen. "Money for Manpower," *Museum News,* 53:7 (April 1975), pp. 20-21.♦ Federal funds are available and museums are eligible to apply at the local level for temporary assistance.

Erney, Richard A. *Director–Staff Relations.* AASLH Cassette Tape no. 13. Nashville, Tenn.: American Association for State and Local History, 1971. 1 cassette tape, 57 minutes.♦ Discusses what to look for in recruiting staff, how to build staff competence, how to keep staff effective and content, involvement in staff personal problems, recognizing the director's own biases, how to keep staff well-informed; and concludes with general guidelines for director behavior.

Evans, Bruce H. "Up Against the Ivory Tower," *Museum News,* 52:8 (May 1974), pp. 14-17.♦ Discusses need for communication network among curators.

Gamble, Kathryn E., et al. "Museum Staff Members: Are We Neglected," *The Museologist,* 118 (March 1971), pp. 6-13.

Gladstone, M. J. *A Report on Professional Salaries in New York State, based on a Survey Sponsored by the New York State Association of Museums with Financial Assistance from the New York State Council on the Arts.* New York: New York Association of Museums, distr. by Cranford Wood, Inc., 1972. 47 pp., tables. ♦ Comparative data on salary practices of related institutions, and earning prospects for those considering a museum career.

Glover, Wilbur H. "Toward a Profession," *Museum News,* 42:5 (January 1964), pp. 11-14.

Grant, Alicia. "How Good is MOMA'S PASTA?" *Museum News,* 52:9 (June 1974), pp. 43-44.♦ Professional and Administrative Staff Association of the Museum of Modern Art, New York.

Gray, Peter. "Academic Tenure—Would It Suit Museums?" *Museum News,* 51:9 (May 1973), p. 17.

Grimmett, Archie. "Affirmative Action Can Work," *Museum News,* 54:1 (September/October 1975), pp. 24-25, 72.♦ Guidelines for establishing an affirmative action program that will widen opportunities for minorities and women in the museum work force.

Guthe, Carl E. "Correlation of Museum Positions and Standards," *Curator,* I:2 (1958), pp. 5-12.

Guthe, Carl E. "The Staff." In *So You Want a Good Museum?* (Washington, D.C.: American Association of Museums, 1967), pp. 13-16.

Hall, Patricia A., comp. "Salaries in Historical Agencies," *History News,* 33:12 (December 1978), pp. 281-288.♦ Fourth in a continuing series of surveys to document salary trends in historical agencies in the U.S.

Hamilton, David K. "Salary and Fringe Benefit Survey of Selected Museums," *Curator,* XIX:3 (September 1976), pp. 183-192.♦ Survey includes eleven natural history museums and 10 art museums.

Hopkins, Kenneth R. " 'If You Can't Stand the Heat . . .': Administration in a Small Museum (Or Even in a Medium Size Museum)," *The Museologist,* 126 (March 1973), pp. 5-11. ♦ Importance of communication with staff; "hire people not jobs."

Hurst, Richard M. "The Administrator in the Middle," *The Museologist,* 145 (June 1978), pp. 10-12.♦ Discusses the job, trials and tribulations and rewards of positions that fall in the category of middle management.

Idelson, Evelyn M. *Affirmative Action and Equal Employment, A Guidebook for Employers.* Washington, D.C.: U.S. Equal Employment Opportunity Commission, for sale by the Superintendent of Documents, U.S. Government Printing Office, 1974. 2 vols., bibliog. references.♦ Standards to be used by employers in setting up affirmative action programs. Affirmative Action in employment practices is the process of taking deliberate steps to hire females and members of minority groups; it is specifically required of companies with government contracts and can be required of any company found to be discriminating. EEOC was created by Title VII of the Civil Rights Act of 1964, amended 1972.

Kaderlan, Norman S. *The Role of the Arts Administrator.* Madison, Wisc.: University of Wisconsin, Center for Arts Administration, 1973. 47 pp., bibliog.♦ Discusses necessity of adapting new methods of management because of requirements of accountability of public funds, complexity of operations. Analyzes role of arts administrator in terms of nature of his activities and in context of relationships with people around him.

Kort, Michele, and Jacquelyn Maguire. "Tenure," *Museum News,* 53:4 (December 1974), pp. 26-27, 49-52. ♦ Study of academic system of tenure which is a means of achieving job security and academic freedom, but system not easily transferable to museum community.

McCausland, Mrs. John D. "The Role of Museum Shop Personnel." In *Section Papers, 63rd Annual Meeting, American Association of*

Museums (New Orleans, La.: May 1968), pp. 57-61.

McGrath, Kyran M. *1973 Museum Salary and Financial Survey.* Washington, D.C.: American Association of Museums, 1973. 110 pp., illus.♦ Includes financial and salary tables, details on fringe benefits provided to museum employees, figures on admission fees and attendance, and other data pertinent to current financial state of museums in the U.S. and Canada.

McManis Associates. *Executive Compensation in Education Associations and Professional Societies.* Washington, D.C.: McManis Associates Management and Research Consultants, 1977. 1 vol., various pagings.

Mariner, Dorothy A. "Professionalizing the Museum Worker," *Museum News,* 50:10 (June 1972), pp. 14-20.♦ Discusses problems confronting museum workers in achieving full professional status and strategies for professionalization.

Mark, Charles C. *Hiring an Executive in the Arts.* Rev. ed. Silver Spring, Md.: The Arts Reporting Service, 1975. 16 pp.♦ Defines the responsibilities of the arts executive and boards of directors of arts organizations, and points to cover in employment interviews.

Marshall, Anne. "Employment in the Eyes of the Law," *Museum News,* 51:7 (March 1973), pp. 27-39.♦ Equal Employment Opportunity Commission compiled a listing of federal laws pertaining to job discrimination based on race, sex, religion and age. Defines discrimination, includes resource information on federal laws and the EEOC and basic guidelines for establishing an affirmative action plan.

Matloff, Maurice. "The Military Curator's Obligation to History," *Curator,* XVII:4 (December 1974), pp. 280-289.

Matthai, Robert A. "In Quest of Professional Status," *Museum News,* 52:7 (April 1974), pp. 10-13.♦ Discusses criteria for selecting curators and educators.

Miller, Kenton R. "Development and Training of Personnel," *Trends,* 10:1 (January/February/March 1973), pp. 27-34. ♦ Discusses influences of mass recreation, research, land use competition, and environmental pollution on park management, and need for personnel to acquire more skills to cope with greater variety of park functions.

Miller, Ronald L. "Collective Bargaining in Museums," *Museum News,* 54:1 (September/October 1975), pp. 26-29, 72. ♦ Discusses patterns of museum collective bargaining.

Miller, Ronald L. "Developing a Personnel Policy Manual," *Museum News,* 57:6 (July/August 1979), pp. 29-32.♦ Reviews how good personnel policies and procedures can improve employee morale and performance and offer opportunities for innovation as an organization assesses its goals and operations.

Miller, Ronald L. *Personnel Policies: A Handbook for Management.* Rev. ed. Washington, D.C.: American Association of Museums, 1980. 200 pp., reading list. ♦ Manual based on a survey of museum personnel policies and intended as a source of information and alternative approaches in writing, revising, evaluating policies and procedures. Includes staffing, affirmative action, termination of employment, leaves of absence, due process, benefits, work assignments, compensation administration, pay practices, education and training, supplemental employment, personnel files, performance appraisal, use of museum property and facilities. First edition published by Smithsonian Institution, 1977; revised and updated for publication by American Association of Museums.

Miner, Mary Green. *Pension Plans and the Impact of ERISA.* Washington, D.C.: Bureau of National Affairs, 1977. 47 pp., forms.

Miner, Mary Green. *Separation Procedures and Severance Benefits.* Washington, D.C.: Bureau of National Affairs, 1978. 53 pp., forms.

Miner, Mary Green, and John B. Miner. *Employee Selection Within the Law.* Washington, D.C.: Bureau of National Affairs, 1978. 568 pp., bibliog., index.♦ Manual for personnel administrators and others involved in the hiring process. Discussion of current legislation and methods of evaluating a given selection process.

"Museum Workers Unite," *Museum News,* 52:9 (June 1974), pp. 46-48.♦ Progress reports from representatives of union or staff associations at the American Museum of Natural History, Art Institute of Chicago, Brooklyn Museum, Field Museum of Natural History, Minneapolis Institute of Arts, Museum Workers Association of New York City.

"Museums and the Fair Labor Standards Act," *Museum News,* 47:1 (September 1968), pp. 30-31.

Nagel, Carlos. "Scratching the Back of the Federal Government," *Museum News,* 52:3 (November 1973), p. 52.♦ Describes the Intergovernmental Personnel Act, an opportunity for the free interchange of people and ideas between federal and state and local governments; discusses application to Museum of New Mexico.

Neustupný, Jiří. "What Is Museology?" *Museums Journal,* 71:2 (September 1971), pp. 67-68 ♦ Discusses theoretical basis of museum work, definition, museological disciplines, general and special museology.

Nicholson, Thomas D. "New York State Museums Salary Surveys," *Curator,* XV:3 (September 1972), pp. 238-247.

Nicholson, Thomas D. "Science and the Scientific Staff at The American Museum of Natural History," *Curator,* XVII:3 (September 1974), pp. 173-189. ♦ Includes text of "Policy to Govern the Conditions of Employment, Service, and Responsibilities of the Professional Staff in Scientific and Educational Departments of The American Museum of Natural History."

Osmond, S.P.; Neil Cossons; and N. J. Abercrombie. "Recruitment, Training and Management in the Museum Profession," *Museums Journal,* 70:3 (December 1970), pp. 109-114.

Parr, Albert Eide. "Is There a Museum Profession?" *Curator,* III:2 (1960), pp. 101-106.

Parr, Albert Eide. "On Museums and Directors," *Curator,* XVI:4 (December 1973), pp. 281-285. ♦ Discusses qualifications of training and experience as applied to technology, science, and history directorships.

Parr, Albert Eide. "A Plurality of Professions," *Curator,* VII:4 (1964), pp. 287-295.

Parr, Albert Eide. "Policies and Salaries for Museum Facilities," *Curator,* I:1 (1958), pp. 13-17. ♦ Discusses difficulty in devising a single system of salary schedules and employment policies for the diversity of skills and professions in museums.

Phillips, Richard P. "A Comparative Wage Study Among Museums," *Western Museums Quarterly,* 4:3 (September 1967), pp. 17-18.

Piazza, Paul. "Fighting the Good Fight," *Museum News,* 53:7 (April 1974), pp. 33-35.♦ Discusses caucus of museum educators at 1973 AAM annual meeting which was instrumental in formation of AAM President's Education Committee to improve communication among all museum educators.

Principles of Association Management. Washington, D.C.: American Society of Association Executives, c1975. 437 pp., bibliog.

Rathbone, Perry T. "Association of Art Museum Directors," *Museum News,* 48:4 (December 1969), pp. 25-27.♦ History and growth of the organization, incorporated June 1969, limited membership.

Redfield, Alden. "Mutual Assistance," *Museum News,* 47:10 (June 1969), pp. 19-20.♦ Describes museum jobs for the handicapped at the University of Missouri, Museum of Anthropology.

"Report on the Annual Survey of Faculty Compensation, 1977-78," *AAUP Bulletin,* 64:3 (September 1978), pp. 193-266.♦ First annual survey conducted in 1958 by the Committee on the Economic Status of the Profession; Committee now uses National Center for Education Statistics for data collection. Tables in the survey project scales of faculty salary and fringe benefits; helpful in comparisons of historical organization salaries and benefits. See also: "Errata and Addenda," *AAUP Bulletin,* 64:4 (December 1978), pp. 316-317.

Reynolds, Barrie. "Are Curators Second-Class Citizens?" *Museum News,* 52:8 (May 1974), pp. 33-35.♦ Good curators are hard to find, hard to keep, and hard to use to their full potential.

Rolfe, W. D. Ian. "Special Temporary Employment (STEP) and Youth Opportunity Programs (YOP) in Museums," *Museums Journal,* 78:3 (December 1978), pp. 132-133.♦Discusses how museums can take advantage of the program in Great Britain which succeeded the Job Creation Programme. See also Frank Atkinson, cited above.

"Salary Survey Results," *Western Museums Quarterly,* 6:1 (March 1969), pp. 13-15.

Sampson, Richard A. "The Role of the Museum Administrator in an Exhibit Program," *Midwest Museums Conference Quarterly,* 25:2 (Spring 1965), pp. 5-6.

Schwalbe, Douglas. "Are You an Amateur Administrator?" *Museum News,* 51:5 (January 1973), pp. 26-27.♦ Discusses differences between organizations with tangible goals—geared toward profit, and those with intangible goals—geared to public service (museums).

Shestack, Alan. "The Director: Scholar and Businessman, Educator and Lobbyist," *Museum News,* 57:2 (November/December 1978), pp. 27-31♦ Debates whether training should emphasize scholarly expertise or administrative ability.

Sowers, Richard F. "The Role of the Business Manager," *Western Museums Quarterly,* 4:4 (December 1967), pp. 13-16.♦ Discusses bookkeeping, purchasing, public relations, budgets, employees duties.

Stitt, Susan. "The Search for Equality," *Museum News,* 54:1 (September/October 1975), pp. 17-23.♦ Chapter from the report of a national museum labor market study, cited below, condensed to point out the salary differences between museum men and women.

Stitt, Susan, and Linda Silun. *The Museum Labor Market: A Survey of American Historical Agency Placement Opportunities.* Sturbridge, Mass.: Old Sturbridge Village, 1976. 244 pp., bibliog., appendix, photocopy.♦ Results of a study conducted by Old Sturbridge Village and funded by the National Endowment for the Humanities; limited number of copies were distributed. Contents include survey methodology, analysis of the labor market, and recommendations.

Swann, Peter C. "The Director Preserved?" *The Museologist,* 117 (December 1970), pp. 4-11.♦ Criticisms discussed include museum response to demands of modern society, directors and public issues, trustees out of touch with needs of democratic society; each demand puts professional director in different position.

Toole, K. Ross. "The Sandwich Man: A Hard Role," *Museum News,* 52:9 (June 1974), pp. 41-42.♦ Describes the role of a museum director.

Towers, Cheryl R. "Commentary–Let's Be Affirmative about Affirmative Action," *Museum News,* 56:5 (May/June 1978), pp. 5-7.

Tuminaro, Dominick, and Ashton Hawkins. "You've Come a Long Way . . . ," *Museum News,* 50:10 (June 1972), pp. 27-35.♦ Three-part article on sex discrimination case at Metropolitan Museum of Art.

Ullberg, Patricia. "Naked in the Garden: Museum Practices after *Museum Ethics,*" *Museum News,* 57:6 (July/August 1979), pp. 33-36.♦ Notes progress made in resolving museum staff conflict of interest problems.

U.S. Department of Labor. Bureau of Labor Statistics. "Occupational Earnings in Selected Metropolitan Areas." In *The World Almanac and Book of Facts 1979* (New York: Newspaper Enterprise Association, 1979), p. 124. ♦ Average weekly earnings for selected office worker occupations in seven metropolitan areas, men and women combined; and average hourly earnings for selected maintenance, custodial, and material movement workers.

Whitehill, Walter Muir. "Professional Staff Relationship," *Museum News,* 44:1 (September 1965), pp. 24-26.

NOTES

College Work-Study Program. The College Work-Study Program, authorized by the Higher Education Act of 1965, provides federal funding to institutions of post-secondary education for 80% of the wages of students in the program. Each state allocates the funds directly to colleges and universities which certify a student's eligibility. Institutions or off-campus, nonprofit and public employers provide the other 20%. Any agency directly receiving or placing students must sign an agreement with the colleges which are encouraged by federal guidelines to refer students to public service organizations. Financial aid officers at universities and colleges administer the program.

Comprehensive Employment and Training Act of 1973 (CETA). CETA provides funds to subsidize employees on community projects. The 1973 act (P.L. 93-203) transferred responsibility for manpower programs from state to local units of government. These local units, Prime Sponsors, administer the program, along with manpower planning councils that represent the client, community, business, labor, education, training agencies and the general public. Nonprofit organizations and public agencies are eligible to employ CETA-funded personnel. CETA funds have been used on almost every level of arts and museum employment including administrator, historic site groundskeeper, special projects coordinator, office aide, guard, artist, technician, researcher, craft demonstrator, and carpenter. Money is provided only for salaries, and after a year's employment, the sponsoring organization is expected to transfer CETA personnel to its own payroll. The act was amended by the Emergency Jobs and Unemployment Assistance Act of 1974, which provided continuing manpower assistance to community organizations. For further information, contact the manpower office at city hall or county office building.

Urban Corps, Urban Corps National Service Center, Suite 201, 1140 Connecticut Avenue, N.W., Washington, D.C. 20036. The Center is a joint project of the International City Management Association and the Urban Corps National Association which represents the local Urban Corps programs. The Center was created to provide technical assistance to localities wishing to establish Urban Corps-type internship programs; to increase public knowledge of the Urban Corps concept; and to encourage more complete integration of service-learning experiences with traditional higher academic work. A community agency, usually the local government, establishes an internship office called an Urban Corps. Administered largely by college students themselves, the program acts as the central supplier of temporary student manpower to all the government departments and sometimes includes public service agencies such as museums and historical societies. An assignment pool is developed based on job forms submitted by the participating agencies; the Urban Corps recruits college students, mainly those eligible for assistance under the federal College-Work Study Program (see above). By contracting with the local college an Urban Corps can obtain a number of these students and pay the matching employer's salary share. A local Urban Corps places students in jobs suited to their qualifications, academic interests and career goals. The Urban Corps handles fiscal arrangements, time cards, and paycheck distribution. Either the college or the Urban Corps may be the paymaster of the students, depending upon the local arrangements.

Volunteer and Guide Personnel

Bay, Ann. "Getting Decent Docents," *Museum News,* 52:7 (April 1974), pp. 25-29.◆ Describes a variety of interpreter programs.

Bloom, Kathryn. "The Junior League and Children's Museums," *Museum News,* 39:7 (April 1961), pp. 20-24.

Bradshaw, Mary Claire. "Volunteer Docent Programs: A Pragmatic Approach to Museum Interpretation," *History News,* 28:8 (August 1973), Technical Leaflet no. 65.

Compton, Mildred S. "A Training Program for Museum Volunteers," *Curator,* VIII:4 (December 1965), pp. 294-298.◆ Programs for both junior and adult volunteers.

Dutro, Leroy. "Volunteers in the de Young Museum Society Art Shop." In *Papers, 64th Annual Meeting, American Association of Museums* (San Francisco, Calif.: 1969), pp. 99-101.

Ferdon, Edwin N., Jr., and Emma M. Cappelluzo. "A Double Duty Docent Program," *Museum News,* 44:7 (March 1966), pp. 20-24.

Fertig, Barbara C., and Anne V. Berrill. "Examining a Delicate Balance," *Museum News,* 56:1 (September/October 1977), pp. 15-20. ◆ Essay on the museum volunteer, reprinted from *The Art Museum as Educator,* edited by Barbara Y. Newsom and Adele Z. Silver (Berkeley: University of California Press, 1977), a collection of case studies and reports with a special section on volunteers. Includes place of the volunteer in the museum, what the volunteer receives, problems in volunteer programs, toward an imaginative use of volunteers.

Flanders, Mary P. "Evaluating Docent Performance," *Curator,* XIX:3 (September 1976), pp. 198-225.◆ Discusses problems and procedures, and applying interaction analysis to a single tour.

Flint, Leroy. "Educational Standards and Volunteer Performance," *Curator,* II:2 (1959), pp. 101-106.◆ Considers educational programs and standards, outlines some critera for programs, and defines role of the volunteer.

George Washington University. Center for Museum Education. *Volunteers in Museum Education.* Edited by Barbara Fertig. Sourcebook no. 2. Washington, D.C.: The Center, 1978. 300 pp., bibliog., list of resources. ◆ Case studies on the structure, training, operation and evaluation of volunteer corps. Includes suggestions for preparing handbooks, keeping records, and alternative services that volunteers may perform.

Graham, Frank P. "Defining Limitations of the Volunteer Worker," *Curator,* VIII:4 (December 1965), pp. 291-293.◆ Essential to have defined responsibilities and mutual regard between paid and non-paid personnel.

Gregg, Richard N. "Training and Using Museum Volunteers," Midwest Museums Conference *Quarterly,* 22:3 (Summer 1962), pp. 30-32.

Hall, Nancy Johnston, and Karla McGray. "The Volunteer as Everyman . . . Woman and Child," *Museum News,* 56:1 (September/October 1977), pp. 27-29.

Heine, Aalbert. "The Care and Feeding of Volunteer Staff Members," *Curator,* VIII:4 (December 1965), pp. 287-290.

Lauffer, Armand, and Sarah Gorodezky. *Volunteers.* With contributions by Jay Callahan and Carla Overberger. Human Services Guide Series, vol. 5. Beverly Hills, Calif.: Sage Publications, Inc., c1977. 87 pp., bibliog.◆ Published in cooperation with the Continuing Education Program in Human Services of the University of Michigan School of Social Work.

McBride, Delbert. "Using Museum Volunteers," *Western Museums Quarterly,* 7:1 (July 1970), pp. 8-10.

Morgan, Mrs. William L. "A Survey of American Museum Docent Programs," *Museum News,* 46:10 (June 1968), pp. 28-30.

"Museums and their Friends," *Museum,* XXIX:1 (1977), entire issue.◆ Includes case studies; examples of contributions by friends and volunteers; results of world-wide survey of Friends of Museums; lists of societies of friends of museums.

National Center for Voluntary Action. *Recruiting Volunteers–Views, Techniques and Comments.* Rev. ed. Washington, D.C.: The Center, 1976. 24 pp.

Naylor, Harriet N. *Volunteers Today–Finding, Training and Working With Them.* Dryden, N.Y.: Dryden Associates, 1973. 198 pp., bibliog., appendices.

O'Connell, Brian. *Effective Leadership in Voluntary Organizations: How to Make the Greatest Use of Citizen Service and Influence.* New York: Association Press, c1976. 202 pp., index.◆ Includes guidelines for fundraising; involvement of minorities; dealing with controversy, dissent and disruption; and evaluation. Emphasis on internal mechanics of volunteerism, distinguishing between role of volunteers and function of staff.

Payson, Hulda Smith. "Volunteers: Priceless Personnel for the Small Museum," *Museum News,* 45:6 (February 1967), pp. 18-21.

Pell, Arthur R. *Recruiting, Training and Motivating Volunteer Workers.* New York: Pilot Books, 1972. 62 pp., bibliog.◆ A guide for professional staffs and volunteer leaders of groups that provide opportunities for volunteers.

Reed, Betty Jane. "Establishing a Community Resource Volunteer Program," *Museum News,* 50:9 (May 1972), pp. 20-24.

Reibel, Daniel B. "The Use of Volunteers in Museums and Historical Societies," *Curator,* XVII:1 (March 1974), pp. 16-26.◆ Discusses role of a volunteer, recruitment, training, organization, discrimination, compensation, and volunteer—museum relationship.

Reibel, Daniel B. "The Volunteer: Nuisance or Savior?" *Museum News,* 49:7 (March 1971), pp. 28-30.

Schindler-Rainman, Eva, and Ronald Lippitt. *The Volunteer Community, Creative Use of Human Resources.* Washington, D.C.: Center for a Voluntary Society, NTL Institute for Applied Behavioral Science, c1971. 148 pp., bibliog.

Seidelman, James E., and Mary Atkins. "Importance of Volunteer Placement," *Curator,* VIII:4 (December 1965), pp. 299-301.

Selby, Roger L. "Bylaws for Volunteer Groups," *Museum News,* 56:1 (September/October 1977), pp. 21-23.

Stevenson, Helen H. "Help for the Museum: Volunteers," *Museum News,* 44:9 (May 1966), pp. 34-37.

Straus, Ellen S. "Volunteer Professionalism," *Museum News,* 56:1 (September/October 1977), pp. 24-26.

Swanson, Mary T. *Your Volunteer Program: Organization and Administration of Volunteer Programs.* Ankeny, Iowa: EPDA Volunteer Coordinators Program, Des Moines Area Community College, 1970. 203 pp., illus., bibliog.♦ A how-to-do-it book; contains extensive list of reference materials including "The Art of Board Membership," and "Working with Volunteers."

Swauger, James L. "Is There Life After Retirement?" *Museum News,* 52:3 (November 1973), pp. 31-33.♦ Describes a project developed by the Carnegie Museum utilizing retired steelworkers as volunteers in the museum. Inset article describes how museums may benefit from federal funds for senior citizens.

Thorpe, Heather G. "Docentry at the University of Michigan Exhibit Museum," Midwest Museums Conference *Quarterly,* 25:2 (Spring 1965), pp. 8-11.♦ Guide services and scheduling system, use of college students, list of do's for docents.

"The Training and Utilization of Volunteers: A Symposium," *Curator,* VIII:4 (1965), pp. 287-301.

Wilson, Marlene. *The Effective Management of Volunteer Programs.* Boulder, Colo.: Volunteer Management Associates, c1976. 197 pp., diagrams, bibliog. references.♦ Includes Look at Volunteerism; Role of a Manager; Motivation; Organizational Climate; Planning and Evaluation; Designing Jobs and Recruiting to Fill Them; Interviewing and Placing Volunteers; Training; Communications; Putting It All Together—Client/Staff/Volunteer/Board.

Wiser, Betty. *Resources for Developing Volunteer Programs: An Annotated Bibliography.* Raleigh, N.C.: Urban Affairs and Community Service Center, North Carolina State University, 1971. 74 pp.♦ Includes Program Development; Resources Available in the Local Community; Financial Resources.

Wriston, Barbara. "Volunteer Programs in Museums of the United States," *The Museologist,* 113 (December 1969), pp. 5-12.♦ Describes volunteer programs at Art Institute of Chicago.

NOTES

National Center for Voluntary Action, 1785 Massachusetts Avenue, N.W., Washington, D.C. 20036. Founded in 1970, the Center seeks to encourage more Americans to become volunteers. It assists communities and organizations in reinforcing, expanding and improving the effectiveness of their volunteer activities, and maintains a clearinghouse on case histories of successful volunteer projects throughout the country. Funded by private gifts and grants from foundations and government, the grant money made available by government is for the development of local Voluntary Action Centers, or seed grants or demonstration money for special projects. The purpose of the local centers is to aid voluntary programs and agencies in achieving the most effective use of volunteer resources. The Center makes available consultants, newsletters, and field services of all kinds. It publishes *Voluntary Action Leadership* (bimonthly), and a collection of booklets designed for leaders of community-based volunteer programs.

Retired Senior Volunteer Program (RSVP). The RSVP is part of ACTION, the federal agency for volunteer service. It offers men and women, age 60 and over, new and varied opportunities for volunteer service in their communities. Federal grants are available for developing and operating these programs, but applicants must have a plan for continuing with non-federal contributions. RSVP programs are organized and operated in local communities by approved public or private nonprofit organizations based in those communities. In RSVP, older people serve in schools, parks, courts, museums, libraries, nursing homes, etc. Assignments are carefully matched to the needs. RSVP volunteers receive no compensation but are reimbursed for out-of-pocket expenses.

6

Financial Management

Proposed budgets get larger (inevitably) and money gets tighter. Finances, and the management thereof, top the list of concerns of historical organizations of all sizes everywhere. And so, even though there are relatively few references, they are placed in a chapter by themselves.

No historical organization can succeed unless there is someone who has mastered basic accounting principles and reporting practices, especially in light of tightened tax requirements and accountability requirements for government support.

The best advice that can be given here is to indicate that no historical organization should be without Gross and Daughtrey, *Museum Accounting Handbook*. It may not make a novice into an expert, but it will make more comprehensible budgeting, purchasing, financial statements, fund accounting, indirect costs, the effects of inflation, and a host of other fiscal basics.

Accounting Advisory Committee. *Report to the Commission on Private Philanthropy and Public Needs, Accounting Advisory Committee.* n.p.: The Committee, 1974. 36 pp., tables, forms.♦ Committee studied present accounting principles and reporting practices followed by each major type of philanthropic organization in financial reporting to the public; surveyed present federal and state regulatory financial reporting requirements; studied the basic financial information appropriate for regulatory reporting; made conclusions and recommendations to the Filer Commission. Provided basis for ASTC museum accounting guidelines and the museum accounting handbook.

Advisory Committee on Endowment Management. *Managing Education Endowments: Report to the Ford Foundation.* 2nd ed. New York?: 1972. 65 pp., bibliog. references, appendices. ♦ Includes statement of the program, history and principles, summary and conclusion.

Aljian, George W., ed. *Purchasing Handbook: Standard Reference Book on Policies,* *Practices, Procedures Utilized in Departments Responsible for Purchasing Management or Materials Management.* 3rd ed. New York: McGraw-Hill, 1973. 1 vol., various pagings, illus., bibliog.

American Institute of Certified Public Accountants. *Accounting Principles and Reporting Practices for Certain Nonprofit Organizations, December 31, 1978: A Proposed Recommendation to the Financial Accounting Standards Board.* New York: The Institute, 1979. 117 pp., forms, charts, appendices. ♦ Statement of Position regarding recommended principles and practices for nonprofit organizations not covered by existing AICPA audit guides, such as cemetery societies, professional associations, private foundations, libraries, civic organizations, labor unions, museums, performing arts organizations, research and scientific organizations, zoological and botanical societies, and other cultural organizations.

Association of Science-Technology Centers. *Museum Accounting Guidelines: Recommended Policies for Preparing Financial*

Statements at Museums. Edited by Victor J. Danilov. Washington, D.C.: The Association, 1976. 20 pp., sample statements, bibliog., index.♦ Includes principles for financial statements, operating funds, cash contributions and pledges, contributed materials and services, auxiliary activities, investments, land, building and equipment, related organizations; and representative financial statements.

Barry, Joseph K. *Financial Management Handbook for Associations.* Washington, D.C.: Association Service Department, Chamber of Commerce of the United States, 1966. 95 pp., appendices.

Bennett, Paul. *Up Your Accountability: How to Up Your Serviceability and Funding Credibility by Upping You Accounting Ability.* Washington, D.C.: Taft Products, 1973. 66 pp., bibliog.♦ Discussion of accounting principles and procedures for nonprofit organizations, focusing on analysis of basic financial statements and narrative reports, development of management information, budgeting, and procedures for recording and controlling daily financial activity through bookkeeping and internal controls.

Blaine, John. "Accountability to the Hand That Feeds You," *Museum News,* 57:5 (May/June 1979), pp. 34-36.♦ Obligation of cultural institutions receiving local public support to demonstrate a continuing need for that support and to account for its use.

Danilov, Victor J. "Museum Accounting Guidelines," *Curator,* XXI:1 (1978), pp. 15-35.♦ Summarizes *Museum Accounting Guidelines. . . .*

Dixon, Robert L. *The Executive's Accounting Primer.* New York: McGraw-Hill, c1971. 328 pp., appendix, index.♦ Includes balance sheet; income statement; flow of funds statement; accounting cycle; inventories; fixed assets and depreciation; basic cost accounting; internal management accounting; federal income taxes; use of computers; recognition of effects of inflation.

Eager, George. "Financial Profile of Small New York State Historical Societies," *The Museologist,* 143 (December 1977), p. 21.

"The Energy and Inflation Fighters," *Museum News,* 53:6 (March 1975), pp. 25-27, 45.♦ List of suggestions for small and large museums on how to stretch dollars, raise new funds, and spend less.

Fenstermaker, Joseph Van. *Cash Management: Managing the Cash Flows, Bank Balances, and Short-term Investments of Nonprofit Institutions.* 1st ed. Kent, Ohio: Kent State University Press, c1966. 59 pp., tables, charts, bibliog.

Gross, Malvern J., Jr. "Evolving Accounting Rules for Private Foundations," *Foundation News,* 16:2 (March/April 1975), pp. 34-39.♦ Accounting principles are a concern of small foundations with current demands for full public disclosure.

Gross, Malvern J., Jr. *Financial and Accounting Guide for Nonprofit Organizations.* 2nd ed. New York: Ronald Press Co., 1972. 541 pp., tables, bibliog., appendix, index. ♦ Comprehensive discussion of AICPA guides for accountants who examine the financial statements of hospitals, colleges and universities, and voluntary health and welfare organizations; also discussion of accounting and reporting problems of nonprofit entities for which no definitive guides exist (as of 1972).

Gross, Malvern J., Jr. "How to Make Your Financial Reports Easy to Understand," *Association Management,* 25:9 (September 1973), pp. 65-70. ♦ Offers examples of financial statements of nonprofit organizations.

Gross, Malvern J., Jr. "Report on Nonprofit Accounting," *The Journal of Accountancy,* 139:6 (June 1975), pp. 55-59. ♦ Background of the Accounting Advisory Committee Report to the Filer Commission.

Gross, Malvern J., Jr., and William H. Daughtrey. *Museum Accounting Handbook.* Washington, D.C.: American Association of Museums, 1978. 158 pp., illus., glossary, bibliog., index.♦ How-to manual to span the gap between minimal or nonexistent accounting background of most museum administrators; problems created by increased government support and tightened tax requirements to which private foundations and donors must now adhere. Includes introduction to the use of the handbook; basic concepts of financial reporting and accounting; bookkeeping systems; aspects of fund accounting; budgeting; contributed services and materials; optional procedures; and the entire ASTC *Museum Accounting Guidelines . . .* (1976).

Guthe, Carl E. "Sources of Income; Operating Budget." In *So You Want a Good Museum?* (Washington, D.C.: American Association of Museums, 1967), pp. 19-26.

Macleod, Roderick K. "Program Budgeting Works in Nonprofit Institutions," *Harvard Business Review,* 49:5 (September 1971), pp. 46-56.♦ Cost accounting of professional services pinpoints sources and uses of funds and facilitates decisions on money allocation. Available in Reprint Series, no. 21123, Management of Nonprofit Organizations series. Address: Reprint Service, *Harvard Business Review,* Boston, Massachusetts 02163.

National Health Council, Inc. *Standards of Accounting and Financial Practices for Non-Profit Voluntary Health and Welfare Organizations.* Rev. ed. New York: National Health Council, Inc.; National Assembly of National Voluntary Health and Social Welfare Organizations, Inc.; United Way of America, 1975. 135 pp.♦ Intended to set uniform standards of accounting and reporting; applicable to historical organizations.

Nelson, Charles A., and Frederick J. Turk. *Financial Management for the Arts: A Guidebook for Arts Organizations.* New York: Associated Councils of the Arts, c1975. 52 pp., illus.♦ Aimed at small organizations with budgets $20,000 to $200,000 which may not have trained business management personnel; contains information and examples of organizational accounting including planning and budgeting, cash management, funds and fund accounting, general accounting scheme and reporting, and financial organization.

Nicholas, D. A. "Recession Money-Managing Pointers," *Museum News,* 54:1 (September/October 1975), pp. 50-51.

Perry, Gail, and Ronald Goldstein. "Taking the Mystery out of Financial Management," *Museum News,* 57:3 (January/February 1979), pp. 45-48.♦ Computer system designed by Metropolitan Cultural Alliance, Boston, to bridge gap between artistic and managerial needs of cultural institutions; aids in financial management and designed in accordance with AICPA accounting guidelines.

Rudd, Jean. "Commentary–A Banker's Novel Views on Nonprofit Money Management," *Museum News,* 57:6 (July/August 1979), pp. 9-14.♦ Describes solution to managing deficit at Art Institute of Chicago, including innovative financing, some unusual banking services, a state education authority, a lobbying effort, and sale of bonds. Reprinted from *Foundation News,* March/April 1979.

Steere, William C. "Proposed Endowments Budget: What It Can Mean for Museums," *Museum News,* 48:6 (February 1970), pp. 21-22.

Sweeny, Allen. *Accounting Fundamentals for Nonfinancial Executives.* New York: American Management Association, 1972. 147 pp., charts, index.

Sweeny, Allen, and John N. Wisener, Jr. *Budgeting Fundamentals for Nonfinancial Executives.* New ed. New York: AMACOM, c1975. 137 pp., index.

Tierney, Cornelius E., and Robert D. Hoffman. *Federal Financial Management: Accounting and Auditing Practices.* New York: Federal Government Division, American Institute of Certified Public Accountants, 1976. 186 pp., diagrams, bibliog.♦ Describes federal government procedures; defines allowable/unallowable costs and in-kind contributions for federal grantees.

U.S. Department of Health, Education and Welfare. Division of Financial Management Standards and Procedures. *A Guide for Non-Profit Institutions: Cost Principles and Procedures for Establishing Indirect Cost and Other Rates for Grants and Contracts with the Department of Health, Education and Welfare.* Washington, D.C.: U.S. Government Printing Office, 1974. 64 pp.

Walker, James P. "Playing the Numbers: A Not So New Racket," *Museum News,* 51:8 (April 1973), pp. 28-29.♦ Method of surmounting accounting problems common to most museums with the aid of a computer.

Wehle, Mary M. *Financial Management for Arts Organizations.* Cambridge, Mass.: Arts Administration Research Institute, c1975. 163 pp., graphs.

Zaenglein, Roger W. "Current Accounting Trends: Their Impact on Historical Societies," *History News,* 31:1 (January 1976), Technical Leaflet no. 87.♦ Reviews basic accounting concepts and discusses trends in financial reporting and recording of certain data.

NOTE

American Institute of Certified Public Accountants, 1211 Avenue of the Americas, New York, New York 10036. Founded in 1887, the Institute is a professional society of accountants certified by the states and territories. Its responsibilities include influencing the development of financial accounting standards, and preparing and grading the national uniform CPA examinations for state licensing bodies. It conducts programs of research, education, surveillance of practice, and communication. It has over 100 committees including accounting standards, auditing standards, federal taxation, management advisory services, and professional ethics; and maintains a library. It publishes *CPA* (monthly); *Journal of Accountancy* (monthly); *Tax Advisor* (monthly); *Management Advisor* (bimonthly); and AICPA Industry Audit Guide Series.

7

Fund Raising

The problem for many, if not most, historical organizations is that there is not enough money to manage. Thus, fund raising. And again planning. The singular importance of comprehensive development programs, the need for self-appraisal, for definition of purposes and goals is stressed in the first section. Happily, there are a good many comprehensive handbooks to light a path. Much murkier is the path to knowledge of the continually changing regulations that lay out the boundaries of the income tax laws, but additional help will be found in the sections on tax and law in Chapter 8.

Many organizations get major financial help today from admissions, sales desks and book stores, food concessions, and the licensing for reproductions. Well-conceived and well-directed, sales of theme-related materials can be an important and integral part of the education program. The others represent a service, but they too can be profitable.

Administrators today must be grantsmen to tap successfully the three springs from whence flow the long green rivers of dollars; 1) foundations and private philanthropy; 2) government—federal, state, and local; and 3) business. The revolution in giving to cultural institutions has resulted in a good list of references which point the way to the gold in them thar hills.

Development Planning

"The Battle of the Budget," *History News*, 32:1 (January 1977), p. 27.♦ Set of questions to ask before raising money; first article in money-raising or money-saving series entitled "The Pocketbook."

Boersma, Larry. "Some Hot Tips on the Membership Market," *Museum News*, 51:8 (April 1973), pp. 16-17.♦ Discusses development of contemporary marketing and fundraising techniques by using a computer to maintain and update information on constituency, their interests, annual contributions and fund-raising prospects.

Edwards, Charles A. "Development in Context," *Museum News*, 56:5 (May/June 1978), pp. 40-43.♦ Development in museums should become more than a synonym for fundraising or miracle working; need to be more assertive.

Fields, Curtis P. "A Ten-Point Funding Program," *History News*, 16:8 (June 1961), pp. 110-112.♦ Planning a campaign to develop display space and pay off long term mortgage; emphasis on status and needs of the organization, guiding principles in campaign, progress and results.

Fishel, Leslie H., Jr. *Finances and Fund Raising*. AASLH Cassette Tape no. 15. Nashville, Tenn.: American Association for State and Local History, 1971. 1 cassette tape, 51 minutes.♦ Emphasis on pre-fundraising steps, determining chain of responsibility for fundraising, inventory of what funds needed for which functions; reviews various foundations as sources of funding, the private individual donor, and the corporate donor.

Gleason, Ron. "Local Fund-Raising Strategies," *Museum News*, 55:7 (July/August 1977), pp. 19-23.♦ Discusses self-appraisal and budget; and sources such as membership, designated gifts, local government, school systems, deferred gifts, corporate support, earned income.

Hardy, James M. *Corporate Planning for Non-Profit Organizations.* Washington, D.C.: Association Press, c1972, 1973. 119 (32) pp., bibliog., illus.♦ Guide to implementing a planning program for both large and small nonprofit organizations.

Lee, James C. *Do or Die: Survival for Nonprofits.* Washington, D.C.: Taft Products, Inc., 1974. 102 pp., diagrams.♦ Emphasis on successful money raising, spending and management which provides organization with ability to produce a desirable product. Self-analysis for a nonprofit organization, professional advice for board members and directors on developing and continuing successful financial and management programs.

Lemaire, Ingrid. *Resource Directory of the Funding and Managing of Non-Profit Organizations.* New York: Edna McConnell Clark Foundation, 1977. 127 pp.♦ Three sections include resource development; sources of information for data and research; management support for nonprofit organizations.

Miller, David E. "Master Planning—One of the Best Approaches to Fund Raising." In *Papers, 64th Annual Meeting, American Association of Museums* (San Francisco, Calif.: 1969), pp. 44-46.

Moss, Helen E. "An Eye on the Future," *Museum News,* 57:6 (July/August 1979), pp. 51-53.♦ Comprehensive development programs that include deferred giving not only provide museums with a vehicle for building an endowment but also provide donors with many tax benefits.

"Museum Financing," *Museum News,* 51:6 (February 1973), special issue.♦ Articles on rituals of fundraising, federal programs, Canadian government programs, the Foundation Center, grantsmanship, and subsidies.

Pizer, Laurence R. "Financing Your History Organization: Setting Goals," *History News,* 33:7 (July 1978), Technical Leaflet no. 106.♦ Discusses need to outline goals, sources for permanent funding, and financing short-term projects.

Safrin, Robert W. "Development and the American Museum." In *Papers, 64th Annual Meeting, American Association of Museums* (San Francisco, Calif.: 1969), pp. 42-43. ♦ Emphasis on development work and rise of fulltime development officer.

Shapiro, Benson P. "Marketing for Nonprofit Organizations," *Harvard Business Review,* 51:5 (September-October 1973), pp. 123-132.♦ Certain business concepts of marketing function can be adopted to enhance operation of nonprofit organizations; three tasks defined are resource attraction (obtaining revenue), resource allocation (dispensing services), and persuasion.

Sheehan, Donald T. "Programming for Fund-Raising," *Historic Preservation,* 18:3 (May-June 1966), pp. 118-125.♦ Discusses definition of purpose, overall plan and preparation, competent counsel.

Trenbeth, Richard P. "This Business of Museum Development," *Museum News,* 40:7 (March 1962), pp. 17-21.♦ Discusses need for establishing comprehensive development programs for more widespread support; need to be willing to compete for foundation resources.

Fund Raising Techniques

Associated Councils of the Arts. *How to Raise Money: Special Events for Arts Organizations.* By Ellen S. Daniels. New York: The Council, 1977. 32 pp.♦ Collection of articles describing fundraising events and projects such as auctions, book fairs, and community calendars.

Bingham, Judith. "Museum Fund-Raising Conferences," *Curator,* XIV:4 (December 1971), pp. 287-292.♦ Discusses the fundraising process and methods.

Blanshard, Paul, Jr. *The KRC Fund Raiser's Manual: A Guide to Personalized Fund Raising.* New Canaan, Conn.: KRC Development Council, 1974. 246 pp., appendix.♦ Manual on capital fund campaigning, special project fundraising, annual giving, deferred giving, and foundation grantsmanship.

"A Compilation of State Laws Regulating Charities," *Giving USA Bulletin,* 16 (December 1978), special issue.♦ Third annual compilation of state legislation, as of December 1978, regulating the solicitation of funds by charitable organizations and professional fundraising counsel and solicitors for 35 states and the District of Columbia. In June of each year the American Association of Fund-Raising Counsel, Inc., also publishes a compilation of pending laws.

Conrad, Daniel Lynn, et al. *Successful Fund Raising Techniques.* 2nd ed. San Francisco: Institute for Fund Raising, c1976. 302 pp., in various pagings, bibliog.

Deferred Giving Programs: Administration and Promotion. Editor: William C. Cassell. Washington, D.C.: American Alumni Council, c1972. 123 pp.♦ Essays on aspects of deferred giving; organizing a successful program; finding and researching prospects; role of volunteers; use of direct mail; servicing donors; bequest program; implications of Tax Reform Act of 1969; pooled income trusts; and charitable remainder trusts.

Edwards, Charles A. "A Fund-Raising Resource Guide," *Museum News,* 55:7 (July/August 1977), pp. 15-17.♦ Lists training programs and workshops; information sources on foundations and individuals and other related references.

Fellows, Margaret M., and Stella A. Koenig. *Tested Methods of Raising Money for Churches, Colleges and Health and Welfare Agencies.* New York: Harper, 1959. 463 pp., illus., bibliog.♦ Discusses use of letters, areas of larger giving, means of maintaining support and developing loyalty.

Finke, Hans-Joachim. "Organizing Capital Fund Drives," *History News,* 33:10 (October 1978), pp. 240–241. ♦ Reprinted from Regional Conference of Historical Agencies (N.Y.), Information Sheet, February 1978.

Flanagan, Joan. *The Grass Roots Fundraising Book: How to Raise Money in Your Community.* Chicago: The Swallow Press, Inc., 1977. 219 pp. ♦ Guide to local fundraising, including publicity, bookkeeping, and large and small fundraising projects.

Hanson, Abel A. *Guides to Successful Fundraising.* New York: Bureau of Publications, Teachers College, Columbia University, 1961. 54 pp.

Humphries, H. R. *Fund Raising for Small Charities and Organizations.* Newton Abbot: David and Charles, 1972. 124 pp., bibliog. ♦ Advice on how to run a committee, how to advertise and promote an event; ideas for raising money, the law and fundraising, and appendix of addresses (British).

Independent Community Consultants, Inc. *A Guide to Funding Sources Research.* Rev. ed. Edited by Earl Anthes, Jerry Cronin, Carolyn Strong. Guide Series Publication no. 2. Hampton, Ariz.: Independent Community Consultants, Inc., 1974, 1977. 20 pp.♦ Lists publications and sources by subject: foundations, government grants, corporate donations, special fundraising programs, planning and management of fundraising programs. Available from Planning and Training Office, Box 141, Hampton, Arizona 71744.

Independent Community Consultants, Inc. *A Guide to Fundraising & Proposal Writing.* Albuquerque, N.M.: Independent Community Consultants, Inc., Design and Planning Assistance Center, 1975. 42 pp.♦ Guide to major steps in fundraising: program planning, funding source researching, writing the proposal, other ways of raising money.

Ketchum, Carlton G. "A Case History: Tools and Procedures." In *Section Papers, 63rd Annual Meeting, American Association of Museums* (New Orleans, La.: May 1968), pp. 100-103.♦ Example of a fund drive.

KRC Development Council. *The KRC Guide to Direct Mail Fund Raising.* Edited by Mitchell Keller. New Canaan, Conn.: The Council, c1977. 205 pp., illus.♦ Describes direct mail fundraising campaigns directed toward new prospects and previous donors. Including budgeting, planning and scheduling, design and layout, use of computers, cost measurement and control, and evaluation of campaign results.

Leibert, Edwin R., and Bernice E. Sheldon. *Handbook of Special Events for Nonprofit Organizations: Tested Ideas for Fund Raising and Public Relations.* New York: Association Press, 1972. 224 pp., illus., bibliog.♦ Ideas such as fairs, bazaars, theater benefits, open houses, etc. that have proved successful for community organizations.

Linton, M. Albert. "Fund Management and Fund Raising," *Museum News,* 44:1 (September 1965), pp. 26-27.

Mirkin, Howard R. *The Complete Fund Raising Guide.* New York: Public Service Materials Center, c1975. 159 pp., bibliog.♦ Description of techniques of raising funds from business and labor, foundations, government, memorial giving, bequests and the general public.

Old Sturbridge Village. *Adventure Into the Past.* Sturbridge, Mass.: 1964. 12 pp., illus.♦ Brochure about the Gift Annuity Plan for deferred gift giving at Old Sturbridge Village.

Phillips, Edgar Hereward. *Fund Raising Techniques–and Case Histories.* London: Business Books, 1969. 189 pp., illus., forms, map.

Schwartz, John J. "The Essentials of Fund-Raising—Annual Capital Campaigns: Case, Plan and Organization." In *Section Papers, 63rd Annual Meeting, American Association of Museums* (New Orleans, La.: May 1968), pp. 96-99.

Seymour, Harold J. *Designs for Fund-Raising: Principles, Patterns, and Techniques.* New York: McGraw-Hill Book Co., 1966. 210 pp., bibliog.♦ Discusses what trustees need to know about philosophy and practice of philanthropy and responsibility for leadership; reviews background for fundraising, campaign procedures, special interest campaigns, and professional help.

Sheridan, Philip G. *Fund Raising for the Small Organization.* New York: M. Evans Co., distr. in association with Lippincott, Philadelphia, 1968. 240 pp.

Sperry and Hutchinson Company. *Ways and Means Handbook: A Chairman's Guide to Money Making Projects.* Fort Worth, Texas: Sperry and Hutchinson Company, 1978. 32 pp.♦ Guide to variety of money-making projects used by PTAs, churches, and other groups; includes planning aids and check lists.

Swann, Peter C. "Fund Raising or Reflections on a Wasted Life," *gazette,* 8:1 (Winter 1975), pp. 16-22.♦ Fundraising campaign of the Royal Ontario Museum.

Teitell, Conrad. "Life Income Plans." In *Section Papers, 63rd Annual Meeting, American Association of Museums* (New Orleans, La.: May 1968), pp. 104-111.♦ Explains deferred gifts and tax benefits under life income plans.

Thomas, Charles V. "The Annual Fund," *Museum News,* 45:3 (November 1966), pp. 34-35.♦ Planning and conducting annual fund

drive; example of Minneapolis Society of Fine Arts.

Warner, Irving R. *The Art of Fundraising.* 1st ed. New York: Harper & Row, 1975. 176 pp., index.♦ Instructions for volunteer fundraisers; includes estimating fundraising goals, selecting campaign leader, publicity, fundraising methods and events, motivations for giving, what to do if fundraising attempts fail. Checklist for planning events.

NOTES

American Association of Fund-Raising Counsel, Inc., 500 Fifth Avenue, New York, New York 10016. Founded in 1935, the Association consists of fundraising counseling firms engaged in managing, planning and consulting regarding financing of hospital, educational, religious, community-fund, and other nonprofit institutions for fundraising programs. It has committees for professional ethics and state legislation. It publishes *Giving USA* (annual); *Giving USA Bulletin* (11/yr.); *Master Calendar* (January), annual listing of meetings and seminars whose agendas include fundraising matters.

Funding Sources Clearinghouse, Inc., 2600 Bancroft Way, Berkeley, California 94704. Founded in 1971, the Clearinghouse is a nonprofit organization serving other nonprofit groups in getting grants from foundations, government agencies, private donors, corporations, etc. It uses a data-bank system, and charges an annual membership fee. The Clearinghouse provides data bank searches for an unlimited number of projects with reports on each prospect, and biographical profiles on foundation officers. They also publish a monthly digest of grant news.

National Society of Fund Raising Executives, 1511 K Street, N.W., Investment Building, Suite 831, Washington, D.C. 20005. Founded in 1960, the Society consists of individual memberships, and local groups of 18 men and women engaged in the direction and execution of fundraising programs for nonprofit organizations, agencies, churches, counseling firms, education, health and welfare organizations and institutions. It encourages the study of research and instruction in the field of fundraising through courses at established institutions of learning and through other means. It holds periodic workshops and seminars dealing with all phases of fundraising, and publishes a *Journal* (semiannual). Formerly National Society of Fund Raisers.

In-House Sources of Income

Albers, Harry R. ". . . And Visions of Royalties Danced in Their Heads," *Museum News,* 52:1 (September 1973), pp. 22-25.♦ Discusses licensing.

"Art Dealers Condemn Booming Reproduction Business," *AVISO,* 1 (January 1979), p. 2.♦ Formal statement issued by Art Dealers Association of America deploring increasing manufacture and promotion of reproductions of works of art by museums and those affiliated with museums. Copies of complete statement available from the Association, 575 Madison Avenue, New York, New York 10022.

"Charging for Admission," *Museums Journal,* 69:3 (December 1969), pp. 131-132. ♦ Session at Annual Conference of the Museums Association, Leicester, 1969. Articles by Francis Cheetham and Marshall A. Cubbon.

Davies, Martin; T. A. Walden; and Andrew Wright. "Charging for Admission," *Museums Journal,* 71:3 (December 1971), pp. 119-124.♦ Pros and cons of admission charges and a resolution on museum admission charges.

De Borhegyi, Stephan; Ralph Weil; and Donald G. Herold. "Museum Sales Desks—Tourist Traps and/or Educational Tools," Midwest Museums Conference *Quarterly,* 24:4 (Fall 1964), pp. 4-7.

Faul, Roberta. "Licensing Programs—A Second Life for Museum Collections," *Museum News,* 54:2 (November/December 1975), pp. 26-33.♦ Discusses licensing items from museum collections for merchandising reproductions.

Grove, Kay. "Museum Cookbooks: For Fun and Profit," *Museum News,* 53:9 (June 1975), pp. 52-59.

"Guidelines for Museum Reproductions," *AVISO,* 5 (1979), p. 5. ♦ Four guidelines for manufacture and promotion of reproductions issued by Association of Art Museum Directors, and statement regarding proliferation

of reproductions. Text and copies of other resolutions available from the Association, P.O. Box 10082, Savannah, Georgia 31412.

Hodupp, Shelley, ed. *The Second Shopper's Guide to Museum Stores.* New York: Universe Books, 1978. 192 pp., illus., bibliog. references. ♦ Includes descriptions, illustrations and buying information on products from art, science, history and special museums; arranged by type of product sold; includes index to museums and museum publications.

King, Carol A. "Let's Eat," *Museum News,* 53:9 (June 1975), pp. 44-49.♦ Discusses food service available to visitors and staff; as a place of entertainment, cultural or educational experience; and as a source of income.

Krahel, David H. "Why a Museum Store?" *Curator,* XIV:3 (September 1971), pp. 200-204.

Morrison, William. "A Museum Sales System for the Future," *Museum News,* 48:4 (December 1969), pp. 22-24.

Munro, Gordon. "Museum Shops from the Outside," *Museums Journal,* 76:4 (March 1977), pp. 143-145.

Museums Association. *Museum Shops.* Information Sheet no. 22. London: The Association, 1978. 16 pp., illus., appendix.♦ A study of museum shops and preparation of guidelines covering objectives; legal position; location, design and display; finance and management; stock and budgetary control; marketing; distribution. Appendix lists museums with shops.

Museums Association. *Reproduction Fees, Photography, etc.: Guidelines for Museums.* Information Sheet no. 20. London: Museums Association, 1975. 12 pp.♦ Addenda insert, 1976, 1 page.

Newcomb, Kathleen K. *The Handbook for the Museum Store: A Reference for Museum Store Managers and Personnel.* Virginia Beach, Va.: Museum Publications, c1977. 51 pp., illus.♦ Includes information on location, size, personnel, budgeting and merchandise. Available from Museum Publications, Box 584, Virginia Beach, Virginia 23451.

Newcomb, Kathleen K. "The Museum Store: Organization and Sales Techniques," *History News,* 23:6 (June 1968), Technical Leaflet no. 46.

Newcomb, Kathleen K. "Outdoor Museum Shops." In *Papers, 64th Annual Meeting, American Association of Museums* (San Francisco, Calif.: 1969), pp. 102-105.

Nickelsberg, Arnold. "The Role of Museum Publishing Programs." In *Section Papers, 63rd Annual Meeting, American Association of Museums* (New Orleans, La.: May 1968), pp. 53-56.♦ Discusses benefits of a good museum publications distribution program to publicize museum in general and to increase museum shop potential.

Peel, Arthur J. *How to Run a Gift Shop.* Rev. ed. Newton Center, Mass.: Charles T. Branford Co., 1953. 152 pp., illus.

Reibel, Daniel B. "Visitor-Financed Programs," *Museum News,* 55:7 (July/August 1977), pp. 27-30.

Rushton, Brian H. "Producing and Selling a Quality Service to Education—Slides," *Museum News,* 46:5 (January 1968), pp. 27-32.

Scher, Lee T. "Museum Sales Shops and the IRS," *Museum News,* 49:10 (June 1971), pp. 20-23.

Sekers, David. "The Educational Potential of the Museum Shop," *Museums Journal,* 76:4 (March 1977), pp. 146-147.

"A Shopper's Guide," *Museum News,* 53:4 (December 1974), pp. 37-39.♦ Visual potpourri of gift items available in museum shops.

"Shops and Sales Desks: The Museum Shop as an Educational Service," *Museum News,* 46:4 (December 1967), pp. 32-39.

Thoma, Marna. "A Salaried Museum Shop: Past and Future." In *Papers, 64th Annual Meeting, American Association of Museums* (San Francisco, Calif.: 1969), pp. 106-108.

Zelermyer, Rebecca. *Gallery Management.* Syracuse, N.Y.: Syracuse University Press, 1976. 159 pp., illus.♦ Guide on opening and managing art galleries; sample forms for keeping necessary controls, directions for inventory, daily sales, receiving materials; section on publicity. Adaptable to museum gift shop operation.

NOTES

Museum Store Association, Inc., c/o Ms. Sydney Boisbrun, Administrative Secretary, 260 Cherry Lane, Doylestown, Pennsylvania 18901. Founded in 1955, the Association is a nonprofit organization formed to stimulate the retail selling of museum-related merchandise, and to encourage an exchange of ideas and friendship among museum store managers, publishers, wholesalers and producers of museum store merchandise. Membership is open to volunteer workers and employees of nonprofit museums, and to museum suppliers. The Association acts as a clearinghouse for procedural information, assists in upgrading museum store merchandise, and sponsors regional workshops and an annual convention. It publishes a *Newsletter,* and summary reports of the annual meeting.

Museum Store Association Newsletter. 1955, 3/yr., membership. Museum Store Association, c/o Ms. Sydney Boisbrun, Administrative Secretary, 260 Cherry Lane, Doylestown, Pennsylvania 18901.

Grants

Grantsmanship

Abarbanel, Karin. "Using the Grants Index to Plan a Funding Search," *Foundation News,* 17:1 (January/February 1976), pp. 44-53.

Alderson, William T. "Securing Grant Support: Effective Planning and Preparation," *History News,* 27:12 (December 1972), Technical Leaflet no. 62.

Annual Register of Grant Support. Orange, N.J.: Academic Media, 1969-. 1 vol.♦ Comprehensive directory of fellowships, grant support programs of government agencies, foundations, and business and professional organizations. Imprint varies. Current edition, 12th, 1978-79; Chicago: Marquis Who's Who Books.

Belcher, Jane C., and Julia M. Jacobsen. *A Process for Development of Ideas.* Washington, D.C.: Government Relations Office, c1976. 152 pp. in various pagings, bibliog.♦ Suggests ways to develop and evaluate ideas within the organization prior to seeking funds; includes proposal writing, lists of source materials, criteria used by various funding sources for reviewing proposals. Available from Government Relations Office, 4416 Edmunds Street, N.W., Washington, D.C. 20007.

Bryant, Mavis. *Writing Grants.* Austin, Tex.: Texas Association of Museums, 1978. 7 pp. ◆ Outline of grant writing for the novice in the field.

Church, David M. *Seeking Foundation Funds.* New York: National Public Relations Council of Health and Welfare Services, Inc., 1966. 39 pp., bibliog. ◆ Essentials of grantsmanship, where to find information about foundations, and how to approach them.

Conrad, Daniel Lynn, et al. *The Grants Planner: A Systems Approach to Grantsmanship.* San Francisco, Calif.: Institute for Fund Raising, c1976. 273 pp., forms, bibliog.

Dermer, Joseph, ed. *How to Get Your Fair Share of Foundation Grants.* New York: Public Service Materials Center, c1973. 143 pp.◆ Includes researching foundations, evaluating chances with foundations, approaching foundations; ten steps to long term foundation relationships; and writing the foundation proposal.

Dermer, Joseph. *How to Write Successful Foundation Presentations.* New York: Public Service Materials Center, c1974. 80 pp.

Dermer, Joseph. *The New How to Raise Funds from Foundations.* 3rd ed. New York: Public Service Materials Center, 1975. 95 pp.◆ Includes a discussion of the 1969 Tax Reform Act and its implications for grant-seekers.

Des Marais, Philip. *How to Get Government Grants.* New York: Public Service Materials Center, 1975. 160 pp.◆ Includes which federal agencies make grants; how to approach them; writing proposals; preparing a budget; administering grants.

Directory of Research Grants, 1978. Compiled by Betty L. Wilson and William K. Wilson. Phoenix, Ariz.: Oryx Press, 1977 -. 293 pp.◆ Includes grant proposal preparation; bibliography; subject head equivalency list; grant names; sponsoring organizations.

Georgi, Charlotte, and Marianne Roos, eds. *Foundations, Grants and Fund-Raising: A Selected Bibliography.* Los Angeles: Graduate School of Management, University of California at Los Angeles, 1976. 67 pp., index.

Grantsmanship: Money and How to Get It.

2nd ed. Chicago: Marquis, 1978. 47 pp., bibliog., appendices.

Grove, Richard. "Taken for Granted: Notes on the Pursuit of Money," *Museum News,* 29:10 (June 1971), pp. 18-19. ◆ Steps in preparing a good proposal.

Hillman, Howard, and Karin Abarbanel. *The Art of Winning Foundation Grants.* New York: Vanguard Press, 1975. 192 pp.◆ Methods to be used in applying for grants; instructions on how to assess chances; how to write proposals; how to follow through after proposal has been submitted.

Hillman, Howard, and Kathryn Natale. *The Art of Winning Government Grants.* New York: Vanguard Press, c1977. 246 pp., bibliog., index.◆ Includes how-to information, a listing of federal agencies, and a section on information sources.

Katzowitz, Lauren. "Foundation Researching: Buy a Service or Do It Yourself?" *Foundation News,* 14:2 (March/April 1973), pp. 36-48.◆ Includes information on the Taft Information System; Foundation Research Service; and other independent nonprofit agencies such as Funding Sources Clearinghouse, Inc. (Chicago), and the Grantsmanship Center.

Lawson, Douglas M. *Basic Techniques for Approaching Foundations.* New York: Douglas M. Lawson Associates, Inc., 1977. 6 pp. ◆ Practical procedures for securing foundation grants; available from Douglas M. Lawson Associates, Inc., 38 East 51st Street, New York, New York 10022.

Levitan, Donald. *Selected Bibliography on Grantsmanship.* Exchange Bibliography no. 641. Monticello, Ill.: Council of Planning Librarians, 1974. 15 pp.

Levitan, Donald, and Clara A. Bonney. *A Resource Guide of State and Philanthropic Grants Information.* Exchange Bibliography no. 1513. Monticello, Ill.: Council of Planning Librarians, 1978. 25 pp.

MacIntyre, Michael. *How to Write a Proposal.* Washington, D.C.: Education, Training and Research Sciences Corp., 1971. 55 pp., illus.

Margolin, Judith B. *About Foundations: How to Find the Facts You Need to Get a Grant.* New York: Foundation Center, c1975. 38 pp., illus.◆ Includes description of the Foundation

Center and its services, samples of reference materials, and how to get useful facts about foundations.

National Directory of Grants and Aid to Individuals in the Arts, International. By Daniel Millsaps and editors of Washington International Arts Letter. 3rd ed. Washington, D.C.: Washington International Arts Letter, 1976. 221 pp.♦ Categories include government grants, private organization and association sources; architecture, arts management, crafts, museum administration, writing, media work.

Overlan, S. Francis. *Federal Grants: Some Practical Notes on Getting and Spending.* Grant Data Quarterly, Selected Report no. 2. Los Angeles: Academic Media, 1967. 10 pp.

Pino, Lewis N. *Nothing But Praise: Thoughts on the Ties Between Higher Education and the Federal Government.* With an additional essay by Kenneth Boulding. Lincoln, Neb.: Nebraska Curriculum Development Center, 1972. 71 pp. ♦ Contents include project approach and proposal review, federal agencies, effects of federal programs, and long term prospect; also suggests how to resubmit grant proposals.

Taft Products. *The Proposal Writer's Swipe File: Twelve Professionally Written Grant Proposals–Prototypes of Approaches, Styles, and Structures.* Jean Brodsky, ed. Washington, D.C.: Taft Products, 1973. 135 pp.

Taft Products. *The Taft Guide to Fund Raising Literature: An Annotated Bibliography.* Washington, D.C.: 1973. 21 pp.

Taft Products. *Taft Information System: A Method for Keeping Current on Foundations.* Washington, D.C.: 1972 -. 2 vols., looseleafe. ♦ Subscriptions include *Foundation Reporter* (semiannual), descriptions of the country's largest private foundations, indexed; *Trustees of Wealth* (semiannual), information about the backgrounds, interests, and affiliations of individuals with key philanthropic decision-making powers; *News Monitor of Philanthropy* (monthly), looseleaf, news service on new developments, profiles of philanthropists, hints on proposal writing, lists of recently-made grants; *Hot Line News Service* (irregular), late-breaking news on events in the foundation field. Address: 1000 Vermont Avenue, N.W., Washington, D.C. 20005.

Urgo, Louis A. *A Manual for Obtaining Government Grants.* Rev. ed. Boston: Robert J. Corcoran Company, c1972. 29 pp.♦ Originally published in 1969 to supplement source references such as the *Catalog of Federal Domestic Assistance;* current edition reflects experiences with organization-oriented grants ranging from community action agencies to cultural institutions.

White, Virginia P. *Grants: How to Find Out About Them and What to Do Next.* 3rd ed. New York: Plenum Press, 1975. 354 pp., bibliog. references, index.♦ Includes a chapter on grantsmanship which defines the role of the grantsperson.

NOTES

The Grantsmanship Center, 1031 South Grand Avenue, Los Angeles, California 90015. The Center, organized in 1972, is a nonprofit, educational institution whose purpose is to promote excellence in funding programs of merit. The Center provides three services to other private nonprofit and governmental agencies. It conducts small-group training workshops on program planning and development, the identification of appropriate private and public sources of funds, and proposal writing. It publishes The Grantsmanship Center *News* (8/yr., subscription) and an extensive series of reprints of articles that have appeared in the newsletter. The Center also maintains an office in Washington, D.C., for outreach to federal agencies.

The Washington International Arts Letter. 1962, monthly except July and December, subscription. Washington International Arts Letter, Box 9005, 115 5th Street, S.E., Washington, D.C. 20003.

Foundations and Private Philanthropy

Andrews, Frank Emerson. *Foundation Watcher.* Lancaster, Pa.: Franklin and Marshall College, 1973. 321 pp., bibliog.♦ Personal record of his five decades of experience in philanthropy and foundations. Includes reports on Cox Committee of U.S. House of Representatives considering charitable gifts made by corporations, and testimony before House Ways and Means Committee regarding Tax Reform Act of 1969.

Andrews, Frank Emerson, ed. *Philanthropic Foundations.* New York: Russell Sage Foundation, 1956. 459 pp., illus., tables, bibliog.◆ Basic volume in the field; gives overview of foundation operations and problems, including legal, tax and policy implications and a chapter on application for grants.

Andrews, Frank Emerson. *Philanthropic Giving.* New York: Russell Sage Foundation, 1950. 318 pp., illus., maps, bibliog. footnotes.

Aschfeld, Jean A. "The Foundation Gift," *Museum News,* 46:1 (September 1967), pp. 29-31.◆ Reviews foundation support to museums.

Commission on Foundations and Private Philanthropy. *Foundations, Private Giving, and Public Policy; Report and Recommendations.* Chicago: University of Chicago Press, c1970, 1971. 287 pp., bibliog. footnotes.

Commission on Private Philanthropy and Public Needs. *Giving in America: Toward a Stronger Voluntary Sector.* Report of the Commission. . . . Washington, D.C.: The Commission, c1975. 240 pp., bibliog., appendices. ◆ Report of the Filer Commission. Part I—Giving and the "Third Sector", Findings of the Commission; Part II—Toward a Stronger Voluntary Sector, Conclusions and Recommendations. See also Stephen E. Weil article, cited below.

Council on Foundations. *New Directions for the Seventies.* Proceedings, 24th Annual Conference, St. Paul, Minnesota, May 29-June 1, 1973. New York: 1973. 125 pp., illus.

Council on Foundations. *The Public/Private Partnership: Conflict or Cooperation.* Proceedings, 22nd Annual Conference, Montreal, May 18-21, 1971. New York: The Council, 1971. 96 pp.

Cuninggim, Merrimon. *Private Money and Public Service: The Role of Foundations in American Society.* 1st ed. New York: McGraw-Hill, 1972. 267 pp.

Cutlip, Scott M. *Fund Raising in the United States, Its Role in America's Philanthropy.* New Brunswick, N.J.: Rutgers University Press, 1965. 553 pp., illus., biblig.

De Bettencourt, Francis G. *The Catholic Guide to Foundations,* 2nd ed. Washington, D.C.: Guide Publishers, 1973. 170 pp.

De Bettencourt, Francis G. *The Guide to Washington, D.C. Foundations.* 2nd ed. Washington, D.C.: Guide Publishers, c1975. 58 pp. ◆ Directory of private grant-making foundations.

Dermer, Joseph. *Where America's Large Foundations Make Their Grants.* Rev. ed. New York: Public Service Materials Center, 1974. 256 pp.◆ Specifics of grant making by large foundations, and listings of grants given and amount, and purpose for which grants were made.

Dorian, Frederick. *Commitment to Culture: Art Patronage in Europe, Its Significance for America.* Pittsburgh: University of Pittsburgh Press, 1964. 521 pp.

Ford Foundation. *Report of the Study for the Ford Foundation on Policy and Program.* Prepared by the Study Committee. Detroit: The Foundation, 1949. 139 pp.◆ Prepared for the guidance of the foundation in its initiating period, it is an important document of general value.

Foundation Center. *The Foundation Center National Data Book.* Introduction by Carol M. Kurzig. New York: 1977. 2 vols.◆ Vol. 1, alphabetical; vol. 2, geographical by states according to amounts of annual grants awarded. Lists more than 21,000 private foundations with brief profiles including principal officer, assets, amount of grants made and gifts received.

Foundation Center. *The Foundation Center Source Book, 1975/76.* New York: Foundation Center, distr. by Columbia University Press, 1976. 2 vols.◆ Authoritative profiles of major grant-making foundations; includes national and major regional foundations; all grants made in the year of record and statements of policies, programs, application procedures and recent fiscal data. Information has more comprehensive statements of programs and listing of grants than in the *Directory.*

Foundation Center. *The Foundation Center Source Book Profiles.* Edited by Carol M. Kurzig, et al. New York: 1978. 1 vol., looseleaf. ◆ Monthly, in-depth analytical profiles of more than 500 of the largest foundations with national or regional programs. Includes detailed factual breakdown of awards by each foundation in subject area, grant type, and recipient type. Cumulative subject index and updates address changes; available through subscription service.

Foundation Center. *Philanthropic Foundations in the United States: A Brief Description.* New York: The Foundation Center, 1969. 35 pp., illus., bibliog. references.

The Foundation Directory. 7th ed. Edited by Marianna O. Lewis. New York: Foundation Center, 1979. 594 pp., graphs, charts, bibliog., appendices, index.♦ Listings include brief descriptions of purpose and activities; original and full statements of programs as well as comprehensive listings of grants are given in the *Source Book.* Information includes name and address, date and form of organization, names of donors, statement of purpose, description of activities, names of officers and trustees, fiscal profile. Four semiannual supplements.

Foundation 500. New York: D. M. Lawson Associates, 1974 -. 1 vol., annual.♦ Fundraising aid that analyzes and categorizes grants given by the top 500 foundations each year. Data files, giving up-to-date information are also available from D. M. Lawson Associates, 39 East 51st Street, New York, New York 10022. Current edition, 5th, 1979.

Foundation Grants Index. New York: distr. by Columbia University Press, 1972 -. 1 vol., annual.♦ Cumulative annual listing of foundation grants which appeared in *Foundation News;* includes grants of $5,000 or more, recipient, type of project supported, and subject category index. Current edition, 1978.

Fox, Daniel M. *Engines of Culture: Philanthropy and Art Museums.* Madison, Wisc.: State Historical Society of Wisconsin for the Department of History, University of Wisconsin, 1963. 90 pp.♦ Interpretation of the patterns of philanthropy that have developed in connection with art museums during the past 150 years.

Frantzreb, Arthur C. *The Prospects of Philanthropy for Museums.* New York: Frantzreb and Pray Associates, Inc., 1970. 8 pp.♦ Address to New England Conference of American Association of Museums, Mystic, Connecticut.

The Future of Foundations. Fritz F. Heimann, ed. Englewood Cliffs, N.J.: Prentice-Hall, 1973. 278 pp., bibliog. references. ♦ Background papers for the 41st American Assembly at Arden House, Harriman, New York, November 2-5, 1972.

Giving USA: A Compilation of Facts Related to American Philanthropy. New York: American Association of Fund-Raising Counsel, 1959 -. 1 vol., annual.♦ Includes donors and recipients; the volunteer; sources of philanthropy (individuals, bequests, foundations, corporations); areas of philanthropic opportunity; tables and graphs.

Hightower, Caroline. "Financing the Arts," *Museum News,* 54:3 (January/February 1976), pp. 44-47, 72-79.♦ One of the research studies sponsored by the Commission on Private Philanthropy and Public Needs (Filer Commission) as part of its information gathering and data base for a comprehensive report and recommendations issued in December 1975.

Lowry, Wilson McNeil. *The Arts and Philanthropy.* Waltham, Mass.: Poses Institute of Fine Arts, 1963. 19 pp.

Martinson, Jean Ann, comp. *International Grants: 1975 Foundation Grants Index Data Bank.* New York: Foundation Center, c1976. 223 pp., indexes.♦ Lists 870 grants awarded by U.S. foundations to recipients both here and abroad. Three sections include individual grant listings; computer-generated statistics on grants awarded; access to individual grants by five indexes.

National Directory of Arts Support by Private Foundations. By Daniel Millsaps and editors of the Washington International Arts Letter. Volume 3. Washington, D.C.: Washington International Arts Letter, 1977. 264 pp., index.♦ Arts Patronage Series no. 6. Updates and expands previous work in Volume 2, but omits the business corporations section. Business support is included by those entities which have established private foundations as a channel for gifts and grants.

Nielsen, Waldemar. *The Big Foundations.* New York: Columbia University Press, 1972. 475 pp., bibliog. references.♦ Information on 33 largest foundations; details attitudes of the various types; suggests improvements in staffing and communication with museum world.

"Patronage for the Visual Arts," *Art in America,* 55:2 (March-April 1967), pp. 24-55.♦ Articles on patronage and democracy; the federal art program; patronage for Britain's art; patronage in Western Europe; patronage under communism.

Robinson, Daniel D. "Private Philanthropy and Public Needs," *The Journal of Accountancy*, 141:2 (February 1976), pp. 46-54.♦ Summary of recommendations of the Accounting Advisory Committee to the Filer Commission which was formed to answer questions concerning such problems as the assembly of information about the operation of private not-for-profit sector in specific fields.

Struckhoff, Eugene C. *The Handbook of Community Foundations: Their Formation, Development and Operation.* New York: Council on Foundations, c1977 -. 2 vols., looseleaf for updating, bibliog., index.♦ Defines and describes community foundations, their history, development and characteristics. Lists all U.S. and Canadian community foundations as of 1975.

Taft, J. Richard. "Foundations and the Arts," *Cultural Affairs*, 1 (1968)—12 (1971).♦ Regular column on investigations of historical development of philanthropies, and new directions and practical advice. Periodical discontinued.

Taft, J. Richard. *Report to the National Endowment for the Arts: Foundation Giving to the Arts.* Washington, D.C.: 1967. 37 pp.♦ Report on Part I of the study "Analysis of Potential Cooperation between Private Foundations, Local Agencies and the Federal Government in the Arts."

Taft, J. Richard. *Understanding Foundations: Dimensions in Fund Raising.* New York: McGraw-Hill Co., 1967. 265 pp., bibliog.

Weaver, Warren. *U.S. Philanthropic Foundations: Their History, Structure, Management and Record.* 1st ed. New York: Harper and Row, 1967. 492 pp., illus.

Weil, Stephen E. "Private Giving for Public Purposes—The Filer Commission Report: Is It Good for Museums?" *Museum News*, 54:5 (May/June 1976), pp. 32-33, 49-51.♦ Outlines objectives of the report and analysis; and includes the 19 Recommendations of the Filer Commission. See also: Commission on Private Philanthropy and Public Needs, cited above.

Zurcher, Arnold John. *The Management of American Foundations: Administration, Policies, and Social Role.* New York: New York University Press, 1972. 184 pp., bibliog. references.

NOTES

Commission on Private Philanthropy and Public Needs. The Commission was established in November 1973 as a privately initiated, privately funded citizens' panel with two broad objectives; to study the role of both philanthropic giving in the United States and that area through which giving is principally channeled, the voluntary "third sector" of American Society; and, to make recommendations to the voluntary sector, to Congress and to the American public at large concerning ways in which the sector and the practice of private giving can be strengthened and made more effective. Membership was drawn from a broad spectrum of American society; John H. Filer served as chairman. The Commission sponsored in the course of its two years in operation more than 85 studies on various aspects of philanthropy and nonprofit activity, including individual reports on all the major areas of charitable nonprofit activity; extensive analysis of the laws and precedents, in the U.S. and abroad, that govern the practice of philanthropy and "third sector" activity; and reports on philanthropy in five cities in different regions of the country. A report on its findings and recommendations was published in 1975, *Giving in America* . . . (cited above). In 1976 the U.S. Treasury Department established an Advisory Committee on Private Philanthropy and Public Needs to assist them in formulating tax and regulatory policy affecting philanthropic and voluntary organizations, and to consider implementation of the Filer Commission report.

Council on Foundations, 888 Seventh Avenue, New York, New York 10019. Founded in 1949 as the National Committee on Foundations and Trusts for Community Welfare, and subsequently became the National Council on Community Foundations, and in 1964 the Council, it is a nonprofit membership organization for independent, community, and company foundations, and also corporations with philanthropic giving programs. It provides consultative and other services to the membership and prospective members. It sponsors meetings to enable grant-making foundations' trustees, officers and executives to keep abreast of current trends in the various fields of foundation interest and to share experience in the administration of philanthropic funds. The membership is also kept informed of legislative and other developments in the philanthropic field. The Council publishes *Foundation News*, bimonthly; *Annual Report; Report on Status, Community Foundations in the United States and Canada,* annual; *Conference Proceedings,* annual; *Newsletter,* irregular; *Handbook on Community Foundations in the U.S. and Canada* (1977).

Foundation Center, 888 Seventh Avenue, New York, New York 10019. Founded in 1956, the Center was established as a nonprofit education organization to acquire, organize, and disseminate information about foundations and the grants they award; to collect and make available published information about the foundation field and about its relationships to government and society, including historical records and supporting reference in related fields. It operates public reference libraries in New York and Washington, D.C., and field offices in Cleveland and San Francisco. It cooperates with special collections in over 55 libraries and foundation offices in 44 states. The Center conducts an Associates Program for organizations and individuals needing direct and frequent access to foundation information through a subscription service which includes assistance by toll free telephone or by mail and weekly taped bulletins of current information, by ordering cost copies of foundation information returns or compilations of research by library staff, or by requesting custom searches for information. The Center publishes *Annual Report; Foundation Directory; Foundation Center Information Quarterly;* reference sources and indexes; and *COM-SEARCH Printouts* series (annual), a computer-generated listing of foundation grants reported in 54 subject categories of giving.

Foundation News: The Journal of Philanthropy. 1960, bimonthly, subscription. Mail to: Council on Foundations, P.O. Box 783, Old Chelsea Station, New York, New York 10011.♦ First published by the Foundation Center, September 1960-December 1971; continued by the Council on Foundations, and includes supplemental sections of the *Foundation Grants Index* prepared by the Foundation Center.

Philanthropic Digest. vol. 20, 1974, 16/yr., subscription. Brakeley, John Price Jones, Inc., 1100 17th Street, N.W., Suite 709, Washington, D.C. 20036.♦ Lists recent foundation, corporate and individual gifts and grants, provides

fundraising ideas and continuing information on tax law changes and government action relating to philanthropy.

Government

Brademas, John. "The American Museum of the Future: The Federal Role," *Museum News,* 48:1 (September 1969), pp. 14-17.

Bridge, R. Gary. "Cultural Vouchers," *Museum News,* 54:4 (March/April 1976), pp. 20-26.♦ Proposed system of control over federal dollars spent in museums by issuing vouchers to consumers who trade it for services at authorized institutions; institutions would redeem them for cash.

Brimble, Alan. "The Taxpayer as Patron," *Museum News,* 50:3 (November 1971), pp. 18-21.♦ Citizens of St. Louis voted to support their museums.

Broughton, John G. "Keeping the Doors Open with State Money," *Museum News,* 52:4 (December 1973), pp. 26-28.♦ History of funding programs and problems in New York State; emphasizes need and rationale for a comprehensive program of state operating aid to accredited museums.

Burdman, Nancy, and Mark Todd. "State Arts Agency Funding," *Museum News,* 57:1 (September/October 1978), pp. 51-54.♦ A report on museum funding on the state level for the last two years.

Cameron, Duncan F. "New York Museum Aid Program," *Museum News,* 49:8 (April 1971), pp. 27-30.

Coe, Linda, comp. *Folklife and the Federal Government: A Guide to Activities, Resources, Funds and Services.* Publications of the American Folklife Center, no. 1. Washington, D.C.: American Folklife Center, Library of Congress; for sale by U.S. Government Printing Office, 1977. 147 pp., bibliog., index.♦ Descriptions of programs administered by fifteen federal government agencies providing funding, archival resources, and technical assistance for members of ethnic, occupational, and regional groups involved in documenting, presenting, and preserving aspects of their shared cultural heritage; museum administration; folk artists; folklorists; and researchers.

"Congressional Hearings on the Arts and Humanities," *Cultural Affairs,* 10 (Spring 1970), entire issue.♦ Edited versions of major statements of individual witnesses as well as responses to questions given at Congressional hearings on National Foundation on the Arts and Humanities.

Endter, Ellen. "Money for Manpower," *Museum News,* 53:7 (April 1975), pp. 20-21.♦ Federal funds are available and museums are eligible to apply at the local level for temporary assistance.

Federal Funding Guide for Local Governments. Washington, D.C.: Government Information Services, 1976 - 321 pp., index.♦ Layman's guide to the federal aid process and to grant programs for the environment, community and economic development, revenue sharing, housing and transportation. Available from Government Information Services, 752 National Press Building, N.W., Washington, D.C. 20045.

Federal Grants Reporter. By Tersh Boasberg, et al.; executive editor, Richard E. Thompson. Washington, D.C.: Federal Grants Information Center, 1976. 2 vols., looseleaf, indexes.♦ Designed to clarify the administration, management and law of grants, it collects, indexes, analyzes and cross-references all relevant federal grants material. It serves as a resource tool for grantor agency personnel and grants managers, administrators, coordinators, lawyers, and comptrollers. Includes a basic reference guide, and individual chapters for each of the 21 major grant-making federal agencies. Subscription includes the Resource book and six bimonthly supplements per year; Federal Grants Information Center, 1820 Jefferson Place, N.W., Washington, D.C. 20036.

Grove, Richard. "A Progress Report: Federal Legislation and Museums," *Museum News,* 44:7 (March 1966), pp. 33-34.♦ Discussion of federal laws benefitting museums; includes support for research and related activities, National Foundation on the Arts and Humanities, and Elementary and Secondary Education Act.

Hartman, Hedy, comp. *Funding Sources and Technical Assistance for Museums and Historical Agencies.* Nashville, Tenn.: American Association for State and Local History, 1979. 144 pp.♦ Explains purposes and objectives of 103 public programs in 22 different agencies. Includes funding sources; technical assistance; exhibition services; other programs and services; national museum assistance agencies; state and regional museum coordinators.

Hightower, John B. "The Museum Aid Program of the New York State Council on the Arts," *Curator,* X:1 (March 1967), pp. 8-12.

Hightower, John B. "Public Money and a Public Mission for American Museums," *Saturday Review,* 55:33 (August 12, 1972), pp. 48-49.♦ Suggests that direct government support for museums is preferable to dependence on trustees and patrons. Also reprinted in *The Museologist,* 124 (September 1972), pp. 20-24.

Kostelanetz, Lucy. "Museum Aid Revisited," *Museum News,* 50:10 (June 1972), pp. 46-48.

Loar, Peggy, and Elizabeth Olofson. "The Newest Federal Acronym," *Museum News,* 57:5 (May/June 1979), pp. 43-45.♦ Discusses funding for general operating support from the Institute of Museum Services.

"Major Bill Signed by Ford," *AVISO,* 11 (November 1976), p. 3.♦ Brief review of legislation and provisions of the Arts, Humanities and Cultural Affairs Act of 1976; funding for the National Endowments; establishment of the Institute of Museum Services; and establishment of challenge grant programs in the arts and humanities endowments.

"Millions for the Arts"; *Federal and State Cultural Programs, An Exhaustive Report.* By the editors of the Washington International Arts Letter. Arts Patronage Series no. 2. Washington, D.C.: Washington International Arts Letter, c1972. 58 pp.

"Museum Services Act," *Museum News,* 52:2 (October 1973), pp. 53-55.♦ Report on Senate subcommittee hearings on the act; history of the bill; list of supporters; and objections raised by opponents.

National Center for Community Action. *Where the Money Is!: Federal Funding for Community Action Agencies and Non-Profit Organizations.* Washington, D.C.: The Center, c1975. 106 pp.♦ Available from the Center, 1711 Connecticut Avenue, N.W., Washington, D.C. 20009.

National Endowment for the Arts. *New Dimensions for the Arts, 1971-1972.* Washington, D.C.: for sale by U.S. Government Printing Office, 1973. 135 pp., illus.

National Research Center of the Arts, Inc. *State Arts Councils.* Special editors: Janet English Gracey and Sally Gardner. New York: Associated Councils of the Arts, 1972. 80 pp., illus.

National Trust for Historic Preservation. *A Guide to Federal Programs: Programs and Activities Related to Historic Preservation.* A Project of the National Trust for Historic Preservation with the cooperation and assistance of the Advisory Council on Historic Preservation and the Legislative Reference Service, Library of Congress. Principal consultant, Nancy D. Schultz. Washington, D.C.: The Trust, 1974. 398 pp., index.◆ Summary information on more than 200 programs and activities of the federal government related to historical research and the preservation of properties, and also those additional programs and activities that might be of interest or benefit to persons working in those fields. Covers 49 permanent agencies, departments, boards and commissions. It provides a tool for identifying sources of technical and financial aid and a means of obtaining a broad understanding of the federal role in cultural preservation. See also: *A Guide to Federal Programs, 1976 Supplement,* 88 pp. Describes 30 new or substantially revised programs.

National Trust for Historic Preservation of the United States. Office of Preservation Services. *A Guide to State Historic Preservation Programs.* A Project of the Office of Preservation Services of the National Trust for Historic Preservation under the auspices of a grant from the National Endowment for the Humanities, with the cooperation and assistance of the State Historic Preservation Officers and staffs. Researched and compiled by Betts Abel; edited by Jennie B. Bull. Washington, D.C.: Preservation Press, 1976. 533 pp.◆ Includes for each state, preservation frameworks, state historic preservation office, preservation programs; comprehensive compilation of state preservation legislation. Separate sections on each of the states and territories are available.

New York (State). Commission on Cultural Resources. *State Financial Assistance to Cultural Resources: Report.* New York: 1971. 163 pp., illus.◆ Criteria for New York's permanent

program of support for the arts and cultural organizations.

Newton, Michael, and Scott Hatley. *Persuade and Provide: The Story of the Arts and Education Council in St. Louis.* New York: Associated Councils of the Arts, 1970. 249 pp.◆ Story of public support for the Arts and Education Fund in St. Louis.

1975-76 Museum Guide to Federal Programs. Washington, D.C.: Association of Science-Technology Centers, 1975. 157 pp., illus.

O'Connor, Francis V. *Federal Support for the Visual Arts: The New Deal and Now.* Greenwich, Conn.: New York Graphic Society, 1969. 226 pp., charts, graphs, tables, bibliog.◆ Report on the New Deal Art Projects in New York City and state with recommendations for present-day federal support for the visual arts to the National Endowment for the Arts.

Oliver, James A. "State Aid to Museums," *Curator,* VI:2 (1963), p. 108.

"Preservation Funding Sources," *Preservation News,* 16:9 (September 1976), p. 12. ◆ Non-exhaustive list of 17 major historic preservation funding sources that have been revised or made available since the publication of the National Trust for Historic Preservation *Guide to Federal Programs.*

Steinbach, Alice, and Mark D. Selph. "Bond Issue Politics," *Museum News,* 57:5 (May/June 1979), pp. 37-42.◆ Tax-exempt financing through general obligation bonds as a viable source of funding; needs carefully coordinated campaign for passage of a bond issue.

"Testimony ... In Support of Federal Budget Increases for the Arts and Humanities," *Museum News,* 48:7 (March 1970), pp. 26-38.

U.S. Congress. House. Committee on Education and Labor. Subcommittee on Select Education. *Arts, Humanities and Cultural Affairs Act of 1975.* Joint Hearings before the Subcommittee on Select Education of the Committee on Education and Labor, House of Representatives, and the Special Subcommittee on Arts and Humanities of the Committee on Labor and Public Welfare, United States Senate, Ninety-fourth Congress, first session, on H.R.7216 and S.1800 ... November 12, 13, 14, 1975. Washington, D.C.: U.S. Government

Printing Office, 1976. 489 pp., bibliog.♦ Includes "National Report on the Arts," by the National Committee for Cultural Resources," pp. 249-283.

U.S. Office of Education. *Catalog of Federal Education Assistance Programs.* Washington, D.C.: Office of Education, for sale by the Superintendent of Documents, U.S. Government Printing Office, 1972 -. 1 vol., annual.♦ An indexed guide to the federal government's programs offering educational benefits to the American people.

U.S. Office of Management and Budget. Executive Office of the President. *Catalog of Federal Domestic Assistance.* Washington, D.C.: U.S. Government Printing Office, 1965 -. various pagings, annual, indexes.♦ Comprehensive listing and description of domestic programs to assist the American people in furthering their social and economic progress. Each program description includes type of assistance provided, purpose for which it is available, who can apply for it and how they should apply. Includes various programs, activities and services which can be requested or applied for by a state or states, territorial possession, county, city, other political subdivision, grouping or instrumentality thereof; any domestic profit or nonprofit corporation, institution or individual, other than an agency of the federal government. Published in October at the beginning of each fiscal year and updated semiannually. Available by subscription; order from Superintendent of Documents, U.S. Government Printing Office, Washington, D.C. 20402.

Van Meter, Elena C. "A Continuing Look: Federal Aid to Museums," *Museum News,* 45:10 (June 1967), pp. 35-38.

"The Washington Connection," *Museum News,* 54:5 (May/June 1976), entire issue.♦ Focuses on some congressional and federal agency activities which directly influence museum interests. Museums and other nonprofit arts organizations are beneficiaries or victims of decisions made in Washington regarding tax reforms, occupational health and safety standards, employee pension benefits, postal regulations, etc.

Winokur, Deanne. "Dateline: Washington– National Endowment for the Humanities Office of Museum Programs," *History News,* 28:7 (July 1973), pp. 162-163.

Yadon, Vernal L. "Arts Commission Funding: The 1969-70 Record," *Museum News,* 49:3 (November 1970), pp. 13-16.

Yadon, Vernal L. "State Arts Commission Funding 1971-74," *Museum News,* 54:5 (January/February 1975), pp. 38-41, 58.♦ Survey and statistical information on budgeting, grant recipients, appropriations and program success of state commissions.

Yadon, Vernal L. "Whence the Funds?" *Museum News,* 49:7 (March 1971), pp. 19-20.♦ Reviews sources of funding for small museums; need for added federal support even in small amounts.

NOTES

America the Beautiful Fund (ABF), 219 Shoreham Building, Washington, D.C. 20005. The Fund is an environment-oriented, nonprofit organization, supported by private contributions, grants from the National Endowment for the Arts and the Lilly Endowment, Inc., to enrich the quality of the natural, historic, and man-made environment. Since 1965 the Fund has supported over 1000 projects throughout the country in environmental planning, civic design, conservation, recreation, and cultural and historic preservation. In addition to providing technical assistance in planning and fundraising, the ABF offers small grants as seed money to initiate projects. To be eligible, a proposal must demonstrate significant community participation and provisions for matching funds. The Fund will make fewer seed grants as emphasis is placed more on technical assistance, but innovative projects will still be given priority. The ABF also offers an Information Exchange as a clearinghouse for local history and preservation projects. It publishes *Better Times,* a quarterly newsletter.

Federal Surplus Property. The U.S. General Services Administration has amended its regulations to include public and nonprofit tax-exempt museums among those eligible to receive surplus property. A brochure describing the donation programs, identifying the various types of eligible entities, and giving the location of the 54 state surplus property agencies responsible for making determinations of eligibility and distribution of property is available from the Institute of Museum Services, Department of Health, Education and Welfare, Washington, D.C. 20202.

Institute of Museum Services (IMS), Department of Health, Education and Welfare, Room 325-H, 200 Independence Avenue, S.W., Washington, D.C 20202. The Institute was enacted by P. L. 94-462 (October 8, 1976) as part of the Arts, Humanities and Cultural Affairs Act of 1976. The IMS consists of a policy-setting National Museum Services Board and a Director. The Board is composed of 20 members (five ex-officio), 15 of whom are appointed by the President with the advice and consent of the Senate, and the Director, appointed and confirmed the same way, serves at the pleasure of the President. The purpose of the act and the Institute is to encourage and assist museums in their educational role, to assist museums in modernizing their methods and facilities, and to ease the financial burden borne by museums as a result of their increasing use by the public. A booklet, "Application for Grants," is available from the IMS office.

National Endowment for the Arts (NEA), 2401 E Street, N.W., Washington, D.C. 20506. The National Endowment for the Arts was created by Congress in 1965 as part of the National Foundation on the Arts and the Humanities. The National Council on the Arts is the advisory body for the NEA. Its goals are to make the arts more widely available; to preserve our cultural heritage; to strengthen cultural organizations; and to encourage creative development of talent. Grants are awarded as fellowships or matching grants in the fields of architecture and environmental arts, dance, education, expansion arts, crafts, folk arts, literature, museums, music, public media, theatre, and the visual arts. The NEA also awards grants to state arts agencies and regional arts groups who work closely with the Endowment in developing arts programs in their areas. Ten regional coordinators serve as direct contact between the agency and the field and provide Endowment information and consultative services to cultural institutions, individuals, and state agencies. NEA publishes *The Cultural Post* (1975, bimonthly, free), covering news from NEA, reports of cultural groups, suggestions for meeting mutual problems, and philosophical viewpoints. Grant application guidelines and information leaflets are available from the Program Information Office, Mail Stop 550, Washington, D.C. 20506.

National Endowment for the Humanities (NEH), 806 15th Street, N.W., Washington, D.C. 20506. The National Endowment for the Humanities was created by Congress in 1965 as part of the National Foundation on the Arts and Humanities. The National Council on the Humanities is the advisory body for NEH. According to the act, the humanities include the following fields: history, history and criticism of the arts, archeology, comparative religion, philosophy, languages, linguistics, literature, jurisprudence, ethics, and those aspects of the social sciences employing an historical or philosophical approach to problems. To encourage and support national progress in the humanities, the Endowment operations are conducted through six divisions, and the Challenge Grant Program: Research Grants; Fellowships; Education Programs; Public Programs; State Programs; and, Special Programs which includes Youth Programs and Special Projects. The Challenge Grant Program was authorized by the Arts, Humanities and Cultural Affairs Act of 1976, and was designed to stimulate increased non-federal support for humanities institutions by offering one federal dollar for every three dollars raised in the private sector. The Endowment's programs serve a variety of constituencies including individuals and nonprofit organizations and institutions such as colleges and universities, education, cultural, professional and community groups, public agencies, radio and television stations. Museums, historical organizations and libraries may receive support from several divisions of the Endowment as well as from State Committees. The Endowment makes three types of grants: outright grants, gifts and matching grants, and combined grants. It publishes a newsletter, *Humanities* (irregular). Brochures and calendar of application dates are available from the NEH Public Information Office.

National Foundation on the Arts and Humanities. The Foundation was established in 1965 by P.L. 89-209 to promote progress and scholarship in the humanities and the arts in the United States. It established the Foundation; the National Endowment for the Arts; and, the National Endowment for the Humanities. It also transferred the National Council on the Arts (established by the National Arts and Cultural Development Act of 1964) to the NEA, and established the Federal Council on the Arts and Humanities.

National Historical Publications and Records Commission, National Archives Building, Washington, D.C. 20408. In 1934, Congress established the National Historical Publications Commission for purposes of promoting the collection and publication of papers of outstanding citizens of the U.S. and other documents as may be important for an understanding and appreciation of the history of the United States. From 1954 to 1964, the Commission functioned in accordance with a program that required it to cooperate with, and encourage governmental and private bodies in collecting and preserving historical source materials, and to plan and recommend historical works and collections of source materials. Since 1964, the Commission has had a more active role in preserving documentary source materials, has allocated grants to federal, state and local agencies, and to nonprofit organizations and institutions. In 1974 the name of the Commission was redesignated to include Records, and its membership and authorization of appropriations were increased The Commission makes plans, estimates, and recommendations for the compilation of historical works and collections of source materials that it considers appropriate for printing or recording at public expense; allocations are made to federal agencies and grants to state and local agencies and to nonprofit organizations and institutions for these purposes. The Commission operates primarily through a national historical publications program, and a national historical records program. Outright, matching, or combined grants may be made; brochures outlining the programs and procedures for applications and grants are available from the Commission.

National Museum Act, Arts and Industries Building, Room 1463, Smithsonian Institution, Washington, D.C. 20560. The objectives of the National Museum Act of 1966, as amended, are to make possible a continuing study of museum problems and opportunities, both in the U.S. and abroad; to encourage research on museum techniques; and to provide support for training career employees in museum practices. Programs offered under the Act are: Professional Training in Conservation and Museum Practices; Special Studies and Research in Conservation and Museum Techniques; Professional Assistance in Conservation and Museum Practices. The Act is administered by the Smithsonian Institution; an Advisory Council of eleven museum profes-sionals assists in establishing the policies governing the grant programs and in evaluating projects for which support is requested. Projects must be of substantial value to the museum profession as a whole, must contribute to the improvement of museum methods and practices, or to the professional growth of individuals entering or working in the museum field. Guidelines are available from the National Museum Act Office.

Business

American Council for the Arts. *A Guide to Corporate Giving in the Arts.* Edited by Susan Wagner. New York: The Council, 1978. 402 pp.♦ Lists 359 corporations and their foundations. Corporation profiles include areas of corporate giving, recent support to arts organizations, activities eligible for support, total contributions budget, and whom to contact.

Brownrigg, W. Grant. *Corporate Fund Raising: A Practical Plan of Action.* New York: American Council for the Arts, 1978. 72 pp., appendix.♦ Discusses phases of fundraising from market identification to post-campaign mop-up.

Buechner, Thomas S. "Corporate Giving and the Arts," *Museum News,* 41:1 (September 1962), pp. 16-20.♦ See also: Part II, *Museum News,* 41:2 (October 1962), pp. 16-20.

Business Committee for the Arts. *Business and the Arts: A Question of Support.* New York: The Committee, n.d. 8 pp.♦ Guidelines for businessmen who support or are contemplating support of the arts.

Business Committee for the Arts. *5,123 Examples of How BCA Companies Supported the Arts in '78 & '79.* New York: The Committee, 1979. 44 pp.

Business in the Arts '70. Gideon Chagy, ed. New York: P. S. Eriksson, Inc., 1970. 176 pp., illus., appendices, index.♦ Summarizes history of business patronage in the arts: a survey of corporate activity, noteworthy programs, and guidelines for formulating programs.

Chagy, Gideon. *The New Patrons of the Arts.* New York: H. N. Abrams, Inc., 1973. 128 pp., illus.♦ Develops the case for a natural continuation of historic support of the arts by commerce and industry.

Council for Financial Aid to Education. Division of Research. *Aid-to-Education Programs of Some Leading Business Concerns.* 7th ed. New York: Council for Financial Aid to Education, Inc., 1970. 183 pp.

Dunlop, Susan. "Corporate Funding of Canadian Museums," *gazette,* 12:1 (Winter 1979), pp. 28-33.

Eells, Richard. *The Corporation and the Arts.* New York: Macmillan, 1967. 365 pp., bibliog. notes.♦ Development of a comprehensive rationale for corporate support of the arts.

Elicker, Paul H. "Commentary—Why Corporations Give Money to the Arts," *Museum News,* 56:6 (July/August 1978), pp. 5-6.♦ Reprinted from *Wall Street Journal,* March 31, 1978, p. 15.

Fremont-Smith, Marion R. *Philanthropy and the Business Corporation.* New York: Russell Sage Foundation, c1972. 110 pp., bibliog. references.

Gingrich, Arnold. *Business and the Arts: An Answer to Tomorrow.* New York: P. S. Eriksson, 1969. 141 pp., illus., bibliog., appendices, index.♦ Four parts: background, rationale, opportunities and examples, outlook.

Gingrich, Arnold. "Business and the Arts, II: A Concern for Public Man," *Cultural Affairs,* 5 (1969), pp. 13-17.

Hunter, Sam. *Art in Business: The Philip Morris Story.* Sponsored by the Business Committee for the Arts. New York: Harry N. Abrams, Inc., 1979. 200 pp., index.

Klepper, Anne, and Kathryn Troy. *Annual Survey of Corporate Contributions, 1977.* Report no. 759. New York: The Conference Board, 1979. 48 pp., tables.♦ Begun in 1976; annual compilation of statistical data and text on where corporate charitable dollars go, with a special section on culture and art. Supersedes *Biennial Survey of Company Contributions.*

Loustau, Nicolie Roscoe. "Corporate Philanthropy and Art Museums," *Curator,* XX:3 (1977), pp. 215-226.♦ Discusses kinds of company support for the arts and museum benefits, and includes references.

Lowry, W. McNeil. "Business and the Arts, I: A Two-Way Partnership," *Cultural Affairs,* 5 (1969), pp. 9-12.

Moonman, Eric, and David Alexander. *Business and the Arts.* London: Foundation for Business Responsibilities, 1974. 11 pp.♦ Two papers on should industry subsidize the arts, and business and the arts—the case against business support.

National Directory of Arts Support by Business Corporations. By Daniel Millsaps and editors of the Washington International Arts Letter. 1st ed. Washington, D.C.: Washington International Arts Letter, 1978. 221 pp.♦ Lists 703 main bodies, 2812 affiliates, divisions and subsidiaries, addresses, names of officers, areas of support. Arts Patronage Series no. 7.

Neiswender, Barbara Hodgins. "Launching a Corporate Membership Program," *Museum News,* 55:7 (July/August 1977), pp. 24-26.

Reiss, Alvin H. "Business: BCA, the First Act," *Cultural Affairs,* 5 (1969), pp. 38-39. ♦ Business Committee for the Arts (BCA).

Reiss, Alvin H. "Business: Rhyme or Reason," *Cultural Affairs,* 4 (1968), pp. 42-44.♦ Examples of business support for the arts.

Reiss, Alvin H. "Business: The Hero at Income Gap," *Cultural Affairs,* 8 (1969), pp. 43-44.♦ Labor's potential as an arts benefactor.

Reiss, Alvin H. "Business: Visual Aid," *Cultural Affairs,* 7 (1969), pp. 36-37.♦ Suggests that corporations should work with arts organizations to develop and circulate their exhibitions for publicity.

Reiss, Alvin H. *Culture and Company.* New York: Twayne Publishing, 1972. 309 pp., bibliog.♦ Analysis of relationship between business and arts groups during a decade of social upheaval, and a blueprint for future planning. Includes arts power, scale of business exploitation, cultural tokenism, commercial business—arts partnerships, new arts programming, the influence of government, labor and minority groups, stockholders influence on corporate social activity, and the fragile arts economy.

Stanton, Frank. "Art: An Integral Part of Corporate Life." In *The Arts: A Central Element of a Good Society* (New York: Arts Councils of America, 1966?), pp. 25-30.♦ Emphasizes importance of arts to business whose support can be through philanthropic aid and through direct acquisition and direct involvement.

The State of the Arts and Corporate Support. Gideon Chagy, ed. New York: P. S. Eriksson, 1971. 184 pp., illus., bibliog.♦ Series of essays on corporate patronage, state of the arts, arts administration, public relations.

Thomas, Charles V. "Cultivating Corporate Support." In *Section Papers, 63rd Annual Meeting, American Association of Museums* (New Orleans, La.: May 1968), pp. 112-115.

Watson, John H., III. *20 Company-Sponsored Foundations: Programs and Policies.* New York: National Industrial Conference Board, 1970. 84 pp.

NOTES

Business Committee for the Arts (BCA), 1501 Broadway, 26th Floor, New York, New York 10036. Founded in 1967, the Committee consists of industrial, corporate, and business leaders of the United States. Membership is by invitation with effort made to maintain distribution by type of industry or business and geographical location. To stimulate support of the arts by the business community, the Committee obtains and interprets existing research and statistical analysis pertaining to support of the arts; provides expert counseling services for corporations interested in starting or expanding programs relating to the arts; keeps corporations informed of opportunities for support of the arts and informs the artistic community about what corporations are doing in the field; helps cultural organizations increase their effectiveness in gaining support from business and industry, and encourages active participation of more businessmen in groups concerned with the advancement of the arts; speaks for business in cooperative endeavors with government and private agencies concerned with the arts. It publishes *Arts/Business* (monthly), newsletter; *BCA News* (quarterly); *Business in the Arts* (annual); informational brochures.

The Conference Board, 845 Third Avenue, New York, New York 10022. Founded in 1916 as The National Industrial Conference Board (1916-1970), it is comprised of business organizations, trade associations, government bureaus, libraries, labor unions, colleges and universities, and individuals. It is a fact-finding institution which conducts research and publishes studies on business economics and management experience. It conducts conferences, courses and seminars; serves as an information source for members; disseminates research data to the public; maintains a library, and maintains an office in Ottawa, Canada. It publishes periodicals, proceedings, statistics, and bulletins.

8

Tax, Law, and Insurance

Outside the ken of the staff of most historical organizations are the highly complex fields of taxes, law, and insurance. In truth, there are few specialists in these fields who can relate specifically to the problems of nonprofit educational institutions. Thus the references cited in this chapter have a special value, for they can light the way to some understanding of the problems as well as their potential solutions.

This is not to suggest that the law is a do-it-yourself field; it does suggest that the well-rounded administrator can give an assist through the cited references to the lawyer who is not a specialist in the not-for-profit area. Here are references to tax exemption, organization, civil rights, art law and the protection of cultural property, federal regulatory practices, contracts and agreements, historic preservation law, and more. Special attention should be given to the Note at the end of the second section, for the publications and courses of study on legal problems of museum administration offered by the American Law Institute-American Bar Association may be the key to fuller understanding.

Property damage, liability, fire and theft, fidelity, medical, and retirement insurance are only some of the subjects covered in the references in section three. Most focus on special cases and problems related to historical organizations. But insurance planning is complex and requires continual review; the assistance of a specialist is advised.

Tax

Advisory Council on Historic Preservation. "Historic Preservation and the Tax Reform Act of 1976," *Report: Compliance Issue,* 5:1 (January-February 1977), pp. 13-16. ◆ Review of tax incentives to encourage preservation of historic structures, prepared by the National Register office for general information purposes only. Material has not been reviewed by Internal Revenue Service; recommended that a tax lawyer be consulted before using any of the tax advantages outlined.

Alderson, William T. "Tax Reform Act," *History News,* 25:5 (May 1970), pp. 108-109.

Art Works: Law, Policy, Practice: Materials and Commentary. Edited by Franklin Feldman and Stephen E. Weil. New York: Practising Law Institute, c1974. 1241 pp., bib-liog., index. ◆ Extensive analysis of source materials relating to newly emerging field of art law; includes purchase and sale of art works, transport, insurance, lending, tax aspects, civil and criminal liabilities, statutes, decisions, treaties, legislative materials, forms, agreements and related documents.

Berlin, Roisman & Kessler. *Law and Taxation: A Guide for Conservation and Other Nonprofit Organizations.* Washington, D.C.: The Conservation Foundation, 1970. 47 pp.

Bolton, Howard A. "How to Avoid Taxes," *Museum News,* 52:1 (September 1973), pp. 26-30. ◆ Discusses the effect of revenue-producing activities on tax-exempt status; liability for federal, state and local taxes; classification as public or private museum; avoiding expensive pitfalls when making money.

Bromberg, Alan R. "Museum: The Legal View and Its Tax Implications," *Museum News*, 44:6 (February 1966), pp. 21-27. ✦ General investigation of museum taxes and the view of the courts concerning museum tax status. Also surveys major taxes and the interpretations given to them.

"Charitable Contributions," *Museum News*, 47:2 (October 1968), p. 17. ✦ Review of tax benefits of charitable contributions, and difficulty in determining fair market value.

Dickenson, Victoria. "Museums and Taxes," *gazette*, 9:4 (Fall 1976), pp. 29-34. ✦ A primer for the Canadian museum worker on tax exemption; appendix of Regional Customs Offices addresses; appendix of a sample form for certification by purchaser.

Dolph, W. E., Jr. "Tax Deductibility and Other Legal Problems," *Western Museums Quarterly*, 4:4 (December 1967), pp. 6-9.

"Exempt Organizations and Their Unrelated Business Income," *Museum News*, 47:10 (June 1969), pp. 15-18. ✦ Refers to Internal Revenue Service regulations.

"Exempt Organizations and Their Unrelated Business Tax," *Museum News*, 48:6 (February 1969), pp. 17-21.

"For the Record . . . Statement Regarding the Effect on U.S. Museums of the Internal Revenue Code," *Museum News*, 51:10 (June 1973), pp. 48-50. ✦ Statement before House Ways and Means Committee regarding effect on museums of the Code, and in particular, the Tax Reform Act of 1969.

Kahn, Douglas A., et al. *Federal Taxation of Estates, Gifts, and Trusts.* Philadelphia: American Law Institute-American Bar Association Committee on Continuing Professional Education, 1975-1979. 974 pp. ✦ Includes 1977 and 1979 paperbound supplements with cover amendments to the gratuitous transfer tax and income tax law of 1978. Main text provides concise explanation of the basic principles of estate and gift taxation and income taxation of trusts.

Liles, Kenneth H. "New Tax Incentives' for Museums," *Museum News*, 45:9 (May 1967), pp. 13-19. ✦ Discusses interpretation of museum structures as publicly supported according to amount and source of support.

McGrath, Kyran M. "Deductibility of Membership Dues," *Museum News*, 47:4 (December 1968), pp. 28-29.

McGrath, Kyran M. "Museums and the Tax Reform Act of 1969," *Museum News*, 48:1 (September 1969), pp. 27-29.

McGrath, Kyran M. "The 1969 Tax Act: Questions and Answers," *Museum News*, 49:5 (January 1971), pp. 21-27.

Milrad, Aaron M., and Ella M. Agnew. "Gifts to Museums, or Do We Look a Gift Horse in the Mouth," *gazette*, 8:1 (Winter 1975), pp. 25-27. ✦ Implications of tax laws on gifts (Canadian).

Murphy, Susan D. "The 1976 Tax Reform Act: It Could Have Been Worse," *Museum News*, 55:7 (July/August 1977), pp. 30-33. ✦ Reviews several provisions affecting charitable donations.

National Trust for Historic Preservation. Office of Real Estate and Legal Services. *Tax Memo: Impact of the Tax Reform Act of 1976 on the Preservation of Historic Properties.* Washington, D.C.: The Trust, January 1977. 19 pp. ✦ Describes the provisions of the Tax Reform Act of 1976 that relate to the preservation of historic property and the conservation of scenic property. Prepared by the Trust counsel as an explanation for persons other than attorneys.

Pearson, Leonard. "The Donor and the Internal Revenue," *Western Museums Quarterly*, 6:2-4 (February 1970), pp. 11-13.

Scher, Lee T. "Legal Notes: On Fund Raising," *Museum News*, 50:4 (December 1971), pp. 14-15. ✦ Some Internal Revenue Service guidelines concerning travel programs and charitable events as fundraisers for museums.

Scher, Lee T. "Museum Sales Shops and the IRS," *Museum News*, 49:10 (June 1971), pp. 20-23. ✦ Gift shop operation must be considered a trade or business which is substantially related to the exercise or performance of exempt functions.

Sievers, Michael A. "To Appraise or Not to Appraise," *Museum News*, 53:7 (April 1975), pp. 18-19, 27. ✦ Discusses abuse of charitable income tax deductions and outlines problems that accompany museum appraising of donations and suggests use of outside experts.

A Tax Guide for Artists and Arts Organizations. Edited by Herrick K. Lidstone. Lexington, Mass.: D.C. Heath, Lexington Books, 1978. 400 pp. ◆ Focuses upon qualifications for exemption from income tax, the allowability of charitable deductions in the context of supporting the arts, the limits of political activities, business activities of exempt organizations, and periodic filing requirements.

Tax Impacts on Philanthropy. Symposium conducted by the Tax Institute of America, December 2-3, 1971, Washington, D.C. By Douglas Dillon and others. Princeton, N.J.: Tax Institute of America, 1972. 234 pp., bibliog. references. ◆ Contents: Role of Private Philanthropy; The Treasury Viewpoint on Impact of 1969 Legislation on Philanthropy; Trends in Philanthropic Giving and Receiving as Affected by the Tax Reform Act of 1969; Effects of Tax Reform Act of 1969 on Role of Private Foundations; Support of Private Philanthropy through the Federal Income Tax Laws.

Tax Problems of Non-Profit Organizations, 1970: *Effects of the Tax Reform Act.* Edited by George D. Webster and William J. Lehrfield. New York: Journal of Taxation, Inc., 1970. 367 pp., bibliog. references. ◆ Papers presented at the Sixth Annual Conference on Tax Problems of Non-Profit Organizations, held in Washington, D.C., February 27-28, 1970, expanded and updated by the authors plus additional material. Available from Journal of Taxation, Inc., 125 East 56th Street, New York, New York 10022.

"Tax Reform Act of 1969," *Museum News,* 48:6 (February 1970), pp. 29-30.

Teitell, Conrad. "Life Income Plans." In *Section Papers, 63rd Annual Meeting, American Association of Museums* (New Orleans, La.: May 1968), pp. 104-111. ◆ Discusses deferred gifts and tax benefits under life income plans.

Treusch, Paul E., and Norman A. Sugarman. *Tax-Exempt Charitable Organizations.* Philadelphia: American Law Institute-American Bar Association Committee on Continuing Professional Education, 1979. 558 pp., tables, appendix, index. ◆ Discusses historical development and construction of the controlling legal concepts in the tax statutes of 1969 and 1976, and in the various regulations, rulings and decisions, past and present, affecting tax-exempt organizations. Includes:

initial qualification of a charitable organization; tax on unrelated business income; private foundations; special organizations; procedure for obtaining public charity status.

U.S. Department of the Interior. Heritage Conservation and Recreation Service. *Information: Technical Corrections to the Tax Reform Act of 1976; Rehabilitation & the Revenue Act of 1978.* Washington, D.C.: November 1978. 2 pp.

U.S. Internal Revenue Service. *How to Apply for Recognition of Exemption for an Organization.* Publication 557, revised October 1976. Washington, D.C.: U.S. Government Printing Office, 1977. 28 pp. ◆ Includes procedures; instructions and sample forms for Articles of Incorporation for exemption under Code Section 501 (c)(3). Also needed, Form 1023, revised periodically, *Application for Recognition of Exemption.* Obtain latest revision of Publication 557 and Form 1023 from nearest Internal Revenue Service office.

U.S. Internal Revenue Service. *Valuation of Donated Property.* Publication 561, revised. Washington, D.C.: U.S. Government Printing Office, 1977. 12 pp. ◆ Includes determining fair market value; making the valuation; appraisals and fees; valuations on various types of property and personal services. Revised periodically; obtain latest revision from nearest Internal Revenue Service office.

Weithorn, Stanley S. *Tax Techniques for Foundations and Other Exempt Organizations.* New York: M. Bender, 1964 -. 1 vol., looseleaf, forms. ◆ Paged by sections and designed for insertion of supplements. Exhaustive volume on federal income, gift, estate and excise taxation as it affects non-profit organizations.

NOTES

Non-Profit Organization Tax Letter. 1964, 18/yr., subscription. Organization Management, Inc., Box 34909, Washington, D.C. 20034. Offices at 13234 Pleasantview Lane, Fairfax, Virginia 22030. Current information on tax-exempt status of organizations including legislative developments, cases and rulings, commentaries, publications, and forecasts.

Philanthropic Digest. vol. 20, 1974, 16/yr., subscription. Brakeley, John Price Jones, Inc., 1100 17th Street, N.W., Suite 709, Washington,

D.C. 20036. Lists recent foundation, corporate and individual gifts and grants, provides fund-raising ideas and continuing information on tax law changes and government action related to philanthropy.

Washington Non-Profit Tax Conference. Annual conference (15th, 1979), sponsored by Organization Management, Inc., Box 34909, Washington, D.C 20034 (13234 Pleasantview Lane, Fairfax, Virginia 22030), for nonprofit organizations and their management and focusing on legislation, judicial decisions, federal tax rulings and practices and including sessions on special problems of museums and galleries. Conference "Speakers Outlines" are published for participants.

Law

American Bar Association. Section of Corporation, Banking and Business Law. Committee on Corporate Law. *Model Non-profit Corporation Act, Revised 1964, with Official Forms and Optional and Alternative Sections.* Practice Handbook D. Philadelphia: Joint Committee on Continuing Legal Education, ALI-ABA, 1964. 119 pp., forms, appendix.

American Law Institute-American Bar Association. Committee on Continuing Professional Education. *Trends in Nonprofit Organizations Law.* Edited by Howard L. Oleck. Philadelphia: The Committee, 1977. 176 pp. ◆ Commentaries on and analyses of current aspects of nonprofit organization law and practice, including such topics as tax exemption, organization, combination, dissolution, external and internal regulation, civil rights matters; parliamentary procedure, kinds of nonprofit organization, and litigation aspects. See also: *Supplement, 1979.*

Amram, Philip W. "The Georgia O'Keeffe Case: New Questions About Stolen Art," *Museum News,* 57:3 (January/February 1979), pp. 49-51ff.

Andrews, F. Emerson, ed. *Legal Instruments of Foundations.* New York: Russell Sage Foundation, 1958. 318 pp., illus., bibliog. ◆ A representative selection of 58 documents from 49 different foundations, and an interpretive introduction. Chapters include Acts of Congress, acts of state legislatures, setting up foundations, wills, trust instruments, corporate

resolutions, certificates of incorporation, constitutions, by-laws, letters of gift, and certain operational documents.

Art Law: Domestic and International. Edited by Leonard D. DuBoff. South Hackensack, N.J.: Fred B. Rothman & Co., 1975. 627 pp., illus., bibliog. references, appendices, indexes. ◆ Compiles numerous scattered doctrines, cases, statutes, and other works; from a two-day conference sponsored by the National Endowment for the Arts, American Society of International Law, Oregon Arts Commission, Northwestern School of Law of Lewis and Clark College, and Oregon Volunteer Lawyers for the Arts. Contents: Counseling the Artist; International Law and the Arts; Authentication of Art.

Art Works: Law, Policy, Practice; Materials and Commentary. Edited by Franklin Feldman and Stephen E. Weil. New York: Practising Law Institute, c1974. 1241 pp., bibliog., index. ◆ Extensive analysis of source materials relating to newly emerging field of art law; includes purchase and sale of art works, transport, insurance, lending, tax aspects, civil and criminal liabilities, statutes, decisions, treaties, legislative materials, forms, agreements and related documents.

Burnham, Bonnie, comp. *The Protection of Cultural Property: Handbook of National Legislations.* Paris: International Council of Museums, 1974. 206 pp., bibliog., appendices. ◆ Assembles, classifies and analyzes in summary form the ensemble of some 145 national legislative texts governing the discovery, ownership, circulation and sale of cultural property. Material is divided in the following categories for each country: title of law, definition of cultural property, rights of ownership and regulation of collectors and dealers, administration, and comments.

Cary, William L.,, and Craig B. Bright. *The Law and the Lore of Endowment Funds: Report to the Ford Foundation.* New York: Ford Foundation, 1969. 82 pp., bibliog. references.

"A Compilation of State Laws Regulating Charities," *Giving USA,* 16 (December 1978), special issue. ◆ Third annual compilation of state legislation, as of December 1978, regulating the solicitation of funds by charitable organizations and professional fundraising counsel and solicitors for 35 states and the District of Columbia. In June of each year the

American Association of Fund-Raising Counsel, Inc., publishes a compilation of pending laws.

DuBoff, Leonard D. *The Deskbook of Art Law.* 1st ed. Washington, D.C.: Federal Publications, Inc., c1977. 1345 pp., bibliog., index.

Duffy, Robert E. *Art Law: Representing Artists, Dealers and Collectors.* New York: Practising Law Institute, c1977. 517 pp., bibliog. references, index. ◆ Updates *Art Works . . . ,* by Weil and Feldman, cited above.

Eaton, Berrien C., Jr., et al. "How to Draft the Charter or Indenture of a Charity so as to Qualify for Federal Tax Exemption: Part I—Charitable Corporations," *The Practical Lawyer,* 8:6 (October 1962), pp. 13-37. ◆ See also: "Part II—Charitable Trusts," 8:7 (November 1962), pp. 87-103.

Federal Bar Association of New York, New Jersey, and Connecticut. *Forgery in Art and the Law; A Symposium.* Edited by Leo M. Draschler and Harry Torczyner. New York: Federal Legal Publications, 1956. 61 pp.

Fellner, Baruch A., and Donald W. Savelson. *Occupational Safety and Health: Law and Practice.* New York: Practising Law Institute, c1976. 417 pp., index. ◆ Includes text of "Occupational Safety and Health Act of 1970," pp. 295-325.

"Foundations, Charities and the Law: The Interaction of External Controls and Internal Policies," *UCLA Law Review,* 13:4 (May 1966), entire issue. ◆ Issue devoted to foundations and the law; nine papers on such subjects as Treasury Department Report on Private Foundations, law of trusts, use for perpetuity, duties and responsibilities of trustees.

Fremont-Smith, Marion R. *Foundations and Government: State and Federal Law and Supervision.* New York: Russell Sage Foundation, 1965. 564 pp., bibliog. footnotes. ◆ Contains a table of the 50 states' legal requirements for charitable trusts.

Grove, Migs. "Volunteer Legal Services for Museums," *Museum News,* 57:5 (May/June 1979), pp. 59-60. ◆ Describes Volunteer Lawyers for the Arts, based in New York City, and lists other VLA organizations in the U.S.

Halpert, Stuart D. *Participation in the Development of Legislative Policy: Some Guidelines for 501(c)(3) Tax-Exempt Organi-*

zations. New York: National Health Council, 1975. 16 pp., bibliog. footnotes. ◆ Focuses on limitations under law on the legislative activities of all those organizations qualifying for tax exemption under Section 501(c)(3) of the IRS Code of 1954 other than private foundations. Available from the Council, 1740 Broadway, New York, New York 10019.

Hollander, Barnett. *The International Law of Art, for Lawyers, Collectors, and Artists.* London: Bowes and Bowes, 1959. 287 pp., bibliog. footnotes.

Hopkins, Bruce R., and John H. Meyers. *The Law of Tax-Exempt Organizations.* Washington, D.C.: Lerner Law Book Co., 1975. 356 pp.

Kettler, Ellen, and Bernard D. Reams, Jr., comps. *Historic Preservation Law: An Annotated Bibliography.* Washington, D.C.: Preservation Press, National Trust for Historic Preservation, 1976. 115 pp., appendices, index. ◆ Includes techniques and case studies, background material and reference, federal, state and local preservation legislation.

Law and the Visual Arts Conference, Portland, Or., 1974. *Law and the Visual Arts.* Leonard D. DuBoff and Mary Ann Crawford DuBoff, eds. Portland, Or.: 1974. 359 pp., bibliog. references. ◆ A conference sponsored by Northwestern School of Law of Lewis and Clark College, American Society of International Law, National Endowment for the Arts, Oregon Arts Commission, Oregon Volunteer Lawyers for the Arts, March 15-16, 1974, Lewis and Clark College, Portland, Oregon. Contents: Counseling the Artist; Artists' Property Rights; Copyright Law, Domestic and International; The Protection of Artistic National Patrimony Against Pillaging and Theft; Museum Acquisition Policies; International Trade in National Art Treasures; Scientific Authentication of Art; The Disposable Past and an Adventure in International Understanding.

Legal and Business Problems of Artists, Art Galleries and Museums: Sources and Materials. By Franklin Feldman and Stephen E. Weil. New York: Practising Law Institute, 1973. 712 pp., forms, bibliog. ◆ Patent, Copyright, Trademark and Literary Property Course Handbook Series, no. 36.

Lindey, Alexander. *Entertainment, Publishing and the Arts: Agreements and the Law; Books, Magazines, Newspapers, Plays, Motion Pictures, Radio and Television, Music, Phono-*

graph Records, Art Work, Photography, Advertising and Publicity, and Commercial Exploitation. New York: Clark Boardman Co., 1963. 2 vols., looseleaf, forms, bibliog. ◆ Supplemented biennially. Contains new forms, practical suggestions, new legal topics, citations, summaries of important cases, law review preferences; Supreme Court decisions on libel, invasion of privacy, free press, etc.; legal aspects of computers; legal aspects of machine copying; legal aspects of community antenna television; impact of taxes on the creative individual; antitrust problems in the field of communication.

McAlee, James R. "The McClain Decision: A New Legal Wrinkle for Museums," *Museum News,* 57:6 (July/August 1979), pp. 37-41. ◆ Result of legal decision indicates that museum staff members engaged in interstate transport of pre-Columbian artifacts could face federal criminal prosecution.

Morrison, Jacob H. *Historic Preservation Law.* 2nd ed. Washington, D.C.: National Trust for Historic Preservation, 1965. 198 pp., illus., bibliog. footnotes, table of cases, index. ◆ References for individuals, organizations, and public officials concerned with maintaining landmarks; compilation of municipal and state statutes, ordinances, court decisions, and enactments.

Morrison, Jacob H. *Supplement to Historic Preservation Law.* New Orleans, La.: The Author, 1972. 98 pp. ◆ Updates first and second editions.

National Trust for Historic Preservation. *Legal Considerations in Establishing a Historic Preservation Organization.* Washington, D.C.: Preservation Press, c1977. 24 pp. ◆ Information sheet on planning and objectives, impact of federal tax laws on nonprofit organizations; descriptions of organization structures (corporate, unincorporated association, "sister organization," charitable trust). Outlines steps in forming an organization, sample articles of incorporation, qualifying for federal income tax exemption, sample bylaws.

Oleck, Howard L. *Non-profit Corporations, Organizations, and Associations.* 3rd ed. Englewood Cliffs, N.J.: Prentice-Hall, 1974. 1000 pp., forms, bibliog. references, index. ◆ Discusses changes in law and practice of nonprofit organizations including Tax Reform Act of 1969 and resulting new regulations and forms, the 1970 Not-For-Profit Corporation Law which repealed Membership Corporations Law of the State of New York, and the Model Non-Profit Corporation Act of the American Bar Association being reviewed. Also includes procedures for organization and management such as articles of incorporation, guidelines for board proceedings and minutes, and various tax considerations.

Oleck, Howard L. *Parliamentary Law for Nonprofit Organizations.* Philadelphia: American Law Institute-American Bar Association, 1979. 160 pp., bibliog., tables, index. ◆ Provides an authoritative, simple set of rules of order and addresses itself to nonprofit organizations in the context of relevant statutory materials and case law. Includes such issues as conflicts of interest and indemnification, liabilities of members, and derivative actions. Chapters cover meetings and notice, mechanics of meetings, motions, ordinary and special motions, debate, voting, voting methods, nominations, elections, committees, officers, directors and members.

Prosser, William L. *Handbook of the Law of Torts.* 4th ed. St. Paul, Minn.: West Publishing Co., 1971. 1208 pp. ◆ Discusses libel, survey of right of privacy.

"Regulations Affecting the Arts." In *Cultural Directory, Guide to Federal Funds and Services for Cultural Activities* (New York: ACA Publications, 1975), pp. 269-282. ◆ Covers major federal regulations affecting the arts and the administrative agencies involved: Department of Justice, Department of Labor, Department of Treasury, FCC, ICC, Library of Congress, U.S. Postal Service.

"Restrictions on Legislative Activities of Non-Profit Organizations," *Museum News,* 47:3 (November 1968), pp. 23-27.

Robert, Henry M. *Robert's Rules of Order Revised.* New York: Morrow, c1915, 1971. 323 pp. ◆ Classic manual on parliamentary law.

Serr, Harold. "Museums and the 1968 Gun Control Act," *Museum News,* 48:3 (November 1969), pp. 22-25.

Silvestro, Clement M. "Articles of Incorporation; Sample Constitution; Sample By-Laws." In *Organizing a Local Historical Society,* rev. ed. (Nashville, Tenn.: American Association for State and Local History, 1968), Appendix I-III.

Simpson, Laurence P. *Handbook of the Law of Contracts.* 2nd ed. St. Paul, Minn.: West Publishing Co., 1965. 510 pp. ◆ Concise treatment of contract law.

"State and Local Laws Governing Museums," Midwest Museums Conference *Quarterly,* 14:4 (October 1954), entire issue. ◆ Survey as of 1954, useful as background information.

Twining and Fisher. *Two Reports on Laws Affecting New York State Museums.* New York: Museum of the City of New York, 1969. 48 pp. ◆ Memorandum of certain statutory laws of the State of New York and the Internal Revenue Code affecting public and private museums, and Memorandum of law pertaining to the labor law of the State of New York as it affects non-profit institutions.

United Nations Educational, Scientific and Cultural Organization. *Index of National Legislations on the Protection of Cultural Heritage.* Paris: 1969. 48 pp.

United Nations Educational, Scientific and Cultural Organization. *Technical and Legal Aspects of the Preparation of International Regulations to Prevent the Illicit Export, Import and Sale of Cultural Property.* Paris: UNESCO, 1962. 11 pp.

U.S. Congress. House. Committee on the Judiciary. Subcommittee on Administrative Law and Governmental Relations. *Oversight on Federal Incorporations.* Hearing before the Subcommittee on Administrative Law and Governmental Relations of the Committee on the Judiciary, House of Representatives, Ninety-fourth Congress, First Session . . . June 11, 1975. Washington, D.C.: U.S. Government Printing Office, 1975. 46 pp., index. ◆ Includes text of "How to Apply for Recognition of Exemption for an Organization," pp. 27-46.

The Visual Artist and the Law. Associated Councils of the Arts, The Association of the Bar of the City of New York, Volunteer Lawyers for the Arts. Rev. ed. New York: Praeger, c1974. 87 pp., forms, bibliog. references.

Wald, Palmer B. "In the Public Interest," *Museum News,* 52:9 (June 1974), pp. 30-32. ◆ Discusses need for procedures and safeguards to insure proper administration and utilization of property held for charitable purposes; property primarily encompasses endowments and collections. Reviews briefly pros and cons of legislative measures, with preference for invoking existing powers of the attorney general and providing a great measure of self-regulation.

Warshaw, Robert S. "Law in the Art Marketplace," *Museum News,* 53:8 (May 1975), pp. 18-23, 50-51. ◆ Reviews two books on art works and the law.

"The Washington Connection," *Museum News,* 54:5 (May/June 1976), entire issue. ◆ Special issue focuses on some congressional and federal agency activities which directly influence museum interests. Museums and other nonprofit arts organizations are beneficiaries or victims of decisions made in Washington such as tax reforms, occupational health and safety standards, employee pension benefits, postal regulations, etc.

Webster, George D. *The Law of Associations: An Operating Legal Manual for Executives and Counsel.* New York: M. Bender, 1975. 891 pp. in various pagings, forms, bibliog., appendices, index. ◆ Updated by supplements. Includes nature of associations, association operation, contracts for meetings, executive employment contract, subsidiary corporations, statistical reporting, ethics, cost accounting, advertising, tax aspects, accounting. Prepared for the American Society of Association Executives, by George D. Webster, its general counsel.

Weil, Stephen E. "If Men Were Angels . . . ," *Museum News,* 56:1 (September/October 1977), pp. 35-41. ◆ Museums must learn to live with good grace in face of the rise of regulations; operations that may have legal consequences include employment and promotion practices, wage and hour law, acquisition policy, copyright, conduct of guards, health and safety practices.

NOTES

ALI-ABA Course of Study on Legal Problems of Museum Administration. The American Law Institute-American Bar Association Committee on Continuing Legal Education has sponsored an annual Course of Study since 1973. It is cosponsored by the Smithsonian Institution with the cooperation of the American Association of Museums. The course is intended to provide those responsible for the administration of museums, as well as their counsel and any other interested lawyers, with an awareness of the legal problems commonly encountered by museums. The emphasis is on practical information and on ways to avoid and solve problems. Questions are considered from an administrator's point of view with an attempt to provide practical insight into day-to-day operations. The course is updated and revised each year to reflect the latest developments and practices; topics include employee relations, acquisition, management and disposal of objects, tax problems, endowment fund management, publications and reproductions, duties and liabilities of trustees and directors, insurance, negligence and other torts, principles and curatorial code of conduct, legislative lobbying, and real estate. Study materials and edited transcripts of the proceedings of the 1973, 1974, 1975 Courses are available from the Committee, 4025 Chestnut Street, Philadelphia, Pennsylvania 19104. The Committee also publishes *ALI-ABA Course Materials Journal* (1976, quarterly), and selected course sessions are tape recorded or videotaped and made available.

Volunteer Lawyers for the Arts, 36 West 44th Street, Suite 1110, New York, New York 10036. Founded in 1969, the Volunteer Lawyers for the Arts (VLA) is a nonprofit organization to assist artists and not for profit organizations who lack the financial ability to retain their own lawyers in dealing with arts-related legal problems. It is funded by the National Endowment for the Arts, the New York State Council on the Arts, individual contributions, and private foundations. Eligible artists and art groups are referred to volunteer attorneys who handle such problems as incorporation, securing tax exemption, negotiating and drafting contracts, and advising on copyright, tax, labor and immigration. Procedures for applying for legal assistance are outlined in a brochure available from the VLA office. The VLA also works to increase the legal profession's awareness of the kinds of arts-related problems and to familiarize them with available solutions. It publishes a newsletter, *Art and the Law* (10/yr.), monographs and pamphlets. It also sponsors workshops for artists and lawyers to discuss legal problems of special interest to both groups, and provides speakers for arts-related topics upon request.

Insurance

Allen, Carl G., and Huntington T. Block. "Should Museums Form a Buyers' Pool for Insurance?" *Museum News,* 52:6 (March 1974), pp. 32-35.♦ Discussion of pros and cons of museum insurance pool.

Art Works: Law, Policy , Practice: Materials and Commentary. Edited by Franklin Feldman and Stephen E. Weil. New York: Practising Law Institute, c1974. 1241 pp., bibliog., index.♦ Analysis of source materials relating to new field of art law; includes insuring works of art.

Babcock, Phillip H. "Insurance: Alternatives to Certificates," *Museum News,* 57:5 (May/June 1979), pp. 56-57.♦ Discusses possibility of simplifying process of borrowing and lending objects by finding alternatives to certificates of insurance.

Block, Huntington T. "Insurance: An Integral Part of Your Security Dollar," *Museum News,* 50:5 (January 1972), pp. 26-29.♦ When physical security system fails, the museum's insurance program is called in. Includes valuation clauses, borrowing objects, and how to buy insurance.

Block, Huntington T., and John B. Lawton. "Insurance." In *Primer on Museum Security* (Cooperstown, N.Y.: New York State Historical Association, 1966), pp. 15-38.

"The British Government's Indemnities Scheme," *ICOM News,* 25:2 (June 1972), pp. 102-103. ♦ Issues indemnities to cover works of art borrowed by British national museums and galleries since British government does not insure, it carries its own risks.

Carmel, James H. "Presentation: Insurance and Protection." In *Exhibition Techniques, Travelling and Temporary* (New York: Reinhold Publishing Corporation, 1962), pp. 174-181.

Concise Explanation of Pension Reform Law, Employee Retirement Income Security Act of 1974 (ERISA). Englewood Cliffs, N.J.: Prentice-Hall, 1974. 96 pp.♦ Major objective of the act is to make qualified pension and profit-sharing plans more fair and effective in providing adequate income to participants upon retirement. Also from same publisher, *Complete Handbook on 1974 Pension Reform Law* (304 pp.).

DuBose, Beverly M., Jr. "Insuring Against Loss," *History News,* 24:5 (May 1969), Technical Leaflet no. 50.

Dudley, Dorothy. "Museum Security: Insurance," *Museum News,* 45:6 (February 1967), pp. 29-31.♦ Describes fine arts policy coverage, insurance reports, purchasing insurance, subrogation, insurance certificates, claims, reporting loss or damage, actual claim, and a summary.

Huebner, Solomon; Kenneth Black, Jr.; and Robert S. Cline. *Property and Liability Insurance.* 2nd ed. Englewood Cliffs, N.J.: Prentice-Hall, 1976. 715 pp., bibliogs., index. ♦ Includes property, fire, marine, and liability insurance.

"Insurance." In *Temporary and Travelling Exhibitions* (Paris: UNESCO, 1963), pp. 105-110.♦ Description of insurance provisions based on policies commonly written for fine arts insurance in Europe and the U.S. Includes bibliography. Museums and Monuments series, no. 10.

"Insurance Policy for Historic Homes," *The Old-House Journal,* 7:2 (February 1979), p. 14. ♦ Discusses St. Paul Insurance Company Historic Home Policy designed to provide reasonable fire insurance coverage for privately owned homes which are either listed on the National Register or in a historic district.

Landais, Hubert. "Museums and Insurance," *ICOM News,* 27:3-4 (1974), pp. 79-82.♦ Discusses insurance on collections and loans.

Lawton, John B., and Huntington T. Block. "Museum Insurance," *Curator,* IX:4 (December 1966), pp. 289-297.

"Loan Agreements, Insurance, Transport, Examination of Works of Art," *Museum,* XXI:3 (1968), pp. 198-202ff.♦ Entire issue devoted to "The Technical Organization of an International Art Exhibition," Expo '67 in Montreal. Includes sample forms, pp. 207-210.

MacBride, Dexter, D., ed. "Appraisals of Objects in Historical Collections," *History News,* 32:7 (July 1977), Technical Leaflet no. 97.♦ Panel of certified appraisers examines seven basic questions of importance to history museums and societies.

McGrath, Kyran M. "Are Your Trustees Pro-

tected?" *Museum News,* 52:6 (March 1974), p. 36. ♦ Describes AAM insurance program for museum trustees.

Mills, Paul Chadbourne. "Insurance: Are Fine Arts Premiums Out of Line?' *Museum News,* 57:5 (May/June 1979), pp. 54-55.♦ Reviews problem of premiums much higher than average paid by other buyers of the same class of insurance with similar loss rates.

Monreal, Luis. "Insurance: Notes," *ICOM News,* 27:3-4 (1974), pp. 76-79. ♦ Includes "ICOM Guidelines for Insurance": general responsibilities and expenses, condition reports, insurance, customs formalities, packing, transport, escorts, physical environment, security, photography and reproduction.

Mowbray, Albert H.; Ralph H. Blanchard; and C. Arthur Williams, Jr. *Insurance, Its Theory and Practice in the United States.* 6th ed. New York: McGraw-Hill, 1969. 661 pp., bibliog.

Museums Association. *An Approach to Museum Insurance.* Information Sheet no. 23. London: The Association, 1978. 8 pp., appendices. ♦ Discusses an overall risk management procedure including identification of risks; measurement of risks; avoidance or reduction, and loss accommodation; risk transfer by insurance; special considerations.

Myers, Gerald E. *Insurance Manual for Libraries.* Chicago: American Library Association, 1977. 64 pp., index.

Nauert, Patricia, and Caroline M. Black. *Fine Arts Insurance: A Handbook for Art Museums.* Washington, D.C.: Association of Art Museum Directors, distr. by American Association of Museums, 1979. 100 pp., appendices, glossary, bibliog. ♦ Contents include risk management, insurance management, responsibility of the museum, policy design, insurance documents, rates and premiums, evaluating policies, procedures for handling loss. Separate chapter on special areas of fragile items, contemporary art, indemnity, U.S. Federal Indemnity Program, and loans. A project of the Fine Arts Insurance Committee of the Association of Art Museum Directors.

Ownbey, Don W. "Are You Properly Insured?" *Western Museums Quarterly,* 4:3 (September 1968), pp. 11-16.

Pfeffer, Irving. "Strategies for Insurance Cost Reduction in Museums," *ICOM News,* 27:3-4

(1974), pp. 82-85.♦ Discusses risk management, alternatives to commercial insurance, catastrophe problem in commercial insurance, efficiency in insurance buying.

Pfeffer, Irving, and Ernest B. Uhr. "The Truth About Art Museum Insurance," *Museum News*, 52:6 (March 1974), pp. 23-31.♦ Report on a major study of art museum insurance undertaken for the Association of Art Museum Directors; concludes that museum losses during 1970-72 were very low.

Pilling, Ronald W. "The Co-Insurance Trap," *The Old-House Journal*, 5:12 (December 1977), pp. 133, 143.

Risk Management Manual. Edited by Irving Pfeffer and Daniel K. Herrick. New York: Association of Art Museum Directors, 1974-. 2 vols., looseleaf ♦ Essays on aspects of insuring museum property. Additions made periodically. Available from the Association, P.O. Box 620, Lenox Hill Station, New York, New York 10021.

Rodda, William H. *Marine Insurance: Ocean and Inland.* 3rd ed. Englewood Cliffs, N.J.: Prentice-Hall, 1970. 522 pp.

Rodda, William H. *The Question-and-Answer Insurance Deskbook.* Englewood Cliffs, N.J.: Prentice-Hall, 1975. 336 pp., index.

"Rules and Deadlines for Indemnification Proposed," *AVISO*, 5 (May 1976), pp. 8-9. ♦ Regulations published in *Federal Register*, April 19, 1976. Arts and Artifacts Indemnification Act authorizes the Federal Council on the Arts and Humanities to make indemnity agreements with any person, nonprofit agency, institution or government for eligible items while on exhibition in the U.S., or elsewhere when part of an exchange exhibition.

Teachers Insurance and Annuity Association of America-College Retirement Equities Fund (TIAA-CREF). *Planning a Retirement Program.* New York: TIAA-CREF, 1973. 47 pp.♦ Includes essential features; retirement resolution; discussion of provisions; salary or annuity option; the TIAA-CREF combined annuity; informing staff members about the plan; retirement planning for clerical-service employees; and the work of TIAA and CREF.

United Nations Educational, Scientific and Cultural Organization. *Committee of Experts on Insurance and Other Forms of Coverage of Risks to Works of Art, Final Report.* Paris: 1974. 18 pp.

Vance, David. "A Proposed Standard Insurance Policy," *Museum News*, 48:1 (September 1969), pp. 21-26.

Williams, Donna. "The National Flood Insurance Program and Historic Preservation," *11593*, 2:4 (August 1977), p. 5.

Williams, R. "The Management of Risks Associated with the Property of Museums," *Museums Journal*, 77:2 (September 1977), pp. 59-60.♦ Discusses identification of risk, measurement of risk, risk elimination, risk reduction, risk accommodation.

NOTES

American Association of Museums, Insurance Programs. For its members, the AAM sponsors two insurance programs: for group insurance and retirement programs, contact David L. Jelinek, 209 South LaSalle Street, Suite 555, Chicago, Illinois 60604; for trustees/officers/museum employees liability insurance, contact Huntington T. Block Insurance, 2101 L Street, N.W., Washington, D.C. 20037.

Arts and Artifacts Indemnification Act, P.L. 94-158, December 20, 1975, provides indemnification for international exhibitions of art and artifacts with a limit of $50 million per exhibit. The State Department is required to certify that exhibitions are in the national interest.

Historic Home Insurance Policy. The St. Paul Fire and Marine Insurance Company has developed and made available a historic home policy for privately owned and occupied homes that are architecturally and historically significant. A house must be nominated for or listed on the National Register of Historic Places or be in a historic district to qualify. The policy is currently available in 19 states and will be extended to others. Further information is available from C. Richard Anderson, Underwriting Officer, Personal Lines Department, St. Paul Fire and Marine Insurance Company, 385 Washington Street, St. Paul, Minnesota 55102.

Teachers Insurance and Annuity Association-College Retirement Equities Fund (TIAA-CREF), 730 Third Avenue, New

York, New York 10017. The Association is a nonprofit, legal reserve life insurance company incorporated in the State of New York in 1918. It was organized by the Carnegie Corporation and the Carnegie Foundation for the Advancement of Teaching to function as an education service organization providing insurance and annuities especially designed for employees of education institutions in the United States and Canada. The Fund was established by a special act of the New York State Legislature and began operations July 1, 1952. TIAA and CREF are financially independent of each other and have separate boards of trustees; the same management administers both companies. TIAA funds plans for retirement income that are financially sound and economical and permit interchange of academic talent among institutions without loss to the staff member of accumulated retirement benefits. It also provides insurance plans for groups of staff members of eligible organizations, including collective life insurance, group life insurance, group major medical expense insurance, and group total disability benefits insurance. TIAA life insurance is also available to staff members of eligible institutions on an individual basis. Eligible institutions are colleges, universities, private schools, and certain other nonprofit institutions engaged primarily in education or research. Publications on retirement planning, group plans, and individual insurance are available.

9

Buildings

The design, the care, the use, and the protection of space shared with the public pose special problems. Out of the experience of others come some guidelines.

Planning, design, and construction comprise a rubric that includes materials and costs, visitor comforts, building codes, adaptive use, and accessibility. The section that follows cites the references that can lead to a good plan for effective building and grounds maintenance; but it should be noted that there are special subject-matter references on the care and restoration of historic buildings/materials in Chapter 5 of Volume 1 in the *Bibliography . . .* series: *Historic Preservation*.

The new awareness of the need for energy conservation, collections care, and use of historic buildings lies at the root of the section on environmental security. Additional references on such environmental factors as air conditioning, humidity control, lighting and insect control are cited in Chapter 5 of Volume 2 in the *Bibliography . . .* series: *Care and Conservation of Collections*.

And finally, the section on physical security comprises all the measures taken to protect the building or site and its contents against dangers caused by natural and human sources, technical failures, and personal accidents. Fire prevention, anti-intrusion devices, guards, curatorial and library security, and working with law enforcement agencies, all are considered. But the underlying theme is the fact that security depends on people.

Planning, Design and Construction

Advisory Council on Historic Preservation. "Adaptive Use: A Survey of Construction Costs," *Report,* IV:4 (June 1976), special issue.♦ Case studies of old buildings converted to new apartments, museums, offices, stores, and theaters to demonstrate that conversion is often less expensive than new construction.

Advisory Council on Historic Preservation. *Assessing the Energy Conservation Benefits of Historic Preservation: Methods and Examples.* Washington, D.C.: The Council, 1979. 91 pp., appendices.♦ Report of a study using a new method to determine energy savings when considering a rehabilitation or construction project.

All India Museums Conference, National Museum, 1971. *Museum Architecture.* Proceedings of the All India Museums Conference, New Delhi, February 1-4, 1971. New Delhi: Museums Association of India, 1972. 91 pp., illus.

Aloi, Roberto. *Musei, Architettura–technica.* Milano: Hoepli, 1962. 544 pp., illus., plans. ♦ Survey of contemporary museum design and display with particular emphasis on European and Italian practice. Text in English and Italian; available from William S. Heinman, Imported Books, New York.

American National Standards Institute. *American National Standard Specifications for Making Buildings and Facilities Accessible to and Usable by the Physically Handicapped.* ANSI A117.1—1961 (R1971). New York: American National Standards Institute, c1961, 1971. 11 pp., figures.♦ The Architectural Barriers Act requires that all buildings funded in whole or part by federal monies be designed free of barriers to handicapped people. The ANSI standards approved in 1961 were reaffirmed with no changes in 1971.

Arbeit, A. A. "The Architect and the Museum," *Museum News,* 43:2 (October 1964), pp. 11-16.♦ Discusses the extent of the services of an architect, and planning and design considerations.

Austin, Richard L. "Accommodating the Handicapped, an Introduction . . . ," *Trends* (January-February-March 1974), pp. 3-4.

Beazley, Elizabeth. *The Countryside on View: A Handbook on Countryside Centres, Field Museums and Historic Buildings Open to the Public.* London: Constable and Company, Ltd., 1971. 207 pp., illus., plans, bibliog., index.♦ Contents include briefing the architect, selecting the building site, planning and use of space, building materials, humidity controls, adaptive use, display, visitor services, security and fire protection, interpretation problems.

Belcher, M. *Floor Coverings.* Information Sheet no. 19. London: The Museums Association, 1973. 9 pp.♦ Discusses diversity of materials available, indicates properties and uses, and includes list of suppliers (British).

Belcher, M. *Wall Coverings.* Information Sheet no. 13. London: The Museums Association, 1972. 11 pp.

Bell, James A. M. *Museum and Gallery Building: A Guide to Briefing and Design Procedure.* Information Sheet no. 14. London: The Museums Association, 1972. 7 pp., bibliog.♦ Provides background to building-design, difficulties experienced by the client, relationship of curator/director with designers and engineers, and includes preparation of an outline brief and basic plan of work adopted by most architects.

Brawne, Michael. *The New Museum: Architecture and Display.* New York: Frederick A. Praeger, 1966. 208 pp., illus., bibliog.♦ Case study and critique of major museums con-

structed in Europe and the U.S. since World War II.

"Building Codes for Preservation," *Preservation News,* 16:11 (November 1976), Supplement, 4 pp.♦ Articles by Russell V. Keune, John F. McCune, III, and Robert J. Kapsch; and a review of National Survey by the Bureau of Standards, published 1975.

"Building Types Study," *Architectural Record,* 152:1 (July 1972), pp. 98-112.

Buildings for the Arts. By the editors of Architectural Record. New York: McGraw-Hill, 1978. 247 pp., index.

Colbert, Edwin H., and Gordon Reekie. "New Space, New Wings," *Curator,* VIII:3 (1965), pp. 212-222.♦ Describes new wing of The Canterbury Museum in New Zealand which reproduced the design of the original building; and a completely modern addition to the Australian Museum in Sydney.

Coleman, Laurence Vail. *Museum Buildings: A Planning Study.* Washington, D.C.: American Association of Museums, 1950. 298 pp., illus., appendix.♦ Reviews museum planning and building including size and cost, location, organization of space, heating and air-conditioning, construction, remodeling. Appendix lists buildings 1814-1949.

"Contemporary Architecture and Museums," *Museum,* IX:2 (1956), pp. 69-132.

Dimatteo, Peter F. "Building Codes and Rehabilitation: Toward a National Uniformity," *Technology and Conservation,* 3:2 (Summer 1978), pp. 30-31.♦ Discusses development of guidelines for rehabilitation and adaptive reuse of existing buildings that do not rely on an economic yardstick for code compliance.

Educational Facilities Laboratories. *Arts and the Handicapped: An Issue of Access.* A Report from the Educational Facilities Laboratories and the National Endowment for the Arts. New York: Educational Facilities Laboratories, 1975. 79 pp., illus. ♦ Reports techniques for eliminating physical and social barriers to the handicapped in various arts facilities.

Educational Facilities Laboratories. *Technical Assistance for Arts Facilities: A Sourcebook.* New York: Educational Facilities Laboratories, 1977. 30 pp., index.♦ Lists national organizations involved in planning, architecture, conservation and the arts, and briefly describes the services offered. Covers planning, financing, acquiring, renovating, designing and maintaining physical facilities.

Ferro, Maximilian L. "Building Codes for Historic and Older Structures: The Massachusetts Approach to Developing Realistic Standards," *Technology and Conservation,* 3:2 (Summer 1972), pp. 26-28.♦ Discusses revisions in the state code renovation requirement proposed by the Advisory Committee on Historic Buildings.

"The Great Museum Debate," *Progressive Architecture,* 50:12 (December 1969), pp. 76-85.♦ Special section on museum construction and types of buildings.

Green, Melvyn, and Patrick W. Cooke. *Survey of Building Code Provisions for Historic Structures.* Washington, D.C.: U.S. Department of Commerce, National Bureau of Standards, for sale by the Superintendent of Documents, U.S. Government Printing Office, 1976. 43 pp., illus.

Gretton, Robert. "Museum Architecture: A Primer," *Museum News,* 44:6 (February 1966), pp. 13-17.

Harrison, Raymond O. "Planning for Action and Growth," *Museum News,* 51:3 (November 1973), pp. 21-24.♦ Discusses a formula for others to use in planning buildings for present and future needs.

Harrison, Raymond O. *The Technical Requirements of Small Museums.* Rev. ed. Technical Papers no. 1. Ottawa: Canadian Museums Association, 1969. 27 pp., illus., bibliog.♦ Includes building materials and equipment, principles of building and interior space planning, site selection, building costs and capital budgets. Illustrated with basic floor plans; appendix on small art gallery requirements by Archie F. Key.

Huxtable, Ada Louise. "Architecture of Museums," *Museum News,* 47:3 (November 1968), pp. 18-19.♦ Comment on Museum of Modern Art exhibit on new museum architecture.

"I. M. Pei's Newest Museum," *Museum News,* 53:1 (September 1974), pp. 34-39.♦ Photo essay on the Herbert F. Johnson Museum of Art, Cornell University, Ithaca, New York.

Kenney, Alice P. "A Test of Barrier-Free Design," *Museum News,* 55:3 (January/February 1977), pp. 27-29.

Lawson, Edward P. "Museum Architecture: The Ohio Historical Center," *Museum News,* 49:5 (January 1971), pp. 12-13.

Malajoli, Bruno. "Museum Architecture." In *The Organization of Museums: Practical Advice* (Paris: UNESCO, 1960), pp. 146-185.

Moe, Christine. *Planning for the Removal of Architectural Barriers for the Handicapped.* Exchange Bibliography no. 1337. Monticello, Ill.: Council of Planning Librarians, 1977. 48 pp.

Molloy, Larry. "The Case for Accessibility," *Museum News,* 55:3 (January/February 1977), pp. 15-17.♦ Discusses 1968 Architectural Barriers Act, and 1973 Rehabilitation Act.

"Museum Architecture," *Museum,* XXVI:3/4 (1974), special issue.♦ Includes glossary; commissioning authority and builder; study and choice of site; social context and place of action; factors affecting the visitor; perception and behavior; physiochemistry of the objects; space and circulation; flexibility and extensibility; aesthetics.

"Museum Architecture: Part I," *Museum News,* 51:10 (September 1972), entire issue.♦ Deals with renovation and new buildings, and solutions to technical problems. Includes articles on total design concept, museum interiors, acoustics, glass, modular walls, renovation.

"Museum Architecture: Part II," *Museum News,* 51:3 (November 1972), entire issue.♦ Includes planning for action and growth; planetariums; environmental preserve in San Diego; landscaping; storage facilities; documentation on new construction; and bibliography.

"Museum Architecture: Projects and Recent Achievements," *Museum,* XVII:3 (1964), entire issue.

"Museums for Learning," *The Architectural Forum,* 135:2 (September 1971), pp. 20-39.♦ Portfolio of museum architecture.

Neal, Arminta. "Museum Fatigue and Human Anatomy." In *Exhibits for the Small Museum: A Handbook* (Nashville, Tenn.: American Association for State and Local History, 1976), pp. 139-146.◆ Discusses visitor comfort as an important part of exhibit design and installation in museums and galleries.

Owens, Gwendolyn J., comp. "A Guide to Information on Accessibility," *Museum News,* 55:3 (January/February 1977), pp. 38-39.

Park, Dave. "Considerations in Accommodating the Handicapped," *Trends* (January-February-March 1974), pp. 8-14.

Park Practice Program. "Trends for the Handicapped," *Trends* (July-August-September 1974), entire issue.◆ Articles on making parks and other recreation areas accessible to the handicapped; list of public and private groups concerned about the handicapped who might provide additional resources and information; summary of laws relating to access to public facilities; report on Georgia's special park for the handicapped.

Parr, Albert E. "Problems of Museum Architecture," *Curator,* IV:4 (1961), pp. 304-327.

"The Planning of Museums and Art Galleries," *Museums Journal,* 63:1-2 (June-September 1963), entire issue.◆ Discusses external and internal planning.

Preservation and Building Codes Conference, Washington, D.C., 1974. *Preservation and Building Codes: Papers from the Preservation and Building Codes Conference, Washington, D.C., May 1974.* Sponsored by the National Trust for Historic Preservation. Washington, D.C.: Preservation Press, 1975. 96 pp., illus., appendices.

Reekie, Gordon. "Toward Well-Being for Museum Visitors," *Curator,* I:1 (1958), pp. 91-94.◆ Discusses visitor comforts such as parking, seats, temperature, lounges.

Smith, Baird M. *A Selected Bibliography on Building Codes and Standards.* Washington, D.C.: Office of Archeology and Historic Preservation, National Park Service, 1977. 4 pp. ◆ Technical Preservation Services Reading List.

Snider, Harold. "The Inviting Air of An Accessible Space," *Museum News,* 55:3 (January/February 1977), pp. 18-20.◆ Staff of National Air and Space Museum consulted handicapped in planning accessible programs.

Stein, Richard G. *Architecture and Energy.* New York: Anchor Press, 1977. 322 pp., illus.,

bibliog. references, index.◆ Examines relationship between architectural design and energy use in buildings.

Stein, Richard G. "Energy and Illumination," *Museum News,* 57:4 (March/April 1979), pp. 43-49.◆ Examines energy use in museums.

"Symposium on Museum Architecture, Access and Circulation," *ICOM News,* 22:1 (March 1969), pp. 39-42◆ Reports conclusions of the symposium covering generalities, the director of a museum, conservation, access and circulation, research agency on museum architecture, bibliography of related literature.

Thompson, C. "Recent Developments in Museum Building," *Museums Journal,* 68:1 (1968), pp. 3-11.

U.S. Department of Housing and Urban Development. Office of Policy Development and Research. *Barrier-Free Site Design.* Washington, D.C.: U.S. Government Printing Office, 1976. 82 pp., illus., bibliog., appendix.◆ Graphically illustrates methods in which site components and facilities (ramps, stairs, drinking fountains, planting, lighting, etc.) have been and can be designed to make them accessible and usable by the elderly and the handicapped. Prepared in cooperation with the American Society of Landscape Architects Foundation.

U.S. Heritage Conservation and Recreation Service. Office of Archeology and Historic Preservation. *The Secretary of the Interior's Standards for Historic Preservation Projects with Guidelines for Applying the Standards.* Developed by W. Brown Morton III and Gary L. Hume. Washington, D.C.: 1979. 46 pp.◆ Standards define the general and specific treatments that may be applied to registered properties. Part I includes definitions; general standards; specific standards for seven project areas: acquisition, protection, stabilization, preservation, rehabilitation, restoration and reconstruction. Part II guidelines, detailing recommended and not recommended techniques for all types of buildings, are designed to assist individual property owners formulate specific plans for acquisition, development and continued use of historic properties in a manner consistent with the intent of the standards.

U.S. Heritage Conservation and Recreation Service. Office of Archeology and Historic

Preservation. *The Secretary of the Interior's Standards for Rehabilitation and Guidelines for Rehabilitating Historic Buildings.* Rev. ed. Washington, D.C.: January 1979. 14 pp.◆ Standards appear in Section 36, Code of Federal Regulations, Part 1208. In the Guidelines, techniques, treatments and methods consistent with the Standards are listed in a "recommended" column; techniques which may adversely affect architectural and historical qualities are listed in a "not recommended" column. Aspects covered include the environment; building site; building structural systems; building exterior features; building interior features; new construction; mechanical services; fire protection; safety and code requirements.

Vance, David. "Planning Ahead—The Registrar's Role in a Building Program." In Dudley and Wilkinson, *Museum Registration Methods* (Washington, D.C.: American Association of Museums, 1968), pp. 267-282.

Webb, Michael. "Museum Architecture," *Museum News,* 50:1 (September 1971), pp. 10-12.◆ The National Gallery of Art addition.

Webb, Michael. "Museum Architecture: Model Museum in New York," *Museum News,* 49:2 (October 1970), pp. 11-12.◆ The Everson Museum, Syracuse, New York.

Webb, Michael. "Museum Architecture: New Children's Museum in Florida," *Museum News,* 49:7 (March 1971), pp. 12-14.

Webb, Michael. "Museum Architecture: New University Art Museum at Berkeley," *Museum News,* 49:8 (April 1971), pp. 11-13.

Webb, Michael. "Museum Architecture: Renewing Museums," *Museum News,* 48:9 (June 1970), pp. 16-17.

Wells, Malcolm B. "Opinion—Eschatology, The Last Word in Exhibit Themes," *Museum News,* 49:5 (January 1971), pp. 9-11. ◆ Discusses design of museum buildings that account for ecological factors such as waste management, utilities, building additions.

Witteborg, Lothar P. "Museum Design—A Logical Approach," *Museum News,* 43:5 (January 1965), pp. 22-25.

Zgolinski, Al. "Cracking the Codes," *Museum News,* 57:3 (January/February 1979), pp. 52-55ff.◆ Article includes the nature of building codes, state energy codes, The Massachusetts Exemption; selected examples of building regulations; American Society of Heating, Refrigeration and Airconditioning Engineers (ASHRAE) guidelines; General Services Administration guidelines, and Executive Order 12003; Energy Performance Standards.

Building and Grounds Maintenance

Brady, George S. *Materials Handbook: An Encyclopedia for Purchasing Managers, Engineers, Executives and Foremen.* New York: McGraw-Hill Book Co., 1929 -. 1 vol., maps. ◆ An encyclopedia of terms and definitions; includes chemicals and metals. Current edition, 10th, 1971.

Bullock, Orin M., Jr. *The Restoration Manual: An Illustrated Guide to the Preservation and Restoration of Old Buildings.* Norwalk, Conn.: Silvermine Publishing Co., 1966. 181 pp., illus., glossary, bibliog.◆ Includes a chapter on maintenance of a restored building.

Carlsson, Ingrid, and Ingmar Holström. *Care of Old Buildings: An Annotated Bibliography.* Stockholm: Statens Institut for Byggnadsforskning, distr. by Svensk Byggtjanst, 1975 -. 1 vol.◆ National Swedish Building Research, Document D7:1975.

Chambers, J. Henry. *Cyclical Maintenance for Historic Buildings.* Washington, D.C.: Interagency Historic Architectural Services Program, Office of Archeology and Historic Preservation, National Park Service, 1976. 125 pp., illus., appendices, notes, bibliog.◆ Technical advice on starting a maintenance program; professional services; employee training; and maintenance techniques for specific materials.

Conover, Herbert S. *Grounds Maintenance Handbook.* 3rd ed. New York: McGraw-Hill, c1977. 631 pp., illus., index.

"Energy," *AVISO,* 1 (January 1978), supplement.◆ Includes Energy Hot Line, Energy Forecast, National Conservation Advisory Council, Bulletin Board, and Energy Money.

"The Energy and Inflation Fighters," *Museum News,* 53:6 (March 1975), pp. 25-27, 45.◆ A list of suggestions for small and large museums on how to stretch dollars, raise new funds and spend less.

"Energy Conservation in Historic Buildings," 11593 (Spring 1978), special issue.♦ Articles on energy conservation in historic buildings and energy conservation statement; federal funding sources; information sources.

Favretti, Rudy J., and Joy P. Favretti. For Every House a Garden: A Guide for Reproducing Period Gardens. Chester, Conn.: The Pequot Press, 1977. 137 pp., illus., glossary.♦ Points out basic characteristics of certain period landscapes and discusses how to construct a period garden; includes glossary of historical plants.

Favretti, Rudy J. and Joy P. Favretti. Landscapes and Gardens for Historic Buildings: Reproducing and Recreating Authentic Settings. Nashville, Tenn.: American Association for State and Local History, 1978. 202 pp., illus.♦ Includes history of various periods of American garden design; how to select the correct period for a particular site; compilation of plant species arranged by periods of use; and a section on maintenance.

Fowler, John. "An Ounce of Prevention," Museum News, 53:3 (November 1974), pp. 19, 61.♦ Discusses impact of standards set forth under OSHA on museum and historic site interpretive programs, and describes a new historic preservation variance.

Garston, Eng. Building Research Station. Cleaning External Surfaces of Buildings. Digest 113. London: Her Majesty's Stationery Office, 1970. 4 pp.♦ Descriptive outline of various techniques for cleaning different materials.

Gratwick, Reginald T. Dampness in Buildings. 2nd ed. London: Crosby, Lockwood Staples, 1974. 375 pp., illus., appendices, index.

Greiff, Constance M. The Historic Property Owner's Handbook. Washington, D.C.: Preservation Press, 1977. 92 pp., illus.♦ Discusses protection and restoration of historic properties with sources of technical information, funding and professional services.

Grow, Lawrence. The Second Old House Catalog. New York: Main Street Press, 1978. 219 pp.♦ Directory of suppliers of period materials for use in restoring old houses.

Holmström, Ingmar, and Christina Sandström. Maintenance of Old Buildings: Preservation from the Technical and Antiquarian Standpoint. Stockholm: National Swedish Institute for Building Research, 1972. 45 pp., illus., bibliog. references.♦ Deals with critical parts of buildings: foundations, walls, facade surfaces, roofs, water drainage, heating. Document 10.

Johnson, Sidney M. Deterioration, Maintenance, and Repair of Structures. New York: McGraw-Hill, 1965. 373 pp., illus., diagrams, tables, bibliog., index.♦ Manual on repair and restoration, prevention of deterioration in steel, concrete and timber structures.

Judd, Henry A. "Before Restoration Begins: Keeping Your Historic House Intact," History News, 28:10 (October 1973), Technical Leaflet no. 67.

Mack, Robert C. The Cleaning and Waterproof Coating of Masonry Buildings. Preservation Briefs series, 1. Washington, D.C.: Interagency Historic Architecture Services Program, Office of Archeology and Historic Preservation, National Park Service, 1975. 4 pp., illus. ♦ Explains proper procedures and consequences of inappropriate techniques.

Malaro, Marie C. "Better Safe Than Sorry," Museum News, 53:1 (September 1974), pp. 16-19.♦ Discusses Williams-Steiger Act of 1970 regarding safe and healthful working conditions.

Martin, D. G. Maintenance and Repair of Stone Buildings. London: Church Information Office for the Council for the Care of Churches, 1970. 15 pp., illus., bibliog.♦ Discusses the nature of stone, causes of decay, repair techniques, structural problems, and mortars.

Matthai, Robert A. "Energy Conservation & Management: A Critical Challenge for Cultural Institutions," Technology and Conservation, 3:1 (Spring 1978), pp. 12-21.♦ Discusses measures that can be implemented to more efficiently regulate the environment and cut operating expenses.

Matthai, Robert A. "The Energy Crisis: It's Our Move," Museum News, 56:2 (November/December 1977), pp. 46-51.♦ Describes steps museums must take to protect collections and their future; includes notes and references.

Matthai, Robert A., ed. *Protection of Cultural Properties During Energy Emergencies.* 2nd ed. New York: Arts/Energy Study and American Association of Museums, 1978. 24 pp.

Melville, Ian A., and Ian A. Gordon. *The Repair and Maintenance of Houses.* London: Estates Gazette, Ltd., 1973. 1050 pp., illus., bibliog., appendix, index ◆ Study of building repair by British Building Surveyors.

Minnich, Richard S. "Safety—An Integral Part of Museum Operations." In *Section Papers, 63rd Annual Meeting, American Association of Museums* (New Orleans, La.: May 1968), pp. 63-78.◆ Describes safety and accident prevention program at Smithsonian Institution regarding employee safety, public safety, fire prevention, radiation safety, pesticides control, motor vehicle and traffic safety, property damage control, tort claim investigation, hazardous detection and control.

Moore, Alma Chestnut. *How to Clean Everything: An Encyclopedia of What to Use and How to Use It.* 3rd ed., rev. and updated. Edited and adapted by Honor Wyatt. New York: Simon and Schuster, c1977, 1979. 192 pp.

Nichols, Ashton. "Energy," *Preservation News,* 17:13 (December 1977), pp. 12ff.

Old House Journal Corporation. *Old House Journal Catalog, 1979.* Brooklyn, N.Y.: The Old House Journal, 1979. 76 pp., illus.◆ Buyers guide to products and services for restoring houses built before 1920.

Peterson, Douglas C. "Ways to Save Energy and Stay Warm," *Historic Preservation,* 31:1 (March/April 1979), pp. 41-48.◆ Includes chart on how to save energy in an old house.

Pinto, Edward H., and Eva R. Pinto. *The Care of Woodwork in the Home: Cleaning, Deworming, Repair and Surface Maintenance of Furniture and Other Movables, as Well as the Protection and Treatment of the Timber of the Structure.* London: Benn, 1955. 34 pp., illus.

Rawlins, F.I.G. "The Cleaning of Stonework," *Studies in Conservation,* 3:1 (April 1957), pp. 1-23.◆ Illustrated summary of methods of cleaning old masonry used at cathedrals and other buildings.

Sack, Thomas F. *A Complete Guide to Building and Plant Maintenance.* 2nd ed. Englewood Cliffs, N.J.: Prentice-Hall, Inc., 1971. 677 pp., illus.

Smith, Baird M. *Conserving Energy in Historic Buildings.* Preservation Briefs no. 3. Washington, D.C.: Heritage Conservation and Recreation Service, Office of Archeology and Historic Preservation, Technical Services Division, 1978. 8 pp., illus., bibliog.◆ Ways to achieve maximum energy savings in historic buildings without jeopardizing architectural, cultural and historical qualities. Also discusses passive measures and recommended preservation retrofitting and its benefits.

Sweetser, Sarah M. *Roofing for Historic Buildings.* Preservation Briefs no. 4. Washington, D.C.: Heritage Conservation and Recreation Service, Office of Archeology and Historic Preservation, Technical Services Division, 1978. 8 pp., illus., bibliog.◆ Concise fact sheet on kinds of materials used historically in roofing, problems that necessitate repair or replacement, and methods of replacement which preserve physical integrity.

Symons, Vivian. *Church Maintenance.* London: Marshall, Morgan & Scott, 1968. 153 pp., illus., diagrams, tables, bibliog., index. ◆ Manual on maintaining fabric of churches.

Williams, Donna, and Baird Smith. "Energy Conservation and Historic Preservation," *11593,* 2:3 (June 1977), Supplement. ◆ Includes national programs and technical considerations.

"The Winter of Our Discontent," *Museum News,* 52:6 (March 1974), pp. 21-22.◆ Discusses effects of long-term shortages on various institutional aspects and need for planning.

NOTES

Acoustical and Insulating Materials Association, 205 W. Touhy Avenue, Park Ridge, Illinois 60068. Founded in 1968 as the Insulation Board Institute, the Association includes manufacturers of architectural acoustical and insulating products concerned with combating noise pollution and providing protection from excessive heat and cold in buidlings. It provides technical information on acoustical and insulating materials through Standards/Specifications Activities, Installation and Maintenance Studies, Public Relations Program, Insulation Board Rating Programs. It also publishes booklets, pamphlets, and manuals.

American National Standards Institute, 1430 Broadway, New York, New York 10018. Founded in 1918, the Institute serves as a clearinghouse for nationally coordinated, voluntary safety, engineering and industrial standards. It approves and drafts standards in the field of library work, documentation and related publishing practices; standards adopted under OSHA; information and processing; construction and demolition operations; photography and motion pictures; security equipment; textiles; and many others. A catalog of a complete set of all American National Standards, and special series, is available from the Institute. Brochures listing standards in special fields are also available. Formerly American Engineering Standards Committee (1928); American Standards Association (1965); United States of America Standards Institute (1969).

Building Research: The Journal of the Building Research Institute. 1964, quarterly, membership/subscription. Building Research Institute, 2101 Constitution Avenue, N.W., Washington, D.C. 20418.

Bulletin of APT. 1969, quarterly, membership. Association for Preservation Technology, c/o Ann Falkner, Box 2478, Station D, Ottawa, Ontario K1P 5W6 Canada.

"Conservation Techniques for Historic Houses." Slide/tape training programs on various aspects of the conservation of historic houses and their furnishings. Topics include "Reading a Building," "Overall Planning for Historic House Restoration," "Victorian House Paint Colors," "Wallpaper and the Historic House," "Curatorial Care—The Environment," "Curatorial Care—Wood Furnishings." The programs are self-contained units consisting of a carousel of slides, cassette, script, printed supplementary materials, and pertinent product samples, and are available for rental or purchase from Education Division, American Association for State and Local History, 1400 Eighth Avenue South, Nashville, Tennessee 37203.

Energy Information Clearinghouse, Box 241, Planetarium Station, New York, New York 10024. The Clearinghouse was initially begun in 1974 under a grant from the National Endowment for the Arts for the purpose of inform-ing museums across the country about federal energy guidelines, problems resulting from the energy shortage, and suggestions for plans to help museums through the energy crisis. Two issues of a newsletter, *Museums-Energy-News,* were published in January and March 1974. The Clearinghouse was revived in the winter of 1977 to continue compiling data on museums' energy-related problems. Articles of interest are published by the American Association of Museums in *Museum News* and *AVISO.* An energy workshop planning committee, chaired by Dr. Robert A. Matthai, was formed to help states and municipalities develop programs and services for museums; to publish self-guiding materials and case studies on energy conservation in museum buildings, and to share information and ideas with other sectors of the cultural community. In 1978, the Arts/Energy Study was begun to assess the energy needs and problems of all types of cultural organizations.

Grounds Maintenance. 1966, monthly, subscriptions. Intertec Publishing Corporation, 1014 Wyandotte Street, Kansas City, Missouri 64105.

Occupational Safety and Health Act, 1971 (P.L. 91-596) provides that requirements are made to insure that injuries to employees be kept to an absolute minimum. Standards were published in the *Federal Register,* 37:243 (December 16, 1972) for "Safety and Health Regulations for Construction," and in 37:202 (October 18, 1972) for "Occupational Safety and Health Standards." Conflict has arisen between the safety requirements of the act and the authentic reenactment of the production of goods and other related museum and historic site programs.

The Old-House Journal. 1973, monthly, subscription. The Old House Journal, 69A Seventh Avenue, Brooklyn, New York 11217.

Environmental Security

Amdur, Elias J. "Humidity Control–Isolated Area Plan," *Museum News,* 43:4 (December 1964), Technical Supplement no. 5.

Boyton, Edgar B. "Climate Control in Restored Buildings." In *Restoration Manual: An Illustrated Guide to the Preservation and Restoration of Old Buildings* (Norwalk, Conn.: Silvermine Publishing Co., 1966), pp. 124-131.

Buck, Richard D. "On Conservation: The Energy Crisis and Museum Collections," *Museum News*, 52:7 (April 1974), pp. 8-9.

Buck, Richard D. "A Specification for Museum Air Conditioning," *Museum News*, 43:4 (December 1964), Technical Supplement no. 5.

Fitzsimmons, K. R. "Termite Control in Historic Landmarks," *Historic Preservation*, 22:4 (October-December 1970). pp. 40-44.

Harvey, John. "Air Conditioning for Museums," *Museums Journal*, 73:1 (June 1973), pp. 11-16.

Hickin, Norman Ernest. *The Insect Factor in Wood Decay: An Account of Wood-boring Insects with Particular Reference to Timber Indoors.* Edited and revised by Robin Edwards. 3rd ed. London: Associated Business Programs, 1975. 383 pp., illus., bibliogs., index.

International Institute for Conservation of Historic and Artistic Works. *Control of the Museum Environment: A Basic Summary.* London: The Institute, 1967. 8 pp.♦ Based on the findings of the 1967 London Conference on Museum Climatology.

Keally, F., and Henry C. Meyer. "Air-Conditioning as a Means of Preserving Books and Records," *The American Archivist*, 12:3 (July 1949), pp. 280-282.

Keck, Caroline K. "On Conservation: Relative Humidity Controls," *Museum News*, 50:8 (April 1972), p. 13.

Lewis, L. Logan. "Air Conditioning for Museums," *Museum*, X:2 (1957), pp. 132-147.

London Conference on Museum Climatology. *Contributions to the London Conference on Museum Climatology, 18-23 September 1967.* Edited by Garry Thomson. London: International Institute for Conservation, 1968. 296 pp., illus., bibliog. references.♦ A study of how the environment in a museum affects its contents and how to ensure that their inevitable ageing processes are slowed. Includes air pollution, humidity control, lighting, climate and museum design.

Matthai, Robert A. "Energy Conservation & Management: A Challenge for Cultural Institutions," *Technology and Conservation*, 3:1 (Spring 1978), pp. 12-21.

Metcalf, Clell Lee, and Wesley P. Flint. *Destructive and Useful Insects: Their Habits and Control.* 4th ed. New York: McGraw-Hill Book Co., 1962. 1087 pp., illus.

Morton, W. Brown, III. "Field Procedure for Examining Humidity in Masonry Buildings," *Bulletin of APT*, 8:2 (1976), pp. 2-19.

National Conservation Advisory Council. "The Control of Environmental Conditions in Situations of Energy Shortage," Midwest Museums Conference *Quarterly*, 38:2 (Spring 1978), pp. 19-20.

Richardson, Stanley A. *Protecting Buildings: How to Combat Dry Rot, Woodworm and Damp.* North Pomfret, Vt.: David & Charles, 1977. 156 pp., illus., bibliog., index.

Stolow, Nathan. "The Microclimate: A Localized Solution," *Museum News*, 56:2 (November/December 1977), pp. 52-63.♦ Describes use of specially designed cases, includes notes and references.

Szent-Ivany, J.J.H. "Identification and Control of Insect Pests." In *The Conservation of Cultural Property with Special Reference to Tropical Conditions* (Paris: UNESCO, 1968), pp. 53-70.♦ Includes identification and control of insects, bibliography, and appendix of book insect repellents.

U.S. Department of Agriculture. *Controlling Household Pests.* Home and Garden Bulletin no. 96, rev. ed. Washington, D.C.: U.S. Government Printing Office, 1971. 32 pp., illus., drawings, recipe table.

U.S. Department of Agriculture. *Controlling Wood-Destroying Beetles in Buildings and Furniture.* By Lonnie H. Williams and Harmon R. Johnston. Leaflet no. 558. Washington, D.C.: U.S. Government Printing Office, 1972. 8 pp., illus., drawings, bibliog.

U.S. Department of Agriculture. *Making Basements Dry.* By Richard H. Rule. Home and Garden Bulletin no. 115, rev. ed. Washington, D.C.: U.S. Government Printing Office, 1970. 10 pp., diagrams.

U.S. Department of Agriculture. *The Old House Borer.* By T. McIntyre and R. A. St. George. Leaflet no. 501, rev. Washington, D.C.: U.S. Government Printing Office, 1970. 8 pp.

U.S. Department of Agriculture. *Protecting*

Log Cabins, Rustic Work, and Unseasoned Wood from Injurious Insects in the Eastern United States. Farmer's Bulletin no. 2104, rev. Washington, D.C.: U.S. Government Printing Office, 1970. 18 pp.

U.S. Department of Agriculture. *Subterranean Termites: Their Prevention and Control in Buildings.* By H. R. Johnston, Virgil K. Smith, and Raymond H. Beal. Home and Garden Bulletin no. 64, rev. ed. Washington, D.C.: U.S. Government Printing Office, 1972. 30 pp., illus., drawings, diagrams, map.

U.S. Department of Agriculture. *Wood Decay in Houses: How to Prevent and Control It.* Home and Garden Bulletin no. 73, rev. ed. Washington, D.C.: U.S. Government Printing Office, 1973. 17 pp., illus., diagrams.

NOTES

American Society of Heating, Refrigeration and Air Conditioning Engineers (ASHRAE), United Engineering Center, 345 East 47th Street, New York 10017. Founded in 1894, the Society is a professional organization of heating, ventilating, refrigeration, and air conditioning engineers. It carries out a number of research programs in cooperation with universities and research laboratories on such subjects as human and animal environmental studies, effects of air conditioning, quality of inside air, heat transfer. Research and general technical programs are conducted through 80 technical committees. It publishes *ASHRAE Journal* (monthly); *ASHRAE Handbook* (annual); *ASHRAE Transactions* (annual); research reports, codes and engineering standards, preprints, and bulletins.

U.S. Agricultural Research Service, Entomology Research Division. Home and Garden Bulletin series, Farmers' Bulletin series, and other leaflets are kept up to date and provide current information on the control of all types of pests in homes and other buildings. Catalog available from Superintendent of Documents, U.S. Government Printing Office, Washington, D.C. 20402.

Physical Security

Alsford, Denis B. "An Approach to Museum Security," *gazette,* 8:3 (Summer 1975), pp. 6-16.♦ Includes environmental condition; ap-proach to physical security; external security; locks; internal security; security staff; curatorial security; fire and flood.

Alth, Max. *All About Locks and Locksmithing.* New York: Hawthorn Books, Inc., 1972. 180 pp., illus.♦ Types and development of locks and keys, re-keying and picking of locks.

American Library Association. Library Technology Project. *Protecting the Library and Its Resources: A Guide to Physical Protection and Insurance.* Report on a study conducted by Gage-Babcock & Associates, Inc. Chicago: Library Technology Project, American Library Association, 1963. 322 pp., illus., bibliog., appendix, index.♦ LTP Publication no. 7.

American National Standards Institute. *American National Standard Practice for Protective Lighting.* American National Standard A85.1 1956 (R1970). New York: Illuminating Engineering Society, 1970. 20 pp.♦ Principles involved in outdoor protective lighting.

Bertschinger, Susan. "Protecting Ontario's Historic Buildings Against the Threat of Fire," *gazette,* 9:3 (Summer 1976), pp. 14-18.♦ Reviews four stages of fire, types of detection at two historic sites, and a comment on maintenance of equipment.

Blair, C. Dean. "Protecting Your Exhibits: Security Methods and Devices," *History News,* 32:9 (September 1977), Technical Leaflet no. 99.

Bostick, William A. *The Guarding of Cultural Property.* Paris: UNESCO, 1977. 40 pp., illus.♦ Study demonstrates the need for improved security measures in museums and the importance of the human element in ensuring adequate protection. Provides practical and technical guidance on the various aspects of the care and treatment of museum collections and the preservation of monuments. Available from Unipub, New York.

Bostick, William A. "What Is the State of Museum Security?" *Museum News,* 46:5 (January 1968), pp. 13-19.♦ Details of a survey of security measures in effect in several large U.S. and European museums.

Brown, Peter. *Site Security.* Nashville, Tenn.: American Association for State and Local History, 1973. 30 minute tape cassette, slide carousel, and supplementary materials.♦ Uses Colonial Williamsburg as a model for ideas for solving many general security problems including theft, fire and malicious mischief.

Carroll, Richard S. "A Low-Cost System of Protecting Paintings," *Museum News,* 41:10 (June 1963), pp. 27-29.

Chapman, Joseph. "Fire," *Museum News,* 50:5 (January 1972), pp. 32-35.♦ Brief overview of how to prevent and detect fire in the museum.

Chapman, Joseph. "Museum Security," *Museum News,* 50:1 (September 1971), pp. 43-45.

Chapman, Joseph. ". . . Stepping Up Security," *Museum News,* 44:3 (November 1965), pp. 18-21.

Chapman, Joseph. "Your Security Questions Answered," *Museum News,* 50:5 (January 1972), pp. 22-25.♦ Questions and answers at security sessions of the AAM Regional Conferences in 1971.

Cole, Richard B. *The Application of Security Systems and Hardware.* Springfield, Ill.: Charles C. Thomas, 1970. 257 pp., illus.♦ Includes lock application, truck protection, lighting and general premises protection techniques; also details of a disaster planning program for small businesses.

Cole, Richard B. *Protect Your Property: The Application of Burglar Alarm Hardware.* Springfield, Ill.: Charles C. Thomas, 1971. 180 pp., illus., bibliog.♦ Advantages and disadvantages of various detection devices and concepts of burglar alarm protection.

Corning, N.Y. Museum of Glass. *The Corning Flood: Museum Under Water.* John H. Martin, ed. Corning, N.Y.: The Museum, 1977. 59 pp., 11 pp., appendices.♦ Story of the restoration of the Corning Museum and Library; with suggestions for planning for such disasters. Appendices include staff, volunteers and sources of assistance in restoring the collections; examples of problems; materials and suppliers.

Cunningham, John E. *Security Electronics.* 1st ed. Indianapolis, Ind.: Howard W. Sams & Co., 1970. 159 pp., illus.

Curtis, Sargent J. [Bob]. *Security Control: External Theft.* New York: Chain Store Age Books, 1971. 372 pp., appendices, index. ♦ Applicable information on detection devices, safes and vaults, locks and keys, and protective lighting.

Curtis, Sargent J. [Bob]. *Security Control: Internal Theft.* New York: Chain Store Age Books, 1973. 361 pp.

Fitzsimmons, Neal. "Emergency Measures and Museums," *Museum News,* 43:6 (February 1965), pp. 23-24.♦ Questions and answers about disaster preparedness and references to sources of answers.

Foramitti, Hans. "A Modern Approach to the Prevention of Thefts of Works of Arts," *ICOM News,* 24:4 (December 1971), pp. 72-73.

Francis, Frank. "Security," *Museums Journal,* 63:1-2 (June-September 1963), pp. 28-32.

Gibbs-Smith, Charles H. *The Art of Observation: A Booklet for Museum Warders.* London: Victoria and Albert Museum, 1971. 16 pp.♦ Discusses the powers of observation of security staff.

Gossin, Francis. "A Security Chief Comments on Guards," *Museum News,* 50:5 (January 1972), pp. 30-31.

Grossman, Albert J. "Television—Museum Watchdog," *Museum News,* 44:3 (November 1965), pp. 22-24.

Healy, Richard J. *Design for Security.* New York: John Wiley and Sons, 1968. 309 pp., illus., bibliog.

Healy, Richard J. *Emergency and Disaster Planning.* New York: John Wiley and Sons, 1969. 290 pp., illus.

Hill, John I. "A Consumer Guide to Security Systems," *Museum News,* 55:7 (July/August 1977), pp. 34-37.

"Hot, Hotter, Hottest," *The Laboratory,* 34:3 (1966), pp. 66-70.♦ A discussion of fire fighting materials.

Howard, Richard F. *Museum Security.* Washington, D.C.: American Association of Museums, 1958. 12 pp.

Hunter, John E. "Emergency Preparedness for Museums, Historic Sites, and Archives: An Annotated Bibliography," *History News,* 34:4 (April 1979), Technical Leaflet no. 114.

Hunter, John E. "Security for Museums and Historic Houses: An Annotated Bibliography," *History News,* 30:5 (May 1975), Technical Leaflet no. 83.

International Council of Museums. *International Symposium on the Problems of Security in Museums, Saint Maximin, 28 May-1 June 1973.* Paris: 1973. 43 pp., bibliog.

Keck, Caroline K. "Conservation: Security Depends on People," *History News,* 29:4 (April 1974), pp. 79, 94. ♦ How to close an historic house.

Keck, Caroline K. "On Conservation: Vandalism," *Museum News,* 50:9 (May 1972), p. 9.

Keck, Caroline K.; Huntington T. Block; Joseph Chapman; John B. Lawton; and Nathan Stolow. *A Primer on Museum Security.* Cooperstown, N.Y.: New York State Historical Association, 1966. 85 pp., illus., graphs, forms, bibliog. ♦ Handbook on methods of building security; includes chapters on insurance and environmental security.

Kissane, Thomas P. "Protecting Works of Art From Theft and Fraud," *Best's Review: Property/Casualty Insurance Edition,* 78:1 (May 1977), pp. 38-42. ♦ Report on growing incidence of theft and fraud; work of the International Association of Art Security and the International Art Registry; and recommends a total security approach.

Leo, Jack. *A Basic Security Checklist for the Small Museum.* Austin, Tex.: Texas Association of Museums, 1978. 2 pp., bibliog. ♦ Also reprinted in Bulletin 10, Oklahoma Museums Association, Oklahoma City; and *RCHA News* (February 1979), Information Sheet no. 45.

McQuarie, Robert J. "Security," *Museum News,* 49:7 (March 1971), pp. 25-27. ♦ Suggestions on preventive measures; includes some information on fire prevention.

Mandelbaum, Albert J. *Fundamentals of Protective Systems: Planning, Evaluation, Selection.* Springfield, Ill.: Charles C. Thomas, 1973. 272 pp., bibliog. references.

Mandell, Mel. *Being Safe.* New York: Saturday Review Press, 1972. 312 pp. ♦ Applicable information regarding security on the job and selection of locks and alarm systems.

Mannings, J. "Security of Museums and Art Galleries," *Museums Journal,* 70:1 (June 1970), pp. 7-9. ♦ General treatment of procedural and physical steps to improve security in an existing museum building including such matters as good housekeeping, structural alterations, better locks, searching of premises after closing, outside lighting, and alarms.

Matthai, Robert A., ed. *Protection of Cultural Properties During Energy Emergencies.* 2nd ed. New York: Arts/Energy Study and American Association of Museums, 1978. 24 pp. ♦ Includes preparing for emergencies, protection of cultural buildings and facilities, blackouts and voltage reductions, protection of collections, sources of further assistance.

Michaels, A. F. "Security and the Museum," *Museum News,* 43:3 (November 1964), pp. 11-16. ♦ Describes security at the Smithsonian Institution.

Morris, John. *Managing the Library Fire Risk.* 2nd ed. Berkeley, Calif.: Office of Insurance and Risk Management, University of California, 1979. 147 pp., illus., bibliog., appendix.

"Museums and the Theft of Works of Art," *Museum,* XXVI:1 (1974), entire issue. ♦ Includes report by Interpol on theft of cultural property; psychoanalytic notes on theft and defacement; ethics of museum acquisitions; museum attendants; need for systematic approach to the protection of museums; problems in Egypt and India; comparison of national laws protecting cultural property, with a selective bibliography; Committee of Experts on the Risks Incurred by Works of Art and Other Cultural Property, Brussels, 19-22 November 1973: Final Report.

National Fire Protection Association. *Fire in Your Home: How to Prevent It, How to Survive It.* NFPA no. SPP52. Boston: National Fire Protection Association, c1978. 55 pp., illus.

National Fire Protection Association. *Fire Protection Handbook.* 14th ed. Boston: The Association, 1977. 1296 pp., illus., diagrams, appendices.

National Fire Protection Association. *Firesafety in the Home: A Security Guide for You and Your Family.* NFPA no. SPP40. Boston: The Association, 1976. 116 pp. ♦ Guide to the prevention of fire in the home, detection and inspection, and living techniques useful in fire protection.

National Fire Protection Association. Committee on Libraries, Museums, and Historic Buildings. *Protecting Our Heritage: A Discourse on Fire Prevention in Historic Buildings and Landmarks.* 2nd ed. Edited by Joseph F. Jenkins. Boston: National Fire Protection Association with the assistance of the American Association for State and Local History, 1970. 39 pp., illus., appendices, glossary of fire protection equipment.◆ Includes ideas and directions regarding losses, evaluation of risk and protection measures, good housekeeping, emergency planning and cost consideration.

Newman, Oscar. *Architectural Design for Crime Prevention.* Washington, D.C.: National Institute of Law Enforcement and Criminal Justice, for sale by Superintendent of Documents, U.S. Government Printing Office, c1971, 1973. 214 pp., illus., bibliog.

Nobelcourt, André. *Protection of Cultural Property in the Event of Armed Conflict.* Museums and Monuments no. VIII. Paris: UNESCO, 1958. 346 pp., illus., bibliog. ◆ Out of print.

Noblecourt, André. "The Protection of Museums Against Theft," *Museum,* XVII:4 (1964), entire issue.◆ Study of many types of alarm systems and mechanical devices to prevent or detect theft, robbery and attacks.

O'Rourke, William J. "Magnetometers for Museum Theft Control," *Curator,* XVI:1 (1973), pp. 56-58.

Pakalik, M. J. "Security and Protection in a Museum," *Curator,* I:4 (Autumn 1958), pp. 89-93.◆ Discusses what needs protecting in a museum; public relations factor in the museum's reputation.

Pellant, Leland T. "Are Museums Going to the Dogs?" *Western Museums Quarterly,* 2:4 (June 1964), pp. 19-22.◆ Use of security dogs in museums.

Probst, Tom. "Electronic Eyes and Ears on Guard," *Museum News,* 44:3 (November 1965), pp. 11-17.

Probst, Tom. "Fire Detection/Fire Protection," *Museum News,* 44:9 (May 1966), pp. 11-17.

"The Protection of Museums Against Theft," *Museum,* XVII:4 (1964), entire issue.◆ Includes analysis and planning, list of detection and defense techniques, practical advice on installations, list of techniques and methods used to prevent and detect theft and raids.

Sands, Leo G. *Electronic Security Systems.* 1st ed. Indianapolis, Ind.: T. Audel, 1973. 281 pp., illus.

"Securing Historic Sites: Atlanta's Protection Plan," *History News,* 31:9 (September 1976), pp. 166-168.◆ Fire and security system at Atlanta Historical Society buildings; includes "Guidelines for Buying Alarm Systems," prepared by U. J. Brualdi, director of product marketing, ADT.

"Security: The Schroder Report," *ICOM News,* 28:4 (1975), pp. 141-147.◆ Article based on comprehensive report on museum security by George H. H. Schroder used as basis for discussion at meeting of ICOM Committee for Museum Security, October 1975. Includes all security measures to be taken to protect museum buildings and contents against dangers caused by natural sources, human sources, technical failures, and personal accidents; report of the meeting; and a bibliography.

Sennewald, Charles A. *Effective Security Management.* Los Angeles: Security World Publishing Co., 1978. 298 pp.◆ Emphasis on large industrial or retail security operation with staff, but applicable chapters include program management, selling security within the organization, relationship with law enforcement, and community relations.

Shirar, Gerald. *Protecting Works of Art.* Washington, D.C.: American Society for Industrial Security, 1978. 221 pp., illus., bibliog.◆ How to protect art objects and irreplaceable valuables from fire, theft, vandalism and other threats.

Sohl, Stanley D. "Tornado in My Museums." In *Papers, 64th Annual Meeting, American Association of Museums* (San Francisco, Calif.: 1969), pp. 56-59. ◆ Describes emergency procedures after a tornado; considerations for flood, fire and civil disorders.

Strickland, Robert L. "An Inexpensive Alarm System for the Small Museum," *Museum News,* 43:10 (June 1965), pp. 24-26. ◆ Building a system for signalling to a central location that a protected object has been moved.

Tillotson, Robert G. *Museum Security.* Edited by Diana D. Menkes. Washington, D.C.: American Association of Museums and International Council of Museums, 1977. 256 pp., illus., bibliog., appendices, index. ♦ Includes architectural planning, psychological aspects of guarding, anti-intrusion devices and detectors, protection against fire, vandalism and environmental damage, internal security, inventory control.

Tobias, Marc Weber. *Locks, Safes, and Security: A Handbook for Law Enforcement Personnel.* Springfield, Ill.: Charles C. Thomas, 1971. 338 pp., illus., bibliog.♦ Detailed information on the basic types of locking mechanisms, their strong and weak points, and their applications.

U.S. Department of Agriculture. *First Aid for Flooded Homes and Farms.* Agriculture Handbook no. 38. Washington, D.C.: U.S. Government Printing Office, 1972. 31 pp., illus., table, recipes, checklist.

Vance, David. "Planning Ahead—The Registrar's Role in a Building Program." In Dudley and Wilkinson, *Museum Registration Methods* (Washington, D.C.: American Association of Museums, 1968), pp. 267-282.♦ Discusses how to plan for security of collections while a museum building is being designed, including a zone of safety concept and providing safe and efficient facilities for movement and handling of objects.

Vandalism and Violence: Innovative Strategies Reduce Cost to Schools. Education U.S.A. Special Report. Washington, D.C.: National School Public Relations Association, 1971. 56 pp., illus.♦ Information on how to curb vandalism and an appendix on security preparedness which is applicable to museum use.

Walch, Timothy. *Archives and Manuscripts: Security.* Chicago: Society of American Archivists, 1977. 30 pp., illus., bibliog., appendices.♦ Includes planning a security program, security staff and patrons, security and the collections, equipment, security against fire and flood, archival security and the law.

Walsh, Timothy J., and Richard J. Healy. *Protection of Assets.* Santa Monica, Calif.: The Merritt Co., 1974 -. 2 vols., looseleaf, illus., bibliog.♦ Chapters on all aspects of protecting assets; periodic supplements.

Ward, Ralph V. "The Museum Security Officer," *Security Management,* 20:1 (March 1976), pp. 30-33.♦ Discusses need for reevaluation of security procedures in cultural institutions as required by the mood and events of the time such as thefts, arson and vandalism. Includes effective access control and utilization of a protective security force.

Wathen, Thomas W. *Security Subjects: An Officer's Guide to Plant Protection.* Springfield, Ill.: Charles C. Thomas, 1972. 172 pp., illus.♦ Discusses the needs and operating procedures of a private guard force.

Weber, Thad L. *Alarm Systems and Theft Prevention.* 1st ed. Los Angeles: Security World Publishing Co., 1973. 385 pp., index.♦ Discusses realities of alarm systems, security weaknesses, and ways in which criminals evade and attack alarm protection.

Weldon, Stephen. "Winterthur: Security at a Decorative Arts Museum," *Museum News,* 50:5 (January 1972), pp. 36-37.♦ Describes the entire system with emphasis on guards and their training, emergency preparedness plans, and positive attitudes toward security preparations.

Wels, Byron G. *Fire and Theft Security Systems.* 2nd ed. Blue Ridge Summit, Pa.: G/L Tab Books, 1976. 192 pp., illus., index.

Windeler, Peter. "Fire: Endangers the Past—for the Future," *Museums Journal,* 70:2 (September 1970), pp. 72-74.

NOTES

American Society for Industrial Security, 2000 K Street, N.W., Suite 651, Washington, D.C. 20006. Founded in 1955, the U.S. and overseas geographic areas are divided into ten regions with chapters on the local level. Membership is open to professionals in business and industry, cultural and educational institutions, and government facilities who are responsible for the security functions of their organization. The Society maintains a library; compiles statistics; maintains a placement service; publishes periodicals and reports; and conducts workshops and seminars. Four standing committees are Security Management, Functional, Administrative, and most recently, Museum, Library and Archive Security. The Society publishes *Security Management,* bimonthly. The Committee on Museum,

Library and Archive Security was established in 1976 in response to an important need in security management programs. Its two main objectives are the planning and promotion of programs designed to assist those charged with security in these institutions, and the planning and promoting of programs and methods to better protect their collections and exhibitions from external threats of theft and vandalism, and internal threats from employees and others associated with the institution's environment. The Committee conducts studies and surveys, acts as a clearinghouse of information, develops standards and guides for use by administrators and staff. Specific topics are featured in the Society's bimonthly magazine.

Burglary Protection Equipment List. Available from the Underwriters Laboratory, 207 East Ohio Street, Chicago, Illinois 60611.

Fire Journal. 1907, bimonthly, membership. National Fire Protection Association, 470 Atlantic Avenue, Boston, Massachusetts 02210.

Identifax Nationwide Registry, 1320 Stony Brook Road, Stony Brook, New York 11790. Established in 1972, the Registry provides a nationwide, computerized system of property registration to help police identify recovered stolen property. Each member has an exclusive code number to mark personal property, office and plant equipment. The number is registered in a data bank, along with name, address and telephone number to which all law enforcement agencies have access through a toll free telephone call. Yearly cost depends on the number of items registered.

National Fire Protection Association (NFPA), 470 Atlantic Avenue, Boston, Massachusetts 02210. Founded in 1896, membership consists of representatives of business and industry, both individual and corporate, public safety officials, including state and municipal fire authorities and building inspectors, fire insurance executives and engineers, colleges, hospitals, libraries and others interested in the protection of life and property against loss by fire. It serves as a clearinghouse for information on fire protection and prevention, and fire fighting. Through some 174 technical committees, it develops and publishes advisory standards on virtually every aspect of fire protection and prevention. It provides field service of specialist engineers to promote electrical fire safety through wider application of National Electrical Code and to solve fire problems associated with storage, handling, and use of flammable liquids and gases. The Association maintains a library; and publishes *Fire News* (monthly); *Fire Command* (monthly); *Fire Journal* (bimonthly); *Fire Technology* (quarterly); *Advance Report* (annual); *Proceedings* (annual); *National Fire Codes* (annual); *NFPA Fire Protection Handbook* (cited above); reference books, standards, laws and ordinances, educational pamphlets, and audiovisual materials. Complete publications and visual aids catalog available from the Association. Among the more than 240 codes, standards and manuals which are kept up to date, appropriate editions are: *Protection of Records,* NFPA 232, 1975; *Archives and Record Centers.* NFPA 232AM, 1972; *Protection of Library Collections,* NFPA 910, 1975; *Protection of Museum Collections,* NFPA 911, 1974.

Safe Manufacturers National Association, 366 Madison Avenue, New York, New York 10017. Founded in 1927, the Association is comprised of manufacturers of burglary and fire resistive safes and fire resistive record containers such as filing cabinets.

Security World: *The Magazine of Professional Security Administration and Practice.* 1964, monthly, subscription. Security World Publishing Company, 2639 South La Cienega Blvd., Los Angeles, California 90034.

Underwriters' Laboratories, Inc., 207 East Ohio Street, Chicago, Illinois 60611. Founded in 1894, Underwriters' Laboratories, Inc. is chartered as a not for profit, independent organization testing for public safety. It maintains and operates laboratories for the examination and testing of devices, systems and materials to determine their relation to life, fire, casualty hazards, and crime prevention. Product Directories of Underwriters' Laboratories, Inc. contain the names of the manufacturers who have demonstrated an ability to produce products, devices, or systems in accordance with the Laboratories' requirements for the product categories covered. They also publish a booklet, "Testing for Public Safety," describing the organization; and, a brochure describing UL's publications and motion pictures. Note especially lists for Fire Protection Equipment (1974), and Accident, Automotive, Burglary Protection Equipment (1973), which are available from the publication department.

10

Printing and Publishing

Historical organizations since their inception late in the 18th century in the United States have always taken seriously their obligation to publish. In so doing, they have informed, they have interpreted, and they have promoted their role as a mirror to the past. In a welter of different kinds of publications, from leaflet to multi-volumed series, they have performed these functions, sometimes very well indeed.

Two large areas, writing and editing/design and production, are treated in the first two sections of this chapter. The former deals with the manuals, the dictionaries, and the compendiums on standards for editing and guidelines for manuscript preparation. The latter reflects the changes that modern technology has brought about in the publishing world. One of the most informative handbooks, covering the history of printing to types of printing paper, is *Pocket Pal . . . ,* published by the International Paper Company.

The confusion about copyright, common law and statutory, national and international, can be cleared up by reference to the final section. The new Copyright Law (Title 17 of the U.S. Code), copyright ownership, exclusive rights, fair use, library reproduction, and other bits of esoterica are covered.

Writing and Editing

Alderson, William T. *Historical Publications.* AASLH Cassette Tape no. 2. Nashville, Tenn.: American Association for State and Local History, 1971. 60 minutes.♦ Discusses the work of the editor, kind of publication the society will sponsor, how to begin a publication, what to publish, frequency and price. Also includes notes on content editing and copy editing.

The American Heritage Dictionary of the English Language. William Morris, ed. New College ed. New York: American Heritage Publishing Co., 1975. 1550 pp., illus.

American National Standards Institute and Council of National Library Associations. *American National Standard for Bibliographic References: Approved December 2, 1976.* New York: ANSI, c1977. 92 pp., bibliog., index.♦ Guidelines for the consistent citation of all types of bibliographic material; rules for the inclusion, style and punctuation of biblio-graphic elements, and the hierarchical levels for these elements; covers preparation of bibliographic references to all common print materials.

Balkin, Richard. *A Writer's Guide to Book Publishing.* New York: Hawthorn Books, c1977, 1979. 236 pp., bibliog., index.

Bernstein, Theodore M. *The Careful Writer: A Modern Guide to English Usage.* 1st ed. New York: Atheneum Pubs., 1965. 487 pp.

Bernstein, Theodore M. *Watch Your Language: A Lively, Informal Guide to Better Writing, Emanating from the News Room of the New York Times.* Great Neck, N.Y.: Atheneum Publishers, 1965. 276 pp.

Chicago. University Press. *A Manual of Style, Containing Typographical and Other Rules for Authors, Printers, and Publishers Recommended by the University of Chicago Press, Together With Specimens of Type.* 12th rev. ed. Chicago: The University of Chicago

Press, 1969. 546 pp., tables, glossary, bibliog., index.♦ Subtitle varies; current volume subtitled, For Authors, Editors, and Copywriters. Contents in three parts: bookmaking; style; production and printing.

Felt, Thomas E. *Researching, Writing, and Publishing Local History.* Nashville, Tenn.: American Association for State and Local History, 1976. 165 pp., bibliog., index.♦ Contents are presented in three major chapters: researching, including note taking and organization, use of libraries, oral history, other research sources; writing, including the writing process, footnotes and quotes, editing; publishing, including design and type styles, production processes, promotion and marketing; and, an annotated bibliography.

Ferguson, Rowena. *Editing the Small Magazine.* 2nd ed., rev. New York: Columbia University Press, 1976. 221 pp., bibliog., index. ♦ Covers the editorial process from planning and editorial policy, procuring and processing manuscripts to pictures, layout and design, and printing. Also includes "The Editor's Bookshelf."

Funk and Wagnall's Modern Guide to Synonyms and Related Words; *Lists of Antonyms, Copious Cross-References, a Complete and Legible Index.* By S. I. Hayakawa and the Funk and Wagnalls Dictionary staff. New York: Funk and Wagnalls, 1968. 726 pp., index.

Jones, Lois Swan. "Let Your Fingers Do the Walking," *Museum News,* 52:8 (May 1974), pp. 36-38.♦ Describes summary and scholarly catalogs, problems of time and money, comparisons of U.S. and Europe in meeting need for well-written catalogs of collections.

Jordan, Lewis, ed. *New York Times Manual of Style & Usage: A Desk Book of Guidelines for Writers and Editors.* New and enl. ed. New York: Quadrangle/New York Times Book Co., c1976. 231 pp.

Modern Language Association of America. *MLA Handbook for Writers of Research Papers, Theses, and Dissertations.* By Joseph Gibaldi, Walter S. Achtert. 1st ed. New York: The Association, 1977. 163 pp., illus., index.♦ Based on William Riley Parker's *The MLA Style Sheet* (1951) as revised in 1970 by John H. Fisher and others.

Morris, William, and Mary Morris. *Harper*

Dictionary of Contemporary Usage. 1st ed. New York: Harper & Row, 1975. 650 pp., bibliog.♦ Prepared with the assistance of a panel of 136 distinguished consultants on usage.

Nicholson, Margaret. *Practical Style Guide for Authors and Editors.* 1967. Reprint. 1st ed. New York: Holt, Rinehart, and Winston, 1971. 143 pp., bibliog. references.

Olsen, Udia G. *Preparing the Manuscript.* 9th ed. Boston: The Writer, Inc., c1978. 154 pp., bibliog., index.

Olson, James C. "The Scholar and Documentary Publication," *The American Archivist,* 28:2 (April 1965), pp. 187-193.♦ Discusses need for selection of source documents for publication and well-managed programs of documentary publication.

Parker, Donald Dean. *Local History: How to Gather It, Write It, and Publish It.* 1944. Reprint. Westport, Conn.: Greenwood Press, 1979. 186 pp., bibliog., index.♦ Contents include sources of information for local history; technique of gathering and organizing material; and methods of publishing.

Skillin, Marjorie E., and Robert M. Gay. *Words Into Type.* 3rd ed. Englewood Cliffs, N.J.: Prentice-Hall, 1974. 585 pp., illus., bibliog.♦ Guide to the preparation of manuscripts for writers, editors, proofreaders and printers.

Strunk, William, Jr., and E. B. White. *The Elements of Style.* 2nd ed. New York: Macmillan, 1972. 78 pp.♦ Includes revisions, an introduction and a chapter on writing by E. B. White.

U.S. Government Printing Office. *Style Manual.* Rev. ed. Washington, D.C.: 1973. 548 pp.

Webster's New Dictionary of Synonyms: *A Dictionary of Discriminated Synonyms with Antonyms and Analogous and Contrasted Works.* Springfield, Mass.: G. & C. Merriam Co., 1973. 909 pp.♦ Published in 1942 and 1951 under the title *Webster's Dictionary of Synonyms.*

Design and Production

Alderson, William T. "Marking and Correcting Copy for Your Printer," *History News,* 24:6 (June 1969), Technical Leaflet no. 51.

American Association for State and Local History. *Newsletter Techniques.* Nashville, Tenn.: The Association, 1975. 20 minute cassette tape, slide carousel, and supplementary materials.♦ Deals with producing a readable newsletter showing techniques of spacing, type style, mastheads, and paper, and the problems they can present in design. Also reviews techniques in cropping and scaling illustrations and in duplicating methods.

American National Standards Institute. *American National Standard for Title Leaves of a Book.* Secretariat: Council of National Library Associations. Approved March 31, 1971. New York: The Institute, 1971. 8 pp.

Arnold, Edmund C. *Ink on Paper: 2, A Handbook of the Graphic Arts.* 2nd ed. New York: Harper & Row, 1972. 374 pp., illus., bibliog.

Bailey, Herbert Smith, Jr. *The Art and Science of Book Publishing.* 1st ed. New York: Harper & Row Publishers, 1970. 216 pp., charts, bibliog., appendix, index.

The Bookman's Glossary. Edited by Jean Peters. 5th ed. New York: R. R. Bowker, 1975. 169 pp., illus., bibliog.♦ Guide to the terminology used in the production and distribution of new and old books; the words in common usage in a bookstore or publisher's office, library or among book collectors. Older definitions have been revised to reflect changes in the industry and new names and terms that are relevant to publishing and the graphic arts have been added.

Boorstin, David. "Art Book Publishing in the 70s," *Museum News,* 54:5 (January/February 1975), pp. 36-37ff.♦ Discusses effects of recessionary economy on art book publishing.

Bostick, William A. "Solving the Problem of the Paper Explosion," *Museum News,* 44:9 (May 1966), pp. 18-23.♦ Hints on operating a printing-duplicating shop, when to go to outside printers, and what process to use.

Cardamone, Tom. *Advertising Agency and Studio Skills, A Guide to the Preparation of Art and Mechanicals for Reproduction.* 2nd rev. & enl. ed. New York: Watson-Guptill Publications, 1970. 159 pp., illus.

Davis, Alec. *Graphics: Design Into Production.* London: Faber, 1973. 154 pp., illus., bibliog.

Derby, Charlotte S. "Reaching Your Public: The Historical Society Newsletter," *History News,* 22:1 (January 1967), Technical Leaflet no. 39.♦ Discusses content and layout.

Dessauer, John P. *Book Publishing: What It Is, What It Does.* New York: R. R. Bowker, 1974. 231 pp., bibliog., glossary, index.♦ Discusses the process from editorial development of an idea through the manufacturing, and marketing and shipment. Includes glossary of terms used in publishing and book manufacturing.

Dunlap, Connie R., et al. "Cataloging in Publication: An LJ Mini-Symposium," *Library Journal,* 99:18 (October 15, 1974), pp. 2573-2583.♦ Need to encourage publishers to print CIP data in the book so that bibliographic information is more readily available to more users, libraries, and processing services.

English, John W. "The Most Democratic Art Form," *Museum News,* 53:8 (May 1975), pp. 36-37.♦ Use of cards to announce exhibitions, communicate information, and serve as souvenirs; also affordable.

Faul, Roberta. "Nothing Succeeds Like Success," *Museum News,* 54:5 (January/February 1975), pp. 33-35.♦ Review of the beginnings and successes of the magazine *Smithsonian.*

Ferguson, Marie D. "Do-It-Yourself Design," *Museum News,* 56:4 (March/April 1978), pp. 38-41.♦ Describes design specifications developed by an outside firm used by Dayton Art Institute to produce consistently attractive, money-saving in-house publications.

Fleming, S. J. "Microfiche and the Museum," *Museums Journal,* 76:4 (March 1977), pp. 159-160.♦ Discusses micropublishing opportunities.

Ford, James L. C. *Magazines for Millions: The Story of Specialized Publications.* Carbondale, Ill.: Southern Illinois University Press, 1969. 320 pp., illus., appendices, index.♦ Study of specialized magazines; appendix includes samples of production, copyflow schedules, hints for writers, list of publishing associations, list of national distributors of national magazines.

Gore, Gary. "Phototypesetting: Getting the Most for Your Money," *History News,* 33:1 (January 1978), Technical Leaflet no. 103.♦ Outlines advantages and disadvantages in the photocomposition process in printing.

Gore, Gary. "Spotting Mechanical Errors in Proof: A Guide for Linecasting Machine Proofreaders," *History News,* 24:12 (December 1969), Technical Leaflet no. 53.

Graphic Arts Typographers, Inc., New York. *Graphic Arts Typebook.* New York: Reinhold Publishing Corp., 1965-66. 2 vols.♦ Vol. 1, Machine Composition, Serif Faces (287 pp.); Vol. 2, Machine Composition, Sans Serifs, Square Serifs, Misc. (255 pp.).

Grove, Kay. "Museum Cookbooks: For Fun and Profit," *Museum News,* 53:9 (June 1975), pp. 52-59.♦ Reviews of publications from ten museums and tips for any would-be cookbook publisher.

Henderson, Bill, comp. *The Publish-It-Yourself Handbook: Literary Tradition & How-to Without Commercial or Vanity Publishers.* 1st ed. Yonkers, N.Y.: Pushcart Book Press, 1973. 362 pp., bibliog.♦ Anthology of articles describing the processes, hazards, and personal woes and rewards of the game. Includes a variety of publications, poems, novels, cookbooks, craftbooks.

Hiles, Paula. *Basic Design of Publications.* Nashville, Tenn.: American Association for State and Local History, 1973. 17 minute tape cassette, slide carousel, and supplementary materials.♦ Learning to use five basic elements of a publications program: overall planning, typography, illustration, layout, and use of color.

Hiles, Paula. *Preparing Camera-Ready Art for Publication.* Nashville, Tenn.: American Association for State and Local History, 1973. 15 minute cassette tape, slide carousel, and supplementary materials.♦ Procedures used in preparing a simple, camera-ready brochure that can be printed in offset or mimeographed.

Huffer, Paul. *Poster Graphics.* Nashville, Tenn.: American Association for State and Local History, 1974. 20 minute cassette tape, slide carousel, and supplementary materials.♦ How to design and execute camera-ready art work.

Hurlburt, Allen. *Publication Design: A Guide to Page Layout, Typography, Format and Style.* Rev. ed. New York: Van Nostrand Reinhold Company, 1976. 134 pp., illus., bibliog., index.

International Paper Company. *Pocket Pal: A*

Graphic Arts Production Handbook. 11th ed. New York: International Paper Company, c1974. 191 pp., illus.♦ A basic handbook on printing and publishing; includes history, printing processes, composition, photoengraving, printing inks, binding, graphic arts terms, printing papers. Revised periodically to include recent innovations in printing; sections of earlier editions still helpful.

Jones, Lois Swan. "Where to Publish? Where to Index?" *Museum News,* 54:5 (January/ February 1975), pp. 30-31ff.♦ A compendium of publications, both American and European, in which research may be issued and list of vehicles produced especially for indexing those publications.

Kjorlien, Robert, and Ernest Graubner. "Out of Print," *Museum News,* 52:5 (January/ February 1974), pp. 60-62.♦ Describes two non-print alternatives to exhibit catalogues, LP records and a slide catalog.

Kullen, Allan. "The Printer and You," *Museum News,* 44:2 (October 1965), pp. 24-30.

Lawson, Alexander. *Printing Types, An Introduction.* Boston: Beacon Press, 1971. 110 pp., illus.

Lawton, H. W. "The Small Museum and Publications," *Western Museums Quarterly,* 4:1 (March 1967), pp. 1-5.

Lee, Marshall. *Bookmaking: The Illustrated Guide to Design and Production.* 1965. Reprint. New York: R. R. Bowker Co., 1972. 399 pp., bibliog., index.♦ Covers every step in the process of designing and producing a book, including creative and practical details on design, layout, costs and papers. Definition of terms; illustrated with examples and diagrams.

Marcus, George H. "These Catalogues Don't Stand on Shelves," *Museum News,* 54:5 (January/February 1975), pp. 25-29. ♦ Discusses publications that are boxed, bagged or bundled, bound in peculiar substances, wrapped or canned.

Melcher, Daniel, and Nancy Larrick. *Printing and Promotion Handbook: How to Plan, Produce and Use Printing, Advertising, and Direct Mail.* 3rd ed. New York: McGraw-Hill, 1966. 451 pp., illus.♦ An encyclopedia for those who have to buy, plan or prepare printing, including specific facts and practical details.

Moore, Ethel. "The Rocky Road to Publication," *Museum News,* 54:5 (January/February 1975), pp. 21-24. ◆ Outline of procedures necessary to produce a worthy publication, and a checklist for book-making novices.

"Museum Photography and Publishing," *ICOM News,* 23:2 (June 1970), pp. 61-62. ◆ Discussion with International Photographers Association on problems experienced in acquiring photographs of museum objects for publication.

National Public Relations Council of Health and Welfare Services, Inc. *Creative Annual Reports.* By Frances A. Koestler. New York: The Council, 1973. 71 pp. ◆ Guide to total conception, writing and production. Available from the Council, 815 Second Avenue, New York, New York 10016.

National Trust for Historic Preservation. *Preservation Press Publications Kit.* Revised. Washington, D.C.: The Preservation Press of the National Trust for Historic Preservation, 1978. 33 items. ◆ Resources describing the nuts and bolts of producing publications, from budgeting and design to paper selection, copyright permissions and proofreaders' marks.

Nelson, Roy Paul. *Publication Design.* 2nd ed. Dubuque, Ia.: W. C. Brown Co., c1978. 295 pp., illus., bibliog., index.

Nickelsberg, Arnold. "The Role of Museum Publishing Programs." In *Section Papers, 63rd Annual Meeting, American Association of Museums* (New Orleans, La.: May 1968), pp. 53-56.

One Book–Five Ways: The Publishing Procedures of Five University Presses. Introduction by Chandler Grannis. Los Altos, Calif.: W. Kaufmann, 1978. 350 pp., illus., bibliog. ◆ Originally published as a workbook for use at the 1977 annual meeting of the Association of American University Presses.

"Publication Design: What Museums are Doing," *Museum News,* 44:2 (October 1965), pp. 31-33.

Putnam, John B. "An Offer You Shouldn't Refuse," *Museum News,* 54:5 (January/February 1975), pp. 42-43. ◆ Nonprofit organizations might consider partnerships with university presses for producing museum catalogs and books.

Rice, Stanley. *Book Design: Systematic Aspects.* New York: R. R. Bowker, c1978. 274 pp. ◆ Manual for book designers in large publishing houses; emphasis on efficient use of modern technology in design and production.

Rice, Stanley. *Book Design: Text Format Models.* New York: R. R. Bowker, c1978. 215 pp. ◆ Emphasis on typographic details and visual examples.

Rosenthal, T. G. "Museum Photography and Publishers," *ICOM News,* 24:1 (March 1971), pp. 44-47. ◆ Discusses increase in art publications which call on resources of museum collections for illustrations, research and information; reviews rights of profession in negotiations with a publisher and insights into attitudes prevalent in publishing field regarding fees, copyright, and access to collections.

Sirois, Gary J. "So You Want to Publish a Newsletter?" *gazette,* 10:2 (Spring 1977), pp. 18-21. ◆ Includes dealing with a printer, printing processes, specifications and mechanics, and brief bibliography.

Smith, Cortland Gray. *Magazine Layout: Principles, Patterns, Practices.* Plandome, N.Y.: The Author, 1973. 208 pp., illus.

Smith, Datus C., Jr. *A Guide to Book-Publishing.* New York: R. R. Bowker Co., 1966. 244 pp., illus., bibliog., index. ◆ Guide to general principles of book publishing.

Walklet, John J., Jr. "Publishing in the Historical Society," *History News,* 21:4 (April 1966), Technical Leaflet no. 34.

White, Jan V. *Editing by Design: Word-and-Picture Communication for Editors and Designers.* New York: R. R. Bowker, 1974. 230 pp., illus. ◆ Demonstrates necessary union between word and picture to get an editorial message across; offers solutions to day-to-day graphic problems encountered in the production of magazines, house organs, newsletters and other publications.

Copyright

Bush, George P., ed. *Technology and Copyright: Annotated Bibliography and Source Materials.* Mt. Airy, Md.: Lomond Systems, Inc., 1972. 454 pp., bibliog. references. ◆ Reference guide to the effects of technology—xerography, microforms, computers, facsimile—on copyright.

Conference for Revision of the Universal Copyright Convention, Paris, 1971. *Conference for Revision of the Universal Copyright Convention, Unesco House, Paris, 5-24 July 1971; Report of the General Rapporteur.* Paris: 1971. 26 pp.

"Copyright Law to Change: Revisions Effective 1978," *History News,* 32:2 (February 1977), p. 38.

Copyright Revision Act of 1976: P. L. 94-553, as Signed by the President, October 19, 1976: Law, Explanation, Committee Reports. Chicago: Commerce Clearing House, c1976, 1977. 279 pp., index.

Cox, Henry Bartholomew. "The Impact of the Proposed Copyright Law Upon Scholars and Custodians," *The American Archivist,* 29:2 (April 1966), pp. 217-227.

Gibbs-Smith, Charles H. *Copyright Law Concerning Works of Art, Photographs, and the Written and Spoken Word.* 2nd ed. Information Sheet no. 7. London: Museums Association, 1974. 14 pp.♦ Brief guide to complexities of copyright law (British) and intended for museums and galleries.

Hilliard, David Craig. "Museums and the New Copyright Law," *Museum News,* 56:6 (July/August 1978), pp. 49-51.

Intergovernmental Conference on Copyright, Geneva, 1952. *Convention Universelle sur le Droit d' Auteur Revisée à Paris le 24 Juillet 1971/Universal Copyright Convention as Revised at Paris 24 July 1971 . . . .* Paris: UNESCO, 1971. 34 pp. ♦ Includes Protocols 1 and 2.

Intergovernmental Conference on Copyright, Geneva, 1952. *Universal Copyright Convention, as revised, with Protocols.* Message from the President of the United States transmitting the Universal Copyright Convention as revised at Paris on July 24, 1971, together with two related protocols. Washington, D.C.: U.S. Government Printing Office, 1972. 59 pp.

Johnston, Donald F. *Copyright Handbook.* New York: R. R. Bowker, 1978. 209 pp., appendices.♦ Topics covered include copyright notices, copyrightable subject matter, deposit copies for Library of Congress, copyright ownership, transfers, exclusive rights, infringement remedies, duration, fair use, library reproduction.

Knoll, Alfred P., and Daniel Drapiewski. "Knowing Your Copyrights," *Museum News,* 55:4 (March/April 1977), pp. 49-51. ♦ Discusses writings, legal standards, museum custom, professional customs and considerations, and includes a checklist of questions surrounding museum professionals' writings.

Nasri, William Z. *Crisis in Copyright.* New York: Dekker, 1976. 174 pp., illus., bibliog., index.

Nimmer, Melville B. "Government: Righting Copyright," *Cultural Affairs,* 12 (Fall 1970), pp. 40-41. ♦ Discusses European copyright law (domaine public payant); royalties continue to be paid for the exploitation of works after they have entered the public domain and put in a fund for the general assistance and encouragement of writers, artists and other creators.

Nimmer, Melville B. *A Preliminary View of the Copyright Act of 1976: Analysis and Text.* New York: M. Bender, c1977. 142 pp.

Ringer, Barbara. "Copyright and the Future of Authorship," *Library Journal,* 101:1 (January 1, 1976), pp., 229-232.

Ringer, Barbara. "Finding Your Way Around in the New Copyright Law," *Publishers Weekly,* 210:24 (December 13, 1976), pp. 38-41.

Ringer, Barbara. *The New Copyright Law.* Philadelphia: American Law Institute-American Bar Association, January 1977. one cassette, 1½ hours, no. V390.♦ Informative lecture reviewing the legislative history of the new copyright law, and examination of fundamental changes made by the law. Includes adoption of a single federal system of copyrights, the establishment of copyright from creation of a work rather than publication, divisibility of copyrights, and reforms in formalities.

Seidel, Arthur H. *What the General Practitioner Should Know About Trademarks and Copyrights.* 4th ed. Philadelphia: American Law Institute-American Bar Association, 1979. 265 pp., tables, appendices, index. ♦ Background on origin of trademark and copyright statutes, the law of unfair competition and trademarks, pertinent definitions, discussion of particular statutes; consideration of practical problems regarding trademarks and copyrights; and new chapter on major changes in the copyright law.

Seltzer, Leon E. *Exemptions and Fair Use in Copyright: The Exclusive Rights Tensions in the 1976 Copyright Act.* Cambridge, Mass.: Harvard University Press, 1978. 199 pp., index.♦ First appeared in April and June 1977 issues of the *Bulletin* of the Copyright Society of the U.S.A.

Stedman, John C. "The New Copyright Law: Photocopying for Education Use," *AAUP Bulletin,* 63:1 (February 1977), pp. 5-16. ♦ Appendix includes pertinent sections of the new law.

Walsh, Frank. "The New Copyright Law: Stronger and More Specific," *Public Relations Journal,* 33:8 (August 1977), pp. 6-7.

Winn, Karyl. "Common Law Copyright and the Archivist," *The American Archivist,* 37:3 (July 1974), pp. 375-386.♦ Discusses common law literary property right which differs from statutory copyright which governs published works protected under the copyright act.

NOTES

Copyright Bulletin: Quarterly Review. 1948, quarterly, subscription. Unipub, Box 433, Murray Hill Station, New York, New York 10016; or, UNESCO, 7, Place de Fontenoy, 75700 Paris, France. Reports on developments in international copyright, including information on documentation meetings and bibliographies.

Copyright Law, Title 17. On October 19, 1976, Congress approved "An Act for the General Revision of the Copyright Law, Title 17 of the U.S. Code, and for Other Purposes" (P.L. 94-553, 90 Stat. 2541). The law is amended in its entirety, with the effective date January 1, 1978. Chapters include: 1—Subject Matter and Scope of Copyright; 2—Copyright Ownership and Transfer; 3—Duration of Copyright; 4—Copyright Notice, Deposit, and Registration; 5—Copyright Infringement and Remedies; 6—Manufacturing Requirement and Importation; 7—Copyright Office; 8—Copyright Royalty Tribunal. Detailed information about specific changes or new provisions are available from the Copyright Office, Library of Congress, Washington, D.C. 20559.

U.S. Library of Congress, The Copyright Office. The basic function of the Copyright Office is the administration of the copyright law of the United States (Title 17 of the U.S. Code). The Office examines claims to copyright in a wide variety of works, registers those claims that meet the requirements of the law, and catalogs all registrations. It conducts correspondence about the claims and supplies general information concerning copyright law and registration procedures. All mail should be addressed to the Register of Copyrights, Library of Congress, Washington, D.C. 20559. The administration of the law was entrusted to the Library of Congress by an act of Congress in 1870, and the Office has been a separate department of the Library since 1897. The collections of the Library have been greatly enriched by its acquisition of a substantial proportion of the copies deposited for registration over the years. The Office is operationally separate from other departments and units of the Library of Congress, and has no authority to provide Library of Congress catalog cards or to assign catalog card numbers. Correspondence concerning cards and the preassignment of numbers should be addressed to CIP Office, Processing Department, Library of Congress, Washington, D.C. 20540. The Copyright Office distributes free of charge instructional circulars, selected reports on hearings, its annual report, a general guide to the new copyright law, studies on specific copyright issues, and copies of the law. Other types of reports and records may be purchased from the Superintendent of Documents or the Library of Congress Photoduplication Service. Specific instructions on how to order materials are included in Circular R2, *Publications of the Copyright Office.*

11

Public Relations

The arts of persuasion are manifold. Here they are applied to planning public relations programs, to membership development, and to publicity.

Omnipresent public relations are the responsibility of everyone in the historical organization, including governing board, staff, volunteers, and members—and the literature makes this apparent. Also apparent is the need for a plan, as will be seen in the citations of successful programs. These analyze impact so that programs may be tailored and promoted to meet the needs that are uncovered.

A strong membership base is vital to the development of the historical organization and depends on many factors. In the second section the factors are discussed in the references, and guidelines for carrying out a dynamic membership program are presented.

Effective communication means using all types of media: journals, newspapers, radio, television, and audio-visual materials. In the final section are listed the handbooks, the guides, and the articles that deal practically with all the media. The sole omission is shouting from the rooftops, for which there are no guidelines, alas!

Planning Public Relations Programs

Achterhoff, Carole R. "How to Lobby for the Arts," *Museum News,* 57:5 (May/June 1979), pp. 19-22.♦ Describes Citizens for the Arts; and its subsidiary Minnesota Citizens for the Arts, which is a political organization with the primary function to educate the voters of the state on the needs and goals of the arts in their respective areas. Includes a lobbying checklist.

Adams, G. Donald. "Survey of Museum Public Relations," *Curator,* XX:2 (1977), pp. 117-120.

Angoff, Allan, ed. *Public Relations for Libraries: Essays in Communications Techniques.* Westport, Conn.: Greenwood Press, 1973. 246 pp., bibliog., index.♦ Essays on public relations programs in all types of libraries.

Banks, Rose K. "The Museum and the Community," *Museum News,* 40:8 (April 1962), pp. 17-21.

Bellow, Corinne. "Museum Public Relations," *ICOM News,* 29:1-2 (1976), pp. 32-37.♦ Discusses subsidiary services, financial support, affiliated societies/volunteers, public relations events, published material, advertising, press, temporary/traveling exhibitions, research, outline of future plans, and bibliography.

Bernays, Edward L., et al. *The Engineering of Consent.* 1955. Reprint. 3rd ed. Norman: University of Oklahoma Press, 1969. 246 pp., illus.

Brown, Henry D., and Lucybeth C. Rampton. *Public Relations, Special Events, and Membership Services.* AASLH Cassette Tape no. 4. Nashville, Tenn.: American Association for State and Local History, 1971. 60 minutes.♦ General points about establishing good relations in a community through involvement in community-related organizations other than the historical society.

Burns, William A. "Museums Without Wax," *Curator,* VI:3 (1963), pp. 226-230.♦ Discusses prospects of public relations departments encroaching on administration, education and personnel relations, and curators.

Burton, Richard. "Museums as Media." In *Papers, 64th Annual Meeting, American Association of Museums* (San Francisco, Calif.: 1969), pp. 145-148.♦ Importance of understanding the capabilities of media.

"Business and the Arts: The New Challenge to Public Relations," *The Public Relations Quarterly,* 15:2 (1970), special issue.♦ Articles on why business needs the arts, business support, communication through arts patronage, and bringing arts to the people.

Cameron, Duncan F. "Putting Public Relations in its Place," *Curator,* IV:2 (1961), pp. 103-107.

Canfield, Bertrand R., and H. Frazier Moore. *Public Relations: Principles, Cases and Problems.* 6th ed. Homewood, Ill.: Richard D. Irwin, Inc., 1973. 486 pp., illus., bibliog.

Christison, Muriel B. "Creating a Climate Within the Museum for an Effective Public Relations Program." In *Papers, 64th Annual Meeting, American Association of Museums* (San Francisco, Calif.: 1969), pp. 149-151. ♦ Discusses need for defining museum objectives and policies, clarifying staff responsibilities, and having proper tools and data.

Cramer, Ted, and Kenneth Beam. "Marketing the Museum," *Museum News,* 57:3 (January/February 1979), pp. 35-39. ♦ Describes marketing/management plan at the North Carolina Museum of Art to create public awareness and increasing attendance.

Cruger, George A. "Eventful Calendars," *Museum News,* 57:3 (January/February 1979), pp. 40-44.♦ Use of calendars of events to communicate effectively with the public.

Cutlip, Scott M., and Allen H. Center. *Effective Public Relations.* 5th ed. Englewood Cliffs, N.J.: Prentice-Hall, 1978. 612 pp., illus., bibliog.

Dale, Edgar. *Can You Give the Public What It Wants? The Need for Better Communication in Editing, Writing, Broadcasting, Advertising, Public Relations and Teaching.* 1st ed. New York: World Book Encyclopedia, 1967. 220 pp.

Davis, Susan Lynn. "Public Relations—An Imperative in Today's Art Museums," *Curator,* XIX:1 (March 1976), pp. 63-72.♦ Includes a brief set of guidelines.

Derby, Charlotte S. "Reaching Your Public: The Historical Society Newsletter," *History News,* 22:1 (January 1967), Technical Leaflet no. 39.

Finlay, Ian. "What Image? What Public?" *Museums Journal,* 64:3 (December 1964), pp. 248-253.

Francis, Frank. "Blowing One's Own Trumpet," *Museums Journal,* 64:3 (December 1964), pp. 233-242.

Frere, Elizabeth, and Robin Jones. "Like It Was with 'Like It Is'," *Curator,* XIII:2 (June 1970), pp. 153-164.♦ Report of orientation film for the Metropolitan Museum of Art.

Gibbs-Smith, Charles H. "The Fault, . . . is . . . in Ourselves," *Museums Journal,* 64:3 (December 1964), pp. 226-233.

Golden, Hal, and Kitty Hanson. *How to Plan, Produce and Publicize Special Events.* Dobbs Ferry, N.Y.: Oceana Publications, 1960. 256 pp., illus.

Gorr, Louis F. "Museums and the Public: Realities and Heresies," *The Museologist,* 132 (March 1975), pp. 3-14.♦ Discusses relationship between the public and the museum on the administrative level, and community involvement and public participation on part of board members and executives.

Haupt, Richard W. *Dealing With Your Public.* AASLH Cassette Tape no. 17. Nashville, Tenn.: American Association for State and Local History, 1971. 45 minutes.♦ Discusses functions of membership both as a base for the historical society and as active arm for community outreach, and ways of involving the historical society in public activities and getting activities publicized.

Hyatt, Dave. *Public Relations: A Handbook for Business, Labor, and Community Leaders.* Ithaca, N.Y.: New York State School of Industrial and Labor Relations, 1963. 94 pp.♦ Basics of public relations goals and methods with which to achieve them; and pointers for utilizing different types of media. New York State School of Industrial and Labor Relations, Cornell University, Bulletin 48.

Ikard, Frank N. "How to Approach Your Congressman." Reprinted from *Congressional Action,* February 22, 1963. 2 pp.

Kotler, Philip. *Marketing for Non-Profit Organizations.* Englewood Cliffs, N.J.: Prentice-Hall, c1975, 1974. 436 pp., illus., bibliog. references.♦ How museums, universities, symphony orchestras and social agencies can analyze their impact on the community and tailor programs and fund-raising activities to meet and fulfill their needs. Assists in defining goals and objectives.

Leibert, Edwin R., and Bernice E. Sheldon. *Handbook of Special Events for Nonprofit Organizations; Tested Ideas for Fund Raising and Public Relations.* New York: Association Press, 1972. 224 pp., illus., bibliog.

McCaskey, Thomas G. "Reaching Your Public: Turning Travelers Into Visitors," *History News,* 20:6 (June 1965), Technical Leaflet no. 29.

Mann, Colin. "The Importance of the Public," *Museums Journal,* 64:3 (December 1964), pp. 220-225.

Moorhead, William S.; Richard Hunt; Theodore Haglett, Jr.; and Michael Straight. "Citizens' Strategies for Strengthening the Role of the Arts in Human Environment," *Curator,* XIV:1 (March 1971), pp. 25-35.♦ Importance of using the democratic process in gaining support for the arts.

Morison, Bradley G., and Kay Fliehr. *In Search of An Audience: How an Audience Was Found for the Tyrone Guthrie Theatre.* New York: Pitman Publishing Co., 1968. 229 pp., bibliog.♦ Topics include market analysis and research; psychological factors; image; ticket sales; attendance; and advertising.

Morrison, Larry. "Public Relations and Public Image," *Museum News,* 57:3 (January/February 1979), pp. 26-34.♦ Discusses two-way process of demonstrating the value of an institution to its publics and responding to their viewpoints and attitudes.

Morrison, William. "Your Public Relations Cards," *Museum News,* 41:5 (January 1963), pp. 11-16.

National Public Relations Council of Health and Welfare Services, Inc. *Creative Annual Reports.* By Frances A. Koestler. New York: The Council, 1973. 71 pp.

Norton, Ruth. "From Soup Bowls to the Stars: A Discussion of Museum Public Relations," *Curator,* II:1 (1959), pp. 5-10.

Phillips, E. Hereward; V. Middleton; and J. Letts. "The Outward Image," *Museums Journal,* 71:3 (December 1971), pp. 108-112. ♦ Public relations of the Museums Association, tourism and the role of museums, and the National Heritage program.

Post, Emily (Price). *Etiquette.* 12th rev. ed. by Elizabeth L. Post. New York: Funk & Wagnalls, c1969. 721 pp., illus.♦ Updates original book, first published in 1922, through extensive revisions and entirely new material.

"Public Relations Section: Museum and Visitors Opinion," *Museum News,* 45:7 (March 1967), pp. 29-34.

"Public Relations Section: The Museum's Role in Education—A Challenge for Public Relations," *Museum News,* 46:6 (February 1968), pp. 27-33.

"Publicity and Public Relations: Views of Museum Directors," *Museum,* IV:4 (1951), entire issue.

Ritchie, James I. *How to Work Effectively with State Legislatures.* Washington, D.C.: American Society of Association Executives, 1969. 49 pp., illus.♦ A guide to the planning and development of legislative programs on the state level, includes pre-election planning, legislative session activity, and preparation and procedures for working with legislators and lobbyists.

Robertson, Alex G., et al. "The Museum and the Community," *Museums Journal,* 73:3 (December 1973), pp. 100-106.♦ Includes university and the museum; museums in education; ship restoration project; and working with community industry.

Sperry and Hutchinson Company. *Public Affairs Handbook: A Guide to Achieving Good Government.* Fort Worth, Texas: c1976. 29 pp., illus.♦ Step by step directions for developing a better understanding of all levels of government and putting the understanding to work to make your influence felt in the areas you choose. Includes building awareness;

hearings and lobbying; summaries of local, state and federal government; and sources of information.

This, Leslie E. "Public Hearing Pointers (and Pitfalls)," *Historic Preservation,* 27:4 (October-December 1975), pp. 36-40. ◆ Guidelines for community action and suggestions for publicity.

This, Leslie E. *The Small Meeting Planner.* Houston, Texas: Gulf Publishing Co., 1972. 234 pp., illus., bibliog.

Thomas, W. Stephen. "The Museum as a Communicator: Use of Information Outlets by Museums in the United States," *The Museologist,* 94 (March 1965), pp. 6-13. ◆ Describes publications as an outlet and other types of outlets such as film, radio and television. Also in: Zetterberg, Hans L. *Museums and Adult Education* (London: Evelyn Adams & Mackay for ICOM, 1968), Appendix E, pp. 63-72.

Vanderbilt, Amy. *Etiquette.* New rev. ed. Garden City, N.Y.: Doubleday, 1972. 929 pp., illus.

Walkey, Frederick P. "How to Appeal to the Community," *Museum News,* 46:2 (October 1967), pp. 29-31.

Wasserman, Paul, and Jacqueline R. Bernero, eds. *Speakers and Lecturers, How to Find Them: A Directory of Booking Agents, Lecture Bureaus, Companies, Professional and Trade Associations, Universities, and Other Groups Which Organize and Schedule Engagements for Lecturers and Public Speakers on All Subjects, with Details About Speakers Subjects and Arrangements.* Detroit: Gale Research Co., 1979. 464 pp., indexes.

Waters, Somerset R. "Museums and Tourism," *Museum News,* 44:5 (January 1966), pp. 32-37.

Wheeler, Robert C. *The Art of Communication.* AASLH Cassette Tape no. 22. Nashville, Tenn.: American Association for State and Local History, 1971. 58 minutes. ◆ Emphasis on public relations as part of every museum function; reviews communications in regard to inner-staff, staff-public and museum-public and includes practical ideas on publicity methods with newspaper, radio, television, news releases, press conferences, newsletter, and special events.

Wheeler, Robert C. "Effective Public Relations: Communicating Your Image," *History News,* 28:3 (March 1973), Technical Leaflet no. 3.

Winick, Charles. "The Public Image of the Museum in America," *Curator,* V:1 (1962), pp. 45-52.

Wonderly, Robert, and Charles Van Horn. "Keep in Touch," *Museum News,* 52:5 (January/February 1974), pp. 65-66. ◆ Describes two national associations that provide informational and educational services on audiovisual technology for administrators seeking to upgrade their institution's communications program.

Wrenn, Tony P. "The Tourist Industry and Promotional Publications," *Historic Preservation,* 16:3 (1964), pp. 111-118.

Yeck, John D., and John T. Maguire. *Planning and Creating Better Direct Mail.* New York: McGraw-Hill, 1961. 387 pp., bibliog.

NOTES

National Communication Council for Human Services, 815 Second Avenue, New York, New York 10017. Formerly called the National Public Relations Council of Health and Welfare Services, the Council is a national nonprofit organization and clearinghouse for nonprofit and governmental relations. It is a membership organization established in 1922 and incorporated in 1937. The Council publishes how-to-do-it manuals, and maintains a public relations loan library for health, welfare, recreation, education, and related organizations subscribing to its services. It also maintains a placement service and conducts public relations institutes and workshops and forms study groups to consider public education-public information problems. The Council publishes *Channels,* a semimonthly newsletter; booklets, pamphlets, and audiovisual materials. In cooperation with the Public Relations Society of America, it published a series of six guides, "Managing Your Public Relations: Guidelines for Nonprofit Organizations" (1977) covering planning and setting objectives, using publicity to best advantage, working with volunteers, making the most of special events, measuring potential and evaluating results, using standards to strengthen public relations.

Public Relations Journal. 1945, monthly, subscription. Public Relations Society of America, 845 Third Avenue, New York, New York 10022.

The Public Relations Quarterly. 1955, quarterly, subscription. Howard Penn Hudson and Mary E. Hudson, Editors and Publishers, 2626 Pennsylvania Avenue, N.W., Washington, D.C. 20037. Incorporates *International Public Relations Review.*

Public Relations Society of America, 845 Third Avenue, New York, New York 10022. Founded in 1948, the Society is a professional organization of public relations practitioners in business and industry, counseling firms, trade and professional groups, government, education and health and welfare organizations. It conducts professional development programs; maintains executive referral service and an accreditation program. It publishes *Public Relations Journal* (monthly); *Public Relations Register* (annual). The Society was formed by a merger of the American Council on Public Relations and National Association of Public Relations Counsel; absorbed the American Public Relations Association in 1961.

Membership Development

Andrews, Francis S. "How to Prospect for Museum Membership," *Museum News,* 45:3 (November 1966), pp. 28-30.

Baker, Mildred. "Museum Membership," *The Museologist,* 98 (March 1966), pp. 15-17.♦ Discusses how to increase membership.

Boersma, Larry. "Some Hot Tips on the Membership Market," *Museum News,* 51:8 (April 1973), pp. 16-17.♦ Development of contemporary marketing and fundraising techniques by using a computer to maintain and update information on the constituency; also use files to develop reports on members and their interests, annual contributions and fundraising prospects.

Brick, Kathleen. "The Computer and a Growing Membership." In *Papers, 64th Annual Meeting, American Association of Museums* (San Francisco, Calif.: 1969), pp. 14-18.♦ Use of a computer in handling membership records, mailings, and promotions.

Chesley, Kenneth L. "How to Develop a Basic Museum Membership Program by Mail," *Museum News,* 46:1 (September 1967), pp. 31-34.♦ See also: "Part II," *Museum News,* 46:2 (October 1967), pp. 28-29.

"Development and Membership Promotion Section," *Museum News,* 45:3 (November 1966), pp. 27-35.

Haupt, Richard W. "Busy County Historical Society Triples Membership Since '56," *History News,* 14:7 (May 1959), pp. 58-59.

Haupt, Richard W. *Dealing With Your Public.* AASLH Cassette Tape no. 17. Nashville, Tenn.: American Association for State and Local History, 1971. 45 minutes.♦ Discusses functions of membership both as a base for the historical society and as an active arm for community outreach.

Lethert, Helen. "New Approaches to Membership," *Museum News,* 45:3 (November 1966), pp. 31-32.♦ Describes the experience of the Minneapolis Society of Fine Art in developing its membership program.

"Letters Used in Membership Drives," Midwest Museums Conference *Quarterly,* 13:3 (July 1953), entire issue.

McCausland, Mrs. John D. "How Effective Programming Gains and Retains Members." In *Papers, 64th Annual Meeting, American Association of Museums* (San Francisco, Calif.: 1969), pp. 10-13.

Meyer, Mrs. James. "Membership Development—The Old Way Is Still Best." In *Papers, 64th Annual Meeting, American Association of Museums* (San Francisco, Calif.: 1969), pp. 5-9.

Neiswender, Barbara Hodgins. "Launching a Corporate Membership Program," *Museum News,* 55:7 (July/August 1977), pp. 24-26.

O'Neill, Mary H. "Membership Potential—The Importance of In-Depth Study." In *Papers, 64th Annual Meeting, American Association of Museums* (San Francisco, Calif.: 1969), pp. 3-4.

Porter, Daniel R. *Membership Promotion and Services.* AASLH Cassette Tape no. 19. Nashville, Tenn.: American Association for State and Local History, 1971. 54 minutes. ♦ Reviews many facets of membership including need for membership, regulations governing membership, details of membership recruitment, membership records-keeping, rewards offered to keep members satisfied, constant re-evaluation of all functions pertaining to membership.

Porter, Daniel R. "Recruiting Members for Your Historical Society," *History News,* 21:8 (August 1966), Technical Leaflet no. 37.

Sperry and Hutchinson Company. *Membership Handbook: A Guide for Membership Chairmen.* Fort Worth, Texas: c1977. 24 pp., illus.♦ Includes membership needs, planning the campaign, staging the campaign, incentives for members, and a campaign organization chart.

Spirer, Louise. "Stalking the Museum Member," *The Museologist,* 142 (September 1977), pp. 3-10.

Trenbeth, Richard P. "Building From Strength Through the Membership Approach," *Museum News,* 46:1 (September 1967), pp. 24-29.

Publicity

Ashford, Gerald. *Everyday Publicity: A Practical Guide.* New York: Law-Arts Publishers, 1972. 90 pp.

Biegel, Len, and Aileen Lubin. *Mediability: A Guide for Nonprofits.* Washington, D.C.: Taft Products, 1975. 110 pp., bibliog. references.♦ Guidebook to assist nonprofit managers with little or no professional media experience in obtaining free media coverage, developing inexpensive public service announcements for radio and television, and advertisements for print media and news releases. Explores advantages and disadvantages of advertising, telethons and news conferences.

Carmel, James H. "Publicity." In *Exhibition Techniques: Traveling and Temporary* (New York: Reinhold Publishing Corp., 1962), pp. 182-191.

Cheney, Jane M. B. "Television . . . Voracious? Veracious? A Museum Experience in Television Production," *The Museologist,* 116 (September 1970), pp. 23-25.♦ The how and success of a series of television offerings of the Children's Museum of Hartford, Inc.

Dierbeck, Robert E. "Television and the Museum," *Curator,* I:2 (Spring 1958), pp. 34-44.♦ Describes programs at the Milwaukee Public Museum, audience, expenditures, and potentials of commercial and educational channels.

Dobrin, Michael. "The Race for Media Space," *Museum News,* 52:3 (November 1973), pp. 21-26.♦ How to develop effective news releases and well-planned mailing list for releases; writing for radio, public service announcements, use of photographs and television.

English, John W. "The Most Democratic Art Form," *Museum News,* 53:8 (May 1975), pp. 36-37.♦ Use of cards to announce exhibitions, communicate information, and serve as souvenirs; also affordable.

Gerald, Rex E. "A Philosophy on Publicity for Museums," *Curator,* VI:2 (1963), pp. 125-130.

Gifford, Philip C. "Museum Materials on Television," *Curator,* II:4 (1959), pp. 356-363. ♦ Experience of television at the American Museum of Natural History; the production, handling of materials, expenses, and points to consider in undertaking television programs.

Golden, Hal, and Kitty Hanson. *Techniques of Working with the Working Press.* Dobbs Ferry, N.Y.: Oceana Publications, 1962. 232 pp., illus.

Gottlieb, Edward, and Philip Klarnet. *Successful Publicity in Your Business and Community Life.* New York: Grossett and·Dunlap, 1964. 96 pp., illus., bibliog.

Harral, Stewart. *The Feature Writer's Handbook, with a Treasury of 2000 Tested Ideas for Newspapers, Magazines, Radio, and Television.* Norman: University of Oklahoma Press, 1966. 342 pp., illus., index.

Hellmann, Doris. "Publicity is for Professionals," *Clearinghouse for Western Museums Newsletter,* 1:2 (1960), pp. 31-33.

Hilliard, Robert R. "A Museum on the Dining Room Table." In *Papers, 64th Annual Meeting, American Association of Museums* (San Francisco, Calif.: 1969), pp. 153-156.♦ Use of television as an effective means of communicating values of the museum.

Jacobs, Herbert Austin. *Practical Publicity, A Handbook for Public and Private Workers.* New York: McGraw-Hill, 1964. 210 pp.

Johnston, Bernice. "Museum Piece," *Western Museums Quarterly*, 5:4 (December 1968), pp. 1-5.♦ Discusses advertising in newspapers.

Johnstone, Paul. "Museums and Television," *Museums Journal*, 64:3 (December 1964), pp. 242-248.

League of Women Voters of the United States. *Media Kit.* Washington, D.C.: The League, 1974-1977. 22 pp.♦ Consists of five pamphlets: "Projecting Your Image: How to Produce a Slide Show"; "Speaking Out: Setting Up a Speakers Bureau"; "Reaching the Public"; "Breaking Into Broadcasting"; "Getting Into Print."

Lickorish, L. J., and J. Letts. "Publicity," *Museums Journal*, 70:3 (December 1970), pp. 115-118.♦ Discussion of museums and the visitor, and a national organization for museum support.

Lillys, William. "Museum TV: Its Genesis," *Museum News*, 51:5 (January 1973), pp. 15-19.♦ History of Boston Museum of Fine Arts involvement in museum television; and, mandate for other institutions to establish a nationwide network of televised museum programs.

McMahon, John H. *Productive Press Relations.* New York: National Public Relations Council of Health and Welfare Services, 1968. 72 pp., illus.♦ Handbook on publicity techniques, news releases, working with editors and publishers, photographs, schedules.

Morgenstern, William V. "Publicity and the Museum," *Museum News*, 23:30 (April 15, 1946), pp. 7-8.

Morton, Terry B. *A Guide to Preparing Better Press Releases.* Washington, D.C.: National Trust for Historic Preservation, 1967. 8 pp., bibliog.

National Association of Broadcasters. *If You Want Air Time: A Handbook for Publicity Chairmen.* Washington, D.C.: 1977. 18 pp.♦ Prepared by the Public Relations Service of the National Association of Broadcasters, 1771 N Street, N.W., Washington, D.C. 20006.

National Trust for Historic Preservation. *Do-It-Yourself Press Kit.* Washington, D.C.: The Trust, 1977. folder, six insertions.♦ Guide to types of news; assistance in obtaining media coverage of group activities; sample

press releases for radio, television and publications.

O'Brien, Richard. *Publicity: How to Get It.* 1st ed. New York: Harper & Row, c1977. 176 pp., index.♦ Techniques for obtaining publicity without hiring a professional.

Ridgway, Rosalyn. "Public Image on the Air," *Museum News*, 57:3 (January/February 1979), pp. 21-23.♦ Opportunities for obtaining public service time on radio and television (PSA).

Shosteck, Robert. "Publicity for the Small Museum," *Museum News*, 44:9 (May 1966), pp. 24-26.

Smith, Roy A. "Reaching Your Public Through Television," *History News*, 20:3 (March 1965), Technical Leaflet no. 26.

Sperry and Hutchinson Company. *Publicity Handbook: A Guide for Publicity Chairmen.* Rev. ed. Cincinnati, Ohio: Consumer Relations, Sperry and Hutchinson Company, 1978. 24 pp., illus.♦ Includes basic checklist, four steps to good publicity, preparing a news release, working with news media, glossary of publicity terms.

Steinberg, Charles S., ed. *Mass Media and Communication.* 2nd ed., rev. & enl. New York: Hastings House, 1972. 686 pp., bibliogs.

"Television Section—Production; Programming of Television," *Museum News*, 45:7 (March 1967), pp. 35-39.♦ Articles on problems and techniques in producing museum programs, and varieties in programming.

Thomas, W. Stephen. "How Do Museums Use the Mass Media? A Report from the United States." In *Museums, Imagination and Education* (Paris: UNESCO, 1973), pp. 123-131.

Upward, Geoffrey C. "How to Publish the News," *Historic Preservation*, 29:2 (April-June 1977), pp. 36-41.

Wazlavek, Michael. "Writing Better Press Releases," *History News*, 33:7 (July 1978), p. 167.♦ Basic do's and don'ts; reprinted from *Alabama Museums*, newsletter of the Alabama State Council on the Arts and Humanities, April 1978.

Williams, C. L. "Museums in Television," *Western Museums Quarterly*, 2:3 (March 1964), pp. 15-18.

The Working Press of the Nation. Burlington, Iowa: National Research Bureau, Inc., 1945 -. 5 vols., annual.◆ Vol. 1—Newspaper and Allied Services Directory; Vol. 2—Magazine and Editorial Directory; Vol. 3—Radio and Television Directory; Vol. 4—Feature Writer and Syndicate Directory; Vol. 5—The Gebbie House Magazine Directory. Current edition, 28th, 1977, edited by Milton Paule.

NOTE

Editor and Publisher: International Yearbook. 1920/21, annual, subscription. Editor and Publisher Company, 850 Third Avenue, New York, New York 10022.

12

Management of Collections

The lot of the curator was probably simpler fifty years ago. Today curators and their bosses have to deal with a multitude of new issues and procedures, such as the ethics of acquisition, the use of computers, and the impact of the changing environment on their collections. And while veiled and sometimes overt allusions to "the plundered past" reel in their heads, they must deal with public disclosure and strictures about their deaccessioning procedures, with donor tax deductions and the latest rulings of the Internal Revenue Service (see also Chapter 8 on tax law and regulations), with selling museum objects in their shops (see also Chapter 7 on in-house sources of income), or the return of Native American artifacts.

All of this means careful management of collections and in this chapter are the materials dealing with collections policies including acquisition/disposal and loans, and with curatorial care, including cataloging as well as storage and handling. It should be noted that Volume 2 of the *Bibliography . . .* on *Care and Conservation of Collections* has additional references under "Environmental Considerations" and "Packing and Shipping." For the research and documentation of artifact, decorative arts, fine arts, and folk arts and crafts collections, consult Volume 4: *Documentation of Collections*.

The application of computer science to the arts and humanities is relatively new, but it has led to the development of practical and sophisticated systems of computerized collection records. The references here emphasize the application of the technology. The basic "bible" is Robert Chenhall's *Museum Cataloging in the Computer Age*.

Collection Policies

Acquisition/Disposal

"The AAMD Takes a Stand," *Museum News*, 51:9 (May 1973), p. 49.♦ Association of Art Museum Directors resolution regarding the ethics of acquisition.

The American Museum of Natural History. "Science Policy Report," *Curator*, XIV:4 (December 1971), pp. 235-240.

Amram, Philip W. "The Georgia O'Keeffe Case: New Questions About Stolen Art," *Museum News*, 57:3 (January/February 1979),

pp. 49-51ff.♦ Report on the recent O'Keeffe vs. Snyder decision and its impact on museums and their administration regarding the rights of the victim of the theft, of the innocent purchaser.

Arnason, H. Howard. "Introducing the International Foundation for Art Research," *Museum News*, 50:8 (April 1972), pp. 28-30.♦ Description of the purposes and work of the Foundation in dealing with questions of authenticity of objects.

Baldwin, Martin. "Policies of Acquisition in Medium-sized Museums," *Museum News*, 25:8 (October 1947), pp. 6-8.

Begemann, Egbert H. "The Price Is Never Right," *Museum News,* 51:9 (May 1973), pp. 32-35.♦ Argues against disposal of works of art for any reason, political, economic or aesthetic.

Boston, D. M. "Specimens or People? Purpose and Discrimination in Acquisition," *Museums Journal,* 69:3 (December 1969), pp. 110-113.

Boylan, Patrick J. "The Ethics of Acquisition: The Leicestershire Code," *Museums Journal,* 75:4 (March 1976), pp. 169-170.♦ Policy printed in full.

Brown, Richard, et al. "Forum," *Museum News,* 51:9 (May 1973), pp. 22-24. ♦ Opinions on public disclosure of museum acquisitions and disposals, and the possible need for a standard policy on acquisitions.

Burcaw, G. Ellis. "Active Collecting in History Museums," *Museum News,* 45:7 (March 1967), pp. 21-22.

Burnham, Bonnie. *Art Theft, Its Scope, Its Impact and Its Control.* New York: International Foundation for Art Research, 1978. 192 pp.♦ Report of the Foundation study to determine the feasibility of a central art theft archive and its role as a deterrent to theft. Includes results of a survey of 238 museums and 64 art dealers in the U.S. and Canada. Also available from Publishing Center for Cultural Resources, New York.

Burnham, Bonnie, comp. *The Protection of Cultural Property: Handbook of National Legislations.* Paris: International Council of Museums, 1974. 206 pp., bibliog., appendices.♦ Assembles, classifies and analyzes in summary form the ensemble of some 145 national legislative texts governing the discovery, ownership, circulation and sale of cultural property. The handbook is intended for use by museums and collectors in administering acquisition policies and for use by governments seeking to prepare new legislations, guide archeologists and other field researchers. Appendices include addresses, UNESCO Recommendations and Conventions, ICOM Ethical Acquisition Code, and bibliography.

Canaday, John. "Reproductions for Small Museums," *The Museologist,* 101 (December 1966), pp. 6-8.♦ Reprinted from the *New York Times,* August 21, 1966. Suggests small museums purchase good reproductions in-stead of spending fortunes on mediocre original works.

Constable, W. G. "Problems and Policies of Acquisition in Large Museums," *Museum News,* 25:7 (October 1, 1947), pp. 5-8.

Corley, Margaret A. "Criteria for the Inclusion of Ethnographic Items in Collections for Small Museums," *Western Museums Quarterly,* 4:2 (June 1967), pp. 9-12.

Craven, Roy C., Jr. "The Looting Continues—A New Solution?" *Museum News,* 52:6 (March 1974), p. 14. ♦ Proposes that UNESCO establish an agency to solicit requests for assistance from countries with threatened patrimony, assign a team of professional world archeologists to assist the country in carrying on the dig, supervise disposition of materials to host country and through sale at open international auction.

Driver, Clive E. "What Can You Do If You Have a Small Museum?" *The Museologist,* 127 (June 1973), pp. 9-16.♦ Discusses acquisitions policy for small museums.

"Ethics of Acquisition," *ICOM News,* 22:3 (September 1969), pp. 49-52.♦ Outline of a campaign to establish a set of professional ethical rules governing museum acquisitions to balance the action taken by UNESCO; also includes excerpts from a few examples.

"Ethics of Acquisition," *ICOM News,* 23:1 (March 1970), pp. 54-57.♦ Two letters written in response to problem presented in *ICOM News* article cited above.

"Ethics of Acquisition," *ICOM News,* 23:2 (June 1970), pp. 49-56.♦ Includes: Meeting of Experts to Study Ethical Rules Governing Museums Acquisitions (Conclusions and Recommendations); Archives—Repression of Clandestine Excavations (Rules formulated by the International Conference on Excavations); UNESCO International Convention for the Prevention of Illicit Trade of Cultural Property; Regarding Illicit Trade in Art Objects, Decisions of Curators of the University Museum, University of Pennsylvania; Guidelines for Biological Field Studies.

Field Museum of Natural History. "Policy Statement Concerning Acquisition of Antiquities," *Curator,* XIV:4 (December 1971), pp. 232-235.

Foramitti, Hans. "Use of Photogrammetry in the Museum Field: A New Application," *ICOM News*, 25:1 (March 1972), p. 38. ◆ Detection of thefts of works of art through photogrammetry.

Forgey, Benjamin. "Lord Byron Cried 'Rape, . . . ," *Museum News*, 48:10 (June 1970), pp. 21-25. ◆ Discusses crisis proportions in traffic of smuggled cultural artifacts.

Gallacher, Daniel T. "That's the Limit: A New Approach for Collections' Management in British Columbia," *gazette*, 10:4 (Fall 1977), pp. 38-43.

"Guidelines: The Ethics and Responsibilities of Museums with Respect to the Acquisition and Disposition of the Collection Materials," *The Museologist*, 131 (July-September 1974), pp. 2-4. ◆ Policy approved by the New York State Association of Museums; includes acquisition of objects for museum collections, deaccessioning and disposing of objects from collections, public disclosure.

Guthe, Carl E. "The Collections." In *The Management of Small History Museums* (Nashville, Tenn.: American Association for State and Local History, 1964), pp. 21-50.

Hamblin, Dora Jane. "The Billion-Dollar Illegal Art Traffic—How It Works and How to Stop It," *Smithsonian*, 2:12 (March 1972), pp. 16-27.

Harrison, Richard. "Why Collect What: The Need for a Collecting Policy," *Museums Journal*, 69:3 (December 1969), pp. 113-115.

Harvard University. News Office. "Harvard University Approves Policy Governing Acquisition of Art Objects from Foreign Countries," *Curator*, XIV:2 (June 1971), pp. 83-87.

Hill, Richard. "Reclaiming Cultural Artifacts," *Museum News*, 55:5 (May/June 1977), pp. 43-46. ◆ Relationship between Iroquois Indians and a local historical society prove that the return of artifacts can be mutually beneficial.

Hoving, Thomas P. F. "A Policy Statement from the Met," *Museum News*, 51:9 (May 1973), pp. 43-45. ◆ History of disposal of objects from the museum's collections and a basic policy statement on deaccessioning and disposal; also a note on New York State attorney general investigation at the museum.

International Foundation for Art Research. *Index of Stolen Art/1977.* New York: The Foundation, 1978. 70 pp., illus. ◆ Catalog of 1200 art thefts and recoveries in 1976-1977.

Jacob, John, and A. Kenneth Snowman. "The Sale or Disposal of Museum Objects," *Museums Journal*, 71:3 (December 1971), pp. 112-116.

MacBride, Dexter D., ed. "Appraisals of Objects in Historical Collections," *History News*, 32:7 (July 1977), Technical Leaflet no. 97. ◆ Panel of certified appraisers examines seven basic questions of importance to history museums and societies.

Meyer, Karl E. *The Plundered Past.* 1st ed. New York: Atheneum, 1973. 353 pp., illus., bibliog., appendices. ◆ An exposé of the international illicit trade in antiquities and an outline of steps that must be taken to prevent the disappearance of man's past. Comprehensive bibliography and full list of major art thefts since 1911.

Milrad, Aaron M. "The New Cultural Property Export and Import Act of Canada: A Measure Respecting Export of Cultural Property and Import of Cultural Property Illegally Exported from Foreign States," *gazette*, 8:3 (Summer 1975), pp. 24-28. ◆ Discussion of purposes, application, benefits, cooperation with other countries, provincial taxes, penalties, as well as detriments. Approved June 19, 1975.

Mitchell, Wallace. "When You Run Out of Money . . . Sell," *Museum News*, 51:9 (May 1973), pp. 36-39. ◆ An art academy sold its art collection at public auction to bolster a faltering endowment income.

Montias, J. Michael. "Are Museums Betraying the Public's Trust?" *Museum News*, 51:9 (May 1973), pp. 25-31. ◆ Discussion of donations, acquisitions and disposals as part of the public domain; selling less valuable objects to supplement limited acquisitions budgets; art auction scheme to benefit both rich museums and the less prosperous.

"More on Acquisitions," *Museum News*, 52:1 (September 1973), pp. 46-48. ◆ Text of policy statements made by the Brooklyn Museum, the Smithsonian, University of California at Berkeley, and Joint Professional Policy on Museum Acquisitions, regarding the acquisition of collection material.

Munger, Elizabeth. "A Policy Statement Concerning the Acquisition of Antiquities," Midwest Museums Conference *Quarterly,* 32:4 (Fall 1972), pp. 3-5.

"Museums and the Theft of Works of Art," *Museum,* XXVI:1 (1974), entire issue. ◆ Includes report by Interpol on theft of cultural property; psychoanalytic notes on theft and defacement; ethics of museum acquisitions; museum attendants; need for systematic approach to the protection of museums; problems in Egypt and India; comparison of national laws protecting cultural property, with a selective bibliography; Committee of Experts on the Risks Incurred by Works of Art and Other Cultural Property (Brussels, 19-22 November 1973); Final Report.

Nason, James D.; Kenneth R. Hopkins; and Bea Medicine. "Finders Keepers?" *Museum News,* 51:7 (March 1973), pp. 20-26.◆ Discusses return to Native Americans of artifacts and skeletal remains in museum collections which is a concern for both museum professionals and native peoples; authors explore issue from own perspectives.

Naumer, Helmuth, and Aubyn Kendall. "Acquisitions and Old Lace," *Museum News,* 51:9 (May 1973), pp. 40-42.◆ Discusses a museum acquisition policy that gives institution a free hand to upgrade and enlarge collections without donor interference; also conducts a periodic survey of collections and a biennial auction.

Neal, Arminta; Kristine Haglund; and Elizabeth Webb. "Evolving a Policy Manual," *Museum News,* 56:3 (January/February 1978), pp. 26-30.◆ Includes acquisitions; deaccession and loan policies; appraisals and donor tax deductions; U.S. and international regulations; photographic policies; objects brought in for examination; selling objects in the museum gift shops; library holdings; private collections; packing and shipping procedures.

Nicholson, Thomas D. "The Australian Museum and the Field Museum Adopt Policy Statement Regarding Collections," *Curator,* XVIII:4 (December 1975), pp. 296-314.◆ Includes text of Australian Museum Policy;and the Field Museum Policy (1972 policy covered certain responsibilities with respect to antiquities only, and the 1976 policy covers

entire range of the Museum's collecting responsibilities). See also: *AVISO,* 5 (May 1976), p. 7.

Nicholson, Thomas D. "NYSAM Policy on the Acquisition and Disposition of Collection Materials," *Curator,* XVII:1 (March 1974), pp. 5-9.◆ Policy adopted to govern certain actions of its member institutions; guidelines entitled "The Ethics and Responsibilities of Museums with Respect to the Acquisition and Disposition of Collection Materials, April 1974," printed in full. See also: *WRC Newsletter,* March 1976, p. 5, and *The Museologist,* 131 (July-September 1974), pp. 2-4.

Nicholson, Thomas D. "The Publication of a Statement of Guidelines for the Management of Collections," *Curator,* XVII:2 (June 1974), pp. 81-90.◆ Article reproduces statement adopted in April 1974 by The American Museum of Natural History relative to the acquisition and disposition of natural history specimens.

Papageorge, Maria. "International—The UNESCO Convention," *Museum News,* 56:6 (July/August 1978), pp. 9-11. ◆ Report on status of the UNESCO Convention on the Means of Prohibiting and Preventing the Illicit Import, Export and Transfer of Ownership of Cultural Property; and implications of legislation.

Rodeck, Hugo G. "Private Collections Policy in Institutions," *Curator,* VII:1 (1964), pp. 7-13.

Silva, P.H.D.H. de. "Ethics of Acquisition," *ICOM News,* 25:1 (March 1972), pp. 37-38.◆ Comment on ICOM recommendations for Field Missions.

United Nations Educational, Scientific and Cultural Organization. *Convention on the Means of Prohibiting and Preventing the Illicit Import, Export and Transfer of Ownership of Cultural Property.* Adopted by the General Conference at its sixteenth session, Paris, 14 November 1970. Paris: 1970. 23 pp.◆ Deals with issues resulting in the increasing theft of art objects, and in the illegal excavation of such sites, particularly in less developed countries, that can destroy scientific values and even the sites themselves. U.S. ratified the Convention in August 1972; implementing legislation pending as of 1979.

United Nations Educational, Scientific and Cultural Organization. *Index of National*

Legislations on the Protection of Cultural Heritage. Paris: 1969. 48 pp.

United Nations Educational, Scientific and Cultural Organization. *Technical and Legal Aspects of the Preparation of International Regulations to Prevent the Illicit Export, Import and Sale of Cultural Property.* Paris: UNESCO, 1962. 11 pp.

Wardwell, Allen. "The Ethics of Acquisitions," *Art in America,* 61:4 (July-August 1973), pp. 6-7.◆ Commentary on the problem of draining Central and South American countries of cultural icons. Includes summaries of the various international conferences and laws relating to this matter and the procedures taken by the Harvard Collections and the Metropolitan Museum of Art to avoid involvement in the unethical practices.

Watkins, C. Malcolm; Grace Cooper; and Gus Van Beek. "Museum Collections: A Consuming Responsibility," *Museum News,* 52:9 (June 1974), p. 35.◆ Discussion of the future of museum collections; visual documentation vs. objects, collections representing contemporary culture, master plans for future collecting, regional repositories, storage factors, disposition of materials, role of museum collections.

Williams, Sharon Anne. *The International and National Protection of Movable Cultural Property: A Comparative Study.* Dobbs Ferry, N.Y.: Oceana Publications, Inc., 1978. 302 pp., bibliog. references, index.◆ Analysis and comparison of past and current laws during war and peacetime.

Young, Rachel M. R. *Museum Enquiries.* Information Sheet no. 11. London: Museums Association, 1972. 4 pp.◆ Concerns queries about objects brought into the museum by the public, methods of dealing with such enquiries. Includes identification, forms, conditions of acceptance, disposals, security, storage, dealers and vendors, and other types of enquiries.

Zelle, Ann. "Acquisitions: Saving Whose Heritage?" *Museum News,* 49:8 (April 1971), pp. 19-24.◆ Viewpoints regarding destruction of archeological sites, smuggling national art treasures, international accusations, illegal export, as expressed by native grave robber, customs official, art dealer, archeologist, state department official and museum director; review of what is being done on international and professional levels; brief bibliography.

Zelle, Ann. "ICOM Ethics of Acquisitions: A Report to the Profession," *Museum News,* 50:8 (April 1972), pp. 31-33.

NOTES

International Foundation for Art Research, 46 East 70th Street, New York, New York 10021. Founded in 1968, the Foundation is a nonprofit organization designed to assist art museums, individual collectors, community institutions, and government agencies in the resolution of questions of authenticity or attribution of works of art that may be in their collections or that may be offered to them as gifts. The Foundation is concerned solely with questions of authenticity and not with matters of evaluation. It is administered by a Board of Directors representing leading collectors, scholars, dealers, lawyers and public officials. Reports are compiled by internationally-recognized art experts who form the Advisory Council. Under the aegis of the Foundation, examinations of works of art are conducted below cost and the owner pays a minimal sum. All monies are applied directly to the cost of the examination and not toward the support of the Foundation. The Foundation makes available information and expertise which has been usually unavailable, and acts as a clearinghouse and administrative and legal framework for experts and scholars within which they can express truly objective opinions. It considers requests from owners of works of art and from institutions and agencies for assistance in the investigation of historical background and in matters where questions of substance arise. The Foundation also maintains a Central Archive for Stolen Art in an effort to combat theft and reduce the resale of stolen art objects. It has conducted a survey to determine the extent and seriousness of museums' experience with thefts. It publishes *Art Theft Archive Newsletter,* 10/yr., listing recent thefts with in-depth information on art security.

Museum Exchange Program (MUSEP). The International Council of Museums has established an ad hoc committee for the purpose of preparing a study on the restitution or return of cultural properties to their countries of origin. The purpose of MUSEP is to encourage institutions in both developed and developing countries to exchange materials from their collections; to give practical assistance for the realization of such exchanges by means of collecting information concerning museums willing to exchange, lend, or borrow, as well as the number, type, and nature of the objects; to establish contacts between museums, with a view to reaching bilateral agreements for exchanges. Guidelines for MUSEP are in the recommendation concerning the international exchange of cultural property, adopted at the UNESCO 19th General Conference, 1976.

Theft Notices, Art Dealers Association of America, 575 Madison Avenue, New York, New York 10022. Published 4/5 times a year, *Theft Notices* is distributed as a complimentary service to those requesting to be on the mailing list. It refers to thefts from museums, dealers, private collectors and artists. The Association was founded in 1962 for art dealers seeking to improve the stature and standing of the art gallery business in the United States. It also handles appraisals of works of art donated to philanthropic institutions.

UNESCO/ICOM Documentation Centre. The Centre maintains an archive of national legislations for the protection of cultural property on microfiche to keep up to date the material compiled for the handbook by Bonnie Burnham, cited above. Related ICOM services include publication of notices of thefts and articles on the destruction of cultural property, and professional statements and editorials on the ethics of acquisition in *ICOM News*.

UNESCO Recommendations. Recommendation Concerning the International Exchange of Cultural Property, adopted by the General Conference at its nineteenth session, Nairobi, 26 November 1976; and, Recommendation for the Protection of Movable Cultural Property, adopted by the General Conference at its twentieth session, Paris, 28 November 1978.

Loans

Cannon-Brookes, Peter. "The Loan of Works of Art for Exhibition," *Museums Journal,* 71:3 (December 1971), pp. 105-107.♦ Proposed standards and code of practice; includes draft conditions of loan.

Freed, Stanley A.; Judith Eisenberg; and Laila Williamson. "Should Museums Charge for Loans? A View from New York," *Curator,* XIX:4 (1976), pp. 257-264.

Hatt, Robert T., and George L. Stout. "Standard Procedure for Intermuseum Loans," *Museum News,* 27:18 (March 15, 1950), pp. 7-8.

Katzive, David H. "Contemporary Art Loans, Trial by Fire," *Bulletin of the American Group-IIC,* 11:1 (October 1970), pp. 1-5.

Landais, Hubert. "Museums and Insurance," *ICOM News,* 27:3-4 (1974), pp. 79-82. ♦ Discusses insurance on collections and on loans.

"Lending Museum Materials," Midwest Museums Conference *Quarterly,* 16:4 (October 1956), entire issue.

"Loan Agreements, Insurance, Transport, Examination of Works of Art," *Museum,* XXI:3 (1968), pp. 198-202, 207-210. ♦ Issue devoted to "The Technical Organization of an International Art Exhibition," Expo '67 in Montreal; includes sample forms.

Manning, Anita. "Converting Loans to Gifts: One Solution to 'Permanent' Loans," *History News,* 32:4 (April 1977), Technical Leaflet no. 94.♦ Includes reviewing the loans, finding the lender, and approaching the lender or heirs; sample letter, Certificate of Gift, loan agreement and conditions form.

Michaels, Peter. "Lender Beware," *Museum News,* 43:1 (September 1964), pp. 11-12.

Pomerantz, Louis. "Art Consumption," *Museum News,* 49:3 (November 1970), pp. 10-11.♦ Discusses need to eliminate low-merit exhibitions and granting highly selective loans, savings in man hours and money, and preservation of irreplaceable cultural treasures.

Shapiro, Harry L. "Borrowing and Lending," *Curator,* III:3 (1960), pp. 197-203.

Sweetman, John. "Picture-lending and Museums: Methods and Possibilities," *Museums Journal,* 63:4 (March 1964), pp. 274-282.

Curatorial Care

Cataloging

Bohem, Hilda. "A Visible File Catalog for Photographic Material," *The American Archivist,* 39:2 (April 1976), pp. 165-166.

Bowditch, George. "Cataloging Photographs: A Procedure for Small Museums," *History News*, 26:11 (November 1971), Technical Leaflet no. 57.

Buck, Anne. "Cataloguing Costume," *Museums Journal*, 76:3 (December 1976), pp. 109-110.♦ ICOM Committee of Museums of Costume study on methods of cataloging dress; analysis of basic information compiled into a list.

Buck, Richard D. "Describing the Condition of Art Objects," *Museum News*, 56:6 (July/August 1978), pp. 29-33.♦ Excerpt about preparing condition reports, from Dudley, et al., *Museum Registration Methods*, 3rd ed., 1979; includes a glossary of terms.

Buck, Richard D. "The Inspection of Collections," *Museum News*, 29:7 (October 1, 1951), pp. 6-8.♦ A system for recording condition.

Chenhall, Robert G. *Nomenclature for Museum Cataloging: A System for Classifying Man-Made Objects*. Nashville, Tenn.: American Association for State and Local History, 1978. 512 pp., index.♦ Provides a hierarchical system for the classification of man-made objects; major part of the system is an expandable word list to be used with or without computerized cataloging processes.

Chenhall, Robert G., and Peter Homulos. "Museum Data Standards," *Museum News*, 56:6 (July/August 1978), pp. 43-48.♦ General statement of data standards that are initial steps in the systematic documentation of collections; includes a glossary of terms and data categories for museum inventory control. Also in *gazette*, 11:3 (Summer 1978), pp. 12-18.

Coleman Laurence Vail. "Accession Policies." In *Manual for Small Museums* (New York: G. P. Putnam's Sons, 1927), pp. 121-126.

Cox, Janson L. "Photographing Historical Collections: Equipment, Methods and Bibliography," *History News*, 28:5 (May 1973), Technical Leaflet no. 63.♦ Deals with kind of photographic equipment necessary to carry out curatorial activities at a small historical society or museum; includes information on techniques needed to produce photographic documentation sufficient for accession records, insurance needs, security standards, and exhibit goals.

De Borhegyi, Stephan F., and Alice Marriott. "Proposals for Standardized Museum Accessioning and Classification Systems," *Curator*, I:2 (1958), pp. 77-86.

Detroit Historical Museum. *Registrar's Manual*. 1961. Reprint. Detroit, Mich.: The Museum, 1973. 12 pp.

"The Documentation of Collections in General Museums," *ICOM News*, 23:3 (September 1970), pp. 55-60.♦ A proposed system of classifying and cataloging, illustrated with sample forms.

Drake, Elena. "Problems of a University Museum Registrar." In *Papers, 64th Annual Meeting, American Association of Museums* (San Francisco, Calif.: 1969), pp. 138-143.

Dudley, Dorothy H., comp. "For the Registrar's Notebook," *Museum News*, 43:6 (February 1965), pp. 31-35.

Dudley, Dorothy; Irma B. Wilkinson; et al. *Museum Registration Methods*. 3rd ed. rev. Washington, D.C.: American Association of Museums, 1979. 346 pp., illus., appendix.♦ Updated, expanded and redesigned, and includes computerizing collections and a glossary of terms. Added appendix on "Shipping, Packing and Insurance."

Graham, John M., II. "A Method of Museum Registration," *Museum News*, 42:8 (April 1964), Technical Supplement no. 2.

Guthe, Carl E. "Documenting Collections: Museum Registration and Records," rev. ed., *History News*, 18:9 (July 1963), Technical Leaflet no. 11.

Hurst, Richard M. "Putting a Collection on Film," *Curator*, XIII:3 (September 1970), pp. 199-203. ♦ Photographing collections for purposes of security and patron service.

Klapthor, Margaret M. "Will It Be There Tomorrow?" *Historic Preservation*, 23:1 (January-March 1971), pp. 59-60.♦ Discusses handling artifacts, condition, and quality of the care of the objects.

Kuhn, Hermann, and Christel Zocher. "Feature Cards for the Storing of Technical Data Which Result from the Scientific Examination of Works of Art," *Studies in Conservation*, 15:2 (May 1970), pp. 102-121.♦ Report on how the card system works and its advantages for reference purposes.

Lewis, Geoffrey D. "Obtaining Information from Museum Collections and Thoughts on a National Index," *Museums Journal,* 65:1 (1965), pp. 12-22.♦ Describes a punched feature card system.

Lewis, Ralph H. *Manual for Museums.* Washington, D.C.: National Park Service, U.S. Department of the Interior; for sale by the Superintendent of Documents, U.S. Government Printing Office, 1976. 412 pp., illus., bibliog., index.♦ Outgrowth of the 1941 volume, *Field Manual for Museums* by Ned J. Burns. Includes four parts: Museum Collections; Museum Records; Furnished Historic Structure Museums; Exhibit Maintenance and Replacement, and eight specialized appendices.

MacDonald, Robert R. "Toward A More Accessible Collection: Cataloging at the Mercer Museum," *Museum News,* 48:6 (February 1969), pp. 23-26.

Manning, Anita. "Data Retrieval Without a Computer," *History News,* 30:9 (September 1975), Technical Leaflet no. 85.

Oddon, Yvonne. "The Documentation of Collections in General Museums," *ICOM News,* 23:3 (September 1970), pp. 55-60.♦ Intended for the curator of a small or medium-sized museum covering miscellaneous fields.

Oddon, Yvonne. "Standard Methods of Field Documentation." In *Field Manual for Museums* (Paris: UNESCO, 1970), pp. 41-57.♦ Contents: significance of identification records, field work documentation equipment, general recommendations, completing identification records, museum use of identification labels, audiovisual documentation, bibliography.

Raine, C. C. "Recording Forms," *Museums Journal,* 70:1 (June 1970), p. 28.♦ A tentative questionnaire for donors to complete in order to record all the details the donor might be able to supply.

"Registrar's Section: Looking Ahead," *Museum News,* 46:3 (November 1967), pp. 28-35.

Reibel, Daniel B. "The Challenge of the Future of History Museums," *Curator,* X:3 (1967), pp. 253-260.♦ Discusses lack of adequate documentation and care; recommends a union catalog of rare items in small collections and steps toward cooperative regional information storage systems.

Reibel, Daniel B. *Registration Methods for the Small Museum: A Guide for Historical Collections.* Nashville, Tenn.: American Association for State and Local History, 1978. 160 pp., illus., bibliog., appendices.♦ How-to manual covering entire registration process; examines role of registrar or curator, collections committee, and board of directors; acquisition, numbering, cataloging, documentation and loans; and includes sample forms.

Ricciardelli, Alex F. "A Model for Inventorying Ethnological Collections," *Curator,* X:4 (December 1967), pp. 330-336.♦ Describes statewide inventory project in Oklahoma to develop a material culture file of ethnological items, compiled on IBM punch cards.

Riefstahl, Rudolph M. "Museum Photography," *Museum News,* 44:2 (October 1965), pp. 21-23.

Roberts, D. Andrew. "Proposals for a Survey of Cataloguing Practice in British Museums," *Museums Journal,* 75:2 (September 1975), pp. 78-80.

Ross, David, and Rene Chartrand. "Guidelines for Cataloguing Military Uniforms," *gazette,* 10:2 (Spring 1977), pp. 24-48. ♦ Includes guidelines, bibliography, list of parts of a military uniform, glossary of terms, diagrams and illustrations. Also available as a 25-page reprint from the Canadian Museums Association.

Roy Choudhury, Anil. *Art Museum Documentation and Practical Handling.* Hyderabad: Choudhury & Choudhury, 1963. 300 pp., illus., forms, bibliog.♦ Designed primarily for use by museums in India, but applicable to museums throughout the world. Follows generally the procedures used by British and European museums in cataloging objects; also describes procedures followed by several major U.S. museums.

Schneider, Mary Jane. *Cataloguing and Care of Collections for Small Museums.* Museum Brief no. 8. Columbia, Mo.: Museum of Anthropology, University of Missouri, 1971. 28 pp., bibliog.

Shelton, L. T. "Accession/Catalog Record System," *Midwest Museums Conference Quarterly,* 36:1 (Winter 1975-76), pp. 8-11.

Smathers, Diane G. "Responsibilities of Curating a Small Costume Collection," *Curator,* XX:2 (1977), pp. 157-162.♦ Includes registration, cataloging, marking, storage, display and research.

Thieme, Mary. *Registration of Museum Objects.* Nashville, Tenn.: American Association for State and Local History, 1974. 20 minute tape cassette, slide carousel, and supplementary materials.♦ Explains how to number, measure, and photograph different artifacts, and distinguishes between source, location, document, classification, and catalog files.

U.S. National Park Service. "Museum Collections." In *Field Manual for Museums* (Ann Arbor, Mich.: Finch Press, 1974), pp. 101-117.♦ Includes purposes, accession policies, accession methods, museum records, and sample forms.

Vanderbilt, Paul. "Filing Your Photographs: Some Basic Procedures," *History News,* 21:6 (June 1966), Technical Leaflet no. 36.

Vileck, Marica; Marian Harrison; and Johanna Hecht. "Scholarship on Cards, The Museum Catalogue," The Metropolitan Museum of Art *Bulletin,* 29:4 (December 1970), pp. 185-188.

Weinstein, Robert A., and Larry Booth. *Collection, Use, and Care of Historical Photographs.* Nashville, Tenn.: American Association for State and Local History, 1977. 222 pp., illus., bibliog., appendix, index.♦ Part I—Philosophy, how to collect photographs, how to receive and start processing collections; Part 2—Technical, preservation and conservation of black and white photographs and related subjects.

Whiting, Alfred F. "Catalogues: Damn 'Em—An Inter-museum Office Memo," *Curator,* IX:1 (1966), pp. 85-87.

NOTE

Registrars' Report. May 1977, monthly, subscription. P.O. Box 112, Bicentennial Station, Los Angeles, California 90048.

Storage and Handling

Ames, Michael M. "A New System of Visible Storage," *ICOM News,* 29:3 (1976), p. 60.

Ames, Michael M. "Visible Storage and Public Documentation," *Curator,* XX:1 (1977), pp. 65-79.

Bartlett, John. "Storage and Study Collections—Museums," *Museums Journal,* 63:1-2 (June-September 1963), pp. 62-63.

Beckman, Thomas. "The Transportation of Art Works." In *Papers, 64th Annual Meeting, American Association of Museums* (San Francisco, Calif.: 1969), pp. 133-137.♦ Methods of shipment including transportation, services, sample tariffs.

Bell, Jan R. "Rolling Your Own—A New System of Textile Storage," *Curator,* XIX:3 (September 1976), pp. 246-249.

Buck, Richard D. "Hazards of International Shipment," *Bulletin of the American Group-IIC,* 6 (May 1966), pp. 15-16.

Buechner, Thomas S. "The Open Study-Storage Gallery," *Museum News,* 40:9 (May 1962), pp. 34-37.

Daifuku, Hiroshi. "Collections: Their Care and Storage." In *The Organization of Museums: Practical Advice* (Paris: UNESCO, 1960), pp. 119-125.

De Borhegyi, Stephan F. "Curatorial Neglect of Collections," *Museum News,* 43:5 (January 1965), pp. 34-40.♦ See also: "Field Manual or Cataloguing Guide," pp. 38-40, designed as a field questionnaire for registrars, curators, field personnel to insure the maximum amount of data and information.

De Borhegyi, Stephan F. "Organization of Archaeological Museum Storerooms," *Museum,* V:4 (1952), pp. 251-260.

Dunn, Walter S., Jr. "Storing Your Collections: Problems and Solutions," rev. ed., *History News,* 25:6 (June 1970), Technical Leaflet no. 5.

Elkin, Paul W. "Treasure in Store: The Bristol Museum Storage Project 1972-1974," *Museums Journal,* 54:2 (September 1975), pp. 57-60.

Fall, Frieda Kay. "New Industrial Packing Materials: Their Possible Uses for Museums," *Museum News,* 44:4 (December 1965), Technical Supplement no. 10.

Fikioris, Margaret A. "A Model for Textile Storage," *Museum News,* 52:3 (November 1973), pp. 34-41.

Force, Roland W. "Museum Collections—

Access, Use, and Control," *Curator,* XVIII:4 (December 1975), pp. 249-255.

Goist, David C. "Packing Methods and Procedures," Midwest Museums Conference *Quarterly,* 37:1-2 (Winter-Spring 1977), pp. 20-24.◆ An outline of packing methods for shipping paintings, and a selected bibliography.

Graham, John, II, and the Curatorial Department of Colonial Williamsburg. "Solving Storage Problems," *Museum News,* 41:4 (December 1962), pp. 24-29.

Greene, Candace S. "Storage Techniques for Ethnology Collections," *Curator,* XXI:2 (June 1978), pp. 111-128.◆ Article adapted from "Storage Techniques for the Conservation of Collections," originally published as Bulletin no. 8 by the Oklahoma Museums Association, in conjunction with the Stovall Museum of Science and History, 1977, pp. 1-20. Deals with storage aspects of conservation; techniques applicable to most types of museum collections.

Gregg, Richard N. "The Modest Museum and Its Borrowing Needs." In *Papers, 64th Annual Meeting, American Association of Museums* (San Francisco, Calif.: 1969), pp. 34-36.◆ Discusses packing and shipping problems.

Harris, Karyn Jean. "Perishable: Handle with Care," *Museum News,* 56:2 (November/ December 1977), pp. 43-45.◆ Handling, documentation and storage of costumes.

Harvey, Virginia I. "Space and Textiles," *Museum News,* 42:3 (November 1963), pp. 28-33.

Jachimowicz, Elizabeth. "Storage and Access," *Museum News,* 56:2 (November/ December 1977), pp. 32-36.◆ Describes a space-thrifty storage system at the Chicago Historical Society for the costume collection.

Keck, Caroline K. "Care of Textiles and Costumes: Adaptive Techniques for Basic Maintenance," *History News,* 29:2 (February 1974), Technical Leaflet no. 71.

Keck, Caroline K. *Safeguarding Your Collection in Travel.* Nashville, Tenn.: American Association for State and Local History, 1970. 78 pp., illus.◆ Provides instructions for pre-shipment, inspection, packing, transporting and insurance. Illustrations show procedures for making photographic records and solving specific packing problems.

Kley, Ronald J. "Curatorial Centers: Strength in Numbers," *Museum News,* 53:7 (April 1975), pp. 14, 27. ◆ Need to initiate and encourage some form of regionalism involving the sharing of facilities and responsibilities for collections.

Lanchner, Carolyn. "A New Kind of Storage." In *Section Papers, 63rd Annual Meeting, American Association of Museums* (New Orleans, La.: 1968), pp. 22-24. ◆ Description of redesigned study-storage area at Museum of Modern Art International Study Center.

Lanier, Mildred B. "Storage Facilities at Colonial Williamsburg," *Museum News,* 45:6 (February 1967), pp. 31-33.

Levin, Judith. "The Arrangement of a Toy Collection in a Folk Department," *Museums Journal,* 66:3 (December 1966), pp. 192-203.◆ Includes collecting and classification, storage, conservation, display and bibliography.

McConnell, Anita. "Mechanical Handling in a Museum Store," *Museums Journal,* 73:2 (September 1973), pp. 63-64.◆ Storage area designed with fixed racking, adjustable shelves, items on pallets for mechanical handling.

Myers, George H. "Rugs: Preservation, Display and Storage," *Museum News,* 43:6 (February 1965), Technical Supplement no. 6

Nylander, Jane G. "Care of Textiles and Costumes: Cleaning and Storage Techniques," rev. ed., *History News,* 25:12 (December 1970), Technical Leaflet no. 2.

Pinckheard, John, and Edward Pyddoke. "A System of Standard Storage," *Museums Journal,* 60:11 (February 1961), pp. 281-284.

Price, Marjorie, and Kysnia Marko. "The Storage of Museum Textiles in Switzerland, West Germany and Holland," *Museums Journal,* 76:1 (June 1976), pp. 25-27.◆ Report of storage facilities in three European museums with important textile collections; emphasis on flat textiles.

Reid, Norman. "Storage and Study Collections—Art Galleries," *Museums Journal,* 63:1-2 (June-September 1963), pp. 64-69.

"A Report on the Storage Conference," *Museum News,* 55:5 (May/June 1977), pp.

17-22.◆ Summary of the final report of the International Conference on Museum Storage, 13-17 December 1976, Washington, D.C., organized by UNESCO and ICOM with cooperation of AAM/ICOM and a National Museum Act grant from the Smithsonian Institution. Focused on complex problems associated with storage facilities including inadequacy of space, poor design of existing storage areas, and absence of satisfactory standards to apply to planning for future facilities.

Reynolds, Barrie. "Some Ideas on the Storage of Ethnographic Material," *Museums Journal,* 62:2 (September 1962), pp. 102-109.

Rowlison, Eric B. "Rules for Handling Works of Art," *Museum News,* 53:7 (April 1975), pp. 10-13.◆ Guidelines helpful in working situations.

Silvester, J. W. H. "Palletization in Small Museum Storage," *Museums Journal,* 73:2 (September 1973), p. 65.

"Solving Storage Problems," *Museum News,* 41:4 (December 1962), pp. 24-29.

Stansfield, G. *The Storage of Museum Collections.* 2nd ed. Information Sheet no. 10. London: Museums Association, 1974. 5 pp., bibliog.

Stranger, Frank M. "The 'Archive' Problems of a Small History Museum," *Western Museums Quarterly,* 5:1 (March 1968), pp. 19-23.

Sugden, Robert P. *Care and Handling of Art Objects.* New York: Metropolitan Museum of Art, 1946. 32 pp., illus., bibliog.◆ Summary of instructions for the care and handling of art objects including paintings, large objects, small objects, textiles and works of art on paper. Intended to establish certain fundamental rules for the protection of objects in motion on museum premises.

Sugden, Robert P. *Safeguarding Works of Art: Storage, Packing, Transportation and Insurance.* New York: Metropolitan Museum of Art, 1948. 80 pp., illus., bibliog.

Texas Historical Commission. Museum Services Department. *Thoughts on Museum Conservation: Storage, Handling and Care of Museum Artifacts.* Austin: The Commission, 1976. 36 pp., bibliog.

U.S. National Park Service. "The Study Collection Room and Its Equipment." In *Field Manual for Museums* (Ann Arbor, Mich.: Finch Press, 1974), pp. 94-100.

Waddell, Gene. "Museum Storage," *Museum News,* 49:5 (January 1971), pp. 14-20.

Walden, Ian. "The Large Scale Removal of Museum Specimens," *Museums Journal,* 71:4 (March 1972), pp. 157-160. ◆ Describes moving objects in large storage space to new quarters, including costs, preparations, techniques and equipment used.

Watson, Thomas C. "Archive and Costume Storage," *Curator,* XIX:1 (March 1976), pp. 29-36.

Computerization of Collections

Bergengren, Göran. "Automatic Data Processing in the Registration of Museum Collections in Sweden," *Museum,* XXIII:1 (1970-71), pp. 56-58.

Bowles, Edmund A. "The Marriage of Museums and Technology," *Museum News,* 51:8 (April 1973), pp. 35-36.◆ Discusses application of computer science to the arts and humanities, and closer ties with IBM Corporation and the museum community.

Cameron, Duncan F. "Museums, Systems and Computers," *Museum,* XXIII:1 (1970-71), pp. 15-17.◆ Suggests that certain computer approaches to museum processes may aid in understanding the museum, in identifying strengths and weaknesses, and other computer applications of merit.

Chenhall, Robert G. *Computers in Anthropology and Archeology.* 1st ed. White Plains, N.Y.: IBM Corporation, c1971. 71 pp., illus., diagrams, bibliog.◆ Manual intended for the professional anthropologist who may know little about computer technology but may feel that the computer might be useful in research. Emphasis on application of computer technology to the field, not on the technology itself.

Chenhall, Robert G. *Museum Cataloging in the Computer Age.* Nashville, Tenn.: American Association for State and Local History, 1975. 261 pp., illus., diagrams, index.◆ Contents include: Computers and Museums; Documenting the Collections; Why Use a Computer; What to Record; Creating the Records; Computer Systems to Do the Work; Putting It All

Together; Computer Networks and Catalogs of the Future.

Chenhall, Robert G. *Museum Information Networks.* Museum Data Bank Research Report no. 5. Rochester, N.Y.: Museum Data Bank Committee, 1975. 19 pp., bibliog.

Chenhall, Robert G. "The Mythical Magic Black Box," *Museum News,* 53:1 (September 1974), pp. 30-33.

Chenhall, Robert G. *Nomenclature for Museum Cataloging: A System for Classifying Man-Made Objects.* Nashville, Tenn.: American Association for State and Local History, 1978. 512 pp., index.♦ Provides an organized hierarchical system for the classification of man-made objects. The major part of the system is an expandable word list to be used with or without computerized cataloging processes.

Chenhall, Robert C. *The Onomastic Octopus.* Museum Data Bank Research Report no. 10. Rochester, N.Y.: Museum Data Bank Committee, 1977. 14 pp.♦ An overview of description of activities and information needs in museums, and to focus on the specific need for a rational system of nomenclature for all of man's artifacts. A preliminary description of the lexicon, *Nomenclature . . . ,* cited above.

Chenhall, Robert G. "Sharing the Wealth," *Museum News,* 51:8 (April 1973), pp. 21-23.♦ Research by National Science Foundation and the Museum Data Bank Coordinating Committee to determine feasibility of establishing a universal computer network to assist museums in many areas of operation.

Cole, Wilford P. "Computers: Second Thoughts on the Second Phase," *Museum News,* 48:10 (June 1970), pp. 19-20, 50.

Computers and Their Potential Applications in Museums. A Conference sponsored by the Metropolitan Museum of Art, April 15, 16, 17, 1968. New York: Arno Press for the Museum, 1968. 402 pp., illus., bibliog. references.♦ Papers presented at the Conference focused on documentary applications, stylistic analysis by computer, visual applications, computerized museum networks, new approaches in museum education.

Cuisenier, Jean. "Feasibility of Using a Data-Processing System in the Musée des Arts et Traditions Populaires, Paris," *Museum,* XXIII:1 (1970-71), pp. 33-36.

Cutbill, J. L. *Computer Filing Systems for Museums and Research.* London: Museums Association, 1973. 23 pp.♦ Results obtained from the operation of the Cambridge Geological Data System to test the computer as an aid to the documentation of a museum collection, and assess this in relation to the IRGMA project and future developments.

Elisseeff, Vadime. "Museums and Computers," *Museum,* XXIII:1 (1970-71), pp. 4-6.

Ellin, Everett. "Computer-Based Information System for the American Museum Community." In *Section Papers, 63rd Annual Meeting, American Association of Museums* (New Orleans, La.: May 1968), pp. 25-30.

Ellin, Everett. "Computer Horizons in the Museum World," *Museum,* XXIII:1 (1970-71), pp. 8-10.♦ Use of computer technology to retain control over museum records.

Ellin, Everett. "Considerations in the Formation of Museum Data Banks in the United States of America," *Museum,* XXIII:1 (1970-71), pp. 20-21.♦ Describes Museum Computer Network project, begun in 1967 by 25 museums in Washington, D.C. and New York City.

Gittins, David. "Computer-based Museum Information Systems," *Museums Journal,* 76:3 (December 1976), pp. 115-118.♦ Discusses museum projects that have involved both the simple and sophisticated use of computers.

Hackmann, W. D. *The Evaluation of a Museum Communication Format: Part I–Collection of Input Data.* Final Report for the period October 1970-September 1972 and extension November 1972-December 1972. Oxford: Museum of the History of Science, 1973. 79 pp. ♦ Outlines the first part of the test of the IRGMA Museums Communication Format in the construction of a detailed catalog of early electrostatic instruments. Report to OSTI on Project SI/56/07. Also available from the Museums Association, London.

Heller, Jack. *On Logical Data Organization, Card Catalogs and the GRIPHOS Management Information System.* Museum Data Bank Research Report no. 3. Rochester, N.Y.: Museum Data Bank Committee, 1974. 21 pp., bibliog.

Information Retrieval Group, Museums Association. Standards Committee. "Ten Years of IRGMA, 1967-1977," *Museums Journal,* 77:1 (June 1977), pp. 11-14.

International Business Machines Corporation. Data Processing Division. *Introduction to Computers in the Humanities.* 1st ed. New York: 1971. 76 pp., illus.

Lewis, Geoffrey. "An Interdisciplinary Communication Format for Museums in the United Kingdom," *Museum,* XXIII:1 (1970-71), pp. 24-26.♦ The work of the Information Retrieval Group of the Museums Association, London.

McAllister, Don E.; Robert Murphy; and John Morrison. "The Compleat Minicomputer Cataloging and Research System for a Museum," *Curator,* XXI:1 (1978), pp. 63-91.

Mandel, Hanni. "Scholarship on Discs, The Museum's Computerized Catalogue," The Metropolitan Museum of Art *Bulletin,* 29:4 (December 1970), pp. 189-190.

Neff, Jeffrey M., and Holly M. Chaffee. "REGIS—A Computerized Museum Registration System," *Curator,* XX:1 (1977), pp. 32-41.

Oehler, Hansgeorg, and Rolf Gundlach. "Electronic Documentation of a Collection of Roman Sculpture Photographs," *Museum,* XXIII:1 (1970-71), pp. 46-52.♦ Describes use of computerized data to obtain print-outs, for comparative research, considering purchases, classification of accessions; includes a model questionnaire.

Peters, James A. "The Time-Shared Computer as an Adjunct to Museum Exhibits," *Museums Journal,* 72:4 (March 1973), pp. 143-145.

Roberts, D. A. *Introduction to the IRGMA Documentation System.* London: Museums Association, 1976. 29 pp.

Rush, Carole E. *An Information System for History Museums.* Museum Data Bank Research Report no. 11. Rochester, N.Y.: Museum Data Bank Committee, 1977. 21 pp., illus.♦ Topics discussed are the analyses required for the design of an integrated record-keeping system and the steps required to implement such a system.

Scholtz, Sandra. *Data Structure and Computerized Museum Catalogs.* Museum Data Bank Research Report no. 2. Rochester, N.Y.: Museum Data Bank Committee, 1974. 8 pp., bibliog.

Scholtz, Sandra. *A Management Information System Design for A General Museum.* Museum Data Bank Research Report no. 12. Rochester, N.Y.: Museum Data Bank Committee, 1977. 15 pp. ♦ Discusses a total accessioning/registration/cataloging system for a general museum.

Scott, David. *The Yogi and the Registrar.* Museum Data Bank Research Report no. 7. Rochester, N.Y.: Museum Data Bank Committee, 1976. 13 pp.♦ Survey of common ground between the registrar and the curator to determine whether common ground, if any, justifies cultivation in the form of data processing.

Swinney, H. J. *Characteristics of History Museum Activity and their Influence on Potential Electronic Cataloging.* Museum Data Bank Research Report no. 8. Rochester, N.Y.: Museum Data Bank Committee, 1976. 8 pp.

Vance, David. "Computer Techniques in Museum Registration." In *Papers, 64th Annual Meeting, American Association of Museums* (San Francisco, Calif.: 1969), pp. 116-132b.

Vance, David. *Computers in the Museum.* White Plains, N.Y.: International Business Machines, 1973. 69 pp.♦ Manual intended to help museum personnel understand the uses of computers in the museum environment. Includes discussion of several museum applications of data entry and recording devices, data formatting and file organization, and information retrieval techniques based on the experience of the Museum Computer Network.

Vance, David. "Museum Computer Network: Progress Report," *The Museologist,* 135 (December 1975), pp. 3-10.

Vance, David. "Museum Computer Network: The Second Phase," *Museum News,* 48:9 (May 1970), pp. 15-20.♦ First phase involved experiments with basic system.

Vance, David. "Museum Computer Network: The Third Phase," *Museum News,* 51:8 (April 1973), pp. 24-27.♦ Describes system's financial and technical developments of the computerized cataloging system with flexibility of cataloging a multitude of museum collections.

Vance, David. *Structure and Content of a Museum Data Bank.* Washington, D.C.: ERIC Document Reproduction Service, 1971. 32 pp.♦ Discusses the logical structure of the data bank from the user's point of view. Compiled for use in a workshop on data collection and data dissemination in museums at the Metropolitan Museum of Art, June 5, 1970. Revised, July 1970 and January 1971. Eric report #048 866, available from ERIC Document Reproduction Service, Computer Microfilm International Corporation, P.O. Box 190, Arlington, Virginia 22210.

Vance, David. *What are Data?* Museum Data Bank Research Report no. 1. Rochester, N.Y.: Museum Data Bank Committee, 1974. 10 pp., bibliog.

NOTES

Information Retrieval Group, Museums Association, 87 Charlotte Street, London W1P 2BX, England. Organized in 1967 for the purpose of preparing a museums communication format based on the initial proposals for an interdisciplinary catalog system, the Group is concerned with the problems of cataloging and indexing and utilization of museum collections, particularly with the use of computers to permit the exchange, amalgamation and manipulation of information for a wide variety of purposes. The British Department of Education, Office for Scientific and Technical Information (OSTI), funded projects to test the communication format which would provide a method for translating relevant data from one storage format into another. See report by Hackman, cited above. The Group published *IRGMA News,* 3 issues only (January 1969, July 1975, January 1977).

Museum Computer Network, Inc., Center for Contemporary Arts and Letters, E 2340 University Library, State University of New York, Stony Brook, New York 11790. The Museum Computer Network, Inc., was formed in 1967 as a loosely organized consortium and housed at the Museum of Modern Art, New York City. It is a nonprofit corporation with museums and similar organizations as its members. Its purpose is to assist museums in the conversion of their inventories and extensive files of related information to a form that can be searched, sorted, and analyzed readily by electronic means. Its primary objective is the formation of a central inventory file of museum holdings and the data base draws on the basic information that normally appears in a museum's card catalog. Museums are supplied with specially designed data sheets and detailed instructions on how to fill them out. As they are computed for each work of art, they are submitted to the Network. Membership is open to any museum or other institution with files of information of interest to museums or their public. Group memberships are available to enable small museums and historical societies to participate. Collections of every description from archeological sites to zoo animals may be suitable for the Network's programming.

Museum Data Bank Committee, Research Reports. Twelve research papers, prepared by members of the Committee and relating to the information needs of museums and related organizations and the application of information science in general and data banks in particular, were published as a series (1974-1977) and are available from the Registrar, Margaret Woodbury Strong Museum, 700 Allen Creek Road, Rochester, New York 14618.

13

Library and Archive Administration

It is difficult to imagine an historical organization without a library collection and archives. It is not so difficult to realize that only the larger institutions have fully trained professionals to administer their collections. They will be well acquainted with most of the references here, which are selected to provide all the necessary guidelines and sources of information for a small staff and/or volunteers to manage well the library and archives collections.

Divided into five sections, this chapter starts with general references, the organizations that will aid and assist and the periodicals that inform and update. It proceeds to the handbooks and manuals on organization and management, with a special selection of references for the small historical museum or organization. It then deals with technical services: the selecting and acquiring that constitute collecting; cataloging; protection and preservation; and finally the processes for reproducing materials. The library and archives collections and their relationship to the public deals with guides, loan procedures, access, and other aspects of administration, but it should be noted that there are other references in related chapters in this volume (on publishing, resources for administration, physical security of buildings, and personnel management), as well as in Volume 3 of the *Bibliography . . .* series, *Interpretation.*

The final section consists of studies and guidelines on design, furnishings and equipment, compendiums produced by professionals seeking to aid and assist in planning library and archival buildings.

General Reference

American Library Association. Editorial Committee. Subcommittee on Library Terminology. *ALA Glossary of Library Terms, with a Selection of Terms in Related Fields.* Prepared under the Direction of the Committee on Library Terminology of the American Library Association by Elizabeth H. Thompson. Chicago: American Library Association, c1943, 1965. 159 pp., appendices.♦ Comprehensive collection of concise definitions of library terms; appendices include tables of book and type sizes and a list of abbreviations used in library terminology.

American Library Association. Headquarters Library. *ALA Publications Checklist, 1979: A List of Materials Currently Available from the American Library Association.* Chicago: 1979. 112 pp., indexes.♦ Provides bibliographic data on every publication currently available from the Association and its units; includes books, pamphlets, journals, membership materials, journal reprints, working documents of ALA, and such audiovisual materials as the cassette programs from the Annual Conference.

American Library Directory: A Classified List of Libraries in the United States and Canada with Personnel and Statistical Data. New York: R. R. Bowker Co., 1923 -. 1 vol., biennial.◆ Current edition, 31st, 1978.

American Library Laws. Edited by Alex Ladenson. 4th ed. Chicago: American Library Association, 1973. 1992 pp., index.◆ State and federal laws pertaining to libraries in effect as of December 31, 1972. Decennial edition in two parts, laws under federal jurisdiction and laws of the states. See also: First Supplement, 1973-1974 (1975); Second Supplement, 1975-1976 (1978).

Anderson, Beryl L. *Special Libraries and Information Centres in Canada: A Directory.* Rev. ed. Ottawa: Canadian Library Association, 1970. 168 pp.◆ Lists special libraries in business, government, industry, research organizations, and special subject departments of university and public libraries. Addenda, 1972.

Annual Review of Information Science and Technology. New York: Interscience Publishers, 1966 -. 1 vol., annual.◆ Issued by American Documentation Institute, 1937-1967; American Society for Information Science, 1968 -. Categories include planning information systems and services, basic techniques and tools, applications, the profession. Current edition, 13th, 1978, edited by Martha Williams.

The Bookman's Glossary. Edited by Jean Peters. 5th ed. New York: R. R. Bowker, 1975. 169 pp., illus., bibliog.◆ A practical guide for those interested in the terminology used in the production and distribution of books new and old; the words in common usage in a bookstore or publisher's office, library, or among book collectors. Older definitions have been revised to reflect changes in the industry and new names and terms that are relevant to publishing and the graphic arts have been added.

The Bowker Annual of Library and Book Trade Information. New York: R. R. Bowker, 1955 -. 1 vol., annual.◆ Title varies. Current edition, 23rd, 1978, edited by Nada Beth Glick.

Carbone, Salvatore, and Raoul Guêze. *Draft Model Law on Archives: Description and Text.* Paris: UNESCO, 1972. 225 pp.◆ Discusses a draft model law to promote efficient national archives and records management systems appropriate for nations in various developmental stages; considers production and right of access, expropriation of documentary sources, state documents, gifts and bequests, and inspection and destruction of documents. Available from Unipub, Box 433, Murray Hill Station, New York, New York 10016.

Directory of State and Provincial Archives. Austin, Texas: Society of American Archivists, 1975. 1 vol.◆ A project of the Society's State and Local Records Committee and issued by the Society and the Texas State Archives. Includes information on staff, research facilities and hours, published guides and archival holdings; also statistical section with comparative data on holdings, budgets, parent agencies. Available from the Society of American Archivists.

Elsevier's Lexicon of Archive Terminology: *French, English, German, Spanish, Italian, Dutch.* Compiled and arranged on a systematic basis by a committee of the International Council on Archives. Amsterdam and New York: Elsevier Publishing Co., 1964. 83 pp.

Evans, Frank B. *Modern Archives and Manuscripts: A Select Bibliography.* Washington, D.C.: Society of American Archivists, 1975. 209 pp., indexes.◆ Guide to writings on archival administration with new chapters on machine-readable records and archives; three chapters on international aspects of archives. Additional subheadings, and a system of decimal numbering has been adopted for the subheadings to facilitate revisions and indexing.

Evans, Frank B.; Donald F. Harrison; Edwin A. Thompson; and William L. Rofes. "A Basic Glossary for Archivists, Manuscript Curators, and Records Managers," *The American Archivist,* 37:3 (July 1974), pp. 415-433.◆ Available as a reprint from Society of American Archivists.

Fang, Josephine R., and Alice H. Songe. *Handbook of National and International Library Associations.* Prelim. ed. Chicago: American Library Association, 1973. 326 pp., appendices, index.

Kruzas, Anthony T., ed. *Encyclopedia of Information Systems and Services: A Guide to Information Storage and Retrieval Services, Data Base Procedures and Publishers, Online Vendors. . . .* 3rd ed. Detroit: Gale Research Company, 1978. 1000 pp., indexes.◆ Description of organizations in more than 30 countries that produce, process, store and use bibliographic and non-bibliographic information.

Mushake, Kathryn. *Glossary of Library Terms.* Chicago: Small Libraries Project, American Library Association, 1969. 15 pp.♦ Supplement A to Pamphlet 7, Small Libraries Project.

New York (State). Office of State History. *Laws Relating to the Management of Local Public Records.* Rev. ed. Albany, N.Y.: 1971. 14 pp.♦ Includes general laws, disposition, disposition of records that have been microphotographed, custody of local public records.

Pinkett, Harold T. "A Glossary of Records Terminology: Scope and Definitions," *The American Archivist,* 33:1 (January 1970), pp. 53-59.

Posner, Ernst. *American State Archives.* Chicago: University of Chicago Press, 1964. 397 pp., bibliog.♦ State by state survey and evaluation of archives; useful for background information. Includes glossary and bibliography on public archives administration in the U.S.

Society of American Archivists. *ADP and Archives: Selected Publications on Automatic Data Processing.* Meyer H. Fishbein, compiler. Chicago: The Society, 1975. 11 pp.♦ Includes references on glossaries, history and methodology, general archival applications, preservation and use of machine-readable records, indexing and information retrieval.

Society of American Archivists. Committee on Records Management. "Writings on Records Management: A Select List," *The American Archivist,* 36:3 (July 1973), pp. 367-371. ♦ See also "Writings on Archives, Current Records, and Historical Manuscripts," cited in Notes below, which includes records management.

U.S. Library of Congress. General Reference and Bibliography Division. *The National Union Catalog Reference and Related Services.* Compiled by John W. Kimball, Jr. Washington, D.C.: Library of Congress, 1973. · 33 pp.♦ Includes general information on the NUC, and procedures for obtaining copies of National Archives holdings, National Technical Information Service materials, translations of foreign publications, and U.S. government

publications. Available from Library of Congress, Union Catalog, Reference Unit, Washington, D.C. 20540.

U.S. National Archives and Records Service. Office of Records Management. *Bibliography for Records Managers.* Washington, D.C.: for sale by the Superintendent of Documents, U.S. Government Printing Office, 1964. 58 pp., glossary.♦ List of books and articles, classified by function (correspondence, forms, reports, surveys, etc.); and a list of periodicals and a glossary.

Watkins, Jessie B., comp. *Selected Bibliography on Maps in Libraries: Acquisition, Classification, Cataloging, Storage, Uses.* Syracuse, N.Y.: Syracuse University Libraries, 1967. 18 pp.♦ Useful list of articles and monographs to 1967, divided by subheadings to cover acquisition, classification, cataloging, storage and use.

Young, Margaret L., et al. *Directory of Special Libraries and Information Centers.* Edited by Margaret Young, Harold Chester Young, Anthony T. Kruzas. 4th ed. Detroit: Gale Research Co., 1977. 3 vols.♦ Vol. 1—Special Libraries; Vol. 2—Geographic and Personnel Index; Vol. 3—New Special Libraries, a Periodic Supplement.

NOTES AND PERIODICALS

The American Archivist. 1938, quarterly, subscription. Society of American Archivists, Ann Morgan Campbell, Executive Director, 330 South Wells Street, Suite 810, Chicago, Illinois 60606.

American Library Association, 50 East Huron Street, Chicago, Illinois 60611. The Association was founded in 1876 for librarians, libraries, trustees, friends of libraries and others interested in the responsibilities of libraries in the educational, social and cultural needs of society. Its Divisions are: Public Library Association (PLA), publishes *Public Libraries* (quarterly); Association of College and Research Libraries (ACRL), with sections on art libraries, community, college and university libraries, and rare books and manuscripts, and publishes *College & Research Libraries* (bimonthly) and *C&RL News* (supplement); Association of Specialized and Cooperative Library Agencies (ASCLA), publishes *Newsletter* (quarterly); American Association of School Librarians (AASL), publishes *School Media Quarterly;* Young Adult Services Division (YASD) and Association for Library Service to Children (ALSC), publishes *Top of the News* (quarterly); Resources and Technical Services Division (RTSD) with sections on resources, cataloging and classification, serials, reproduction of library materials, and publishes *Library Resources & Technical Services* (quarterly); Library Administration and Management Association (LAMA), with sections on buildings and equipment, library organization and management, personnel administration, public relations, circulation services, statistics, and publishes *LAMA Newsletter* (quarterly); Reference and Adult Services Division (RASD), publishes *RQ* (quarterly); American Library Trustee Association (ALTA), publishes *The Public Library Trustee* (periodically); Library and Information Technology Association (LITA), publishes *Journal of Library Automation* (quarterly). Specialized projects applicable to historical organizations include: Small Libraries Project, a series of inexpensive publications on such subjects as staff, buildings and equipment, adult and children's services, organization of collections, audiovisual and local history collections; and, Library Technology Program, a series of studies on technical aspects such as preservation of library materials, physical protection, copying methods, and a bimonthly subscription service with looseleaf binder to *Library Technology Reports* providing information on library supplies, equipment and systems. The Association publishes *American Libraries* (11/yr.), *Choice* (11/yr.), *The Booklist* (semimonthly), monographs and conference proceedings. A complete publications catalog is available.

American Society for Information Science, 1155 16th Street, N.W., Washington, D.C. 20036. Founded in 1937 as the American Documentation Institute, the Society adopted its current name in 1968 to reflect the members' interests in all aspects of the information transfer process. Membership includes information specialists, scientists, librarians, administrators, social scientists and others interested in the use, storage, retrieval and dissemination of recorded specialized information. The Society provides a forum for the discussion, publication and critical analysis of work dealing with the theory, practice, research and development of elements involved in communication of information. Activities include classification and coding systems, in-

dexing, library systems analysis, copyright issues, etc. There are local and student chapters, and among the fourteen Special Interest Groups are Arts and Humanities, Classification Research, Library Automation and Networks, and Reprographic Technology. In 1970 ASIS began the operation of the ERIC (Educational Resources Information Center) Clearinghouse on Library and Information Sciences, a nationwide information system funded by the U.S. Office of Education. It is designed to serve the field of education through the dissemination of information about educational resources and research materials, and is responsible for making available studies of current research and work in the field of library and information sciences. The Society holds annual meetings, regional meetings, seminars and workshops. It operates a placement service and is affiliated with the American Federation of Information Processing Societies and the American Library Association. It publishes a *Journal* (bimonthly); *Information Bulletin* (10/yr.); *Handbook and Directory* (annual); *Annual Review of Information Science and Technology; Information Science Abstracts* (bimonthly); *Proceedings of the ASIS Annual Meeting;* and other books and pamphlets.

Annotation. 1973, quarterly, limited circulation. National Historical Publications and Records Commission, National Archives Building, Washington, D.C. 20408.

Archivaria. 1975, semiannual, subscription. Association of Canadian Archivists, c/o Public Archives of Canada, Room 349, 395 Wellington Street, Ottawa, Ontario, K1A ON3, Canada. Supersedes *Canadian Archivist.*

ARLIS/NA Newsletter. 1972, quarterly, membership. ARLIS/NA Newsletter, c/o Sherman Clarke, 779 Princeton Blvd., Wilkinsburg, Pennsylvania 15221.

Art Libraries Society of North America, c/o Sherman Clarke, 770 Princeton Blvd., Wilkinsburg, Pennsylvania 15221. The Society was founded in 1972 by interested art librarians who realized the need for communication, cooperation, and an international forum for ideas, projects, and programs on the visual arts. Membership is open to practicing art librarians, and those interested in the visual arts, architecture and the new methods and approaches to handling materials in these fields. Regional chapter participation is actively encouraged, and chapters are located in states, large regions and metropolitan areas. ARLIS/NA maintains liaison with ARLIS/United Kingdom, International Federation of Library Associations, and the Council of National Library Associations. The Society sponsors seminars and workshops and an annual conference, and is working on an Art Documentation Project in collaboration with Queens College, a national union catalog of art periodicals, a handbook on art librarianship, a cooperative venture to standardize methods of collecting and organizing exhibition catalogs, and improving the art librarian's awareness of high standards in art book manufacture and design. Publications include *ARLIS/NA Newsletter; Directory of Members; Standards for Staffing Art Libraries: Primitive Art Guide* (2 vols.); and a series of articles on *Classification in the Visual Arts.*

Association of Records Managers and Administrators, P.O. Box 281, Bradford, Rhode Island 02808. Founded in 1975, the Association includes administrators, supervisors, specialists and others interested in the study of efficient records-making and records-keeping. It conducts research in standardized alphabetical filing, shelf filing methods and equipment, machine processed data control, microfilm systems, records protection, forms/reports management, and retention practices. It collaborates with the American Standards Association on office practices and equipment. Programs include awards, placement service, speakers bureau, and correspondence course; and committees on curriculum, ecology, research and education. The Association publishes *ARMA Records Management Quarterly; Newsletter,* quarterly; directory of officers and chapter presidents; "Rules for Alphabetical Filing as Standardized by ARMA," and "Records Management Workshop." The Association was formed by a merger of the Association of Records Executives and Adminstrators and the American Records Management Association.

Association of Research Libraries, 1527 New Hampshire Avenue, N.W., Washington, D.C. 20036. Founded in 1932 for university, public, private and governmental research libraries, the purpose of the Society is to identify and solve problems fundamental to large research libraries so that they may efficiently serve the needs of students, faculty and the research community generally. It has committees on university library standards,

manuscripts and rare books, national periodicals system; and joint committee with Association of College and Research Libraries (American Library Association).

Canadian Library Association, 151 Sparks Street, Ottawa, Ontario, K1P 5E3, Canada. Founded in 1946, the Canadian Library Association is a nonprofit voluntary organization which seeks to develop high standards of librarianship and of library and information services by encouraging the development of efficient and effective library operations, and by increasing public awareness of and support for libraries. Constituent divisions of the Association represent the interests of college and university libraries, public libraries, school and special libraries, and library trustees. Its headquarters is divided into four departments: publishing services, membership, programs and accounting. Activities of the Association include development of a National Library; microfilming early Canadian newspapers and documents of historical importance; development of standards for libraries and library technical programs; library school scholarships and children's book awards; international liaison with other library associations such as American Library Association and International Federation of Library Associations. Publications include *Canadian Library Journal* (bimonthly); *Canadian Periodical Index* (11/yr.); *Canadian Reference Sources* (1973) and *Supplement* (1975); *Canadian Materials* (3/yr.); *Anglo-American Cataloguing Rules* (joint publisher with American Library Association).

Canadian Library Journal. 1944, bimonthly, membership. Canadian Library Association, 151 Sparks Street, Ottawa, Ontario K1P 5E3, Canada.♦ Formerly *Canadian Library.*

College and Research Libraries. 1939, bimonthly, membership. Association of College and Research Libraries, American Library Association, 50 East Huron Street, Chicago, Illinois 60611.

International Council on Archives, 60 rue des Francs-Bourgeois, 75003 Paris, France. Founded in 1948, the Council is a federation of national and international archival associations, archival institutions and individuals in 99 countries, formed to encourage preservation of archives and advance their administration; to simplify the use of existing archives by making their contents more widely known, encouraging greater freedom of access, and making reproductions more readily available. It was created under the auspices of UNESCO. It sponsors a quadrennial International Congress on Archives and an annual International Archival Round Table Conference. It has committees on archival terminology; automation; guide to sources of the history of nations; microfilming; sigillography. It publishes *Archivum,* annually.

Library Journal. 1876, semimonthly (September-June), monthly (July-August), subscription. Subscriptions to Subscription Service Department, R. R. Bowker, Box 67, Whitinsville, Massachusetts 01588.

The Library Quarterly: *A Journal of Investigation and Discussion in the Field of Library Science.* 1931, quarterly, subscription. University of Chicago Press, 5801 Ellis Avenue, Chicago, Illinois 60636.

Library Resources and Technical Services. 1957, quarterly, membership/subscription. American Library Association, Resources and Technical Services Division, 50 East Huron Street, Chicago, Illinois 60611.

Library Technology Reports. 1965, bimonthly, subscription. American Library Association, 50 East Huron Street, Chicago, Illinois 60611. A service to provide information on library systems, equipment and supplies to the library profession, published by the Library Technology Program.

The Manuscript Society, Audrey Arellanes, Executive Secretary, 1206 N. Stoneman Avenue #15, Alhambra, California 91801. Founded in 1948, the Society is for collectors, dealers, librarians, curators, writers and historians interested in autographs and original related material such as manuscripts, letters and documents. It holds an annual meeting; publishes *Manuscripts* (quarterly) and a membership directory. Formerly National Society of Autograph Collectors.

Manuscripts. 1948, quarterly, membership. The Manuscript Society, Audrey Arellanes, Executive Secretary, 1206 N. Stoneman Avenue #15, Alhambra, California 91801.

National Historical Publications and Records Commission, National Archives Building, Washington, D.C. 20408. In 1934, Congress established the National Historical Publications Commission for purposes of promoting the collection and publication of papers of outstanding citizens of the U.S. and other documents as may be important for an understanding and appreciation of the history of the U.S. From 1954 to 1964 the Commission functioned in accordance with a program that required it to cooperate with, and encourage governmental and private bodies in collecting and preserving historical source materials, and to plan and recommend historical works and collections of source materials. Since 1964, the Commission has had a more active role and has allocated grants to federal, state and local agencies, and to nonprofit organizations and institutions, and has had its membership increased to include representatives of related organizations. In 1974, the name of the Commission was redesignated to include Records, and its membership and authorization of appropriations were increased again. The Commission makes plans, estimates, and recommendations for the compilation of historical works and collections of source materials that it considers appropriate for printing or recording at public expense. Allocations are made to federal agencies and grants to state and local agencies and to nonprofit organizations and institutions for these purposes. The Commission operates primarily through a national historical publications program, and a national historical records program. Outright, matching and combined grants may be made under each program; a brochure outlining guidelines and procedures for applications and grants is available from the Commission.

Prologue: *The Journal of the National Archives.* 1969, quarterly, subscription. The National Archives, Washington, D.C. 20408.

Resources and Technical Services Division, American Library Association, 50 East Huron Street, Chicago, Illinois 60611. The Division is a type-of-activity division of the Association for librarians interested in the acquisition, identification, cataloging, classification and preservation of library materials. It publishes *Library Resources and Technical Services* (quarterly).

Society of American Archivists, Ann Morgan Campbell, Executive Director, 330 South Wells Street, Suite 810, Chicago, Illinois 60606. Founded in 1936, the SAA is a professional society of archivists concerned with management of current records, archival administration and the custody of historical manuscripts in government, business, and semipublic institutions. It publishes *SAA Newsletter* (bimonthly); *The American Archivist* (quarterly); *SAA Directory* (biennial); and a Basic Manual Series (1977) on Archives and Manuscripts.

Special Libraries. 1910, monthly (September-April), bimonthly (May-August), subscription. Special Libraries Association, 235 Park Avenue South, New York, New York 10003.

Special Libraries Association, 235 Park Avenue South, New York, New York 10003. Founded in 1909, the Association is an international organization of professional librarians and information experts who serve manufacturing concerns, banks, corporations, law firms, newspapers, advertising and insurance agencies, transportation companies, research organizations, museums, hospitals, business branches and other departments of public and university libraries, federal, state, and municipal government bureaus, associations and other organizations in the fields of business, medicine, science, technology and the social sciences. Its purpose is to promote the collection, organization and dissemination of information in specialized fields and to improve the usefulness of special libraries and information services. It publishes *Special Libraries* (10/yr.); *Technical Book Review Index* (10/yr.); *Scientific Meetings* (4/yr.)

"Writings on Archives, Current Records, and Historical Manuscripts," is a bibliography published annually in *The American Archivist* since 1956. Topics include general literature; management of records; activities of archival agencies and related organizations; buildings and equipment; handling of records and manuscripts; preservation and rehabilitation; arrangement and description; photographic processes; use and publication of records; special types of records and manuscripts; recruitment and training. Compilers include Lester W. Smith, Grace Quimby, Frank B. Evans, Patricia A. Andrews, Carmen R. Delle Donne, Nora P. McCarthy, and Isabel V. Clarke.

Organization and Management

American Library Association. Audio-Visual Committee. *Guidelines for Audiovisual Materi-*
als and Sources for Large Public Libraries. Chicago: The Association, 1975. 40 pp., glossary, index.♦ Designed for larger library systems who wish to establish audiovisual services or strengthen existing collections and services.

Anderson, Frank J. "A Sense of History: Some Notes on the Establishment and Maintenance of a Local History Collection in a Public Library," *Library Journal,* 83:13 (July 1958), pp. 2003-2007.

Archer, H. Richard, ed. *Rare Book Collections: Some Theoretical and Practical Suggestions for Use by Librarians and Students.* Chicago: American Library Association, 1965. 128 pp., bibliog., appendix.♦ Chapters include development of rare book collections, acquisition, organization, processing, cataloging and classification, care and maintenance, physical housing and equipment, access and service, rare book library and the public.

Archive-Library Relations. Edited by Robert L. Clark, Jr. New York: R. R. Bowker, 1976. 218 pp., bibliog., index.♦ Essays by Robert L. Clark, Jr., Frank G. Burke, Miriam I. Crawford, Frazer G. Poole, Robert L. Brubaker, and an annotated bibliography by Marietta Malzer, focusing on benefits of libraries and archives working together.

Art Library Manual: *A Guide to Resources and Practice.* By Philip Pacey. London and New York: R. R. Bowker in association with the Art Libraries Society, 1977. 423 pp., bibliog.♦ Handbook on organizing, managing and documenting materials that specialize in art and design. Includes general art bibliographies, reference material, art publications, periodicals and serials, theses and primary sources.

Benedon, William. *Records Management.* Englewood Cliffs, N.J.: Prentice-Hall, 1969. 272 pp., illus., glossary, index.♦ Covers elements of a records management program including inventorying, retention scheduling, storage, forms management, vital records protection, reports management, microfilming, filing systems, and correspondence control.

Bernhard, Genore H. *How to Organize and Operate a Small Library.* Fort Atkinson, Wisc.: Highsmith Co., c1975. 47 pp., illus., appendices.♦ Subtitle: A Comprehensive Guide to the Organization and Operation of a Small Library for Your School, Church, Law Firm,

Business, Hospital, Community, Court, Historical Museum or Association.

Berry, Elizabeth, and John Thompson. "Records Management," *Museums Journal,* 77:1 (June 1977), pp. 7-10.♦ Report of a joint committee of representatives from The Society of Archivists and the Museums Association, working on a memorandum of policy for areas of common concern to both professions.

Bibliography and the Historian: The Conference at Belmont of the Joint Committee on Bibliographical Services to History, May 1967. Edited by Dagmar H. Perman. Santa Barbara, Calif.: CLIO, 1968. 176 pp., bibliog. footnotes.♦ Based on studies prepared for the conference held under the auspices of the American Historical Association and the National Endowment for the Humanities. Emphasis on inadequacy of present bibliographical aids and an examination and evaluation of developments in bibliographical control of monographs, serials and documents by libraries and other depositories of historical source materials.

Bloomberg, Marty, and G. Edward Evans. *Introduction to Technical Services for Library Technicians.* Littleton, Colo.: Libraries Unlimited, 1971. 175 pp., illus., bibliog.

Bordin, Ruth B. A., and Robert M. Warner. *The Modern Manuscript Library.* New York: Scarecrow Press, 1966. 151 pp., bibliog.♦ Standard text for the manuscript curator, dealing with all aspects of the work.

Burnette, O. Lawrence, Jr. *Beneath the Footnote: A Guide to the Use and Preservation of American Historical Sources.* Madison: State Historical Society of Wisconsin, 1969. 450 pp., bibliog., index.♦ Concerned with the origins and evolution of those institutions and practices involved in the care and use of primary forms of American historical evidence.

"Care and Editing of Manuscripts." In *Harvard Guide to American History,* rev. ed. (Cambridge, Mass.: Belknap Press of Harvard University Press, 1974), Volume 1, pp. 21-36.♦ Chapter on handling and preservation, calendaring and indexing, dating of manuscripts, copying of manuscripts, editing and printing.

Cave, Roderick. *Rare Book Librarianship.* London: C. Bingley; and Hamden, Conn.: Linnet Books, 1976. 168 pp., illus., bibliog., index.♦ Introductory manual on the treatment of rare books and special collections, including acquisition, processing, restoration, housing and organization of these materials.

Collins, Marcia R., and Linda Anderson. *Libraries for Small Museums.* 3rd ed. Columbia, Mo.: Museum of Anthropology, University of Missouri-Columbia, c1977. 48 pp., illus., bibliog.♦ Handbook on basic library administration including organizing, cataloging, processing, ordering, circulation, financing.

Cook, Michael Garnet. *Archives Administration: A Manual for Intermediate and Smaller Organizations and for Local Government.* Folkestone, Eng.: William Dawson & Sons Ltd., 1977. 258 pp., illus., bibliog., index.

Drazniowsky, Roman, comp. *Map Librarianship: Readings.* Metuchen, N.J.: Scarecrow Press, 1975. 548 pp., illus., bibliog.♦ Articles on all phases of map forms, classification, processing, and a bibliography.

Duckett, Kenneth W. *Modern Manuscripts: A Practical Manual for Their Management, Care and Use.* Nashville, Tenn.: American Association for State and Local History, 1975. 375 pp., illus., appendices, notes, glossary, bibliog., index.♦ Focuses on practical and technical aspects of the management of manuscript collections; role of the curator from fundraiser to microfilmer and conservator; mechanics and ethics of acquisitions; physical care and conservation; bibliographic control; information retrieval; non-manuscript material; use of collections; and public service.

Evans, Frank B. *Archives and Manuscripts.* AASLH Cassette Tape no. 14. Nashville, Tenn.: American Association for State and Local History, 1971. 1 cassette, 55 minutes.♦ Discusses distinction between three areas of specialization in the collecting and use of printed and written materials: libraries, archives, manuscript collections; and reviews origin and purpose of these areas.

Hart, Katherine. "Administering the Local History Collection," *Texas Libraries,* 29:3 (Fall 1967), pp. 187-202.

Heintz, Ingeborg. *The Organization of the Small Public Library.* Paris: UNESCO, c1963. 66 pp., illus., bibliog.

Hobbs, John L. *Local History and the Library.* Completely revised and partly rewritten by

George A. Carter. 2nd ed. London: A. Deutsch, 1973. 344 pp., illus., bibliog., appendix.♦ Includes value and use of local history; printed, manuscript, and local records; care and treatment of archives; exhibitions and publicity; use of local research materials; problems of organization and administration; staffing; cataloging, indexing, classifying local material.

Holbert, Sue E. *Archives and Manuscripts: Reference and Access.* Chicago: Society of American Archivists, 1977. 30 pp., bibliog., appendices.♦ Basic Manual series; includes access policy, security, restrictions and references, fair use, loans, and personnel.

Hull, David, and Henry D. Fearnley. "The Museum Library in the United States, A Sample," *Special Libraries,* 67:7 (July 1976), pp. 289-298.♦ Statistical survey of general conditions and problems of the museum library.

Irvine, Betty Jo. *Slide Libraries: A Guide for Academic Institutions and Museums.* Littleton, Colo.: Libraries Unlimited, 1974. 219 pp., illus., tables. ♦ Discusses slide librarianship, staffing, classification and cataloging, use of standard library techniques and tools, production methods and equipment, storage and access systems, physical facilities; and, a selected bibliography and directories of distributors and manufacturers of equipment and supplies, slide sources, and slide libraries.

Jenkinson, Hilary. *A Manual of Archive Administration.* Rev. 2nd ed., with an introduction and bibliography by Roger H. Ellis. London: P. Lund, Humphries & Co., Ltd., 1965. 261 pp., illus., bibliog. notes.♦ One of the basic texts of the profession, though technical information has been superseded.

Kane, Lucile M. *A Guide to the Care and Administration of Manuscripts.* 2nd ed. Nashville, Tenn.: American Association for State and Local History, 1966. 74 pp., illus., bibliog.♦ Provides basic information on the care of historical manuscripts, including chapters on establishing controls, organizing and sorting collections, evaluation, preservation and cataloging.

Kaser, David. "The Library in the Small Historical Society," *History News,* 20:4 (April 1965), Technical Leaflet no. 27.♦ Discusses acquisitions, processing and circulation.

Leahy, Emmett J., and Christopher A.

Cameron. *Modern Records Management: A Basic Guide to Records Control, Filing, and Information Retrieval.* New York: McGraw-Hill, 1965. 236 pp., illus.

Lipton, Barbara. "The Small Museum Library," *Special Libraries,* 65:1 (January 1974), pp. 1-3.

McCree, Mary Lynn, and Timothy Walch, eds. "Setting Priorities for Historical Records: A Conference Report," *The American Archivist,* 40:3 (July 1977), entire issue.♦ Articles on surveys of historical records; intellectual control of historical records; professional archival training; conservation and preservation; preservation and use of state and local records; archival research centers.

Map Workshop Panel, McGill University, 1969. *Recent Practices in Map Libraries: Proceedings.* New York: Special Libraries Association, 1971. 36 pp., illus.♦ Sponsored by the Geography and Map Division of Special Libraries Association; reprinted from various issues of *Special Libraries,* 1969, 1970, 1971. Includes map librarianship; published sources of information about maps and atlases; map cataloging; equipment; automation; repair and preservation of map materials.

Menzeńska, Mary Jane. *Archives and Other Special Collections: A Library Staff Handbook.* New York: School of Library Service, Columbia University, 1973. 87 pp., forms, appendices, glossary, bibliog.♦ Chapters on handling and care; general policies; acquisitions and accessioning; evaluation, retention and disposal; arrangement and boxing; control, access and publicity; sample copies of finding aids; sample of a record groups classification for archives.

Mittal, R. L. *Library Administration: Theory and Practice.* 3rd enl. ed. Delhi: Metropolitan Book Co., 1973. 676 pp., bibliog. footnotes.

"Museum Division Issue," *Special Libraries,* 42:5 (May-June 1951), entire issue.

"Museum Libraries," *Special Libraries,* 50:3 (March 1959), entire issue. ♦ Articles on photograph and slide collections in art libraries, art libraries and librarians, presidential library, historical society library, art museum libraries, planning new libraries.

Myers, Gerald E. *Insurance Manual for Libraries.* Chicago: American Library Association, 1977. 64 pp., index.

Petrucci, Armando. "Archives and Libraries: Possibilities of Collaboration," *UNESCO Bulletin for Libraries,* 20:2 (March/April 1966), pp. 65-70.

"Rare Books and Special Material in Museum Libraries: A Roundtable," *Special Libraries,* 52:1 (January 1961), pp. 9-21.

Ratner, Jane Faux. "Local History Collections: The Practical Problems," *Library Journal,* 101:19 (November 1, 1976), pp. 2231-2235.♦ Discusses local history collections in public libraries; security and service; legalities such as copyright and libel; and staffing.

Schellenberg, Theodore R. *Modern Archives: Principles and Techniques.* 1956. Reprint. Chicago: University of Chicago Press, 1975. 247 pp.♦ Examines the management of governmental records at all levels and offers valuable background material for archivists.

Society of American Archivists. College and University Archives Committee. *Forms Manual.* Madison, Wisc.: 1973. 236 pp. ♦ Handbook of forms used by archives in educational institutions throughout the U.S. and Canada. Includes forms used in records management, appraisal, inventory and description, collecting policies and procedures, accessioning, arrangement, description, reference and research services, reproduction, oral history, and statistical reports.

Sommer, Frank H. "A Large Museum Library," *Special Libraries,* 65:3 (March 1974), pp. 99-103.♦ Philosophy and organization of the Henry Francis duPont Winterthur Museum Library.

Special Libraries Association. *Objectives and Standards for Special Libraries.* New York: 1964. 9 pp.♦ Reprinted from *Special Libraries,* 55:12 (December 1964), pp. 671-680.

Special Libraries Association. Illinois Chapter. *Special Libraries: A Guide for Management with Revisions through 1974.* By JoAnn Aufdenkamp and others. Edward G. Strable, editor. New York: The Association, 1975. 74 pp., illus., bibliog.♦ Covers acquisition, organization and dissemination of materials, staff, space and equipment, and planning and budgets.

Stevenson, Gordon, ed. "Trends in Archival

and Reference Collections of Recorded Sound," *Library Trends,* 21:1 (July 1972), entire issue.♦ Includes scope and purpose of phonorecord archives, oral history, preservation of sound recordings, copyright and archival collections of sound recordings.

Thompson, Enid T. *Local History Collections: A Manual for Librarians.* Nashville, Tenn.: American Association for State and Local History, 1978. 100 pp., illus., bibliog., appendix, index.♦ Chapters include collecting local history; materials of local history; legal aspects; conservation, cleaning, mending and other chores; processing local history; services; training volunteers; special projects. Appendix includes organizations, sources of supplies, publication addresses.

U.S. National Park Service. "The Park Library." In *Field Manual for Museums* (Ann Arbor, Mich.: Finch Press, 1974), pp. 240-254.

Usilton, Bertha. "The Museum Library," *Museum News,* 42:2 (October 1963), pp. 11-14.

Walton, Clyde C., ed. "State and Local History in Libraries," *Library Trends,* 13:2 (October 1964), entire issue.♦ Topics include libraries of privately supported historical societies; acquisition and organization of local historical materials; use of local historical materials; ownership of local historical materials; trends in preservation; problems of maps; manuscript and newspaper collections.

Weihs, Jean Riddle; Shirley Lewis; and Janet MacDonald. *Nonbook Materials: The Organization of Integrated Collections.* In consultation with the CLA/ALA/AECT/EMAC/CAML Advisory Committee on the Cataloguing of Nonbook Materials. 1st ed. Ottawa: Canadian Library Association, 1973. 107 pp., bibliog., appendices, index.♦ Includes cataloging policy, cataloging rules, and storage guidelines for nonbook materials. Also distributed by the American Library Association.

Young, Virginia G., ed. *The Library Trustee, A Practical Guidebook.* 3rd ed. New York: R. R. Bowker, 1978. 256 pp., bibliog., appendix, index.

Young, Virginia G. *Trustee of a Small Public Library.* Rev. ed. Small Libraries Project Pamphlet no. 1. Chicago: American Library Association, 1978. 12 pp.

Technical Services

Collecting: Selection and Acquisition

American Book Prices Current: *A Record of Literary Properties Sold at Auction in the United States.* New York: Dodd, Mead & Co., 1894/95 -. 1 vol., annual.♦ Five-year indexes. Current edition, vol. 84, 1978, auction season September 1977-August 1978, published by American Book Prices Current, 121 East 78th Street, New York, New York 10021.

American Book Trade Directory. New York: R. R. Bowker, 1915 -. 1 vol., annual.♦ Alphabetically arranged, by state and city, U.S. and Canadian book outlets in cities; with a guide to the special type of stock carried. Also includes a directory of U.S. book publishers, and U.S. and Canadian wholesalers and distributors of paperbacks and magazines, remainder dealers, etc. Issues 1915-1946 have no numbering but constitute 1st-10th eds. Title varies: 1915-1922, American Book Trade Manual; 1925-1949, American Booktrade Directory. Current edition, 24th, 1978-79; revised annually by Jacques Cattell Press.

Autographs and Manuscripts: *A Collector's Manual.* Edited by Edmund Berkeley, Jr., Herbert E. Klingelhofer, and Kenneth W. Rendell. New York: Charles Scribner's Sons, 1978. 565 pp., illus., bibliog., glossary, index.♦ Collection of articles by recognized authorities on every phase of collecting. Sponsored by the Manuscript Society.

Benjamin, Mary A. *Autographs: A Key to Collecting.* Corr. and rev. with a new preface and a selected list of reference works. New York: W. R. Benjamin Autographs, 1963. 313 pp., illus., tables, bibliog., index.♦ Introduction to the study and collecting of autographs including history, evaluation, forgeries; facsimiles and detection; care and preservation of collections; arrangement of collections.

Berner, Richard C. "On Ephemera: Their Collection and Use," *Library Resources & Technical Services,* 7:4 (Fall 1963), pp. 335-339.

Book Collecting: A Modern Guide. Edited by Jean Peters. New York: R. R. Bowker, 1977. 288 pp., bibliog., appendix.♦ Twelve essays on major aspects of book collecting: antiquarian books, manuscripts, bibliography, fakes and forgeries, physical care of books, and appraisal.

Bookman's Price Index. An Annual Guide to the Values of Rare and Other Out-of-Print Books. Detroit: Gale Research Co., 1964 -. 1 vol., annual.♦ Current edition, vol. 16, 1979.

Books in Print: *An Author-Title-Series Index to the Publishers' Trade List Annual . . . .* New York: R. R. Bowker Co., 1948 -.♦ Two author and two title volumes; supplement published in spring. Current edition, 1979-1980.

Bradley, Van Allen. *The Book Collector's Handbook of Values.* 3rd ed. rev. & enl. New York: Putnam, c1978. 590 pp., illus.♦ Alphabetical, author-title listing of selected rare books published since 1800.

Brichford, Maynard J. *Archives and Manuscripts: Appraisal and Accessioning.* Chicago: Society of American Archivists, 1977. 24 pp., bibliog., appendix.♦ Basic Manual series; includes characteristics of records; administrative, research, archival values; appraisers and appraisal techniques; gift, sale and tax appraisals; accessioning.

Brooks, Philip C. "The Selection of Records for Preservation," *The American Archivist,* 3:4 (October 1940), pp. 221-234.

Brubaker, Robert L. "Clio's Midwife: Collecting Manuscripts at a State Historical Library," *Illinois Libraries,* LD Pub. 82 (June 1965), pp. 1-7.

Carter, John. *ABC for Book Collectors.* 4th rev. ed. New York: Alfred A. Knopf, 1966. 208 pp.♦ Comprehensive listing of the terminology of book collecting.

Conner, Seymour V. "A System of Manuscript Appraisal," *History News,* 22:5 (May 1967), Technical Leaflet no. 41.

Directory of American Book Specialists: Sources for Antiquarian and Out-of-Print Titles. New York: Continental Pub. Co., 1972. 172 pp.♦ Directory of bookmen in the U.S. and Canada specializing in antiquarian and out-of-print titles.

Duniway, David C. "Conflicts in Collecting," *The American Archivist,* 24:1 (January 1961), pp. 55-63.

Fleckner, John A. *Archives and Manuscripts: Surveys.* Chicago: Society of American Archivists, 1977. 28 pp., bibliog.♦ Basic Manual series; describes surveys of records and papers not in immediate custody; administering

170

the survey; publicity, forms and surveyors; and completing the field work.

Ford, Stephen. *The Acquisition of Library Materials.* Rev. ed. Chicago: American Library Association, 1978. 232 pp., bibliog., appendices, glossary, index.♦ Emphasis on topics that are of concern to all libraries regardless of size, including planning for acquisitions, bibliographies used in searching, purchasing, out-of-print books, serials, gifts and exchanges, centralized processing.

Kaiser, Barbara J. "Problems with Donors of Contemporary Collections," *The American Archivist,* 32:2 (April 1969), pp. 103-107.

Kemp, Edward C. *Manuscript Solicitation for Libraries, Special Collections, Museums, and Archives.* Littleton, Colo.: Libraries Unlimited, 1978. 204 pp., bibliog. references, index.

Lehmann-Haupt, Hellmut, ed. "Current Trends in Antiquarian Books," *Library Trends,* 9:4 (April 1961), entire issue.

Lewis, David L. "Appraisal Criteria for Retention and Disposal of Business Records," *The American Archivist,* 32:1 (January 1969), pp. 21-24.

Menkus, Belden. "Viewpoint," *History News,* 26:4 (April 1971), pp. 77-78.♦ Pleads a case for preserving today's records as the materials with which tomorrow's historian will work.

Parker, J. Carlyle. "Genealogy Part II: Basic Reference Tools for American Libraries," *Wilson Library Bulletin,* 47:3 (November 1972), pp. 257-261.♦ Suggests what books to order in setting up a genealogical section in the library such as how-to-do-it books, pamphlets, place name literature, family histories, county histories, census, indexes, church records.

Pinkett, Harold T. "Accessioning Public Records: Anglo-American Practices and Possible Improvements," *The American Archivist,* 41:4 (October 1978), pp. 413-421.

Pinkett, Harold T. "Selective Preservation of General Correspondence," *The American Archivist,* 30:1 (January 1967), pp. 33-43.

Rapp, Brigid, et al. "Collecting Resources for Historic Preservation," *Preservation News,* 17:3 (March 1977), Supplement.♦ Articles on collection and organization of special library materials relating to historic preservation; description of the National Trust for Historic Pres-

ervation library and sources; classifying materials; managing architectural records and newspaper clippings, and a source list.

The Reader's Adviser: *An Annotated Guide to the Best in Print in Literature, Biographies, Dictionaries, Encyclopedias, Bibles, Classics, Drama, Poetry, Fiction, Science, Philosophy, Travel, History.* 11th ed. rev. & enl. Edited by Winifred F. Courtney. New York: R. R. Bowker, 1969. 2 vols.

Sterne, Edward L. *Is My Old Book Valuable? With Hints on Selling.* 3rd ed. rev. & enl. Taneytown, Md.: Antiques Publications, 1966. 60 pp., illus., bibliog.

Tannen, Jack. *How to Identify and Collect American First Editions: A Guide Book.* New York: Arco Publishing Company, c1976. 147 pp.♦ Guide to building a collection including definition of terms and list of American publishers and their methods of denoting first editions.

Winterich, John T., and David Randall. *A Primer of Book Collecting.* 3rd rev. ed. New York: Crown Publishers, 1966. 228 pp., illus., index.♦ First edition, 1927, revised editions in 1935 and 1946. Includes: first edition and blood relations; association books; what makes a rare book rare; the factor of condition; the mechanics of collecting; the pursuit of the point; dollars and cents; tools of the trade.

Wulfekoetter, Gertrude. *Acquisition Work: Processes Involved in Building Library Collections.* Seattle: University of Washington Press, 1961. 268 pp., bibliog.

NOTES AND PERIODICALS

AB Bookman's Weekly/Antiquarian Bookman. 1948, weekly, subscription. AB Bookman's Weekly, Box 1110, Newark, New Jersey 07101. Source for advertising and locating out-of-print books.

Publishers Weekly: *The Book Industry Journal.* 1872, weekly, subscription. Orders to R. R. Bowker Company, Subscription Service Department, Box 67, Whitinsville, Massachusetts 01588.

University Microfilms, Inc., 300 N. Zeeb Road, Ann Arbor, Michigan 48106. Source of facsimiles of out-of-print books.

Cataloging

Akers, Susan Grey. *Akers' Simple Library Cataloging.* By Arthur Curley and Jana Varlejs. 6th ed., completely rev. and rewritten. Metuchen, N.J.: Scarecrow Press, 1977. 338 pp., illus., bibliog., index.

American Library Association. Small Libraries Project. *The Vertical File.* Chicago: The Association, 1963. 4 pp.

American Library Association. Subcommittee on the ALA Rules for Filing Catalog Cards. *ALA Rules for Filing Catalog Cards.* Prepared by the ALA Editorial Committee's Subcommittee on the ALA Rules for Filing Catalog Cards. Pauline A. Seely, chairman and editor. 2nd ed. abridged. Chicago: 1968. 94 pp.♦ See also full edition, 2nd ed., 1968, 260 pp., edited by Pauline A. Seely.

Anglo-American Cataloguing Rules. Prepared by the American Library Association, et al.; edited by Michael Gorman and Paul W. Winkler. 2nd ed. Chicago: American Library Association, 1978. 620 pp., bibliog. references, index.♦ New edition to incorporate already agreed revisions to AACR 1; to harmonize with British and North American texts of AACR 1; to incorporate international standards and international agreements; to take developments in library automation into account; to incorporate changes arising from proposals for change coming from any source.

Anglo-American Cataloging Rules. Prepared by the American Library Association, the Library of Congress, and the Canadian Library Association. General Editor: C. Sumner Spaulding. Chicago: American Library Association, 1967. 400 pp.

Bartlett, James, and Douglas Marshall. "Maps in the Small Historical Society: Care and Cataloging," *History News,* 34:1 (January 1979), Technical Leaflet no. 111.♦ Basic elements of map preservation, storage and retrieval using a card catalog.

Berner, Richard C. "The Arrangement and Description of Manuscripts," *The American Archivist,* 23:4 (October 1960), pp. 395-406.

Berner, Richard C. "Manuscript Collections and Archives—A Unitary Approach," *Library Resources & Technical Services,* 9:2 (Spring 1965), pp. 213-220.♦ Discusses cataloging techniques, based on premise that biblio-graphic characteristics of archives and manuscript collections are fundamentally the same and that these characteristics are essentially different from those of published items.

Bodem, Dennis R. "The Use of Forms in the Control of Archives at the Accessioning and Processing Level," *The American Archivist,* 31:4 (October 1968), pp. 365-369.♦ Review of examples of accessioning and progress forms submitted by archival agencies, noting essential factors and types.

Bogar, Candace W. *Annotated Bibliography of Published Literature on the Cataloging and Classification of Films, Pictures, and Slides in Architecture, City Planning and Art.* Exchange Bibliography no. 405. Monticello, Ill.: Council of Planning Librarians, 1973. 17 pp.♦ Emphasis on constructive suggestions for specific classification and cataloging systems to meet the needs of various patrons. Standard cataloging tools not included except for those which specifically deal with nonbook materials of a pictorial nature.

Boggs, Samuel W., and Dorothy C. Lewis. *The Classification and Cataloging of Maps and Atlases.* New York: Special Libraries Association, 1945. 175 pp., illus., forms, map, bibliog., index.♦ Still useful for the identification of projections and the determination of scales. Out-of-print; available from University Microfilms, Inc.

Bordin, Ruth B. "Cataloging Manuscripts—A Simple Scheme," *The American Archivist,* 27:1 (January 1964), pp. 81-86.

Brown, Lloyd Arnold. *Notes on the Care and Cataloguing of Old Maps.* 1941. Reprint. Port Washington, N.Y.: Kennikat Press, 1970. 110 pp., illus., bibliog.♦ Includes storage and equipment, classification, cataloguing, and cartographic nomenclature.

Cutter, Charles Ammi. *C. A. Cutter's Three-figure Author Table.* Swanson-Swift revision. Chicopee, Mass.: distr. by H. R. Huntting Co., 1969. 29 pp.♦ Mounted on boards and spiral bound; also *Instruction Book,* 4 pp., in pocket of main work.

Daily, Jay E. *Organizing Nonprint Materials: A Guide for Librarians.* New York: M. Dekker, 1972. 190 pp., illus., bibliog.

Dewey, Melvil. *Dewey Decimal Classification and Relative Index.* 19th ed. Albany, N.Y.:

Forest Press, division of Lake Placid Education Foundation, 1979. 3 vols.♦ Vol. 1—Introduction, Tables; Vol. 2—Schedules; Vol. 3—Relative Index.

Dunkin, Paul S. *How to Catalog a Rare Book.* 2nd ed., rev. Chicago: American Library Association, 1973. 105 pp., bibliog.♦ Practical guide to cataloging rare books; shows how to examine a book to determine how it differs from other editions or printings of the same title.

Dunn, Walter S., Jr. "Cataloging Ephemera: A Procedure for Small Libraries," *History News,* 27:1 (January 1972), Technical Leaflet no. 58.

Evans, Frank B. "Modern Methods of Arrangement of Archives in the United States," *The American Archivist,* 29:3 (April 1966), pp. 241-263.

Falco, Nicholas. *Manual for the Organization of Manuscripts in the Long Island Division of the Queens Borough Public Library.* Jamaica, N.Y.: Queens Borough Public Library, 1978. 140 pp., diagrams, forms.♦ Guidance in the care and servicing of manuscript materials; not intended to be exhaustive but covers virtually all aspects of the subject. Also not intended directly for other libraries or historical societies but useful especially to smaller organizations and those with no professional manuscript curator or archivist.

Finch, Jean L. "Some Fundamentals in Arranging Archives and Manuscript Collections," *Library Resources & Technical Services,* 8:1 (Winter 1964), pp. 26-34.♦ Includes bibliography and sample card forms.

Gilbert, Karen Diane. *Picture Indexing for Local History Materials.* New ed. Monroe, N.Y.: Library Research Associates, 1973. 36 pp., bibliog., index.♦ Manual on the scope and method of indexing local history pictorial material based on system used at the Newark Public Library, New Jersey. Includes indexing procedure, indexing by locality, nongeographic and special subject headings, storage and retrieval.

Gilley, Beulah L. "Declassifying the Slide Secrets," *Museum News,* 52:6 (March 1974), pp. 45-48.♦ Reports on a number of classification systems used by museums, universities and libraries, and recommends some procedures for the care and development of museum slide libraries.

Gordon, Robert S. "Suggestions for Organization and Description of Archival Holdings of Local Historical Societies," *The American Archivist,* 26:1 (January 1963), pp. 19-39.

Gould, Geraldine N., and Ithmer C. Wolfe. *How to Organize and Maintain the Library Picture/Pamphlet File.* Dobbs Ferry, N.Y.: Oceana Publications, 1968. 146 pp., illus., forms.

Gracy, David B. *Archives and Manuscripts: Arrangement and Description.* Chicago: Society of American Archivists, 1977. 49 pp., bibliog., index.♦ Basic Manual series; includes arrangement, description, and handling special record material such as diaries, maps, microforms.

Hague, Donald V., and Catherine Hammond. "A System for Cataloging Museum Periodicals," *Museum News,* 55:7 (July/August 1977), pp. 38-40.

Hale, Richard W., Jr. "The Cataloging of Microfilm," *The American Archivist,* 22:1 (January 1959), pp. 11-13.

Holmes, Oliver W. "Archival Arrangement—Five Different Operations at Five Different Levels," *The American Archivist,* 27:1 (January 1964), pp. 21-41.♦ Discusses levels of arrangement: depository, record group, within the record group, filing units within series, documents within file units; and boxing, shelving and labeling.

Horn, Andrew H., ed. "Special Materials and Services," *Library Trends,* 4:2 (October 1955), entire issue.♦ Includes maps, newspapers, prints, pictures, photographs, musical scores and recordings, films, microfilm, pamphlets, posters, clippings, manuscript collections.

Jasenas, Michael. "Cataloging Small Manuscript Collections," *Library Resources & Technical Services,* 7:3 (Summer 1963), pp. 264-273.♦ Reviews technical details; cites sample forms.

Johnson, Sheila G. "Geographic Arrangement of Topographic Maps," *Special Libraries,* 68:3 (March 1977), pp. 115-118.

Kansas. Traveling Libraries Commission. *Step-by-Step Library Organization: A Basic Organization Manual for Libraries with Book Collections of 5,000 or Less.* By Zelia J. French. Topeka, Kans.: The Commission, 1959. 36 pp., illus.♦ Setting up a workable card file for books and circulation records necessary to the operation of a small library. Out-of-print; photocopies available from the Kansas State Library, 535 Kansas Street, Topeka, Kansas 66603.

Larsgaard, Mary. *Map Librarianship: An Introduction.* Littleton, Colo.: Libraries Unlimited, 1977. 330 pp., bibliog., index.

"Library of Congress Rules for Cataloging a Collection of Manuscripts," *History News,* 12:11 (September 1957), pp. 85-88.

Matthis, Raimund E., and Desmond Taylor. *Adopting the Library of Congress Classification System: A Manual of Methods and Techniques for Application or Conversion.* New York: R. R. Bowker, 1971. 209 pp., illus., bibliog., appendices.♦ Includes reclassification, cost data, cataloging and mechanical decisions.

May, Ruby S. "Cataloging and Indexing Historical Collections," *Special Libraries,* 66:4 (April 1975), pp. 217-222.

Miller, Shirley. *The Vertical File and Its Satellites: A Handbook of Acquisition, Processing and Organization.* Littleton, Colo.: Libraries Unlimited, 1971. 220 pp., bibliog.♦ Discusses locating, cataloging and handling of pamphlets, clippings, local history materials, maps, and pictorial materials.

New York (State). Office of State History. *A Filing System for Historical Information.* Albany: 1973. 17 pp.♦ Includes purpose of a filing system, equipment needed, preparing folders and labels, setting up and expanding the filing system, and an outline of subject headings.

Newark, N. J. Free Public Library. *The Picture Collection: Subject Headings.* By William J. Dane. 6th ed. Hamden, Conn.: Shoe String Press, 1968. 103 pp.♦ A revision and expansion of the list of subject headings first published in 1910 as part of the picture collection by J. C. Dana.

Newman, John, and Patricia Richter. "Indexing Local Newspapers," *History News,* 33:8 (August 1978), Technical Leaflet no. 107.♦ Includes scope of the index, staff, format, specific entries, subject headings, and examples.

Paris. International Documentation Center. *Museum Classification Scheme.* 3rd ed. Paris: UNESCO-ICOM Documentation Centre, 1968. 27 pp.♦ A book classification system. Also: *Index to the Classification Scheme,* published by the Center, 1968, 48 pp.

Perica, Esther. *Newspaper Indexing for Historical Societies, Colleges and High Schools.* Monroe, N.Y.: Library Research Associates, 1975. 55 pp., bibliog., index.♦ Includes guidelines for creating an index, what to index, preparing catalog cards, and general indexing rules.

Radoff, Morris L. "Guide to Practical Calendaring," *The American Archivist,* 11:2 (April 1948), pp. 123-140.♦ Continued in 11:3 (July 1948), pp. 203-222. Includes what materials should be calendared; the calendarer—staff or outsider; materials in one or more depository; printing; length; basic abbreviations; arrangement of calendar entries; physical form of entry; punctuation; names of principals, titles, place, syntax of abstract; length of document; size of page; names of individuals; previous printing; enclosures; preparation of index.

Schellenberg, Theodore R. *The Management of Archives.* New York: Columbia University Press, 1965. 383 pp.♦ Defines principles and techniques of arrangement and description of documentary materials; considers the difference between archival and library methods.

Sears List of Subject Headings. 11th ed. Edited by Barbara M. Westby. New York: H. W. Wilson Co., 1977. 654 pp.

Semowich, Charles J., and Enid T. Thompson. "Post Card Collections in the Local Historical Society," *History News,* 34:8 (June 1979), Technical Leaflet no. 116.

Simons, Wendell W., and Luraine C. Tansey. *A Slide Classification System for the Organization and Automatic Indexing of Interdisciplinary Collections of Slides and Pictures.* Santa Cruz: University of California, 1970. 263 pp., appendices, index.♦ Discusses need for new classification, suggests method of automatic indexing, and classification schedules for history, art, and science.

Society of American Archivists. *Inventories and Registers: A Handbook of Techniques and Examples.* Chicago: The Society, 1976. 36 pp., bibliog.♦ A compilation of examples of representative finding aids from various institutions with brief explanations of the use to which they are or might be put.

Stewart, Milo V. "Organizing Your 2 x 2 Slides: A Storage and Retrieval System," *History News,* 31:3 (March 1976), Technical Leaflet no. 88.

U.S. Library of Congress. Subject Cataloging Division. *Library of Congress Subject Headings.* 8th ed. Washington, D.C.: Cataloging Distribution Service, Library of Congress, 1975. 2 vols.◆ Previous editions have title: Subject headings used in the dictionary catalogs of the Library of Congress. Incorporates material through 1973; kept up to date by quarterly cumulative supplements.

U.S. National Archives. *Principles of Arrangement of Records Followed in the National Archives.* Staff Information Papers no. 18. Washington, D.C.: 1951. 14 pp.

Volkersz, Evert. "Neither Book nor Manuscript: Some Special Collections," *Library Resources & Technical Services,* 13:4 (Fall 1969), pp. 493-501.◆ Cataloging, classification and filing innovations proven successful in achieving bibliographic control over American almanacs, ephemera, objects, pamphlets, pictorial, rare map and scrapbook collections. Also comments on research potentials of these materials.

Western Association of Map Libraries. *Maps in the Local Historical Society.* Stockton, Calif.: Conference of California Historical Societies, 1973. 38 pp., notes, bibliog.

Wynar, Bohdan S. *Introduction to Cataloging and Classification.* 4th rev. ed. Littleton, Colo.: Libraries Unlimited, 1971. 344 pp., glossary, bibliog., index.

NOTE

National Union Catalog. The National Union Catalog represents works cataloged by the Library of Congress and by libraries contributing to its cooperative cataloging program. It constitutes a reference and research tool for a large part of the world's production of significant books as acquired and cataloged by the Library of Congress and other North American Libraries. The NUC contains currently issued LC printed card entries for books, maps, pamphlets, atlases, periodicals and other serials, regardless of imprint date, and is regularly printed in nine monthly issues, three quarterly cumulations, and in annual and quinquennial cumulations. The LC catalog publishing program began with *A Catalog of Books Represented by Library of Congress Printed Cards* (1942-1946), and . . . *Supplement* (1948); and continued with *The Library of Congress Author Catalog, 1948-1952* (1953); *The National Union Catalog, A Cumulative List* (quinquennial cumulations: 1958, 1963, 1969, 1973, 1979). Other comprehensive catalogs are published for Register of Additional Locations, Subject, Films, Monographs, Music, Microform Masters, Manuscript Collections and Newspapers. The publication of the NUC Pre-1956 Imprints was begun in 1968 and makes available in book form the total catalog maintained on cards by the Library of Congress since 1901. The NUC contains main entries, essential added entries and cross references. The majority are reproduced from tapes and include tracings, LC call number, Dewey decimal class number, card number and name of other libraries if copy was supplied by them. Entries represented by LC printed cards are prepared in accordance with the *Anglo-American Cataloging Rules* and LC policies concerning the application of these rules.

Protection and Preservation

American Library Association. Library Technology Project. *Protecting the Library and Its Resources: A Guide to Physical Protection and Insurance.* Report on a study conducted by Gage-Babcock & Associates, Inc. Chicago: Library Technology Project, American Library Association, 1963. 322 pp., illus., bibliog., appendix, index.◆ Part I—physical protection, includes types of physical losses, fire defense measures, fire protection equipment, role of fire protection in library planning; Part II—insurance, includes valuation, coverage, insurance practices, liability insurance, workmens compensation, model insurance policy for libraries. Appendix covers salvage and restoration of damaged materials, evaluation for insurance purposes, liability for copyright infringement.

Bahr, Alice. *Book Theft and Library Security Systems, 1978-79.* White Plains, N.Y.: Knowledge Industry Publications, c1978. 128 pp., bibliog., index.

Banks, Paul N. "Environmental Standards for Storage of Books and Manuscripts," *Library Journal,* 99:3 (February 1974), pp. 339-343.♦ Covers humidity, air cleanness, ventilation, ltght, exhibition, shelving and transportation, storage of microfilm, disaster control, monitoring system, and references.

Bohem, Hilda. *Disaster Prevention and Disaster Preparedness.* Berkeley, Calif.: University of California, Task Group on the Preservation of Library Materials, 1978. 23 pp., appendices.♦ List of factors and options, to suit individual situations, to be considered in the formulation of disaster plans. Includes a plan (prevention and action), checklist, sources of assistance, and telephone assistance.

Bommer, Michael, and Bernard Ford. "Cost Benefit Analysis for Determining the Value of an Electronic Security System," *College and Research Libraries,* 35:4 (July 1974), pp. 270-279.♦ Discusses an electronic security system; two methods for estimating rate of book loss.

Burns Security Institute. *National Survey on Library Security.* Briarcliff Manor, N.Y.: The Institute, 1973. 38 pp., charts.♦ Report of the Institute, a private research unit, which undertook a national survey on library security, covering book theft, security controls, fire and burglar alarms, guards, book recovery, major security problems. Available from the Institute, 320 Old Briarcliff Road, Briarcliff Manor, New York 10510.

Cunha, George D. M., and Dorothy Grant Cunha. *Conservation of Library Materials: A Manual and Bibliography on the Care, Repair and Restoration of Library Materials.* 2nd ed. Vols. 1 and 2. Metuchen, N.J.: Scarecrow Press, 1971 -. 406, 414 pp., illus., diagrams, graphs, appendices, glossary, index.♦ Contents: History of Bookbinding; Materials; Enemies of Books; Conservation (environmental); Conservation (of materials); Conservation in the Tropics; Repair and Restoration; Book Repair; Map Repair; Restoration of Manuscripts, Prints, Drawings, Seals, Films, Tapes and Discs.

Darling, Pamela W.; Paul N. Banks; and Frazer G. Poole. "Books in Peril: A Mini-Symposium on the Preservation of Library Materials," *Library Journal,* 101:20 (November 15, 1976), pp. 2341-2351.♦ Discusses starting a local preservation program, cooperative approaches to conservation, and proposed National Preservation Program of the Library of Congress.

DeWitt, Donald L., and Carol Burlinson. "Leather Bookbindings: Preservation Techniques," *History News,* 32:8 (August 1977), Technical Leaflet no. 98.

Feipel, Louis N., and Earl W. Browning. *Library Binding Manual.* Prepared under the direction of the Joint Committee of the American Library Association and the Library Binding Institute. Chicago: American Library Association, 1951. 74 pp., illus., bibliog., appendix, glossary, index.♦ An elementary book on the binding, care and preservation of printed materials, and covering minimum requirements for the ordinary run of books and other printed material usually found in the library collection.

Hasznos, Lola. "Modern Methods for the Protection of Archival and Library Material: Care and Restoration of Badly Damaged Documents," *UNESCO Bulletin for Libraries,* 24:6 (November/December 1970), pp. 302-304.

Henderson, James W., and Robert C. Krupp. "The Librarian as Conservator," *The Library Quarterly,* 40:1 (January 1970), pp. 176-191.

Horton, Carolyn. *Cleaning and Preserving Bindings and Related Materials.* 2nd ed. rev. Conservation of Library Materials, Pamphlet 1. Chicago: Library Technology Project, American Library Association, 1969. 87 pp., illus., bibliog.♦ Provides much practical advice for the novice, including information on reconditioning a library, sorting books and identifying problems, and treatment of worn and damaged books, list of supplies and equipment, sources of supply, and a glossary.

Hunter, John E. "Emergency Preparedness for Museums, Historic Sites, and Archives: An Annotated Bibliography," *History News,* 34:4 (April 1979), Technical Leaflet no. 114.

Kathpalia, Yash Pal. *Conservation and Restoration of Archive Materials.* Paris: UNESCO, 1973. 231 pp., illus., bibliog.♦ Examines specific problems of conservation and restoration of archive materials in regions with unfavorable climatic conditions.

Kinney, John M. "Archival Security and Insecurity," *The American Archivist,* 38:4 (October 1975), pp. 493-497.

Kish, Joseph L., et al. *Protection of Vital Records: A Special Report by the Association of Records Executives and Administrators, Inc.* Washington, D.C.: Department of Defense, Office of Civil Defense, 1966. 24 pp., bibliog.

Ladenson, Alex. "Library Security and the Law," *College and Research Libraries,* 38:2 (March 1977), pp. 109-117.♦ Includes a model law relating to library theft, and references.

Library Association. Research and Development Committee. *The Care of Books and Documents.* Research Publication no. 10. London: The Association, 1972. 23 pp., bibliog.

Mason, Philip P. "Archival Security: New Solutions to an Old Problem," *The American Archivist,* 38:4 (October 1975), pp. 477-492.♦ Case studies of major manuscript thefts, and suggestions for the prevention and detection of archival theft.

Morris, John. *Managing the Library Fire Risk.* 2nd ed. Berkeley, Calif.: Office of Insurance and Risk Management, University of California, 1979. 147 pp., illus., bibliog., appendix.♦ Written primarily for library board members and library directors; compendium for architects, fire protection professionals, and others concerned with planning and maintenance of buildings.

National Fire Protection Association. *Archives and Records Centers.* NFPA 232AM. Boston: 1972. 26 pp.♦ Provides guidance on fire protection for file rooms of 50,000 cubic feet in volume to largest known archives or records centers.

National Fire Protection Association. *Protection of Library Collections.* NFPA 910. Boston: 1975. 28 pp.♦ Recommended practices with case histories, new construction and guidance to save lives and property.

National Fire Protection Association. *Protection of Records.* NFPA 232. Boston: 1975. 93 pp.♦ Standards and criteria for fire-resistive vaults, file rooms, safes, containers and devices, and management of records. Appendices give data on vault construction, record classifications and forms.

Preservation of Paper and Textiles of Historic and Artistic Value: *A Symposium spon-*sored by the Cellulose, Paper and Textile Division at the 172d Meeting of the American Chemical Society, San Francisco, California, August 30-31, 1976. John C. William, ed. Washington, D.C.: American Chemical Society, 1977. 403 pp., bibliog. references, index.♦ Collection of symposium papers covering paper manufacturing and permanent paper, new deacidification processes, salvage of water damaged books, and causes of paper deterioration. Symposium also covered care and preservation of textiles; estimation of permanence.

Priest, Ernest H.; Luta M. Sewell; and Lester J. Cappon. "Creation of Records: The Program of Colonial Williamsburg," *The American Archivist,* 14:2 (April 1951), pp. 117-125.♦ Describes materials and equipment used, distribution of copies, and establishment of higher standards in the creation of records in view of long-time research value of the materials created by the project.

"Rare Book Division Protected by New Fire Prevention System," *Library of Congress Information Bulletin,* 34:19 (May 9, 1975), pp. 181ff.♦ Brief article on new automatic fire extinguishing system which uses a low temperature refrigerant gas, Halon 1301, to quench flames without damage to materials or harmful effects to humans.

Rhoads, James B. "Alienation and Thievery: Archival Problems," *The American Archivist,* 29:2 (April 1966), pp. 197-208.

Riley, William J. "Library Security and the Federal Bureau of Investigation," *College and Research Libraries,* 38:2 (March 1977), pp. 104-108.

Santen, Vernon, and Howard Crocker. "Historical Society Records: Guidelines for a Protection Program," *History News,* 27:9 (September 1972), Technical Leaflet no. 18.

Schefrin, R. A. "Barriers to and Barriers of Library Security," *Wilson Library Bulletin,* 45:9 (May 1971), pp. 870-878.

Seminar on the Application of Chemical and Physical Methods to the Conservation of Library and Archival Material, Topsfield, Mass., 1971. *Library and Archives Conservation: The Boston Atheneum's 1971 Seminar. . . .* Edited by George M. Cunha and Norman P. Tucker. Boston: Library of the Boston Atheneum, 1972. 255 pp., illus., bibliog. references.♦ Includes materials; fungus deterioration; insect damage; control of light; acid deterioration; environmental control; storage.

Smith, Richard D. "Guidelines for Preservation," *Special Libraries,* 59:5 (May-June 1968), pp. 346-352.♦ Recommends a written preservation policy for each library.

Walch, Timothy. *Archives and Manuscripts: Security.* Chicago: Society of American Archivists, 1977. 30 pp., illus., bibliog., appendices.♦ Basic Manual series; includes planning a security program, security staff and patrons, security and the collections, equipment, security against fire and flood, archival security and the law.

Walch, Timothy. "The Improvement of Library Security," *College and Research Libraries,* 38:2 (March 1977), pp. 100-103.♦ Discusses practical and low-cost measures to improve security, and the services of the Archival Security Program of the Society of American Archivists.

Waters, Peter. *Procedures for Salvage of Water-Damaged Library Materials.* Washington, D.C.: Library of Congress, 1975. 30 pp., illus.

NOTES

Archival Security Program, Society of American Archivists, Timothy Walch, Associate Director, 330 South Wells Street, Suite 810, Chicago, Illinois 60606. The SAA Archival Security Program was established in 1975 with the assistance of the National Endowment for the Humanities and serves as a clearinghouse for information on theft and security in libraries and archives. The major facets of the program include a national register of lost or stolen archival materials; a newsletter; and a consultant service. The National Register of Lost or Stolen Archival Materials was established to publicize missing items and is updated bimonthly and sent to dealers and curators across the country. There is no charge for listing missing items; nor is the service restricted to SAA members. Forms for the registration of missing items are available from the SAA office. The Society provides consultants to archival institutions in need of competent experts to advise them in areas of security systems and internal archival procedures. Applications are available from the SAA office.

The Society publishes *Archival Security Newsletter* (bimonthly), devoted to archival security. It includes notices and accounts of recent thefts and prosecutions, and articles on various security systems and related matters. The newsletter is published as a supplement to the *SAA Newsletter* and as part of the Register. The Society has also published a manual on archival security (1977), cited above.

Conservation Administration News. 1979, quarterly, subscription. c/o Robert H. Patterson, Director of Libraries, P.O. Box 3334 University Station, Laramie, Wyoming 82071. Devoted to varied aspects of preservation of library and archival materials; directed to librarians and archivists who may lack expertise in conservation but must plan and execute programs in their institutions; includes advice and assistance on preventive programs.

Library & Archival Security. vol. 3, no. 1 (January 1979), quarterly, subscription. The Haworth Press, 149 Fifth Avenue, New York, New York 10010. Covers specific areas of security planning, policies, procedures for both libraries and archives; includes book theft, electronic security systems, fire security, protection of special collections, circulation control.

Reproduction Processes

Benjamin, Curtis G. "Regulation of Photocopying: A World-Wide Quandry," *Library Journal,* 100:15 (September 15, 1975), pp. 1481-1483.

Buyer's Guide to Micrographic Equipment, Products and Services. Silver Spring, Md.: National Micrographics Association, 1976 -. 1 vol., illus.

Costigan, Daniel M. *Micrographics Systems.* Silver Spring, Md.: National Micrographics Association, 1975. 228 pp., illus., tables, appendices, notes, index.♦ NMA Reference Series no. 16.

Dearstyne, Bruce W. "Microfilming Historical Records: An Introduction," *History News,* 32:6 (June 1977), Technical Leaflet no. 96.

Eckles, Robert B. "The Importance of Photocopy Projects for Local and Regional History," *The American Archivist,* 25:2 (April 1962), pp. 159-163.

Fleming, S. J. "Microfiche and the Museum," *Museums Journal,* 76:4 (March 1977), pp. 159-160.♦ Discusses micropublishing opportunities.

Hawken, William R. *Copying Methods Manual.* Chicago: Library Technology Program, American Library Association, 1966. 375 pp., illus., appendices, bibliog., glossary.♦ Comprehensive study of the processes which can be used to copy library materials and documents, with special discussion of the characteristics of originals which govern their reproducibility and of methods and techniques for producing full-size copies, microcopies, and eye-legible copies from microforms. Appendices include the acquisition of reproductions of research materials, document reproduction services in libraries, a discussion of copyright problems, a list of domestic and foreign standards, an annotated bibliography by Allen B. Veaner, and a glossary.

Hawken, William R. *Enlarged Prints from Library Microforms: A Study of Processes, Equipment and Materials.* Chicago: Library Technology Program, American Library Association, 1963. 131 pp., illus.♦ Analysis of equipment in regard to use in library and archives, including technical data, cost, warranty, and operating and maintenance instructions.

Hawken, William R. *Photocopying from Bound Volumes: A Study of Machines, Methods and Materials.* Chicago: Library Technology Program, American Library Association, 1962. 208 pp., illus.♦ Evaluation of the processes and the equipment available for use as a guide to basic copying procedures and a handbook for the operator of copying machines.

La Hood, Charles G., Jr., and Robert C. Sullivan. *Reprographic Services in Libraries: Organization and Administration.* LTP Publication no. 19. Chicago: Library Technology Program, American Library Association, 1975. 74 pp., bibliog., index.

Leisinger, Albert H. *Microphotography for Archives.* Washington, D.C.: International Council on Archives, 1968. 52 pp., bibliog.♦ Discussion of various types of microforms with emphasis on roll microfilm; microfilm equipment; guidelines on archival operations.

Lewis, Chester M. "Interrelationship of Microfilm, Copying Devices and Information Retrieval," *Special Libraries,* 53:3 (March 1962), pp. 130-134.

Librarian's Copyright Kit: *What You Must Know Now.* Chicago: American Library Association, 1977. 11 item packet.♦ Includes guide to new copyright law; new interlibrary loan form; guidelines on photocopying and display warning; bibliography. Descriptive brochure available on request.

Libraries and Copyright: *A Summary of the Arguments for Library Photocopying.* Washington, D.C.: American Library Association, 1974. 50 pp., bibliog. references.♦ Addresses copyright questions from librarian's viewpoint in regard to copying machines, interlibrary communication, and growth of educational community which has created demand for copied material and a redefinition of permissable copying.

Microforms In Libraries: A Reader. Edited by Albert James Diaz. Weston, Conn.: Microform Review, c1975. 428 pp., bibliog.♦ Articles by various authors on organizing the microform collection, bibliographic control, applications, standards and specifications, and user reactions.

Nasri, William Z. *Crisis in Copyright.* New York: Dekker, 1976. 174 pp., illus., bibliog., index.♦ Discusses photocopying processes and fair use.

Nitecki, Joseph Z., comp. and ed. *Directory of Library Reprographic Services: A World Guide.* 6th ed. Weston, Conn.: Published for the Reproduction of Library Materials Section, RTSD-American Library Association by Microform Review, c1976. 178 pp., and microfiche in pocket, bibliog.

Saffady, William. "Microfilm Cameras, a Survey of Features and Functions," *Special Libraries,* 68:1 (January 1977), pp. 1-6.

Saffady, William. *Micrographics.* Littleton, Colo.: Libraries Unlimited, 1978. 238 pp., illus., bibliog., index.♦ Discusses microformats, microform reading room, uses of microforms, computer-output-microfilm, and micropublishing.

Seltzer, Leon E. *Exemptions and Fair Use in Copyright: The Exclusive Rights, Tensions in the 1976 Copyright Act.* Cambridge, Mass.:

Harvard University Press, 1978. 199 pp., index.♦ Discusses photocopying processes and fair use.

Skipper, James, ed. "Photoduplication in Libraries," *Library Trends,* 8:3 (January 1960), entire issue.

Statement on the Reproduction of Manuscripts and Archives for Commercial Purposes. Chicago: Association of College and Research Libraries, American Library Association, 1977. 1 p.♦ Statement developed by the Committee on Manuscript Collections of the Rare Books and Manuscripts Section of ACRL, approved as policy by the ACRL Board of Directors, on January 31, 1977. Reprinted from *C&RL News,* no. 5 (May 1977), pp. 143-144.

"Survey and Bibliography of Microreproduction Forms, Equipment, Techniques, and Problems," *Special Libraries,* 51:2 (February 1960), pp. 59-76.

U.S. Library of Congress. *Specifications for the Microfilming of Newspapers in the Library of Congress.* Washington, D.C.: 1972. 17 pp., bibliog.

U.S. Library of Congress. Photoduplication Service. *Specifications for the Microfilming of Books and Pamphlets in the Library of Congress.* Washington, D.C.: Library of Congress, for sale by the Superintendent of Documents, U.S. Government Printing Office, 1973. 16 pp., illus., bibliog.

U.S. National Archives and Records Service. Office of Records Management. *Computer Output Microfilm.* Washington, D.C.: for sale by the Superintendent of Documents, U.S. Government Printing Office, 1975. 46 pp., illus., tables, appendices.♦ Emphasizes systems design and economic analysis. Records Management Handbook series.

U.S. National Archives and Records Service. Office of Records Management. *Microfilming Records.* Washington, D.C.: General Services Administration, National Archives and Records Service, Office of Records Management; for sale by Superintendent of Documents, U.S. Government Printing Office, 1974. 168 pp., illus., charts, tables, appendices.♦ Records Management Handbook series.

U.S. National Archives and Records Service. Office of Records Management. *The*

Microform Retrieval Equipment Guide. Washington, D.C.: for sale by Superintendent of Documents, U.S. Government Printing Office, 1974. 90 pp., illus., tables, appendices. ♦ Detailed guidance on the selection of microfilm readers, reader printers, and other microform display and reference equipment; defines critical factors in selecting various types of microfilm equipment used in information retrieval. Records Management Handbook series.

Veaner, Allen B. *The Evaluation of Micropublications: A Handbook for Librarians.* Chicago: Library Technology Program, American Library Association, 1971. 59 pp., illus., bibliog.♦ Evaluates technical aspects of micropublications including archival permanence.

NOTES

"Developments in Copying, Micrographics, and Graphic Communications," is an annual review of trends, techniques and equipment, and references in the summer issue of *Library Resources & Technical Services.* Author varies. Summer 1978 review includes discussion of impact of new copyright law.

Microform Review. 1971, 4/yr., subscription. Microform Review, Rogues Ridge, Weston, Connecticut 06880. Forum of timely articles on micropublishing (reprography); Allen B. Veaner and Alan M. Meckler, editors.

National Micrographics Association, 8728 Colesville Road, Suite 1101, Silver Spring, Maryland 20910. Founded in 1945, the Association serves manufacturers of equipment and supplies for micro-reproduction; and users (government, business, industrial, technical, education, library, etc.) making microcopies of documents and records. It conducts educational programs to stabilize and improve production and use of microfilms. The Association publishes *Proceedings* (annual); *Micrographics Today* (10/yr.); *Journal of Micrographics* (bimonthly); *Glossary of Micrographics; Guide to Micrographic Equipment* (2 vols.); and an annual buyer's guide. In 1974, the Wisconsin Chapter established a micrographics technician apprenticeship program, approved by the Wisconsin Department of Industry, Labor and Human Relations, Division of Apprenticeship and Training.

Library/Archives and the Public

Angoff, Allen, ed. *Public Relations for Libraries: Essays in Communications Techniques.* Westport, Conn.: Greenwood Press, 1973. 246 pp., bibliog., index.◆ Essays on public relations programs for various types and sizes of libraries.

Burke, John G., and H. Paxton Bowers. "Institutional Censorship: A Proposal for an Effective Mechanism to Protect the Researcher," *Library Journal,* 95:3 (February 1, 1970), pp. 468-469.◆ Discusses right of access to library materials and protection for the researcher.

Daifuku, Hiroshi. "Museums and Research." In *The Organization of Museums: Practical Advice* (Paris: UNESCO, 1960), pp. 68-72.

Federal Library Committee. *Guidelines for Library Handbooks.* Washington, D.C.: U.S. Government Printing Office, 1972. 8 pp. ◆ Pointers on content, format, and design, and a list of supplementary readings; useful recommendations for preparing guides to a collection's scope and use.

Foster, Edith. *The Library in a Small Community.* Small Libraries Project Pamphlet no. 14. Chicago: Small Libraries Project, Library Administration Division, American Library Association, 1963. 8 pp.

Glazer, Frederick. "Selling the Library," *Library Journal,* 99:11 (June 1974), pp. 1518-1520.◆ Suggests creating a demand for services so that libraries will receive a larger share of public money.

Gregory, Lee H. "Local History and the Rural Library," *Library Journal,* 81:1 (January 1, 1956), pp. 54-56.

Harrison, Caroline. "Education and the Museum Library," *Museum News,* 42:5 (January 1964), pp. 33-36.◆ Describes integration of science museum library into total education program, including construction and furnishing the library, and establishing a liaison position in the library.

Holbert, Sue E. *Archives and Manuscripts: Reference and Access.* Chicago: Society of American Archivists, 1977. 30 pp., bibliog., appendices.◆ Basic Manual series; includes access policy, security, restrictions and references such as guides, interviews, fair use, loans; and personnel.

Lucas, E. Louise. "Library Services to Staff and Public," *Museum News,* 26:19 (April 1, 1949), pp. 6-7.

"Publicity with a Purpose . . . For Libraries on a Shoestring," *Library Journal,* 99:6 (March 15, 1974), pp. 862-863.◆ An informed and involved public is the best guarantee of a library's financial health and vitality.

Robotham, John S., and Lydia La Fleur. *Library Programs: How to Select, Plan and Produce Them.* Metuchen, N.J.: Scarecrow Press, 1976. 295 pp., illus., bibliog., index.

Rubincam, Milton. "What the Genealogist Expects of an Archival Agency or Historical Society," *The American Archivist,* 12:4 (October 1949), pp. 333-338.

Sager, Donald J. "Libraries and the Arts: Working with Foundations, How to Start a Local Arts Council," *Wilson Library Bulletin,* 45:8 (April 1971), pp. 744-749.◆ The cultural domain of a community includes a library.

Society of American Archivists. Committee on Professional Standards. "Standards for Access and Appraisal of Gifts," *The American Archivist,* 37:1 (January 1974), pp. 153-155.◆ Discusses proposed standards concerning access to research materials in archival and manuscript repositories, and the appraisal of gifts.

Stone, J. H., and J. W. Cortada. "Libraries and Local Historical Societies: The Need for Cooperation," *Journal of Library History,* 6:4 (October 1971), pp. 360-364.

Suhler, Sam A. *Local History Collection and Services in a Small Public Library.* Chicago: American Library Association, 1970. 11 pp., bibliog.◆ Useful suggestions for small local libraries including local historical society libraries, and deals with newspapers, magazines, books, manuscripts, maps, vertical file materials, tape recordings, and pictorial materials.

Swartz, Roderick G., et al. "Humanities in the Library: The Role of the National Endowment for the Humanities," *Wilson Library Bulletin,* 46:5 (January 1972), pp. 426-445.◆ Review by several authors of NEH funded programs to make libraries more humanistic: orientation projects, pride in heritage series, staff participation, adult education, communication arts programs.

Thomson, Sarah Katharine. *Interlibrary Loan Procedure Manual.* Chicago: Interlibrary Loan Committee, American Library Association, 1970. 116 pp., bibliog.

Buildings and Equipment

American Library Association. Library Technology Project. *Permanence and Durability of Library Catalogue Cards.* A Study conducted by W. J. Barrow for the Library Technology Project. Chicago: The Association, 1961. 39 pp., illus., diagrams, tables, bibliog.

"Annual Buyer's Guide 1978," *Library Journal,* 103:15 (September 1978), pp. 1584-1621.◆ List of firms offering products or services of particular interest to libraries. Includes Product Directory and Suppliers' Directory.

Barrow, W. J. "Archival File Folders," *The American Archivist,* 28:1 (January 1965), pp. 125-128.◆ Study of file folders suitable for archival use; more fully reported in *Permanence/Durability of the Book* series.

Bartkowski, Patricia, and William Saffady. "Shelving and Office Furniture for Archives Buildings," *The American Archivist,* 37:1 (January 1974), pp. 55-66.

Berkeley, Bernard. *Floors: Selection and Maintenance.* Chicago: Library Technology Program, American Library Association, 1968. 316 pp., illus., tables, bibliog., index.◆ Chapters devoted to detailed descriptions of the properties of the major categories of floors and floor coverings; installation and maintenance techniques; selection critera and maintenance practices and equipment.

Brawne, Michael. *Libraries: Architecture and Equipment.* London: Pall Mall Pub., 1970. 188 pp., illus., plans, bibliog. references, index.

Duchein, Michel. *Archive Buildings and Equipment.* Munchen: Verlag Dokumentation, distr. by Unipub, New York, 1977. 201 pp., illus., bibliog., index.◆ International Council on Archives Handbooks series, 1.

Galvin, Hoyt R., and Martin Van Buren. *The Small Public Library Building.* Paris: UNESCO, 1958. 133 pp., illus., bibliog.

Gondos, Victor, Jr. "Archival Buildings—Programming and Planning," *The American Archivist,* 27:4 (October 1964), pp. 467-484.

Gondos, Victor, comp. *Reader for Archives and Records Center Buildings.* Washington, D.C.: Committee on Archival Buildings and Equipment, Society of American Archivists, 1970. 127 pp., illus., bibliog.◆ Writings by archival specialists on record containers, film records management, and records and fire protection.

Jones, James V. "Furniture for Library Offices and Staff Work Areas," *Library Trends,* 13 (1965), pp. 448-454.

Kurth, William H., and Ray W. Grim. *Moving a Library.* New York: Scarecrow Press, 1966. 220 pp., illus., plans, appendix.◆ Describes moving the National Library of Medicine, with emphasis on planning.

Langmead, Stephen, and Margaret Beckman. *New Library Design: Guidelines to Planning Academic Library Buildings.* New York: J. Wiley & Sons Canada, c1970. 117 pp., illus., plans, bibliog.

Lewis, Chester M., ed. *Special Libraries: How to Plan and Equip Them.* A Project of the New York Chapter. New York: Special Libraries Association, 1963. 117 pp., illus., bibliog. ◆ Selective guide containing basic information on major considerations involved in structural and space requirements as well as equipment; annotated bibliography.

Library Buildings Institute, Detroit, 1965. *Libraries: Building for the Future; Proceedings of the Library Buildings Institute and the ALTA Workshop Conducted at Detroit, Michigan, July 1-3, 1965.* Chicago: American Library Association, 1967. 208 pp., illus., plans. ◆ Includes pitfalls in planning and building libraries, factors and criteria for planning, specific features of different types of structures, planning technical processing areas, previous mistakes in planning, and the trustees role in planning and building.

Library Equipment Institute, 1st, University of Miami, 1962. *Library Furniture and Equipment; Proceedings of the Three-day Institute.* Chicago: American Library Association, 1963.

68 pp.♦ Presentations deal with furniture selection; bookstack selection; specification writing and bidding procedures; and methods and equipment for catalog card reproduction, photocopying and microtext copy.

Library Equipment Institute, 2d, St. Louis, 1964. *The Library Environment: Aspects of Interior Planning; Proceedings.* Edited by Frazer G. Poole. Chicago: American Library Association, 1965. 69 pp., illus., charts, tables. ♦ Librarians, designers and experts from commercial firms consider five major aspects of library interiors: informal furnishings, lighting, audio facilities, flooring, and transport of people and books.

Library Equipment Institute, 3d, New York 1966. *The Procurement of Library Furnishings: Specifications, Bid Documents, and Evaluation; Proceedings.* Edited by Frazer G. Poole and Alphonse F. Trezza. Chicago: American Library Association, 1969. 150 pp., forms, plans.♦ Recommendations based on discussions with library representatives, architects, designers, and library equipment manufacturers.

Metcalf, Keyes DeWitt. *Library Lighting.* Washington, D.C.: Association of Research Libraries, 1970. 90 pp., bibliog.

Metcalf, Keyes DeWitt. *Planning Academic and Research Library Buildings.* New York: McGraw-Hill Book Co., 1965. 431 pp., illus., bibliog., appendices, glossary.♦ Sponsored by the Association of Research Libraries and the Association of College and Research Libraries under a grant by the Council on Library Resources. Selective annotated bibliography included. Comprehensive manual dealing with the problems involved directly or indirectly in the planning and construction of academic and research libraries, including objectives, finances, traffic problems, furniture and equipment, space requirements, mechanical facilities, construction period.

Myller, Rolf. *Design of the Small Public Library.* New York: R. R. Bowker, 1966. 95 pp., illus.♦ Manual describing steps in planning and implementation of a building program for public libraries in smaller communities.

Novak, Gloria. *Energy and Library Buildings: A Bibliography on Energy Conservation in Buildings.* Chicago: Library Administration and Management Association, American Library Association, 1978. 160 pp.

Roth, Harold L., ed. "An Analysis and Survey of Commercial Library Supply Houses," *Library Trends,* 24:4 (April 1976), entire issue.♦ Includes computers, book wholesaler services, serial subscription agencies, microform hardware and suppliers, automated turn-key systems, audiovisual suppliers, library binders, library supplies, commercial cataloging services.

Special Libraries Association. New York Chapter. *Planning the Special Library; A Project of the New York Chapter, SLA.* Edited by Ellis Mount. SLA Monograph no. 4. New York: 1972. 122 pp., bibliog., index.♦ Compiled from a series of papers presented at a Seminar sponsored by the New York Chapter of SLA, April 1971, and may be treated as a sequel to the planning guide by Lewis (1963), cited above. Includes initial concepts, layout, interior design, selection of furniture and equipment, procedures for moving and remodeling; two checklists and a bibliography, and a brief classified list of manufacturers and suppliers of library equipment.

Speyers-Duran, Peter. *Moving Library Materials.* Rev. ed. Chicago: Library Technology Project, American Library Association, 1965. 63 pp., illus., bibliog.♦ Includes planning the move, moving methods, and specifications and contract forms.

Thompson, Godfrey. *Planning and Design of Library Buildings.* 2nd ed. London: Architectural Press, 1977. 189 pp., illus., bibliog., index.♦ Includes updated and expanded essay on alteration or conversion of existing buildings, and enlarged bibliography. British counterpart of Metcalf, *Planning Research and Academic Library Buildings,* cited above.

Van Buren, Martin. "What to Look for When Buying Shelving," *Library Journal,* 90:7 (April 1, 1965), pp. 1614-1617.

APPENDIX
Periodicals Cited

AAM Bulletin. see AVISO.

AAUP Bulletin. 1915, 4/yr., membership/ subscription. American Association of University Professors, Suite 500, One Dupont Circle, N.W., Washington, D.C. 20036. Beginning February 1979: *Academe: The Bulletin of the AAUP,* combining *AAUP Bulletin* and *Newsletter.*

AB Bookman's Weekly/Antiquarian Bookman. 1948, weekly, subscription. AB Bookman's Weekly, Box 1100, Newark, New Jersey 07101.

AIA Journal. 1944, monthly, qualified personnel/subscription. American Institute of Architects, 1735 New York Avenue, N.W., Washington, D.C. 20006.

ARLIS/NA Newsletter. 1972, quarterly, membership. Art Libraries Society of North America, c/o Sherman Clarke, 779 Princeton Blvd., Wilkinsburg, Pennsylvania 15221.

ARMA Records Management Quarterly. 1975, quarterly, subscription. Association of Records Managers and Administrators, Box 281, Bradford, Rhode Island 02808. Formerly *Records Management Journal* (1963-1975).

ASHRAE Journal. 1894, monthly, membership/subscription. American Society of Heating, Refrigeration and Air Conditioning, United Engineering Center, 345 East 47th Street, New York, New York 10017.

The American Archivist. 1938, quarterly, subscription. Society of American Archivists, Ann Morgan Campbell, Executive Director, 330 South Wells Street, Suite 810, Chicago, Illinois 60606.

American Libraries. 1907, 11/yr., membership/subscription. American Library Association, 50 East Huron Street, Chicago, Illinois 60611. Formerly *ALA Bulletin.*

American Quarterly. 1949, 5/yr., membership. American Studies Association, 4025 Chestnut Street, Philadelphia, Pennsylvania 19174.

American Society for Information Science. *Bulletin.* 1974, 10/yr., subscription. American Society for Information Science, 1155 16th Street, N.W., Washington, D.C. 20036. Supersedes *ASIS Newsletter.*

American Society for Information Science. *Journal.* 1950, bimonthly, subscription. American Society for Information Science, 1155 16th Street, N.W., Washington, D.C. 20036. Formerly *American Documentation.*

Annotation. 1973, quarterly, limited circulation. National Historical Publications and Records Commission, National Archives Building, Washington, D.C 20408.

The Architectural Forum. 1892-1974, 10/yr. Whitney Publications, Inc., 130 East 59th Street, New York, New York 10022. Ceased publication with March 1974 issue, absorbed by *Architecture Plus,* Informat Publishing Corporation, 1345 Sixth Avenue, New York, New York 10019.

Architectural Record. 1891, monthly, subscription. Architectural Record, 1221 Avenue of the Americas, New York, New York 10020.

Archival Security Newsletter. 1975, bimonthly, subscription. Archival Security Program, Society of American Archivists, 330 South Wells Street, Suite 810, Chicago, Illinois 60606. Published as a supplement to the *SAA Newsletter.*

Archivaria. 1975, semiannual, subscription. Association of Canadian Archivists, c/o Public Archives of Canada, Room 349, 395 Wellington Street, Ottawa, Ontario K1A ON3. Succeeds *Canadian Archivist.*

Art and the Law. 1974, 10/yr., subscription. Volunteer Lawyers for the Arts, 36 West 44th Street, Suite 1110, New York, New York 10036.

Art in America. 1913, bimonthly, subscription. Subscriptions to: Art in America, 1255 Portland Place, Boulder, Colorado 80302.

Art Theft Archive Newsletter. 1979, 10/yr., subscription. International Foundation for Art Research, 46 East 70th Street, New York, New York 10021.

Arts/Business. 1971, monthly, membership. Business Committee for the Arts, 1501 Broadway, 26th Floor, New York, New York 10036.

Association Management. 1949, monthly, subscription. American Society of Association Executives *Journal;* absorbed Society's *ASAE News* and *Here's How,* as of January 1963.

AVISO. 1975, monthly, membership. American Association of Museums, 1055 Thomas Jefferson Street, N.W., Washington, D.C. 20007. Succeeds *AAM Bulletin* (1968-1975).

BCA News. 1968, quarterly, free. Business Committee for the Arts, 1501 Broadway, 26th Floor, New York, New York 10036.

Best's Review: *Property/Casualty Insurance Edition.* 1899, monthly, subscription. A.M. Best Company, Inc., Editorial Offices, Oldwick, New Jersey 08858.

Better Times. 1976, quarterly, subscription. America the Beautiful Fund, 219 Shoreham Building, Washington, D.C. 20005.

Building Research: *The Journal of the Building Research Institute.* 1964, quarterly, membership/subscription. Building Research Institute, 2101 Constitution Avenue, N.W., Washington, D.C. 20418.

Bulletin. 1961, monthly, membership. Museums Association, 87 Charlotte Street, London W1P 2BX, England.

Bulletin of APT. 1969, quarterly, membership. Association for Preservation Technology, c/o Ann A. Falkner, Box 2478, Station D, Ottawa, Ontario K1P 5W6, Canada.

Bulletin of the American Group-IIC. see *Journal of the American Institute for Conservation.*

Canadian Library Journal. 1944, bimonthly, membership. Canadian Library Association, 151 Sparks Street, Ottawa, Ontario K1P 5E3, Canada.

Choice. 1964, 11/yr., subscription. Subscriptions to: 100 Riverview Center, Middletown, Connecticut 06457. Publication of the American Library Association, Association of College and Research Libraries.

Clearinghouse for Western Museums Newsletter. see *WRC Newsletter.*

College and Research Libraries. 1939, bimonthly, membership. Association of College and Research Libraries, American Library Association, 50 East Huron Street, Chicago, Illinois 60611.

Congressional Action. 1956, weekly while Congress is in session, membership. Chamber of Commerce of the United States, 1615 H Street, N.W., Washington, D.C. 20006.

Conservation Administration News. 1979, quarterly, subscription. c/o Robert H. Patterson, Director of Libraries, P.O. Box 3334, University Station, Laramie, Wyoming 82071.

Copyright Bulletin: *Quarterly Review.* 1948, quarterly, subscription. UNESCO, 7, Place de Fontenoy, 75700 Paris, France. Also available from Unipub, Box 433, Murray Hill Station, New York, New York 10016.

Cultural Affairs. 1967-1971, quarterly. Associated Councils of the Arts, succeeded by American Council for the Arts, 570 Seventh Avenue, New York, New York 10018. Publication ceased with no. 16, August 1971.

Curator. 1958, quarterly, subscription. American Museum of Natural History, 79th Street at Central Park West, New York, New York 10024. Volume 20, no. 4 (December 1977) contains cumulative index to Vols. 1-20, arranged by author, title, and subject.

11593: *Information Related to Responsibilities of the Secretary of the Interior, Section 3, Executive Order 11593.* June 1976, bimonthly, free on request. Office of Archeology and Historic Preservation, Heritage Conservation and Recreation Service, Washington, D.C. 20240.

Fire Journal. 1907, bimonthly, membership. National Fire Protection Association, 470 Atlantic Avenue, Boston, Massachusetts 02210.

Fire News. 1916, 10/yr., membership. National Fire Protection Association, 470 Atlantic Avenue, Boston, Massachusetts 02210.

Foundation Center Information Quarterly. 1972, quarterly, subscription. Foundation Center, 888 Seventh Avenue, New York, New York 10019.

Foundation News. 1960, bimonthly, subscription. Subscriptions to: P.O. Box 783, Old Chelsea Station, New York, New York 10011. Published by the Council on Foundations.

gazette. 1975, quarterly, membership. Canadian Museums Association, P.O. Box 1328, Station B, Ottawa, Ontario K1P 5R4, Canada. Published bimonthly, 1966-1974; succeeded by quarterly, begun Winter 1975.

Giving USA Bulletin. 1955, 11/yr., subscription. American Association of Fund-Raising Counsel, Inc., 500 Fifth Avenue, New York, New York 10016. Formerly American Association of Fund-Raising Counsel *Bulletin.*

Grantsmanship Center News. 1973, 8/yr., subscription. The Grantsmanship Center, 1031 South Grand Avenue, Los Angeles, California 90015.

Grounds Maintenance. 1966, monthly, subscription. Intertec Publishing Corporation, 1014 Wyandotte Street, Kansas City, Missouri 64105.

Harvard Business Review. 1922, bimonthly, subscription. Subscriptions to: Subscription Service Department, 108 10th Street, Des Moines, Iowa 50305. Published by Graduate School of Business Administration, Harvard University.

Heritage Canada. 1974, bimonthly, membership. Heritage Canada, P.O. Box 1358, Station B, Ottawa, Ontario K1P 5R4, Canada. Combines *Heritage Canada,* quarterly, and *Heritage Conversation.*

Historic Preservation. 1949, bimonthly, membership. National Trust for Historic Preservation, 1785 Massachusetts Avenue, N.W., Washington, D.C. 20036.

History News. 1941, monthly, membership (includes Technical Leaflet). American Association for State and Local History, 1400 Eighth Avenue South, Nashville, Tennessee 37203.

ICOM News/Nouvelles de l'ICOM. 1948,

quarterly, membership. International Council of Museums, 1 rue Moillis, 75732 Paris, France.

Inside SEMC. bimonthly, membership/ subscription. Maralynn Troutman, Editor, Arkansas Arts and Humanities Office, Continental Building, Suite 500, Markham and Main Streets, Little Rock, Arkansas 72201. Newsletter of the Southeast Museums Conference, American Association of Museums.

The Journal of Accountancy. 1905, monthly, subscription. American Institute of Certified Public Accountants, 1211 Avenue of the Americas, New York, New York 10036.

Journal of Library History, Philosophy and Comparative Librarianship. 1966, quarterly, subscription. University of Texas Press, Austin, Texas 78712.

Journal of Micrographics. 1967, bimonthly, subscription. National Micrographics Association, 8728 Colesville Road, Suite 1101, Silver Spring, Maryland 20910. Formerly *NMA Journal.*

Journal of the American Institute for Conservation. Vol. 16, no. 2 (1976), biannual, subscription. American Institute for Conservation, Martha Morales, Executive Secretary, 1522 K Street, N.W., Suite 804, Washington, D.C. 20005. Succeeds *Bulletin of the American Group-IIC* (1960-1972), and *AIC Bulletin* (1972-1976).

Journal of World History. 1953-1972, quarterly. UNESCO; distributed by Unipub, Inc., Box 433, Murray Hill Station, New York, New York 10016. Succeeded by *Cultures,* devoted to cultural life in all manifestations, national, regional, and international; contemporary; and includes cultural studies, international cultural relations, cultural development, and the elaboration of cultural policies.

Laboratory. 1928, 4/yr., free. Fisher Scientific Company, 711 Forbes Avenue, Pittsburgh, Pennsylvania 15219.

Library & Archival Security. 1979, quarterly, subscription. The Haworth Press, 149 Fifth Avenue, New York, New York 10010.

Library Journal. 1876, semi-monthly (September-June), monthly (July-August), subscription. Subscriptions to: Subscription Service Department, R. R. Bowker, Box 67, Whitinsville, Massachusetts 01588.

Library Quarterly; *A Journal of Investigation and Discussion in the Field of Library Science.* 1931, quarterly, subscription. University of Chicago Press, 5801 Ellis Avenue, Chicago, Illinois 60636.

Library Resources & Technical Services. 1957, quarterly, membership/subscription. Resources and Technical Services Division, American Library Association, 50 East Huron Street, Chicago, Illinois 60611.

Library Trends. 1952, quarterly, subscription. Subscriptions to: University of Illinois Press, Subscription Department, Urbana, Illinois 61801. Published by University of Illinois Graduate School of Library Science, Urbana, Illinois.

Living Historical Farms Bulletin. 1970, bimonthly, membership. Association for Living Historical Farms and Agricultural Museums, c/o John T. Schlebecker, Smithsonian Institution, Washington, D.C. 20560.

Manuscripts. 1948, quarterly, membership. The Manuscript Society, Audrey Arellanes, Executive Secretary, 1206 N. Stoneman Avenue #15, Alhambra, California 91801.

Maryland Historical Magazine. 1906, quarterly, subscription. Maryland Historical Society, 201 West Monument Street, Baltimore, Maryland 21201.

Metropolitan Museum of Art. *Bulletin.* 1942, new series, quarterly, subscription. Metropolitan Museum of Art, Fifth Avenue and 82nd Street, New York, New York 10028.

Microform Review. 1971, 4/yr., subscription. Microform Review, Rogues Ridge, Weston, Connecticut 06880.

Micrographics Today. 1967, 10/yr., membership. National Micrographics Association, 8728 Colesville Road, Suite 1101, Silver Spring, Maryland 20910. Formerly *Micro News Bulletin.*

Midwest Museums Conference. *The Quarterly.* 1941, quarterly, membership/subscription. L. G. Hoffman, Editor, Davenport Municipal Art Gallery, 1737 West 12th Street, Davenport, Iowa 52804. Newsletter of the Midwest Museums Conference, American Association of Museums.

MPMC Newsletter. 1960, quarterly, membership/subscription. David L. Hartman, Editor, Denver Museum of Natural History, City Park, Denver, Colorado 80205. Newsletter of the Mountain/Plains Museums Conference, American Association of Museums.

museogramme. 1973, monthly, membership. Canadian Museums Association, P.O. Box 1328, Station B, Ottawa, Ontario K1P 5R4, Canada.

The Museologist. 1935, quarterly, membership. Robert W. Ott, Editor, Division of Art and Museum Education, 273 Chambers Building, Pennsylvania State University, University Park, Pennsylvania 16802. Newsletter of the Northeast Museums Conference, American Association of Museums.

Museum. 1948, quarterly, subscription. UNESCO, 7 Place de Fontenoy, 75700 Paris, France. Distributed by Unipub, Inc., Box 433, Murray Hill Station, New York, New York 10016. Also available, reprints from Vols. 1-10 (1948-1957) from Kraus Reprint, division of Kraus-Thomson Organizations Limited, FL-9491 Nendeln, Liechtenstein; and, Index, Vols. 1-25 (1948-1973).

Museum News. 1924, 6/yr., membership. American Association of Museums, 1055 Thomas Jefferson Street, N.W., Washington, D.C. 20007.

Museum Scope. 1976, bimonthly, subscription. Alden Redfield, Editor, Suite 5, Strollway Centre, 111 South 9th Street, Columbia, Missouri 65201.

Museum Store Association Newsletter. 1955, 3/yr., membership. Museum Store Association, c/o Mrs. Sydney Boisbrun, Administrative Secretary, 260 Cherry Lane, Doylestown, Pennsylvania 18901.

Museums Journal. 1901, quarterly, membership. Museums Association, 87 Charlotte Street, London W1P 2BX, England. Also available: technical indexes for 1930-1955, and 1956-1966; Vols. 1-75 in microform from Oxford Microform Publications Ltd., Blue Boar Street, Oxford OX1 4EY, England.

NEMA News. 1976, quarterly, membership/subscription. Katherine Smith, Editor, DeCordova Museum, Sandy Pond Road, Lincoln, Massachusetts 01773. Newsletter of the New England Museums Association, American Association of Museums.

Nebraska History. 1918, quarterly, membership. Nebraska State Historical Society, 1500 R Street, Lincoln, Nebraska 68508.

Newsweek. 1933, weekly, subscription. Newsweek, Inc., 444 Madison Avenue, New York, New York 10022.

Non-Profit Organization Tax Letter. 1964, 18/yr., subscription. Organization Management, Inc., Box 34909, Washington, D.C. 20034.

The Old-House Journal. 1973, monthly, subscription. The Old-House Journal, 69A Seventh Avenue, Brooklyn, New York 11217.

Parks and Recreation: *Journal of Park and Recreation Management.* 1903, monthly, subscription. National Recreation and Park Association, 1601 North Kent Street, Arlington, Virginia 22209.

Philanthropic Digest. 1974, 16/yr., subscription. Brakely, John Price Jones, Inc., 1100 17th Street, N.W., Suite 709, Washington, D.C. 20036.

The Practical Lawyer. 1955, 8/yr., subscription. ALI-ABA Committee on Continuing Legal Education, 4025 Chestnut Street, Philadelphia, Pennsylvania 19104.

Preservation News. 1961, monthly newspaper, membership. National Trust for Historic Preservation, 1785 Massachusetts Avenue, N.W., Washington, D.C. 20036.

Progressive Architecture. 1920, monthly, subscription. Reinhold Publishing Company, 600 Summer Street, Stamford, Connecticut 06904.

Prologue: *The Journal of the National Archives.* 1969, quarterly, subscription. The National Archives, Washington, D.C. 20408.

Public Relations Journal: *A Journal of Opinion in the Field of Public Relations Practice.* 1945, monthly, subscription. Public Relations Society of America, 845 Third Avenue, New York, New York 10022.

The Public Relations Quarterly. 1955, quarterly, subscription. Howard Penn Hudson and Mary E. Hudson, Editors and Publishers, 2626 Pennsylvania Avenue, N.W., Washington, D.C. 20037. Incorporates *International Public Relations Review.*

Publishers Weekly: *The Book Industry Journal.* 1872, weekly, subscription. Subscriptions to: Subscription Service Department, R. R. Bowker, Box 67, Whitinsville, Massachusetts 01588.

RCHA News. 1972, monthly, membership. Regional Conference of Historical Agencies, 314 East Seneca Street, Manlius, New York 13104.

Real Property, Probate and Trust Journal. 1966, quarterly, subscription. American Bar Association, Section of Real Property, Probate and Trust Law, 1155 East 60th Street, Chicago, Illinois 60637.

Registrar's Report. 1977, monthly, subscription. P.O. Box 112, Bicentennial Station, Los Angeles, California 90048.

Report. 1975, 8/yr., on request. Advisory Council on Historic Preservation, 1522 K Street, N.W., Washington, D.C. 20005. Includes: Special Issues and Compliance Issues; succeeds *Newsletter* (1973-1974).

Saturday Review. 1924, weekly, subscription. Saturday Review, Inc., 488 Madison Avenue, New York, New York 10022. Formerly *Saturday Review/World.*

Security Management. 1972, bimonthly, subscription. American Society for Industrial Security, 2000 K Street, N.W., Suite 651, Washington, D.C. 20006. Formerly *Industrial Security* (1954-1972).

Smithsonian. 1970, monthly, subscription. Smithsonian Associates, 900 Jefferson Drive, S.W., Washington, D.C. 20560. Succeeds *The Smithsonian Journal of History* (1966-1969).

Special Libraries. 1910, 10/yr., subscription. Special Libraries Association, 235 Park Avenue South, New York, New York 10003.

Studies in Conservation. 1952, quarterly, membership/subscription. International Institute for Conservation of Historic and Artistic Works, 6 Buckingham Street, London WC2N 6BA, England.

Technology and Conservation. 1976, quarterly, free to qualified persons, subscription to others. The Technology Organization, Inc., 1 Emerson Place, Boston, Massachusetts 02114.

Texas Libraries. 1909, quarterly, subscription. Texas State Library and Historical Commission, Box 12927, Capitol Station, Austin, Texas 78711.

Trends. 1968, quarterly, subscription. National Recreation and Park Association, Park Practice Program, 1601 North Kent Street, Arlington, Virginia 22209.

UCLA Law Review. 1953, 5/yr., subscription. University of California School of Law, Los Angeles, California 90024.

UNESCO Bulletin for Libraries. 1947, bimonthly, subscription. UNESCO; distributed by Unipub, Inc., Box 433, Murray Hill Station, New York, New York 10016.

U.S. Library of Congress. *Information Bulletin.* 1942, weekly, free to libraries. Order to: LC Central Services Division, U.S. Library of Congress, 19 First Street, S.E., Washington, D.C. 20540.

The Virginia Magazine of History and Biography. 1893, quarterly, subscription. Virginia Historical Society, William M. E. Rachal, Editor, Box 7311, Richmond, Virginia 23221.

Voluntary Action Leadership. 1970, bimonthly, free. National Center for Voluntary Action, 1785 Massachusetts Avenue, N.W., Washington, D.C. 20036. Incorporates *Voluntary Action News* since 1976.

The Washington International Arts Letter. 1962, monthly except July and December, subscription. Washington International Arts Letter, Box 9005, 115 5th Street, S.E., Washington, D.C. 20003.

Western Museums Quarterly. see *WRC Newsletter.*

Wilson Library Bulletin. 1914, monthly September/June, subscription. H. W. Wilson Company, 950 University Avenue, Bronx, New York 10452.

WRC Newsletter. 1975, quarterly, membership/subscription. Joan Pursell, Editor, Santa Barbara Museum of Natural History, 2559 Puesta del Sol Road, Santa Barbara, California 93015. Newsletter of the Western Regional Conference, American Association of Museums. Succeeds *Western Museums Quarterly* (1963-1974), and *Clearinghouse for Western Museums Newsletter* (1958-1962).

NOTE

For current information and addresses for specialized organizations and periodicals, consult the following:

Gale Research Company. *Encyclopedia of Associations.* Detroit: 1967 -. 3 vols.♦ Volume 1—National Associations of the U.S.; Volume 2—Geographic and Executive Index; Volume 3—New Associations and Projects (with periodic supplements). Current edition, 13th, 1979.

Ulrich's International Periodicals Directory. New York: R. R. Bowker Company, 1932 -. 1 vol. ♦ Biennial new editions and supplements issued in alternating years. Current edition, 17th, 1977-1978.

Index

191